WOMEN of IRELAND

BIOGRAPHIC DICTIONARY

Kit & Cyril Ó Céirín

TírEolas

IRISH BOOKS AND MEDIA

First published in 1996 by Tír Eolas
Newtownlynch, Kinvara, Co. Galway.

Text copyright © Kit and Cyril Ó Céirín.
Illustrations © listed sources.

Editorial advisers: Annette Möcker, Mary Healion-Shelley.
Picture research: Anne Korff.

British Library Cataloguing in Publication Data.
A catalogue record for this book is available from the British Library.
ISBN 1-873821-06-9

Published in the USA 1996 by
IRISH BOOKS AND MEDIA, Inc.
1433 Franklin Avenue East
Minneapolis, Minnesola 55404-2135

ISBN 0-937702-16-1

Library of Congress Catalog card number: 96-78096

Cover and layout: Anne Korff, Johan Hofsteenge.
Typesetting: Johan Hofsteenge
Printed in Ireland by Betaprint International Ltd.

DEDICATION

•

*To the young and future generations
of mná na hÉireann, the women of Ireland,
not only in Ireland itself,
but in the 'four corners of the world'.*

ACKNOWLEDGEMENTS

We wish to express our appreciation to the following who generously contributed their time and knowledge to this first edition: Michael Barry; Deasún Breathanach; Walter Bridgeman; Barbara and Ken Burke, (Florida); Sara and Gabriel Casey; Pat Cooke, Aer Rianta; John Coyle; Antoin Daltún; Beatrice Dixon; Brian Doyle (Ennistymon Library); Lelia Doolan; Jimmy Drumm; Embassy of the Kingdom of Morocco, Dublin, (Deirdre Dunne); Seán Eustace (Coleaiste Muire gan Sunál, Luimneach); Martha Foley; Michael Geraghty; Noel Henry; Sr. David Hopkins, Archivist, Dominican Sisters; Blanaid Irvine; Sr. Mary Jordan, Franciscan Missionaries of Africa; Bill Kerins, (Mass. USA); Babe Larkin; Gerry Linnane; Elizabeth Marsden; Múinteoirí Náisiúnta na hÉireann, Head Office, (Liz. Burke, Michelle Harnett, Michael Moroney); Máire Ní Murchú, Anne O'Connor, Archivist, Alexandra College; Edward O'Loughlin, UCG Library; Marie Peoples; Sr. Martha Magdalen Power, (Sisters of Charity); Sr. Patricia Quinlan, (Convent of Mercy Kinsale); Cilian Roden, Joe and Christine Scallan; St. Dimpna - en Gasthuismuseum, Geel (Frieda Van Ravensteyn); Sean Spellissy; Sr. Theodore, (Holy Faith Sisters); Dr. Hilda Tweedy; Professor John Waddell; Women's Commemoration and Celebration Committee (Joy Rudd); Women's Studies Centre, UCG.

A special word of thanks is due to Alan Hayes, Women's Studies Centre, UCG, for his most generous sharing of information with us.

We are also much indebted to our publisher Anne Korff, to our editorial advisers Annette Möker and Mary Healion-Shelley, and to our indexor Bernie Small.

Míle Buíochas.

ACKNOWLEDGEMENTS FOR ILLUSTRATIONS

National Library of Ireland, illus. 1, 4, 9, 14, 15, 21, 23, 31, 34, 38, 39, 49, 53, 57, 58, 64, 66, 67, 68, 76, 77.

National Gallery of Ireland, illus. 5, 7, 8, 11, 18, 20, 27, 28, 30, 32, 33, 44, 46, 50, 52, 56, 61, 65, 74, 75.

Hugh Lane Municipal Gallery of Modern Art, Dublin, illus. 26, 41, 62, 70.

An Post, illus. 2, 25. Liam de Paor, illus. 3. G.A. Duncan, illus. 6, 10, 42, 45, 54. Comhaltas Ceoltóiri Éireann, illus. 12. St. Clare's Convent, Kenmare, illus. 13. Ulster Museum, Belfast, illus. 16. National Musuem of Ireland, illus. 17. Irish Traditional Music Archive, illus. 19. Steve Mac Donogh, illus. 22. Victoria & Albert Museum, London, illus. 24, John Cussen, Newcastle West Historical Society, illus. 29. Gerry Linnane, illus. 35. The Hulton Deutsch Collection, illus. 36, 40. Edward Sweeney, illus. 37. SIPTU, illus. 43. The Cork Examiner, illus. 45. Foxford Resources Ltd., illus. 48. RTE, illus. 51. Private Collection, illus. 55. National Botanic Gardens, illus. 59, 60, 63. Alexandra College, Dublin, illus. 69. John James Mahon, illus. 71a & b. Frank Dolan, Westport, illus. 72. The Birr Scientific and Heritage Foundation, illus. 73.

Special thanks to Pauline Goodwin for her enthusiasm and time in assisting the publisher to locate photographs. To Mary McFeely of the National Gallery of Ireland; David McLoughlin, Elizabeth M. Kirwan and Colette O'Daly of the National Library of Ireland for their kind assistance.

FOREWORD

Mary Robinson's election to the Presidency of Ireland in 1991, however immeasurable its impact as yet, has given an unprecedented impulse to the awakening of interest in women's studies. The result of this will, ideally, be the reinstatement of the women's story into the Irish psyche, into the mainstream of Irish historical research and, eventually, into the classrooms of the Irish educational system.

"I want this Presidency to promote the telling of stories," declared President Robinson in her first address to the Irish people, "stories of celebration through the arts and stories of conscience and of social justice. As a woman I want women who have felt themselves outside history to be written back into history ..."

The origin of this Dictionary of Irishwomen's Biography lies in our response to these words from our first woman President to *mná na hÉireann*, the women of Ireland. Subsequent visits to libraries, hours spent delving into history books, and an existing personal collection of biographies convinced us of what historian Margaret Ward called, 'the collective amnesia,' regarding the roles and achievements of women in Irish historiography and even in the Irish mind. A pressing need for such a reference book was clear. The potential of such a work, to open hearts and minds to the stories of these women, spurred us into action.

Once we began to plan this book it became immediately apparent there was a need for some criteria as to who could be considered as 'Irish' and who might be selected from the thousands of choices. Apart from a straightforward decision to exclude any living person (the dictionary or biography we had in mind was not to be a 'Who's Who') the selection has often been subjective, personal and, on occasion, constrained by time and other contingencies. We wanted our selection to be as representative and diverse as reasonably possible: to provide evidence of Irish women acting and achieving, in as many areas as was feasible over the centuries, and rising above dictates or limitations placed on them by society or circumstances. We are conscious, however, there are many areas to which we could only make the occasional bow.

An area of particular concern was to indicate family background and, wherever possible, historical context; we also aimed to provide some flavour of each subject's life. We undertook to make the material accessible and meaningful to a potential international readership and to the younger generation of Ireland who, perhaps, have not had an opportunity such as our own to become familiar with almost two millennia of Irish history. To this end we have included much detail, explicatory and expository, which we hope will prove useful to many readers without appearing overly-pedantic to the rest. Students, researchers, and readers with a particular interest in women's studies, will find a comprehensive index and a supplementary section in which the subjects of the entries are classified according to occupations, pursuits, etc. An appendix of more than one hundred explanatory notes has been added as a further aid.

Factual errors and omissions are the responsibility of the authors alone; we hope to be afforded the opportunity to amend any such in a future edition. In particular we beg the lenity of our readers in regard to the orthography of Gaelic names and words and to what may appear as the arbitrary use of both original Gaelic names and their Anglicised forms. There is no standard to adhere to, for the benefit of the general reader, other than to Anglicise everything and, to do that, we would consider debasing and distorting.

Finally, we hope this Dictionary of Irishwomen's Biography will not only be of interest to the general reader, and of use to the specialist, but will also play some part in putting the women's story back into Irish history.

Cyril and Kit Ó Céirín.
Lios Dúin Bhearna, July 1996.

AIKENHEAD, MARY (MOTHER MARY AUGUSTINE) (1787-1858), founder of the Irish Sisters of Charity. Born Cork city January 19, 1787. Her father, a wealthy doctor, was the son of a protestant Scots military officer. Her mother came from a Roman Catholic merchant family, the Stacpooles. For health reasons Mary was fostered out to a poor Roman Catholic family on the outskirts of the city and the experience was to influence her enormously. Following the death of her father, who became a convert to Roman Catholicism on his death bed, she too converted at the age of fifteen and dedicated herself to working with the poor. A visit to Dublin led to the coadjutor bishop of the city, Dr. Murray, advising Mary to enter the novitiate at the Bar Convent in York, England. In 1815 she returned to Dublin with Alicia Walsh and at the North William Street Orphanage, their first house, they took vows of religion. Mary, now Mother Mary Augustine, was appointed Superior-General of the newly-constituted Congregation of the Irish Sisters of Charity, an un-cloistered order vowing service to the poor for 'pure love of God'. Final papal confirmation of the order's constitution had to wait until 1833. The order, providing poor schools, hospitals and refuges for women, set up several convents in Dublin as well as in Cork (1826), Waterford (1842), Galway (1844), and Clonmel (1845). When called on by Dr. Murray during the cholera epidemic of 1832, the Sisters of Charity ran two small hospitals in Dublin until, two years later, Mother Mary Augustine founded the first Roman Catholic hospital in the city since the Reformation, the famous St. Vincent's Hospital, then in St. Stephen's Green. In 1838, the Irish Sisters of Charity became the first Roman Catholic women religious to work in Australia. Despite being bed-ridden or a near-invalid with chronic spinal problems for almost three decades, Mother Mary Augustine worked incessantly until her death in Dublin on July 22, 1858. Her last official act was the establishment of a convent at Benada Abbey, Co. Sligo. "Labour," she advised her Sisters, "as if all depended on our poor endeavours, all the while convinced that God is all-sufficient." Her congregation has since spread to England Scotland, the USA, Venezuela, Zambia and Nigeria. The cause for her beatification has been approved by the papacy.

ALEXANDER, CECIL FRANCES, née HUMPHREYS, (1818-1895), hymn-writer. Born Co. Wicklow and moved, aged fifteen, to Strabane, Co. Tyrone, where her father, Major Humphreys, was land steward to the Duke of Abercorn. As a Sunday school teacher, Cecil composed hymns for children, two books of which were published in 1848, *Hymns for Little Children* and *Verses for the Holy Season*. The former, containing the much-loved 'All Things Bright and Beautiful', went into sixty-nine editions and her carol, 'Once in Royal David's City', is still a Christmas favourite. She continued to write all her life, publishing several volumes of spiritual poetry and other hymns including her most famous, 'There is a Green Hill Far Away'. She donated the bulk of the publications to a school for deaf children founded by her sister Anne in Strabane. At thirty-two, she married a young Derry-born curate, William Alexander, who became known as a theologian, author and poet and was made Bishop of Derry in 1867. Cecil Alexander did not live to see her husband made Primate of All Ireland, having died two years previously in Derry on October 12, 1895.

ALLGOOD, MOLLY. See under O'NEILL, MÁIRE.

*1. **Sara Allgood** playing the title role in* Kathleen Ni Houlihan *by W.B. Yeats, Abbey Theatre, Dublin.*

ALLGOOD, SARA (1883-1950), actress. Born Drumcondra, Dublin. She was apprenticed to an upholsterer as a young girl and later joined the nationalist women's association, Inghinidhe na hÉireann, to be 'discovered' by its drama coach, William Fay. After a short period with his National Theatre Society she played in the opening night of LADY GREGORY'S *Spreading the News* at the Abbey Theatre, Dublin, in 1904. Sara made a lasting impact on audiences in such plays as Yeats' *Cathleen Ní Houlihan* and Synge's *Riders to the Sea,* for the next decade, by exemplifying the characteristic restrained style of acting associated with the Fay brothers and the Abbey. During this period she also completed highly successful tours of England and America with the company. In 1915 she played the female lead in *Peg O' My Heart,* a lightweight comedy that was so successful it toured for several years, being especially popular in Australia and New Zealand. Sara married her leading man, Gerald Henson, in Melbourne, Australia, but when he died within two years she returned to Ireland and the Abbey Theatre. She secured her place in Irish theatrical history by playing the tragic female leads in Sean O'Casey's *The Plough and the Stars* and *Juno and the Paycock.* Several successful tours of England and America followed and she appeared in a number of American films, including versions of *Juno* and *Riders to the Sea.* Sara opted to remain in Hollywood at the outbreak of the Second World War and she appeared in many more films, though only in cameo roles and bit parts. She died, poor and forgotten, twelve years later on September 13, 1950, survived by her sister MOLLY ALLGOOD, who had followed her to fame on the Abbey stage and who also ended her career playing bit parts in films.

ATTRACTA (ATHRACHT), SAINT (c. 410-c. 470), virgin saint, patron of the diocese of Achonry, in north Connaught. It is generally accepted that Attracta was of Donegal origin as the *Martyrology of Donegal* states she was daughter to one Tighernach of Cill Saile, probably a petty chieftain. She was professed by St. Patrick and, at his command, established her cell or convent at Lough Gara, Co. Sligo, at a spot where seven roads met so that it might be as accessible as possible for the needy. A great *bruighean* or hostel for the poor and sick she built at Killaraght flourished for more than a thousand years until destroyed in 1539. Her name is associated with several other ecclesiastical foundations in the diocese of Achonry and an unusually large amount of folklore about her life and miracles survived among the people of the surrounding Coolavin district until recent times. She is the patron of the diocese of Achonry and a pilgrimage was made to a well at Killaraght on August 11, her feast day, up until this century.

AYLWARD, MARGARET LOUISA (1819-1889), social worker, founder of the Sisters of the Holy Faith. Born November 23, 1810, in Waterford at the beginning of the Roman Catholic revival in the post-penal era. Margaret was a daughter of one of the several wealthy Roman Catholic merchant families in the thriving seaport. Her mother, a Murphy, had a similar background. She and her nine sisters and brothers were sent to expensive schools. Margaret spent an extended period at the Ursuline Convent in Thurles, Co. Tipperary and was nearly twenty when she returned home. She applied herself for four years to the type of charitable work which, in that period, was not uncommon among middle class ladies of all denominations. She entered MARY AIKENHEAD's Irish Sisters of Charity but left again possibly in protest with the founder's handling of an internal discipline problem. After three years, in which she guided her family through a period of severe financial and emotional difficulties, Margaret made a second abortive attempt to become a nun. In 1846, as the Great Famine raged, she moved to Dublin and became wholeheartedly involved in working with the Ladies Association of Charity of St. Vincent de Paul for the Spiritual and Temporal Relief of the Sick Poor, a lay middle-class relief and catechizing group. Some years later with her friend, Margaret Kelly, she set up a branch of the Ladies Association in one of the city's worst slum areas, St. Michan's and St. Mary's in north central Dublin. With the help of a small committee Margaret soon had a team of one hundred and fifty middle-class women engaged in serious relief work as well as in religious instruction. The team's corporeal works of charity were made possible by endless fund-raising. While accepting help from the local clergy Margaret conducted the Association's affairs with an independence unusual for a woman of her day. She attacked the city's wealthy Roman Catholics and the official Church, then engaged in a spate of church-building, for neglecting the poor. The work of the Ladies Association brought them into direct confrontation with the protestant proselytizing group, the Irish Church Missions, founded at the height of the Famine and drawing on state support. Margaret's group believed that providing food depots, poor houses, and residential homes for children on strict denominational lines, was a cynical attempt, by the Mission, to induce mass conversion. The Ladies Association responded aggressively by attempting to recover children from protestant care. As a further response, Margaret Aylward planned and directed a system, from 1857, by which destitute children could be reared by selected foster mothers on small farms in the environs of the city: St. Brigid's Orphanage, working in conjunction with the diocesan clergy, was administered by volunteer staff and entirely supported by donations. Some three thousand children were taken into care in the thirty years of Margaret's management. In 1860, in a complicated legal case, she was charged with kidnapping and sentenced to six months imprisonment for not producing a particular child. Bitter public controversy ensued in which the London *Times* accused the Archbishop of Dublin of inciting 'fanatical women' to steal children. Although subjected to unusually harsh treatment Margaret continued to manage her charities from prison. On her release she set about establishing a series of small poor schools, especially in areas where protestant proselytizers were hardest at work, setting up ten in all. Realising that the Ladies Association required some permanent form Margaret allowed the small group of fellow workers, with whom she had lived for some years under self-imposed religious rule, to become a canonically approved institution under the control of her bishop. This resulted in the founding of the Sisters of the Holy Faith in 1868. Even so, she maintained her independent approach in the face of episcopal interference where she considered the welfare of the poor to be at stake. Margaret Aylward died on October 11, 1889. By the end of the century the Holy Faith order had twenty-three schools in Dublin and Leinster and St. Brigid's Orphanage operated for another half century. Having accepted an invitation in 1947 to meet a demand for Roman Catholic education in Trinidad, the order set up foundations in the USA, New Zealand and Australia over the next twenty years.

BALL, FRANCES (MOTHER MARY TERESA)

(1794-1861), educator and founder of the Sisters of Loreto. Born January 6, 1794, at 63 Eccles Street, Dublin, the youngest child of a wealthy silk merchant who had exhibited moral courage by converting to Roman Catholicism in the political climate of the period. Frances was educated in England, from age nine to fourteen, at the Bar Convent, York. Back in Dublin she choose to enter religious life while still in her mid-teens. Archbishop Murray, a family friend who had been instrumental in the establishment of the Sisters of Charity in Dublin to nurse the sick, advised her of the necessity for Roman Catholic schools in the city. Frances returned to the Bar Convent to be prepared for the task and was professed there, in the Institute of the Blessed Virgin Mary (IBVM), in 1816. Mother Mary Teresa returned to Dublin, with two novices and five years teaching experience, to found the autonomous Irish branch of the Institute intended to provide day and boarding schools for girls and free schooling for poor children. In May 1822 she opened the first school, with a total of twelve pupils, in a small rented house in Harold's Cross. The penal laws against Catholic education had become relaxed and the Archbishop was able to purchase Rathfarnham House, a sizeable property then on the outskirts of the city, for the nuns. Mother Mary Teresa, who proved to be an exceptional organiser and administrator, built up a convent and boarding school and named it 'Loreto Abbey'. The Sisters of the Irish IBVM became known as the 'Ladies of Loreto' (or Loretto). After Catholic Emancipation (1829), Loreto Abbey was greatly enlarged and many novices joined the order. Loreto schools played an important role in the revival of Catholic education, especially that of middle class girls. Under Mother Mary Teresa's direction the Sisters answered invitations to set up boarding, day and free schools outside Dublin. Navan, Co. Meath, was the first foundation in 1833. Today there are nine in Ireland. At the request of the

Bishop of Calcutta she sent Sisters to India in 1841 to found the first Loreto foreign mission. Others followed in Mauritius (1844), Gibraltar (1845), Canada (1847), England (1851), and Spain (1855). When Mother Mary Teresa died in Dublin, on May 19, 1861, there were thirty-eight Loreto foundations administered from the original mother-house in Rathfarnham. The Loreto Sisters continued to expand their mission and today are involved in educational, social and pastoral work in South Africa, Australia. Kenya, the United States of America and Peru.

BALL, MARGARET, née BERMINGHAM (*c.* 1515-c. 1584), recusant. Daughter of the Corballis, Co. Meath, branch of the Norman-Irish house of Bermingham. She married a wealthy Dublin merchant, Alderman Bartholomew Ball, in 1530. Her husband was Lord Mayor of Dublin 1553-1554. Both families were strong supporters of the Roman Catholic Reformation and Margaret, widowed in her early fifties, not only refused to obey the ordinances of the English Reformed Church but also became actively engaged in Roman Catholic catechetics with her chaplain. She ran a school for 'good scholars and devoted followers' in her home and established a network with other wealthy Dublin recusant families and their servants. In the late 1570s she was arrested during a mass in her house and both she and the priest were imprisoned for a short period. When Viscount Baltinglass and Baron Nugent were forced into rebellion in 1580 and supplied by merchants in Dublin, many members of the best families of the Pale were arrested on suspicion of complicity and executed or imprisoned. It was in this situation that Walter Bermingham, Margaret's eldest son, attempted to follow in his father's footsteps and become Lord Mayor. To persuade him to remain faithful to Rome his mother convened at her home 'many Roman Catholic bishops, priests and other learned men' to debate the issues involved and dissuade him. He chose the protestant side, became Lord Mayor in 1580, and immediately had his mother and her chaplain arrested. 'Worn out by the filth of the prison, by her sufferings and by her infirmities,' she died in about 1584 while still imprisoned in Dublin Castle. The cause of Margaret Bermingham (with sixteen other martyrs of the period) has been proved acceptable to the Roman Congregation for the Causes of Saints and her formal beatification is in process.

BALL, MARY (1812-1898), naturalist. Born in Cork into an affluent Anglo-Irish family. She is one of the earliest Irish women scientists and among the first in a series of 19th century Irish gentlewomen to contribute significantly in the field of natural history. Her brother John was also a notable scientist and botanist. Mary assembled important collections of insects (now on permanent display in the Museum of Trinity College Dublin), lepidoptera, shells (the shell *Rissoa Balliae* has been named after her) and flora. It was, however, considered 'unladylike' to be seriously concerned with such matters before the advent of her contemporary, MARY WARD, therefore many of Mary Ball's observations are incorporated in the publications of male contemporaries as, for instance, in William Thompson's *Natural History of Ireland* (1849-1856), the standard book on the subject for almost half a century, in A.H. Haliday's *Irish Lepidoptera* and in books by Continental naturalists. Even her study of stridulation (insects making rasping sounds with their legs), the first of its kind recorded, was published under her brother's name. Mary Ball enjoyed her 'pastime' into old age and was still touring with the Belfast Naturalist's Field Club until she died in her eighties.

BARBER, MARY (1690-1757), poet. Believed to be born in Dublin. She married an English tailor in Capel Street, Dublin, and appears to have lived in poor circumstances. Mary was one of the first women poets in the English language in Ireland and was fortunate that her work gained the notice of the ageing Dean Swift who became a patron. Much of her verse was written for her children, for instance a poem for her son to be 'spoken by him in school, upon his master's bringing in a rod,' or another 'to be spoken by him at his first putting on breeches.' However, if her subjects were domestic, she was able to satirise the follies of society through them. Swift may have introduced her to other patrons including the wife of the Lord Lieutenant. She published *Poems on Several Occasions* (1734) by subscription in London. Although there was good response the book earned her little money. Swift came to the rescue by allowing her to publish his *Polite Conversations* which proved successful financially and she appears to have kept poverty at bay until her death two decades later.

What is it our Mammas bewitches,
To plague us little Boys with breeches?
To Tyrant Custom we must yield,
Whilst vanquish'd Reason flies the Field...

BARNACLE, NORA (1884-1951), wife of James Joyce. Born Galway, daughter of a baker. At twenty, she went to Dublin to escape poverty and worked as a chambermaid in Finn's Hotel, Leinster Street, where she began a relationship with James Joyce, an occasional teacher and singer, who was two years younger. They went to Zürich where Joyce taught English and began to write his book of short stories, *Dubliners*. Two children, Georgio and Lucia Anna, were born before their parents married in 1931. The family's poor circumstances, due mainly to Joyce's growing drink problem, was relieved only by the patronage of some rich American ladies. Nora, despite her lack of schooling and disinterest in literature (she always felt her consort should have followed his singing career) made a lasting impression on Joyce's literary and artistic friends because of her individuality and unconventionality. Her life was bleak and often isolated. She moved with Joyce to Zürich in 1940, shortly before his death, and survived him by eleven years. In the latter years of her life, Nora gradually reverted to the Roman Catholicism her husband had so trenchantly renounced. She died in Zürich in 1951. Today, Nora Barnacle is something of a cult-figure to feminists and other admirers not only for her personality but also because of her constancy in the face of vicissitudes with the genius with whom she had chosen to live.

BARNEWELL, MARGERY (*c*. 16th-17th century), recusant nun. Born into a branch of the Roman Catholic 'Old English' family of Trimbleston, which, following the collapse of the House of Kildare, was already split in its political and religious loyalties. Some leading members of the family were prepared to take over church lands and to war against the King's 'English rebels and Irish enemies.' Margery was thirty years old before she 'received the blessed veil from a certain Roman Catholic bishop . . . according to the old Irish custom.' At this time convents in the accepted sense were not tolerated in the Pale (the territory on the east coast, including Dublin, under full control of the English monarchy) as acts had been passed by the 'Reformation parliament' in Dublin to dissolve the abbeys. For this reason Margery may have remained in her own home or in a private place of retirement. In about 1578 a spy reported her to Loftus the protestant Archbishop of Dublin. When arrested, she refused to abjure the Roman faith and was imprisoned. Her family, probably embarrassed by such recusancy, contrived Margery's escape on a French vessel bound for St. Malo in Brittany. She had a young girl with her who was most likely an attendant. At St. Malo, the pair were attacked by drunken crew members and escaped by jumping overboard but their voluminous garments saved them from drowning. They were recognised in the city by a merchant from Dublin and were welcomed by the local bishop. In fulfillment of a vow Margery journeyed, apparently on foot, to the shrine of Santiago de Compostella in northern Spain where her young companion died. She continued on to Rome and other places of pilgrimage. Returning to Ireland she lived as best a Roman Catholic nun could during that period, practising her religion in secret, and 'passing her life amidst honest, chaste women and devout virgins.' Evidently Margery's example attracted a relatively large number of women to religious life so that by 1607, some time after her death, the Jesuit Henry Fitzsimons was urged to return from Flanders to Dublin to minister to them.

BARRINGTON, MARGARET (*c.* 1896-1982), novelist and short-story writer. Born Malin, Co. Donegal, where her father was a district inspector of police. She was educated in schools in Donegal, Kerry and Dublin before attending Trinity College Dublin. She married the historian Edmund Curtis in 1918 but the marriage was dissolved. In 1926 she married Liam O'Flaherty who had established himself the previous year as a major new writer. They had one child and separated after six years. The details of Margaret's subsequent life are blurred. It is known that she went to England where she worked as a journalist. Always in sympathy with the radical left, she assisted in organising support for the Republicans during the Spanish Civil War. She had already published some sketches and short stories without much reaction before a novel, autobiographical in content, *My Cousin Justin* (1939), marked her as a promising writer. However, the Second World War intervened and Margaret was next found helping refugees from the Nazi terror. She was involved in left wing political activities for a time before going to west Cork where she lived for thirty years in some isolation. In her old age, she discovered a large number of short stories, written several decades earlier, and submitted them to a publisher. The result was *David's Daughter, Tamar* (1982), which received unusual critical acclaim. Margaret Barrington had, however, died a short time previously.

BARRY, MOTHER GERALD (CATHERINE) (1881-1961), educator and religious administrator, co-founder of Barry College, Miami. Born March 11, 1881, in Inagh, Co. Clare, one of eighteen children. Her father was a prosperous well-educated farmer. Catherine emigrated as a young woman to America where several members of the family preceded her and where two of her brothers had entered religious life. When she was thirty-two she entered the Dominican Sisters of Adrian, taking the names Mary Gerald. After serving as teacher, principal, and novice mistress she was appointed Mother General of her order in 1933 and held this post until her death almost thirty years later. During her term of office Mother Gerald saw membership increase threefold and encouraged hundreds of Sisters to obtain third level qualifications. Numerous educational foundations for females were set up by the order under Mother Gerald's administration. These included two senior colleges, four girls high schools, seventy parochial schools, a teachers college (Nassau, Bahamas), a business women's residence, an academy and two missions in Santo Domingo. In 1940, with her brothers Patrick, then Bishop of St.

Augustine, and William, Monsignor of St. Patrick's Church, Miami Beach, and their friend John Thompson, a Baptist attorney, Mother Gerald founded Barry College, a leading liberal arts college for women, in Miami. The College was affiliated to the Roman Catholic University of America and received a charter to confer degrees from the State of Florida. Mother Gerald served as president of the College board for about two decades. Today the curriculum encompasses theology and philosophy, language and literature, natural and social sciences, fine arts and community services including nursing. In 1960 the College, and Dominican schools in general, began a co-ordinated service for the many Cuban refugees arriving in Florida at this time. Mother Gerald received honorary degrees from the Universities of Santo Domingo, Notre Dame and Loyola for her work in education. In l952 she was the first executive chairperson of the Sisters' Committee for the National Congress of Religious in the US. She presided, in 1956, at the meeting of religious superiors of North America. This led to the permanent Conference of Major Superiors of Women's Religious Institutes. She died on November 20, 1961, at Adrian, Michigan, where she had entered the Dominican Sisters almost a half century before. A collection of her letters to her community was published in 1962 under the title, *The Charity of Christ Presses Us.*

BARRY, 'JAMES' MIRANDA STUART (1795-1865), army surgeon. Born Co. Cork, one of two daughters of the painter, James Barry, who lost his position as professor at the British Royal Academy and was expelled from that institution four years after Miranda's birth. When he died wretchedly poor, in l806, he commended his family to his former patrons, the Earl of Buchan and General Francisco Miranda, a political exile from Venezuela, (in whose honour, Barry's daughter Miranda had been named). Their mother brought both children to Edinburgh where they were sustained by the Earl. Miranda Barry studied science privately from an early age and, determined to become a doctor, readily accepted a proposal by the General that she should practice in Venezuela. Women were barred from university education at that time but Miranda gained entry to Edinburgh University by pretending to be a boy - 'James' - and, although said to have been petite and effeminate, she attracted little attention before qualifying as a physician in 1812. By then General Miranda's Venezuelan revolution had failed and 'James' continued her deception in order to study surgery in Guy's Hospital, London, before joining the British army in 1813, possibly with the connivance of her patron. Following two years as staff surgeon at Plymouth, England, she was posted as assistant surgeon to the Cape Colony, where she worked for a dozen years. While the 'prevailing opinion (was) that he was a female', Barry was so successful a practitioner that this was overlooked and she was promoted to Medical Inspector for the Colony. However, she made enemies in attempting to improve conditions there, especially because of her efforts on behalf of prisoners, the mentally-ill, and non-whites. She received a suspended prison sentence for refusing on principle to obey a superior's command and was subsequently posted to other outposts of the British Empire. In 1836 she was appointed Principal Medical Officer on the island of St. Helena. Again, on a matter of principle, she ran foul of her superiors and was charged with 'conduct unbecoming an officer and a gentleman'. For the next twenty-one years, Miranda served successively in the Windward and Leeward Islands in the Caribbean, in Malta, Corfu and, finally, Canada where she was Inspector-General of all British hospitals. Ill health forced her to leave army service in 1859 and she retired with a small pension to lodgings in Marylebone, London, where she died five years later. It was only then the discovery of her true sex became public knowledge and (even though the Army Command had probably been aware of her true sex for half a century) a planned military funeral was countermanded. She is credited with having carried out the second successful caesarean operation in modern medical history and with being the first medical doctor to encourage the use of official female nurses for female hospital patients.

BARRY, TERESA (MOTHER MARY TERESA) (*c.* 1815-1900), nursing pioneer and administrator. Born in Cork city and taken to the United States at the age of two by spinster aunts, Honora and Mary O'Gorman, after the death of her mother, and reared by them in Baltimore, Maryland. In 1829 yellow fever struck Carolina and Georgia, leaving large numbers of destitute children and orphans, many of them coloured, in its wake. Teresa's aunts and a friend, Miss Burke, answered the call for assistance from the Roman Catholic Archbishop of Charleston. After arriving in Charleston, they set up a religious community, The Sisters of Charity of Our Lady of Mercy, using a modification of the St. Vincent de Paul rule, and opened their first school. At fifteen Teresa took vows and, as Sr. Mary Teresa, began to teach. The early years of poverty and struggle seemed hopeless for the tiny community but by 1836, when cholera swept through Charleston, the Sisters were numerous enough to play a significant role in nursing the sick. In 1841, Sr. Mary Teresa was appointed principal of their school for coloured children. At the age of twenty-nine she was made Reverend Mother of the religious community. During the Civil War twenty years later, Mother Mary Teresa turned the Charleston foundation into a

hospital. Because of their work with battle casualties and prisoners the nuns were asked to set up a hospital for the military at White Sulphur Springs in West Virginia. Mother Mary Teresa, with five of her community, set off in a wagon on the one hundred and fifty mile trail across the Allegheny and Appalachian mountain wilderness to establish the military hospital: she almost immediately detoured, with three of her party, to fight a yellow fever outbreak in Wilmington, North Carolina. The city of Charleston was destroyed during the war and, with it, all the foundations of the Sisters of Charity but Congress later granted twelve thousand dollars to the community as 'a testimonial of appreciation and gratitude from the American people.' Mother Teresa spent the remaining thirty-five years of her life overseeing the extension of the order's network of schools, orphanages, and hospitals in Charleston and West Virginia. She died, after seventy-one years as a nun, on May 18, 1900.

BARTON, ROSE MAYNARD (1858-1929), artist. Born at Rochestown, Co. Tipperary, daughter of a wealthy solicitor; the painters LETITIA HAMILTON, her sister Eva, and the author and painter EDITH SOMERVILLE, were close relations. Rose was educated by a governess from whom she first learned to draw. In her late teens she studied art in London, with the noted watercolour artist Paul Naftel, and in Paris under Henri Gervex, who introduced her to Impressionism. Once back in Ireland, she was initially too taken up with a heady social life to employ her talents seriously. Rose exhibited for the first time, in 1878, at the Royal Irish Academy in Dublin and at the Royal Academy in London in 1880. From this time onwards she worked mainly in the British capital where her attractive watercolours, mostly of townscapes and casual subjects captured in her own impressionistic genre, sold well. In 1898 Rose produced more than ninety illustrations for Frances Gerrard's book, *Picturesque Dublin, Old and New*, and, in 1904, she wrote and richly illustrated *Familiar London*. She enjoyed a highly successful career as a professional artist; examples of her work are in many public and private collections, including the National Gallery of Ireland and the Hugh Lane Municipal Gallery in Dublin, the Ulster Museum in Belfast and the Crawford Municipal Art Gallery in Cork. Rose Barton died at her home in Knightsbridge, London, in October 1929.

BATES, DAISY MAY, née O'DWYER (*c.* 1862-1951), anthropologist and journalist. Born in Co. Tipperary. She claimed direct descent from the Gaelic lords, the O'Dwyers of Kilnamanagh, whose power was broken in the mid-17th century. Some branches, mostly protestant, survived as landed gentry in or near their ancestral territory and supplied at least eight generals to the British army. Daisy professed to have belonged to one of the better-off protestant branches but recent research indicates she was from a poor Roman Catholic family. In fact, given the history of the period, the two accounts may not be incompatible. Circumstantial evidence suggests that, although Daisy was to work intermittently as a freelance journalist, she had a private income for at least the first half of her long life. It is difficult to separate fiction from fact in the various accounts of Daisy Bates' remarkable career and some particulars in the following description are open to question. Because her family broke up she may have been reared by grandparents or in an orphanage and trained as a governess in a charity school. In her early twenties she emigrated to North Queensland, Australia, and married twice before returning alone to Ireland, leaving a baby son behind. She then appears to have worked for some years as a journalist in London and was sent (by her own account) by the London *Times* to investigate the ill-treatment of Aborigines in Western Australia. Daisy was reunited for a time with her possibly bigamous cattle drover husband, Jack Bates, and her son, on an outback farm on the northwest coast. She then accompanied the Roman Catholic Bishop of Perth on a four-month trek to a mission further north in the wilderness. The party barely escaped with their lives to Broome. Here, while working on a cattle station, Daisy studied the local aboriginal people and used her remarkable talents to gain admittance to their hidden social life and rites. According to an article she published in the *Australasian* journal, twenty years later, Daisy then bought a herd of eight hundred cattle and, with a team of drovers, set off to drive them to her husband's cattle station a thousand miles south. She made a thousand pounds profit. For most of the following eight years she lived as a nomad with the aboriginal peoples of south west Australia and continually recorded their way of life. By 1920 Daisy, who had also taken up lecturing, was recognised as an authority on the indigenous peoples and was invited to take part in university expeditions and science conferences. She was even requested to organise an exhibition of native life for the Prince of Wales. On the other hand she got little financial support for her work. At almost sixty years of age, Daisy moved to the arid Nullarbor Plain of South Australia where she spent twelve years living with the Aborigines. She nursed and defended them (she was made a Justice of the Peace, the first woman in the state to be so appointed) while continually recording their ways. 'It was now impossible for me to relinquish the work,' she once wrote. 'I realized they were passing from us'. Daisy produced a relatively large amount of journalistic work at this time to make the Aborigines' plight known to the outside world.

In 1933, Daisy Bates was brought, by an Australian Government committee, to Canberra to advise on the future of the aboriginal peoples; her advice (to give them enough land to live on protected from intrusion) was ignored. She was awarded an OBE in 1934. In 1938 she published her monumental work, *The Passing of the Aborigines,* in Britain; it did not appear in Australia for another eight years and then only after she had received a Commonwealth Literary Fellowship. Finding herself a misfit in western society Daisy went back, at about eighty years of age, to the Aborigines of the Murray River Basin east of Adelaide. It is on record that, during this period, she once prevented police from raiding a native camp by threatening them with a shotgun. In 1945 ill health forced Daisy to leave the outback and the Australian Government finally came to her aid by granting her a much-needed pension of five guineas a week. Daisy Bates died in an Adelaide nursing home six years later. The invaluable records of her research were given to the National Library of Australia at Canberra and remain unpublished to date.

BEE, SAINT. See under BEGHA, SAINT.

BEERE, THEKLA JUNE (1901-1991), civil servant and chairperson of the Irish National Commission on the Status of Women (1970-1972). Born in Dublin, where her father was a Church of Ireland rector, she was first educated by her mother as delicate health prevented her from attending school. At the age of fourteen she entered Alexandra College, Dublin. When she began a degree course in law, and legal and political science, at Trinity College Dublin, in 1919, she was the only female student in the law school. Although she graduated with distinction, there was little scope for a young woman of Thekla's background and education in the

Ireland immediately following the break with Britain and the ensuing Civil War. She could only find employment as a third grade clerk with the Irish civil service but at least this new service, composed mainly of personnel from the previous British imperial system, offered a measure of security and potential for advancement. In the event, her position afforded her the opportunity to avail of a Rockerfeller Scholarship that enabled her to spend three years studying in universities in the USA. These included Harvard College, Boston, and Berkeley College, California. Thekla returned to the civil service and by a combination of determination, diplomacy, and toughness, gained steady though slow promotion despite the covert prejudice against women's advancement existing within the service. By her retirement in 1966 she had, as parliamentary secretary to the Department of Transport and Power, reached the highest position ever obtained by a woman. (Four decades were to pass before this achievement was repeated). In her capacity as parliamentary secretary Thekla was chief negotiator, on behalf of the government, in talks with the US Department of Commerce regarding opening Dublin Airport to large American airlines; she needed all her shrewdness and firmness to uphold the Irish government's committment to Shannon Airport. In 1970, some years after her retirement, Thekla accepted chairmanship of the National Commission on the Status of Women, whose terms of reference include making 'the recommendations and the steps necessary to ensure the participation of women on equal terms with men in the political, social, cultural, and economic, life of the country'. The Beere Report (1972), which led to forming the Council for the Status of Women, is looked upon as a watershed in the struggle for women's equality. Thekla Beere was appointed to various influential boards and committees including the council of her old school, Alexandra College; she was also governor of Dublin's Rotunda Hospital. In 1976 a small group of people concerned with the promotion of the status of women in Ireland attempted to persuade the government party to propose her as a nationally-acceptable candidate in the elections for the Presidency of Ireland. She was awarded an honorary LL.D. by Trinity College Dublin, in 1960. Thekla Beere, a keen hill walker all her life, was a founder member of An Óige (1932), the national youth-hostel organisation, with which she maintained close links up to her death at the age of ninety.

BEGHA (BEE, BEGU?), SAINT (7th century), virgin saint. Little is known with certainty about this saint; perhaps the lives of near-contemporaries with similar names have been confused. Best known in Britain as Saint Bee, Begha was the daughter of an Irish king, most likely in Leinster. Determined to follow the life of a religious, she evaded the marriage arrangement made for her by going to the north-west coast of England, the area now known as Cumberland. Here, on the headland which still bears her name, she set up a hermitage, probably with a small community that included a confessor. At this time much of Northumberland had reverted to the control of pagan Saxon kings but King Oswald, who had lived in Ireland from childhood, reclaimed his kingdom in 634 and sent for Christian missionaries. St. Aidan led the Northumbrian mission from Iona and Begha joined him from Cumberland. It is generally accepted that she may be identified with one Heiu whom Bede recorded as being professed by Aidan and is thus credited as the first woman religious in this important kingdom. She was given charge of a convent established at Hartlepool. Later, when the royal princess Hilda was professed, Begha abdicated in her favour.

According to her Acts, she returned to her first foundation which later received grants from King Oswald and successive Anglo-Saxon kings. St. Bees, the monastery named after her, flourished until the Reformation. Other mediaeval writings suppose her to have gone to Yorkshire or to Whitby; since at least the 12th century Begha has also been identified with a Saint Begu whose relics were venerated by the monks of Whitby after the translation of those of the princess Hilda to Glastonbury. Her feast day in Ireland is on September 6. Melvyn Bragg has based his novel *Credo: An Epic Tale of the Dark Ages* (1995) on the literary survivals of this saint's life.

BEHAN, KATHLEEN, née KEARNEY (c. 1889-1984), Dublin character and wit. Born Capel Street, Dublin, into a tenement family with strong republican and cultural antecedents, among them Nioclás Ó Cearnaigh, the last recognised Gaelic scribe and *file* in Co. Louth. Her parents' poverty resulted in Kathleen being admitted to Goldenbridge Orphanage at the age of nine. In her early teens, influenced by her brother Peadar who wrote the words of *A Soldier's Song*, later to become the Irish national anthem, she became associated with the republican movement. During the 1916 Rebellion Kathleen carried despatches to Patrick Pearse and James Connolly. When her first husband died in 1918, leaving her with two small children, she worked as housekeeper for MAUD GONNE MACBRIDE and became known as a 'character' to the literary and artistic circle in Dublin. In 1922 she married Stephen Behan, a house painter, who was imprisoned for two years by the Free State Government as a result of revolutionary activities. Their most famous son, Brendan, born in 1923, was followed by four other children. Although the family remained poor the children grew up in an extraordinary atmosphere of singing, conversation, and literature, in both English and Irish. Kathleen's life was dominated for some decades by the IRA activities of her relatives and immediate family. Brendan was sentenced to three years Borstal detention and later imprisoned. He emerged in the 1950s as a writer and playwright and 'Dublin character'. Another son, Dominic, became a celebrity as a folk singer and song writer. Because of her sons' fame, Kathleen, now in her eighties, was drawn into the limelight and appeared on many TV shows in Britain and Ireland. At the age of ninety she made a long-playing record and, at ninety-five, published an autobiography *Mother of All the Behans* (1984). Vibrant and talkative as ever, she died in Dublin that same year.

BELL, LAURA (1829-1894), courtesan, social missionary and preacher. Born in Co. Antrim, where her father was a land bailiff, she worked as a shop-girl in Belfast before taking to prostitution in Dublin. Although still in her teens, Laura was soon a celebrity in the fashionable society of that city. After moving to London she became infamous as the 'Queen of Whoredom'. She married the wealthy Captain Thistlethwayte and the couple were notorious for their profligacy at their home in London's Grosvenor Square. At thirty-one she was 'converted', became an evangelical preacher and social missionary, and was supported in this work by her husband. Through the next three decades, now a respected figure, she closely co-operated with Prime Minister Gladstone in his social schemes to 'rescue London prostitutes'. After her husband's death Laura Bell retired to a cottage in Hampshire where she died a few years later.

BELLAMY, GEORGE ANNE (*c*. 1727-1788), actress. Born Fingal, Co. Dublin, the illegitimate child of Lord Tyrawley and a young Quaker woman who later married a sea-captain named Bellamy. Lord Tyrawley sent George to be educated at a French convent but her mother enticed her back to England and put her on the stage. She made her debut, age seventeen, at Covent Garden and soon became a sensation at Garrick's Drury Lane Theatre as much for her looks and charms as her acting talents. George became notorious for her numerous love affairs, bigamous marriage, and rivalry with another infamous Dublin-born actress, PEG WOFFINGTON. That rivalry reached its height when Woffington stabbed her in a fit of rage. Soon after the incident Woffington had a breakdown and died and George stepped into her shoes to become the leading lady in London theatre. Her attraction decreased in middle age and only a Covent Garden benefit in 1785 rescued her from abject poverty. George used the money to publish a six-volume account of her tempestuous career, *Apology* (1785), which duly caused a sensation but brought little financial return. She died in obscurity, in London, three years later.

BENNETT, LOUIE (1870-1956), labour leader and suffragist. Born Temple Hill, Dublin, into an affluent protestant business family She was educated at Alexandra College, Dublin, in England and Germany. She had attempted to become a singer and writer, publishing two romantic novels, *The Proving of Priscilla* (1902) and *A Prisoner of his Word* (1908), before becoming active in the suffrage movement in Dublin with her life long friend and co-worker, HELEN CHENEVIX. The pair founded the Irish Women's Suffrage Federation in 1911 with Louie as its first secretary. She worked in association with HANNA SHEEHY SKEFFINGTON on the journal *Irish Citizen*. Under Hanna's influence she was drawn into the developing Irish labour movement, and in 1913 became deeply involved

ÉIRE 32
EUROPA

VOTES
FOR
WOMEN

LOUIE BENNETT (1870-1956) SUFFRAGETTE, TRADE UNIONIST.

*2. **Louie Bennett,** Irish postal stamp, issued 1996.*

in the Dublin general strike. In the same year Louie co-founded the Irish Women's Reform League and, affiliating it to the Suffrage Federation, brought the social and economic plight of women workers and suffrage issues under the one banner. At the outbreak of the First World War she joined the Women's International League for Peace and Freedom and energetically campaigned for peace as a member of its international executive. After the 1916 Rising she became general secretary of the Irish Women Workers Union (IWWU), a position she retained for the next forty years, during which time she was never without the able assistance of Helen Chenevix. Louie transformed the IWWU into a powerful organisation and brought about much reform especially for printing and laundry workers. Her election as president of the Irish Trade Union Congress in 1931 made her the first woman to hold that position. She was in the forefront of the protest against the Conditions of Employment Bill (1935) which she saw as an attempt by the new Fianna Fáil Government to restrict employment opportunities for women, 'a deadly encroachment upon the liberty of the individual'. She also acted as chairperson of a committee formed by the National Council of Women in Ireland to investigate all legislation affecting women's rights and to promote their

interests. A member of the Irish Labour Party's Administrative Committee, she stood unsuccessfully in the 1944 general election as a labour candidate. In 1945 she led the strike of one thousand five hundred laundry workers in Dublin which established the right of the workers to two weeks annual holidays. She again held the office of president of the Irish Trade Union Congress in 1946-1947. Louie Bennett retired from active participation in the trade union and labour movements in 1955 at the age of eighty-five: she died in November of the following year in Killiney, Dublin.

BERMINGHAM, MARGARET. See under BALL, MARGARET.

'BETTY, LADY' (*c.* 1750-*c.* 1807), public hangwoman. Evidently born and raised in Co. Kerry where she married a small farmer named Shugrue. Said to have been evicted as a widow and took to the roads with two young children. She and a son eventually settled in Roscommon. She ran a lodging house for many years until murdering a lodger for his money. 'Betty' had not realised this was her son recently returned from foreign parts. She was sentenced to death but no hangman could be found on the morning of the execution. This is possibly because the other condemned prisoners were Whiteboys, members of a local peasant secret society. The authorities accepted her offer to act as executioner in return for her freedom. It is said she hanged twenty-five men on the first day, incurring the opprobrium and fear of the ordinary people. They nicknamed her 'Lady Betty'. She continued to work as public executioner for the Connaught circuit, especially at Roscommon Jail, for many years. A number of United Irishmen, condemned for insurgency, met their death at the hands of 'Lady Betty'. Her death sentence was lifted by the Lord Lieutenant in 1802 in appreciation of these latter services. She died inside the jail precincts where she had been given quarters for her protection from the time she had begun her nefarious work.

BLACKBURN, HELEN (1842-1903), pioneer campaigner for women's rights, trade unionist and author. Born Knightstown, Valencia Island, Co. Kerry, on May 25, 1842, where her father, an engineer and inventor, was a quarry manager; the family moved to London when she was seventeen. Helen got involved in the movement for women's suffrage at an early age believing that the vote was essential for women's emancipation. At thirty-two she became secretary of the London Central Committee for Women's Suffrage, a post she held for twenty-one years. During this period she was also involved with similar associations and trade unions, one of which, the British National Union of Working Women, sent her as a delegate to the Trades Union Congress in 1881. In that year she published the first of many authoritative books on women's rights and conditions, *A Hand Book for Women engaged in Social and Political Work*. At the same time she was appointed editor of *The Englishwoman's Review*, and established a close co-operation with its owner E.J. (Jessie) Boucherett. From 1895 onwards Helen withdrew from her committee and secretarial activities and wrote *The Women's Suffrage Calendar* (1896-1897), as well as *Condition of Working Women and the Factory Act*s, an important book published by Jessie Boucherett in 1896, promoting their ideas about self-help for women and opposition to legislation regarding women workers. The authors' commitment to the latter concept of self-determination caused them to oppose the extension of the Factory Acts to women and led to controversy within the trade union movement. To this end she and Jessie also established the Freedom of Labour Defence League in 1899. Helen's record of the suffrage movement in the British Isles, *Women's Suffrage* (1902), is still a source book. This was followed by *Women Under the Factory Act*, in conjuction with Nora Wynne, and published posthumously in 1903, as Helen Blackburn had died in London on January 11 of the same year. She is buried in Brompton Cemetery, London.

BLACKBURNE, E. OWENS (*c.* 1848-1894), pen-name of Elizabeth Casey, author. Born Slane, Co. Meath, in comfortable circumstances and educated at Trinity College Dublin. Although having severe eye trouble in her teens Elizabeth chose to become a journalist and writer and went to London in 1873 to further her career. She became a prolific journalist and had early success with a novel, *A Woman Scorned* (1876), which was previously serialised in the *Nation*. Some twenty novels followed in quick succession, including *The Way Women Love* (1877), *The Glen of Silver Birches* (1880) and *The Heart of Erin* (1882). She is mainly remembered for her important work, *Illustrious Irish Women* (1887), the first compilation of its kind and one which is referred to by researchers in women's studies today. E. Owens Blackburne died in a house fire in Fairview, Dublin, in 1894.

BLAKE, LADY EDITH, née OSBORNE (1845-1926), naturalist and painter. Born Newtown Anner, Clonmel, Co. Tipperary, the estate of her maternal grandfather, Sir Thomas Osborne, MP and Sheriff of Waterford; her father, Ralph Bernel, assumed the name Osborne on his marriage. Her mother encouraged her daughters to paint (Edith's sister Grace, later Duchess of St. Albans, also became an accomplished artist) and invited professional painters to their estate. Edith began to paint plants and insects in her teens but it was not until her marriage to Henry Arthur Blake, in 1874, that she began to make important contributions to natural history. Her husband served in the British Colonial Service and Edith followed him, for two decades, on his postings to the various countries in which he became governor, the Bahamas, Newfoundland, Jamaica, Hong Kong and Ceylon. She studied and painted plant and insect life in all these regions, producing valuable scientific information, especially for the British Museum of Natural History, London. Among those of particular account were some two hundred illustrations of Jamaican lepidoptera (butterflies, moths, etc.,) still on display there. Her many floral watercolours of exotic flowers are in private collections.

BLESSINGTON, MARGUERITE, COUNTESS OF, née POWER (1789-1849), socialite and author. Born Knockbrit, Clonmel, Co. Tipperary. Daughter of a once wealthy magistrate and merchant who forced her to marry a British army officer at fifteen. She ran away after three months ill-treatment, lived with another army officer for ten years and, having educated herself, became popular for her beauty and charm in Dublin salons and society. When her husband was killed in a brawl, Marguerite married Charles Gardiner, Earl of Blessington. Her own salon in Dublin and that in her husband's mansion at St. James' Square, London, became famous and she added to her reputation by publishing sketches of London society. In 1822 she toured the Continent with her husband, met Lord Byron in Genoa and, about this time, began a life-long liaison with her husband's son-in-law, Count d'Orsay. After the Earl died in 1829 Marguerite returned to London with d'Orsay. Her financial position was greatly reduced and she turned to writing for profit. Her first novel, *Grace Cassidy or The Repealers* (1833), topical at this time of Repeal agitation, proved financially successful. It was swiftly followed with three biographical travel-

books, *Conversations with Lord Byron* (1834), *The Idler in Italy* (1839) and *The Idler in France* (1841). These effusive works were extremely popular in the fashionable society of the day and did much to popularise the Grand Tour, now that travelling on the Continent was becoming more comfortable. Marguerite re-established her dazzling salon, wrote several other novels and edited two annuals, *The Book of Beauty* and *The Keepsake*. However, the famine in Ireland had had a disastrous effect on the income from her estates and, in spite of making a large income from her literary work, she and d'Orsay had to go to France in May 1849 to escape creditors. Marguerite, Countess of Blessington, died in Paris of apoplexy a month later, on June 4.

BLINNE, SAINT. See under MONINNA, SAINT.

BONNY or BONNEY, ANNE (c. 1700), pirate. Born in one of the English colonies on the coast of Cork, most likely Kinsale or Baltimore, Anne was said to have been the illegitimate daughter of an attorney. Her father brought the child to Charleston, Carolina, in North America, where many of the Cork English were settling. She grew up on his plantation and then ran off with a seaman to New Providence, now Nassau, in the Bahamas, about 1720. 'Bonny' was possibly her married name. Some accounts say Anne's husband sold her, not unwillingly on her part, to 'Calico' Jack Rackham, a small-time pirate captain. Aboard Rackham's sloop, she was to discover another female disguised in male attire, one Mary Read, an ex-British soldier. Both Read and Bonny, wearing 'Men's Jackets, and long Trouzers, and Handkerchiefs tied about their Heads; and ... a Machet and Pistol in their Hands,' took part in boarding ships as pirates. Rackham and company were captured and brought to trial in Jamaica on a charge of seizing seven fishing boats and four merchant vessels during their piratical rampage about Jamaica in the autumn of 1720. At a court of the vice-admiralty, held in Jamaica on November 28, 1720, the entire crew were sentenced to death for acts of piracy. Anne Bonny was reprieved on account of pregnancy, released from prison, and disappeared from the public eye. Daniel Defoe gave an account of her in his celebrated *History of the Pyrates* (1724) and Jamaican court evidence supports the basic facts of his story.

BOURKE or de BÚRCA, HONORA, LADY LUCAN and DUCHESS OF BERWICK (c. 1674-1698), wife of Patrick Sarsfield, hero of the Williamite War. Born at the family seat of De Búrca in Portumna Castle, Co. Galway, daughter of the 7th Earl of Clanrickarde; her mother was a MacCarthy of the Earls of Clancarty. Her father supported the Jacobite cause and commanded a regiment in the army of King James II. Honora was probably educated in Dublin by the Benedictine nuns. At about sixteen years of age she married one of Ireland's wealthiest Roman Catholics, the Jacobite Brigadier General Patrick Sarsfield of Lucan, Co. Dublin. Sarsfield, who previously fought for King James II in England, had accompanied the king to Ireland in 1689 and, in campaigning against the Williamites for two years, became a heroic figure to Irish Jacobites. Honora is said to have been with her husband during both the famous sieges of Limerick and emigrated to France with him in the 1691 'Flight of the Wild Geese' after the Jacobite defeat. While Sarsfield, now a general in the French army, went on campaign in Flanders Honora and their child were given refuge in the Jacobite Court of St. Germaine. The young Lady Lucan impressed both the depressed St. Germaine Court and the glorious Court of Versailles by her vivacity and beauty and is said to have introduced Irish and English dancing to Versailles. Sarsfield was killed at the battle of Landen in 1692. In 1695 Honora married the Marshal Duke of Berwick much to the displeasure of King James, the Duke's natural father, but relations soon improved and the couple were given a suite at Versailles where their son, James Francis FitzJames, was born. Ill health forced the Duchess to move to Languedoc where she died at Pezenas in 1698. Her husband brought Honora's body back to Pontoise where she was buried in the English convent. John Francis Sarsfield, her eldest son, became a colonel in the Spanish and French armies and was killed in action at the age of twenty-four. Her son James, later Duke of Liria, was the Spanish Ambassador to the Russian Court and ancestor of the powerful Spanish family, the Dukes of Alba.

BOWEN, ELIZABETH DOROTHEA COLE (1899-1973), novelist. Born Dublin, June 7, 1899. She lived in Dublin and at Bowen's Court, the family estate in Kildorrery, Co. Cork. The Bowens, originally Welsh Protestants, were prosperous members of the colonist land-owning class. Elizabeth was educated in England and began writing at twenty. Her first book, *Encounters*, a collection of short stories, was published in 1923. The same year she married Alan Cameron who was soon to be Secretary for Education for the City of Oxford, where the couple settled. She published another collection of short stories, *Ann Lee's and Other Stories* (1926), followed by several novels: *The Hotel* (1927), *Friends and Relations* (1931), *To The North* (1932), *The House in Paris* (1936), and *The Death of the Heart* (1936) which is considered one of her best. During this period she also wrote two more books of short stories and three books of a biographical nature: *The Last September* (1929) describing life in a 'big house' during the War of Independence, *Bowen's Court* (1942), a history of the Bowen family in Ireland, and *Seven Winters* (1942), childhood reminiscences. After the war she became a broadcaster and lecturer on literary subjects while producing a steady stream of publications including books of short stories and essays. Her next novel, *The Heat of the Day* (1949), was a Book Club Choice in the United States. She wrote three more, *A World of Love* (1955), *The Little Girls* (1964), *Eva Trout* (1968), and a further collection of stories, *A Day in the Dark* (1965). Elizabeth Bowen is recognised as one of the more important of modern Irish-born novelists and won many honours, including a CBE in 1948, for her writings. She returned to her beloved Bowen's Court in 1952 after the death of her husband but the upkeep proved too much of a burden. She returned to England eight years later and settled at Hythe, Kent. Elizabeth Bowen died in London, February 22, 1973.

BOWEN, GRETTA (1880-1981), artist. Born Dublin, January 1, 1880. She married Matthew Campbell from Belfast and they lived in Arklow, Co. Wicklow, before moving to Belfast. Her husband died in early middle age and Gretta ran a boarding house to support and educate her family. Two of her sons, George and Arthur, became painters with the former being celebrated in Ireland and abroad, particularly in Spain. Gretta began to paint in her seventies almost by chance and, not wishing to be known as the mother of an established painter, exhibited in Belfast under her maiden name. She became widely known as 'the Irish Grandma Moses' because of her age and primitive style, and her recollected scenes from early child-hood attracted many commissions from England, the USA and France. In 1979, her hundredth year - and the year her famous son, George, died - she contributed to the first International Exhibition of Naïve Art, held in London. Gretta Bowen died, aged one hundred and one, on April 8, 1981.

BRACKEN, JOSEPHINE (*b.* 1876), Philippino revolutionary. Born in Belfast, August 9, 1876. Her mother, the wife of a British army corporal, died in childbirth and Josephine was adopted by her godparents, Mr. and Mrs. George Taufer, who brought her to Hong Kong where Mr. Taufer was a boiler engineer. At nineteen she accompanied her foster-father to the Philippines where he had gone to visit a noted physician, Dr. Jose Rizal, for treatment of an eye disease. Dr. Rizal had been campaigning for ten years against the Spanish occupation of the area and seeking reforms in both government and religious affairs. Josephine and the doctor fell in love. With a new insurrection imminent Rizal was arrested, tried in Manila, and sentenced to death as a traitor to Spain. Josephine was permitted to marry the Malay patriot minutes before his execution. Almost immediately, insurrection broke out in the provinces of Panzasina, Zombales and Llocas and the young widow, with her new sister-in-law, joined the rebel forces. At first Josephine did nursing duties but then appears to have taken part in the fighting for some weeks. While on a mission to procure arms she got to Japan, went from there to America, and became unable to rejoin her comrades in the Philippines. She returned to Hong Kong in 1897, when she was twenty-one, and published the story of her involvement in the rebellion and of her marriage. Nothing is known of her subsequent life.

BRAY, SAINT. See under BREAGE, SAINT.

BRAYTON, TERESA (1866-1943), poet. Born Kilbrook, near Kilcock, Co. Kildare, of tenant farming stock. Having attended the local national school Teresa later worked as an assistant teacher at a school in Newtown, Co. Kildare, for many years. She attracted some attention with the publication of her verse in the national press before emigrating to America at the age of forty. In America she supported the Irish Republican Brotherhood by organising fund-raising activities, lecturing on Irish politics and history and distributing pamphlets. She came back to Ireland on a number of occasions and met many leaders of the republican movement. She continued to write in America and *Songs of the Dawn and Irish Ditties* was published in 1913. About this time her poem *The Old Bog Road*, published in a local Cavan newspaper, inspired a young girl, Madeleine King (later O'Farrelly), to compose the air which made it one of the most popular of all Irish immigrant songs. Collections of Teresa Brayton's verse include *Flame of Ireland* (1926) and *Christmas Verses* (1934).

BREAGE (BREACA, BREAG and BRAY), SAINT (5th and 6th century), missionary and hermit. Patron of Breage, Cornwall. An account of her life, kept in her church in Breage, states that Breage was a native of Lagonia, which may indicate that she came from the province of Leinster or was a member of the Laguni people, perhaps from the Louth area. It appears that she was a contemporary of St. Brigid and entered a convent founded by the latter in Magh Breagh ('Campus Breacae'), now Co. Louth. An early wave of Irish missionaries to Cornwall brought her there as one of a large company of men and women which included (under the Cornish form of their names), Sinwan, Erc, Elwen, Crewern and Helen, all of whom played important roles in the history of the Christian church there. It is said they landed at Reyver, moved inland to Penrith, and met a hostile reception from the local chief, Theodorick or Tewder, when some were killed. Breage retreated to Reyver or Pencair and set up her hermitage there. Not uncommon with the hermits of her time she attracted many people to her and is said to have established religious centres in Trenwith and Talmeneth as well as at Breage, the settlement named after her, overlooking Mount's Bay. As many miracles were believed to have occurred at her tomb, it became a place of pilgrimage. Her feast day is not known but, for many centuries, a pilgrimage was made on June 5.

BRIDGEMAN, JOANNA (MOTHER JANE FRANCIS) (*c.* 1812-1888), nursing pioneer and administrator. Born Ballagh, Ruan, Co. Clare, into a prominent wealthy family, a member of whom had been elected MP and involved in the struggle for Catholic Emancipation. Her mother, Lucy Reddan, was related to Daniel O'Connell with whom the family visited. In 1819, after her mother's death and her father's remarriage, Joanna was sent to an aunt, Mrs. Mary Anne Burke, who took her to Limerick where she was setting up a Magdalen Asylum for 'destitute girls'. When a cholera epidemic struck the city in 1832 Joanna assisted her aunt in nursing the sick. In 1838, after the newly-formed Sisters of Mercy had opened a convent in the city, she became a postulant after an unusually short noviceship and, when professed the following year by the founder, CATHERINE McAULEY, took the name Sister Jane Francis. Later, her aunt was to follow her into the order, becoming Mother Mary Anne Burke. In the famine year 1844, on the request of a rich widow from Kinsale, Co. Cork, the Sisters from Limerick set up St. Joseph's convent there. Joanna, as superior, was now Mother Jane Francis and, with her small team of five nuns, began to visit the sick and feed the starving poor. The Sisters received funding from Rome, America, and from the Society of Friends (Quakers). The following year they opened a school and soup kitchen for seven hundred children. This was followed by an orphanage and industrial school housing one hundred and fifty girls employed in needlework and lace-making as indentured servants. The Kinsale community grew rapidly and, in 1844, the first daughter house was established in San Francisco, USA, by MOTHER BAPTIST RUSSELL and Mother Mary Anne Burke. In 1849 a second daughter house was founded in Derby, England. During a cholera outbreak in 1849 the guardians of the Kinsale workhouse, which had more than two thousand inmates, requested the nuns to take over the Kinsale hospital, relaxing the rules to allow the women to carry out their vocation of religious instruction along with their nursing. When Florence Nightingale and her contingent of nurses needed help during the Crimean War, an appeal was made to the Irish Sisters of Mercy. Mother Jane Francis volunteered and was assigned to take fifteen nursing nuns to the war zone. She was soon in conflict with Miss Nightingale and the situation was greatly exacerbated by the racial antagonism of the British Secretary of State for War to the Irish nuns. Once the problems were overcome, especially those arising from the Sisters' vow of obedience to their religious superior, they nursed first at Scutari (now Uskudar in Turkey) and then took over Kouali Federal Hospital. Here they introduced a system of nursing and management later adopted by Nightingale in the scheme for military nursing she submitted to the War Office. The Sisters, having spent the last six months of the war at the Crimean front, were never officially given credit for their services by the British Government and their role in developing the system of modern nursing has only been recognised internationally in recent years. Mother Jane Francis remained in Kinsale for the rest of her life where eventually the nuns were teaching a thousand children free of charge, in their schools, and providing school meals in winter. Not long before her death she wrote a textbook, *God in His Works*, which was used internationally in Sisters of Mercy primary

schools. Mother Jane Francis died at her convent in Kinsale on February 11, 1888, having directed the establishment of daughter houses in Newry, Co. Down, Clonakilty and Skibbereen, Co. Cork, Doon, Co. Limerick, Ballyshannon, Co. Donegal, and abroad in Derby, England, as well as in San Francisco and Cincinnati, USA. The order now manages Kinsale Hospital, runs primary and secondary schools in the town and has missionary outposts in Peru and Kenya.

BRIGID (BRIGIT, BRIGHID, BRÍD, BRIDE), SAINT (*c.* 455 - c. 525), abbess and one of the three patron saints of Ireland. Few ascertainable facts are available about her life. Born most likely near Croghan, now in Co. Offaly, or at Faughart, near Dundalk, Co. Louth, into a lowly subject people named Fatharta. Her mother, Broicsech, was a slave-woman and may have been a Christian. Her father was most likely a *flaith* (chief of a military group), although it has also been suggested he was a druid. Her maternal uncle, MacCaortin, was a bishop under St. Patrick. Her mother may have been sold when Brigid was still young and according to one tradition she herself was sold to a druid whom she later converted. Many legends concerning her unbounded charity indicate she may have risen to a position of importance in either the household of the druid or of her father. Her determination to live as a Christian religious is demonstrated by her refusal to marry (some tradition even mentions a match with the king of Ulster) in contravention of the familial-social conventions of tribal life. Some circumstantial evidence suggests that she may have become a leading figure in the cult of the goddess Brigit or of some sun-god; however, while the goddess was patron of poetry, metalwork, and medicine, the historical Brigid had no connection with these arts. The 7th century hagiography by Cogitosus states that the Patrician bishop,

3. **St. Brigid, a** *carved figure at White Island, Co.* *Fermanagh.*

MacCaille, received her religious profession and that she founded a church and monastery in Cill Dara, now Kildare, probably towards the end of the 5th century. As abbess, Brigid soon became the most important Christian leader in Leinster and, although an early story credits her consecration as a bishop and she is represented with a bishop's staff in at least one early monument, she had, in fact, her own bishop, Conlaed. Nevertheless, she and the later abbesses of Kildare appear to have exercised an authority approaching jurisdiction over all churches and church lands attached to the monastery in Kildare. These extended not only throughout most of Leinster but to those parts of her *paruchia* as far away as Kilfenora, in north Clare. Brigid's Kildare foundation was unique in Ireland in that it was a double monastery with males and females who lived apart but followed the same rule and used the same church. Brigid, it seems, travelled widely throughout central Ireland, perhaps to the west coast, and may have converted several women who held important positions in pagan cults. At any rate, her example inspired countless women to follow a vocation into religious life.

Like Catherine of Siena and Teresa of Avila she combined the life of a contemplative with one of activity and organisation, but, above all, she has been noted for her impassioned charity. Known as the 'Mary of the Gael', she became the most beloved and invoked of all the saints in the Gaelic-speaking world and a vast amount of myth and legend is associated with her. Her principle feast day is observed on February 1, the first day of spring. She died in about 525 and was buried at the right hand side of the altar in Kildare and, significantly, Bishop Conlaed was buried opposite her. In 878, perhaps because of the incursions of the Northmen or as a symbol of church unity, her body was removed to Downpatrick, Co. Down. In 1185 St. Malachy, in another symbolic gesture, had her remains placed in the grave containing St. Patrick and St. Columcille, the other two patron saints of Ireland. Her cult, probably carried by Irish missionaries, attained remarkable popularity not only in Britain and Brittany, but in the Walloon area in Belgium, Liguria in Italy, as well as Köln, Mainz and Schotten in Germany. Part of her skull is in the Church of St. John the Baptist in Lumiar, a suburb of Lisbon, Portugal, where there is a curious tradition that Broicsech, the saint's mother, had been a native of that country's Hispania region from which she had been taken captive by Irish raiders.

BRIGIDA, SAINT. See under MAURE AND BRIGIDA.

BRIGIDA, SAINT, OF FIESOLE (9th century), patron of Fiesole, Italy. An Italian version of this saint's life referring to Scotia, the contemporary Latin name for Ireland, creates the mistaken belief she was born in Scotland. Authorities such as Colgan, in *Acta Sanctorum Hiberniae* (1645), have produced circumstantial evidence to show she was Irish although it is unusual that Irish sources do not give a place of birth or a genealogy. These state only that she was born in the reign of Aedh Oirdnidhe, king of Ireland, which lasted from *c.* 798 to 817. This dating agrees with an Italian 'life' of her brother that claims he came to Italy in the time of Emperor Ludovicus Pius whose reign began in 815. The Italian *Acta S. Brigidae* states that Brigida's family were of great wealth and distinction. Her older brother Andrew - almost certainly a name taken with religious vows - was a novice with Bishop Donatus (i.e. the Irishman, Donnchad) whom he accompanied on a pilgrimage to Rome and settled at Fiesole, then a major city of Hetruria, Tuscany, where Andrew founded a monastery. How Brigida came to Fiesole remains a mystery:

hagiographies insist that forty years after her brother's exile she was, to her utter bewilderment, transported there by an angel to spiritually assist her brother on his death-bed as 'an intercessor before our Lord.' After Andrew's death she made a hermitage in a wood near Fiesole and remained there in prayer and penance until her death. The significance of Brigida's life can be gauged by the fact that not only was she mentioned in the several Italian versions of the life of Donatus and Andrew but was also thought worthy of her own *Acta* and assigned a feast day on February 1, the same as her famous predecessor, BRIGID of Kildare. Brigida is said to have died in about the year 880. The fact that Irish sources do not mention any hermitage or convent in Ireland in connection with her indicates that she accepted the 'white martyrdom' of exile at a young age.

BRODERICK, THE HON. ALBINIA or NÍ BHRUADAIR, GOBNAIT (1863-1955), republican. Daughter of Viscount Middleton (Co. Cork) and his wife, Augusta Freeman. Sister of the first Earl of Middleton, leader of the Unionists in the south of Ireland, and granddaughter of Baron Cottesloe. Albinia spent most of her youth on her father's estate at Peper Harrow in England and rebelled against almost everything in her family background. She was a mature woman before fully asserting her independence and training as a nurse in Jervis Street Hospital, Dublin. Influenced by the Gaelic League she went to the Donegal Gaeltacht to learn Irish and, unlike many other notables in the early League, gained an excellent command of the language. Albinia Gaelicised her name to Gobnait Ní Bhruadair and, as the League grew more revolutionary, became an ardent nationalist. She eventually joined the radical women's organisation, Cumann na mBan, and shocked acquaintances by converting to Roman

Catholicism. Although somewhat eccentric and absolutely in rebellion against her class and conditioning, Gobnait was fearless, sincere and generous. At forty-seven and financially independent after her father's death, she went to live near Sneem, Co. Kerry, where she nursed the

4. The Hon. Albinia Broderick and Mary MacSwiney.

sick in their homes during an outbreak of smallpox. In 1912 Gobnait financed the building of a hospital for the poor, 'Baile an Chúnaimh' in west Cork, which she ran for the next twenty years. She sheltered IRA members on the run and her house was raided several times by Black and Tans, an infamous auxiliary force of British troops: she was shot on one occasion while effecting the escape of a wanted man. Gobnait was friendly with DR. KATHLEEN LYNN and worked with the White Cross distributing food to dependants of IRA volunteers and others left impoverished by the War of Independence. In 1920 she was elected, for Sinn Féin, to Kerry County Council. During the Civil War, she was jailed in Kilmainham by the Free State Government for her republican sympathies. Gobnait represented Munster at the Sinn Féin Árd-Fheis (Convention) in 1926, a crucial time when most of the prominent members of the organisation were defecting to Fianna Fáil. In 1929, following a period of renewed IRA opposition to the Free State Government, and during the campaign by Cumann na mBan to influence and intimidate jurors in trials of republicans she was, as an officer of Cumann na mBan, subjected to harassment and raiding by government forces on an almost daily basis. In 1933 she resigned from Cumann na mBan with MARY MacSWINEY and others who disagreed with policy changes that committed the organisation to social radicalism. The dissidents formed the right-wing Mná na Poblachta (Women of the Republic). With her own money Gobnait set up a republican journal, *Saoirse*. When she died, on January 16, 1935, she left what remained of her wealth 'for the benefit of the republicans as they were in 1919-1921'.

BROOKE, CHARLOTTE (*c.* 1740-1793), author. Born Co. Cavan, one of twenty-two children of the noted writer Henry Brooke, who was a poet, dramatist, novelist, anti-Jacobite propagandist and friend of Swift. Charlotte was the only surviving member of that family when her father died in 1783 and was soon threatened by poverty because of unwise investments. She turned to writing as a source of income and, in 1789, published her first and most remarkable book, *Reliques of Irish Poetry*, a collection of translations into English of Gaelic poetry and song with their Irish originals. Although it is generally agreed that her English versions are stilted and hardly poetic, translation of Gaelic poetry had never been attempted on such a scale. The book was a watershed, not only in the history of the Irish language but also in Anglo-Irish literature, as it introduced new elements from the Gaelic into composition in English which helped to bring about a distinctive Irish literature in the latter language. In 1791 Charlotte published *School for Christians*, a collection of exemplary dialogues for children. In 1792 she produced an edition of the works of her father, considered a noteworthy enterprise on account of their bulk and diversity, and these brought her some financial reward. Charlotte Brooke died the following year in Longford.

BROWNE, FRANCES (1816-1879), poet and children's story-teller, known as the 'blind poetess of Donegal.' Born Stranorlar, Co. Donegal, on January 16, 1816, into the large family of the village postmaster. She became purblind from smallpox in infancy. From a young age Frances contributed verse to magazines such as *The Irish Penny Journal, Hood's Magazine,* and *Athenaeum*. In 1844 she published a collection of verse, *Star of Atteghei*, which was not only well received but also attracted the attention of the British prime minister, Sir Robert Peel who, out of sympathy for her physical handicap, awarded Frances a civil-list pension of twenty pounds annually. At the age of thirty-one, during the Great Famine, she moved to London and settled there permanently. She published several volumes of poetry, among them *Lyrics and Miscellaneous Poems* (1848), and *Pictures and Songs of Home* (1856), along with novels, children's stories and an autobiography. Her collection of fairy tales, *Granny's Wonderful Chair and the Stories it Told* (1857), ran into two editions but was then forgotten until 1877, two years before her death, when the stories were retold by another author. The original, thus rediscovered, became an international best-seller but Frances Browne did not live to enjoy her triumph. She died in London on August 25, 1879.

BRUINSEACH (BRUINNECH), SAINT (5th or 6th century), probable patron of St. Buryan, Cornwall, England. Bruinseach was the daughter of one Crimhthann of Magh Trea, now Moytra in Co. Longford. Her name (more correctly 'Bruinnech', which means 'the pregnant one' or 'the mother') is almost certainly an appellation given to her because of her history. She entered religious life under the direction of Saint Liadhan at her community, Cill Liadhuin, now Killion, near Birr, Co. Offaly. The convent had close connections with the nearby foundation of Liadhan's son, St. Ciarán of Saigir. Dimma, a chieftain of the Uí Fiachrach on the western side of the Shannon, desired Bruinseach so much that he, with a band of his men, raided the convent and abducted her to his fortress in Uí Fiachrach where he 'extorted from her the rights of a husband.' Ciaran went to her rescue but was rebuffed by Dimma until, confronted by the saint's miraculous powers, he unwillingly released the girl. Ciarán returned her, pregnant by now, to his mother's care. Dimma came again to abduct her but another miracle, through Ciarán's power, made him a penitent. Ciarán then raised the girl from the death-swoon into which she had fallen. Bruinseach lost the baby which is doubtlessly why the epithet, Ceal or Caol, has been applied to her, i.e. 'the slender mother'. Nothing else is recorded of her subsequent life in Ireland but her significance may be assessed in that she was venerated at Cill Liadhuin and at her homeplace, Magh Trea, and is mentioned in various martyrologies and calendars. A feast day is assigned to her on May 29. It is difficult, however, to see why Bruinseach was so honoured if she is not the same person as

St. Buriana of Cornwall, one of the vanguard of the remarkable religious diaspora from Ireland to that country in the fifth and sixth centuries. It is not implausible, given the possible implications of the Dimma affair, that Bruinseach imposed upon herself the 'white martyrdom' of exile. According to the *Martyrologium Anglicanum* (1608) Buriana was of noble parents in Ireland and 'thence passed over to England' where she lived, 'in the practice of great virtue' on the promontory of Cornubia in Cornwall. Although the earliest written record of her is found in an Anglo-Saxon charter of 943, almost nothing else is definitely known of Buriana as her Acts, said to have been preserved in the cathedral at Exeter for many centuries, have not been recovered. While no mention of her mission to Britain has been discovered in Irish sources, neither is there any mention of Bruinseach's death or place of death, which is highly unusual. It is hardly coincidence that, up to the 1600s, both saints shared the same feast day of May 29. A church bearing Buriana's name in the Hundred of Penwith, a very ancient Cornish foundation, was continually rebuilt and added to, according to records, since the 8th century. In the 15th century a church dedicated to her was built on the site of her original foundation. The modern town of St. Buryan, half-way between Penzance and Land's End, takes its name from her. It has been suggested that the exile of Buriana was of critical importance as an impetus to the wave of religious settlement in south-west Britain from Ireland in the subsequent century.

BRYANT, SOPHIE, née WILLOCK (1850-1922), educator, suffragist, author and historian. Born Dublin, daughter of the Rev. W.A. Willock who played a significant role in the Commission for National Education in Ireland. She grew up in counties Cork and Fermanagh and was educated privately by her father and governesses. When Sophie was thirteen the family moved to London where she won a scholarship to Bedford College. At nineteen she married a doctor but was widowed the following year. She began teaching mathematics and German at the North London Collegiate School, a pioneering 'ladies' high school. In 1881 Sophie took a BA in Mental and Moral Science and Mathematics and three years later became the first woman D.Sc. in Moral Science. She was then appointed headmistress of her school and devoted herself to the cause of secondary education for women. She served on the educational committees of the London County Council and the University of London, on the Board of Studies in Pedagogy and on the Bryce Commission on Secondary Education (1894). Besides contributing articles on education and philosophy to many journals, she wrote several books on moral and religious education, the most noted being *Educational Ends* (1887), *Short Studies in Character* (1894), and *Moral and Religious Education* (1920). Sophie was drawn into the women's movement and politics. As a member of the Women's Liberal Federation she became president of the Hampstead Suffrage Society and was one of the leaders of the march of the National Union of Suffrage Societies in 1908. She never lost interest in Ireland, even to the extent of becoming a Home Rule activist; she founded the English Home Rule Propagandist Organisation and, proclaiming that 'freedom is a condition of all development,' lectured on Home Rule platforms in England and in Ireland. Sophie played an important if forgotten role in the resurgence of interest in Irish studies and wrote several books in this field including *Celtic Ireland* (1889), *The Genius of the Gael: a Study in Celtic Psychology and its Manifestations* (1913). *Liberty, Order and Law under Native Irish Rule*, was published posthumously in 1923. Despite these other interests, Sophie Bryant remained committed to women's secondary education and did not relinquish her post as headmistress until 1918. A well-known Alpine climber, she was lost in an avalanche on Mont Blanc in the French Alps on August 12, 1922.

5. *Selina Bunbury, c. 1825, by Harriet Bunbury.*

BUNBURY, SELINA (1802-1882), travel writer and novelist. Born Kilsaran, Co. Louth, into a wealthy Methodist family. After her husband's bankruptcy, Selina's mother moved the family of fifteen to Dublin. At the age of seventeen she began to work as a teacher while already writing her first book, *Visit to my Birthplace* (1820), which ran into twelve editions. Over the next fifteen years she wrote several books about Ireland, including *Cabin Conversations* (1827), *Early Recollections* (1829) and *Tales of my Country* (1833), and several novels, all of which sold well. The books concerning Ireland are a mine of information for social historians today because of their wide-ranging descriptions of pre-famine

Ireland. Selina moved to Liverpool, England, in 1830 and continued to write while looking after her twin brother, perhaps even supporting him financially. Her mostly historical novels like *The Star of the Court or the Maid of Honour and Queen of England, Anne Boleyn* (1844) proved popular. After her brother's marriage in 1845 she began to travel widely on the Continent and over the next dozen years wrote a series of extraordinary travel-books covering Italy, Scandinavia, Austria, the Pyrénées, and even Russia which she visited as the Crimean War came to an end. Subsequently, she continued to produce novels, her large output including *Coombe Abbey* (1857), which ran to eight volumes, *Sir Guy d'Esterre* (1859), *Florence Manvers* (1865), *Lady Flora* (1870). A devout Methodist, she also wrote numerous tracts and chap-books of evangelical short fiction. Selina Bunbury died in Cheltenham, England, in 1882.

BURIANA, SAINT. See under BRUINSEACH, SAINT.

BURKE, HONORIA. See under DE BURGO, HONORIA.

BURKE SHERIDAN, MARGARET (1889-1958), opera singer. Born October 15, 1889, in Castlebar, Co. Mayo. Her father was a descendant of the extraordinary literary and artistic Sheridan family, one of whom had married into an old aristocratic family, the Burkes of Mayo. However the family's wealth had dwindled and her father held the position of postmaster in Castlebar. Orphaned at the age of twelve Margaret became a permanent boarder at the Dominican Convent, Eccles Street, Dublin. Here she was first trained in singing by Mother Clement Burke who, recognising her potential, arranged for further training under Dr. Vincent O'Brien who was then tutoring the future

6. Margaret Burke Sheridan in 1950.

operatic tenor John McCormack. She began to sing on Dublin stages and was a prize winner at the Feis Ceoil in 1909. By organising benefit concerts O'Brien helped Margaret to raise the necessary funds to study at the Royal Academy of Music, London. She was to remain there for some years through the generosity of her patrons, Lord and Lady de Walden of Chirk Castle, North Wales. The inventor Marconi became her next and most influential patron. Margaret broke off an unofficial engagement with an Irish MP to study in Rome, eventually coming under the guidance of great teachers such as Martino and Corelli. She made her successful operatic début as Mimi in Puccini's *La Bohème* in Rome (1918) before a distinguished audience which included King Vittori Emanuele III. She sang in La Scala, Milan for the first time in 1920 and was thereafter considered one of the greatest sopranos of all time. The Italians adored her because she sang and acted with great emotion. "For a feeling, for an ideal," she once said, "I would give my life." 'La Sheridan' became the principal singer at La Scala, sang with Gigli at Rimini, and Puccini coached her personally for his opera *Manon*. She made many guest appearances at Covent Garden, London, where audiences were again captivated not only by her voice but also by her impassioned characterisation and beauty. It was here she met and began a difficult relationship with the managing director, Colonel Eustace Blois. Margaret's relatively short career ended abruptly at the conclusion of the 1936 season. She suffered from throat illnesses and was deeply affected by the traumatic ending of her affair with Blois who died shortly afterwards. For the following twenty years she lived between Dublin and New York where she was a member of the Advisory Committee of the Arts Foundation. Although her operatic success is commemorated by a bronze plaque in the La Scala opera house, Milan, and she was fêted in London, Margaret was never paid more than scant attention from the conventional Roman Catholic bourgeoisie in Dublin except 'to be mildly witty at her expense'. Having spent her latter years in growing isolation, Margaret Burke Sheridan died in St. Vincent's Hospital on April 16, 1958, and was buried in Glasnevin Cemetery, Dublin.

BURYAN, SAINT. See under BRUINSEACH, SAINT.

BUSHE, LETITIA (*c.* 1710-1757), artist. Born Dangan, Co. Kilkenny, youngest daughter of a genteel family with landed connections; her father was secretary of Commissioners of Revenue. She was possibly the first Irish woman artist who can be described as a professional. It is not known where or how Letitia trained but she may have been instructed by a visiting artist from the Continent. She worked mainly in watercolours, occasionally used oils, and was known to paint miniatures. She lived a somewhat peripatetic life, leaving her apartment in Dublin to stay with families such as that of Mrs. Delaney, wife of the Dean of Down, and others in different parts of the country. Genteel young ladies like Letitia Bushe, who could teach art besides having 'a turn for conversation that is not common' and 'inexhaustible' good humour, would have been much in demand as companions in isolated country houses where the female occupants suffered from extreme boredom. In the early 1740s Letitia visited England, probably in the capacity of companion, and painted in London, Bath and Bristol. A small amount of her work still survives, including views of Bray, Co. Wicklow and London. Other drawings preserved through engraving have among them one of Killarney, dated 1751, which may well be the first representation made of that famous place. Letitia Bushe died in Dublin on November 17, 1757.

7. 'A view of the village of Bray, Co. Wicklow,' *painted 1736 by* **Letitia Bushe.**

BUTLER, MOTHER MARIE JOSEPH (JOHANNA)

(1860-1940), educator, founder of the Marymount schools and colleges in the USA and Europe; candidate for canonisation. Born July 22, 1860, at Ballynunnery in south west Kilkenny where her father, a descendant of the earls and dukes of Ormond, had a large estate. Her mother was from a Roman Catholic Anglo-Irish family. Although she attended a local school and later a convent school in nearby New Ross, it was Johanna's mother who laid the foundation for her education and religious training. At sixteen, as an outgoing young lady who moved in local society with grace and a good horsewoman, Johanna surprised her parents by asking their permission to enter a French convent, the Congregation of the Sacred Heart of Mary in Béziers. This had been founded twenty-five years earlier to provide a modern education for upper class girls. She took the name Marie Joseph and was professed in 1890, in Portugal, where she had gone to teach in a convent school. Mother Marie Joseph remained in Portugal for a further twenty-two years, first as teacher and later as superior. In 1903 she was sent by her order to Long Island, New York, to take charge of the Congregation's school, its second foundation in the USA. Moreover, Mother Marie Joseph was charged with the responsibility of extending the order's activities and influence in North America; in particular, she hoped to establish an institution of higher education for Roman Catholic girls which would match the best of secular colleges. In 1907 when a cousin gave her a site for a school in Tarrytown, New York, Mother Marie Joseph

8. 'A preliminary investigation', *painted 1898 by* **Mildred Anne Butler.**

requested her order to send Sister Gerard Phelan as her assistant. Sr. Gerard, a fellow Kilkenny-woman, had graduated from Cambridge University and served for a dozen years as headmistress in a school in Westmorland, England. She was to be Mother Marie Joseph's collaborator and confidante for the next thirty-two years. Together they founded the first Marymount school at Tarrytown that opened, with only one pupil, in 1908. Ten years later the first Marymount College also opened at Tarrytown. This four-year liberal arts institute had a charter from the University of the State of New York and granted Bachelor degrees from 1924. Sr. Gerard, having completed postgraduate studies in education in American universities, took responsibility for carrying out educational policy. Mother Marie Joseph's talents for administration and business meant she was the driving force behind the founding of three Marymount

colleges and seventeen schools established in the USA during her lifetime. The first of these schools outside New York opened in Los Angeles in 1921. Already the Marymount system, based on high academic and religious development, was known for its emphasis on social and physical training and for preparing young women from affluent families for their changing role and responsibility in society. Marymount students were also trained for social service and relief work among the poor. A 'Mariemonte' opened in Paris in 1923. In 1926 Mother Marie Joseph was elected Mother General of her order and embarked on the establishment of more Marymount schools outside the USA. While continuing the order's expansion in America she founded twenty-three new Marymount institutions, both schools and novitiates, in Italy, Canada, Brazil, England and Ireland. She died on April 23, 1940, in

Tarrytown, New York, on the day following the celebration of her sixtieth year as a nun. Mother Marie Joseph was noted for her spirituality and the cause for her canonisation was officially opened within eight years of her death. Her religious writings were collected and published in 1954 under the title *As an Eagle*. Mother Marie Joseph's educational work was continued by Mother Gerard who, having replaced her as Superior-General, doubled the number of the order's foundations over the next twenty years and expanded its work into Africa.

BUTLER, MILDRED ANNE (1858-1941), painter. Born Kilmurry, near Thomastown, Co. Kilkenny, into a branch of the once-powerful Norman-Irish family of the Butlers of Ormond. Her father, Captain Edward Butler, was a watercolorist and draughtsman. She painted from an early age, but received no training until she entered the Westminster School of Art in London in her mid-twenties. In 1885 the young painter was encouraged by receiving a prize in the Dublin Amateur and Artist's Society. She studied with Naftel and Calderon in London and exhibited in the Dudley Gallery in Piccadilly in 1888. Two years later Mildred exhibited for the first time with the Watercolour Society of Ireland and continued to do so regularly for the next forty-six years. In 1894 she left Ireland for Cornwall, England, where she was much influenced by two fellow Irish artists, Norman Garstin and Stanhope Forbes. In 1896 Mildred's work was accepted by the British Royal Academy and she was elected to the Royal Watercolour Society. She spent most of the latter half of her life at home in Kilmurry, living in quiet seclusion, but making many visits to England and the Continent. A prolific painter, Mildred faithfully recorded many scenes of the life and surroundings of the Butler house, specialising in large-scale scenes of gardens, farmyards, and flowers, and also becoming a noted natural history painter. As women of her class did not need to sell their work they were looked on as 'amateurs' by the artistic establishment. However, Mildred Butler sold many paintings to members of the British and Continental aristocracies, including the British Queen Mary. Although she continued to paint and exhibit up to the age of seventy-eight, her work was swiftly forgotten until it underwent a remarkable revival of popularity forty years after her death, which occurred at Kilmurry House in 1941. Her paintings hang in London's Tate Gallery and, among others, in the National Gallery of Ireland and the Hugh Lane Municipal Gallery, Dublin.

CAOILINN (CAELFIND, CAELAINN), SAINT (8th century), virgin saint. Very little is known about Caoilinn and what is known was recorded because of her associations with the Ciarraige people of Connaught who venerated her for many centuries as their patron saint. According to tradition she was baptised by St. Patrick. She was granted lands for her religious foundations at Termonmore, in Kilkeevin, outside what is now Castlereagh, Co. Roscommon. When a branch of the Ciarraige people from Munster took refuge in that province in the 6th century reign of Aed, the king granted them relatively large tracts of land in mid-Connaught. Caoilinn, herself one of the Ciarraige Luachra (being 'daughter of Cael, son of Fionnchadh of the race of Ciar') was guarantor of the arrangement. She could have belonged to an earlier migration of the Ciarraige people and at what may have been a venerable old age, be considered a figure of great moral authority. Early histories record that when the king condoned an attempt by the native nobles to poison Coirbri Mac Conaire, the Ciarraige chief, at a royal feast, the plot was made known to Caoilin in a vision and she exposed it. As a result the Ciarraige retained possession of their territory where they remained autonomous under the paramount chieftainship of the O'Connors until the early fifteenth century. The saint's well at Termonmore was a place of pilgrimage for centuries. Her feast day is kept on February 3.

CARBERY, ETHNA (1866-1911), poet and nationalist propagandist. Born Anna Johnston at Ballymena, Co. Antrim, into a protestant Unionist family. She became a convert to the 'Irish Ireland' movement and, subsequently, to Irish nationalism, so much so that she assumed the more 'Irish' pen-name of Ethna Carbery when she began writing poems which appeared in periodicals such as the *Nation* and *United Ireland*. With ALICE MILLIGAN, who had come from a similar background, Ethna founded a monthly journal, the *Northern Patriot*. In 1896, although still without a political programme, the pair founded and edited another journal, the *Shan Van Vocht*, which helped to propagate the idea of separation from the British Empire. During the 1798 centenary celebrations Ethna Carbery toured the country lecturing on the United Irishman Rebellion. In 1900 she was present at the inaugural meeting of Inghinidhe na hÉireann, the separatist women's movement founded by MAUD GONNE MACBRIDE, and was appointed one of four vice-presidents. Ethna and her husband, the poet and writer Seamus MacManus, went to America in 1899 intending to make a living from their literary talents and knowledge of Irish folklore and history, something Ireland had failed to afford them. She wrote prolifically, starting with *Will O' The World's End*, an adaptation of folktales, and a collection of verse, *The Four Winds of Eirinn* both published in 1902. While the latter has not stood the test of time, it was widely read and saw several reprints during the early part of the century as it appealed to Irish-American

sentiment at the time. *The Passionate Hearts*, a collection of short stories, followed in 1903, and *In the Celtic Past*, tales from Irish history, in 1904. Ethna Carbery died in America in 1911 at the age of forty-five. Her early death and her husband's subsequent writings about their life together, their love for each other and for Ireland, caused them to be much romanticised in nationalist circles. Her verse, although conventional and slight, stimulated the early Sinn Féin movement as well as American support for Irish nationalism. Her evergreen ballad, 'Roddy McCorley', is still sung.

CARNEY, WINIFRED (WINNY) (1887-1943), socialist, trade unionist, revolutionary, secretary and confidante of James Connolly. Born December 4, 1887, at Bangor, Co. Down, into a large lower middle-class family with strong Roman Catholic and nationalist leanings. After convent secondary school education she joined the Gaelic League. Her involvement, in her early twenties, in suffragist and socialist movements set her apart from her peers. Through her friendship with Thomas Johnson, future parliamentary leader of the Irish Labour Party, and his wife Marie, Winny was drawn into militant trade union activities and worked with James Connolly, then Ulster organiser for the Irish Transport and General Workers' Union (ITGWU). In 1912 she co-founded and became secretary of the Textile Workers Union, which was, in effect, the female branch of the ITGWU. Winny worked closely with Ellen Gordon and Connolly to organise the mill girls during this period of labour agitation. In 1913, during the mass lockout of unionised workers in Dublin, she supported the workers by fundraising in Belfast and staged a welcome for Connolly there on his release from prison. Supporting Connolly's views on militancy following the experiences of 1913, she worked increasingly in a secretarial capacity for him and prepared herself, through military and first-aid training with Cumann na mBan, for the revolution she saw as a necessary start to a just society. Privy to all Connolly's plans, Winny came to Dublin at his request to assist him in preparations for the Easter Rebellion in 1916, typing mobilisation orders and dispatches. Although ordered by Pearse to leave she remained with the insurgents in the General Post Office until the capitulation, earning the sobriquet, 'the typist with the Webley'. She was interned with almost eighty other women, all members of the Citizen Army, but while most were released after some months, she and fellow trade-unionist HELENA MOLONEY were detained in Aylesbury Prison until Christmas, 1916. Imprisonment may have precipitated the ill health from which she would suffer for the rest of her life but it also hardened her resolve to assist in bringing about radical social change. She stood as Sinn Féin candidate for the Belfast Victoria ward in the 1918 General Elections, being one of only two women nominated, both by Sinn Féin (the other was COUNTESS MARKIEVICZ). Having frightened off potential support from conservative nationalist Roman Catholics by advocating a workers' republic - and being a woman - she scraped a tiny three hundred and ninety-five votes against almost ten thousand for the Unionist candidate. While Winny always regarded herself as an 'extreme anarchist', she now devoted her energies to the trade union movement, eschewing nationalist politics. Nevertheless, during the War of Independence, she sheltered many republicans, including Countess Markievicz, and suffered police raids and several prison sentences. She continued her work for the ITGWU in both Dublin and Belfast and for the then highly radical Northern Ireland Labour Party. In 1928 she married George McBride, a Marxist trade-unionist who had

earlier been a Unionist Labour activist. Both were ostracised by their families as a result. In 1930 she joined the Belfast Socialist Party but chronic ill health meant that she could give it little more than token support. Winifred 'Winny' Carney died on November 21, 1943, almost unnoticed and forgotten.

CAVANAGH, KIT (CHRISTIAN), known also as CHRISTIAN DAVIES and MOTHER ROSS (1667-1739), soldier. Born Dublin, into the family of a prosperous protestant brewer. She was reared there and on her father's small farm at Leixlip, Co. Kildare. Kit's family broke up in unusual circumstances at the onset of the Williamite/Jacobite War of 1689; her father, although a protestant, joined the Jacobite army while mother and daughter favoured the Orange side and were imprisoned as a result. Her father's properties were confiscated following the Williamite victory and Kit went to live with an affluent aunt in Dublin whose inn she was soon to inherit. She married her aunt's manservant, Richard Welsh, and had two children before he was press-ganged into the British army which needed men to fight against the French in Holland. Leaving her children in the care of a relative, Kit disguised herself as a man and enlisted to find her husband. In Holland she was transferred to the cavalry and served in her husband's regiment, the Scots Greys, in the campaign of 1702-1703, being wounded on more than one occasion. She did come across Richard who appears to have 'married' another woman. Kit remained in Marlborough's army until, at the battle of Ramillies (1706), she was wounded again and her true sex discovered. She became a celebrity in her regiment and the military authorities, while discharging her from the army, ordered a new marriage service for her with Richard. She continued to follow him as a sutler, supplying food to troops, and becoming known as 'Mother Ross.' After her husband was killed at the battle of Malplaquet (1710), Kit married a grenadier from her former regiment who was also killed shortly afterwards. Rewarded by the army with a shilling-a-day pension she returned to Dublin, set up a food and liquor shop, and married once more. Her latest husband, an ex-soldier named Davies, re-enlisted. Kit followed him to London, set up shop there, and raised the money to buy him out. Two days later he got drunk and re-enlisted again. Having become impoverished in her later years, Kit was given refuge in the Chelsea Pensioner's Hospital. Here she was reunited with her husband once again, having prevailed upon the hospital authorities to give him a position as sergeant. While nursing him in a bout of fever she contracted the illness and died on July 7, 1739, and was buried with military honours. A celebrated figure in her time, Daniel Defoe wrote Kit's biography, *The Life and Adventures of Mrs. Christian Davies commonly named Mother Ross* (1740).

CENTLIVRE, SUSANNA, née FREEMAN (1667-1722), playwright. Born Co. Tyrone, into an English colonist farming family who had been grantees in the Plantation of Ulster. Susanna had some elementary schooling before running away to England, at fifteen, from an unhappy homelife and disagreeable domestic service. An under-graduate at Cambridge dressed her in men's clothes and kept her for some years, as a houseboy, in his university rooms. She is next discovered in London where, taking advantage of the fact that women were now allowed to perform in the theatre, she had become an actress. Susanna married twice but both young gentlemen were killed in duels. She began to write drama and one of her plays, *The Perjured Husband*, was performed in Windsor Castle with her in the leading role. On that occasion, the royal chef Joseph Centlivre, a Frenchman, fell in love with her. They married and went to live in Charing Cross where her salon attracted many distinguished men of letters. Happily married and financially well-off, she became a prolific writer of successful plays, among them *The Wonder! A Woman Keeps a Secret* (1714) and *A Bold Stroke for a Wife* (1718). She died in London on December 1, 1722, and is buried in the church of St Martin-in-the-Fields. The inscription on her tomb pays tribute to her career as the first in a long line of female theatrical notables with an Irish background: 'Here lies Susanna Centlivre née Freeman from Ireland. Playwright'.

CHAMBERLAINE, FRANCES. See under SHERIDAN, FRANCES.

CHENEVIX, HELEN (*c.* 1870-1963), suffragist, trade unionist and peace campaigner. Born in Dublin, daughter of a Church of Ireland bishop, and attended Alexandra College, Dublin, before becoming one of the first women graduates of Trinity College Dublin. Having been active in the suffragist movement for some time, she and her life-long friend and neighbour, LOUIE BENNETT, founded the Irish Women's Suffrage Federation in 1911 to link together the many suffrage societies of the period throughout the country. Out of the Federation grew the Irish Women's Reform League in Dublin which monitored legislation affecting women, campaigned for the provision of school meals and called for technical education for girls. The following year Helen was on the platform of a mass meeting of women, in Dublin, to demand the inclusion of female suffrage in the proposed Home Rule Bill. When Louie Bennett was given the responsibility of re-organising the Irish Women's Workers' Union (IWWU) in 1917, she invited her friend to help and from this on, inspired by religious commitment, Helen made it her life's work to improve the lot of women workers. When the IWWU was first registered as a trade union in 1918, she and Louie were made honorary secretaries. The union rapidly increased membership and campaigned forcefully and successfully for better conditions and wages for laundresses, box makers and textile workers. For forty years, Helen Chenevix and Louie Bennett were to hold centre stage in the story of Irish trade unionism. In 1935, Helen was a trade union representative at the League of Nations Conference on the Status of Women in Geneva. She was among the organisers of the campaigns against the Conditions of Employment Bill of 1935 and against some articles in the 1937 Constitution on the grounds that they attacked women's rights. During the economic depression caused by the Second World War she practically ran the IWWU and made a major contribution to the Torch and Distaff Guild which played an important role in supplying basic necessities to unemployed women. Helen was elected to Dublin Corporation and was acting Lord Mayor of Dublin in 1942 and again in 1950. The following year she was elected president of the Irish Trade Union Congress. She became general secretary of the IWWU in 1955. During these years she focused her efforts on the improvement of working conditions for psychiatric nurses and on the provision of decent housing for women factory workers as well as playgrounds for children in the inner city. True to her religious convictions Helen was an active campaigner for peace and attempted to promote world peace through trade unionism. She was a member of the Fellowship of Reconciliation, the Women's International League of Peace and the Irish Pacifist Movement (of which she was vice-president), and supported the campaign for nuclear disarmament in her later years. In 1957, the year after the death of her great friend and

co-worker Louie Bennett, Helen relinquished office within the IWWU. For some years afterwards she rented a room at the Union's headquarters from which she continued to promulgate her gospel of disarmament and pacifism.

CLARKE, KATHLEEN, née DALY (1878-1972), revolutionary and politician. Born Frederick Street, Limerick, into a family of small business people with an exceptionally strong republican background. Her father had been imprisoned for involvement in the Fenian Rising and an uncle was imprisoned for life for Fenian activities in Britain. Her mother, while rearing nine children, ran a successful dressmaking business. At the age of eighteen, after her father's death, Kathleen opened her own dress shop. She emigrated to New York, in 1901, to marry Tom Clarke, her uncle's close friend from Millbank Prison in England where the latter had served fifteen years. The couple ran a successful farm and market-garden business until they returned to Ireland in 1907 and opened a tobacconists and news-agency. Kathleen supported her husband's attempts to organise another rebellion against British rule. She was active in Cumann na mBan from its inauguration in 1914, organising the central branch and heavily involved in lecturing and pamphleteering, while rearing three children. The Supreme Council of the IRB entrusted her with details of the intended 1916 Rising and with the task of reorganising the republican movement should the rebellion fail. During the Rising, she was arrested and taken to Dublin Castle and, on her release, following the executions of both her husband and brother, formed the first Committee of the Irish Volunteer Dependants Fund to aid the dependants of the deceased or imprisoned insurgents. It was Kathleen who gave Michael Collins his first position in authority in the republican movement by appointing him secretary. In 1918 she became vice-president of Cumann na mBan and was one of four women elected to the executive of the new Sinn Féin. She campaigned against conscription and, on the pretext of suspected treasonable conspiracy with Germany, was jailed for nine months in Holloway Prison, England, with MAUD GONNE and COUNTESS MARKIEVICZ. In 1919 she was elected alderman for Wood Quay and Mountjoy wards in the Dublin municipal elections and chaired the north city republican courts set up by Sinn Féin. At the same period, she was also highly involved in the White Cross which had come to the aid of war victims throughout Ireland. Kathleen, elected to the second Dáil in 1920, fiercely opposed the Treaty with the other six women deputies. She chaired the failed negotiations to avoid the Civil War and lost her seat in the elections immediately afterwards. She left Sinn Féin in 1926 and, with Countess Markievicz, joined the newly-formed Fianna Fáil and was elected to its executive. Having served as a senator from 1927 to 1936, she became the first woman Lord Mayor of Dublin in 1939. Kathleen opposed de Valera on the Conditions of Employment Bill (1935): along with JENNIE WYSE POWER, she protested that the Bill was in contradiction to the 1916 Proclamation in its sections affecting women. She protested again, and on the same grounds, against de Valera's 1937 Constitution and in the 1940s actively campaigned against the treatment of republican prisoners by the Fianna Fáil Government. When her term of office as Lord Mayor ended, after five years, in 1944, she resigned from Fianna Fáil and, four years later at the age of seventy-one, stood unsuccessfully for the newly-formed Clann na Poblachta Party in the general elections. Kathleen Clarke was conferred with an Honorary Doctorate of Law by the National University of Ireland during the 50th anniversary of the Easter Rising and was given a State funeral in the Pro-Cathedral, Dublin, after dying in her son's Liverpool home on September 29, 1972.

CLARKE, MARGARET. See under CRILLEY, MARGARET.

CLARKE, MOTHER MARY FRANCES (1803-1887), pioneer in women's education in the USA, founder of the Sisters of Charity of the Blessed Virgin Mary, and of Clarke College, Dubuque, Iowa. Born Dublin, March 12, 1803. She arrived in Philadelphia in 1833 as a missionary teacher with three other young Irish girls and, under the direction of Fr. Terence Donaghoe, founded the Sisters of Charity of the Blessed Virgin Mary for the education of young women. In the same year she also set up her first school. Ten years later, on the request of the bishop of Dubuque, Iowa, Mother Mary Frances opened a convent and school in that city. In co-operation with Fr. Donaghoe, then vicar-general of the diocese, she set up St. Mary's Female Academy in 1843. She continued her pioneering work in the late 19th century, providing women's colleges after Fr. Donaghoe's death and, in 1879, founded Mount St. Joseph College on a sixty-acre campus in Dubuque. This was to become an early liberal arts university for women and was granted its permanent charter in 1901. Now known as Clarke College, it is still one of the foremost institutions of its kind in the United States. Two years before her death in Dubuque on December 4, 1843, her order received its final approbation from the papacy.

CLEARY, BRIDGET, née BOLAND (1869-1895), exorcism victim. Born Cloneen, near Fethard, Co. Tipperary, daughter of a cottier. She married Michael Cleary, a farm labourer and small-holder, and lived with him in the townland of

Ballyvuldea, Fethard. When Bridget was still childless at twenty-six she went into a rapid physical, and possibly mental, decline. Her husband, abetted by a local herbalist, became convinced she was a fairy changeling. Michael, her father, and other relatives began an exorcism on the evening of March 14, 1895, which culminated in her death by burning the following night. The perpetrators then attempted to rescue the 'real' Brigid Cleary from a nearby fairy fort. Following the discovery of her remains in the back garden all involved, including the herbalist, were charged with murder and, after a reduction to the charge of manslaughter, those present at the exorcism received varied sentences, Her husband got twenty years hard labour. Bridget Cleary's fate, which caused a sensation at the time, is presented by anthropologists as an extreme example of the age-old belief in 'changelings', and is remembered in the children's skipping rhyme:

Are you a witch, or are you a fairy,
Or are you the wife of Michael Cleary?

CLERKE, AGNES MARY (1842-1907), astronomer and writer. Born in Co. Cork. Her father was a bank manager and the family lived in various parts of Ireland in her youth. He was also an amateur astronomer and classical scholar and had lasting influence on his daughters who were educated at home. Through her father's prompting Agnes Mary had taken an interest in astronomy at an early age and had started to write a history of the science at fifteen. Agnes Mary and her elder sister Mary Ellen, a novelist and poet, were inseparable all their lives. In their late twenties the sisters went to Italy where they remained for seven years and contributed to Italian magazines and periodicals. Agnes Mary began to publish articles on astronomy in the *Edinburgh Review* while still in Italy. In 1877 they settled in London and continued as journalists while Agnes Mary completed her *Popular History of Astronomy during the Nineteenth Century* (1885) which was recognised as a standard work. During the next five years she visited observatories in the Cape of Good Hope, Copenhagen, Stockholm and St. Petersburg. The result of her research is presented in *System of the Stars* (1890). Agnes Mary was one of the first women to receive recognition as an astronomer and contributed articles on the subject and its history to the *Encyclopaedia Britannica* and the *Dictionary of National Biography*. She was honoured by the British Royal Institute in 1892. *Problems in Astrophysics* was published in 1903, the year she was made Honorary Member of the Royal Astronomical Society, and *Modern Cosmogonies* followed in 1905. She never entirely lost her early interest in classical literature and published *Familiar Studies in Homer* in 1892. Agnes Mary Clerke died in London in 1907 within a year of her sister's death.

CLIVE, KITTY, née RAFTER (1711-1785), actress and playwright. Born in Ulster to a ne'er-do-well lawyer who brought her to London. At sixteen, while working in a lodging house, she was discovered by actors from the nearby Drury Lane Theatre and began a career that lasted for some forty years. Within two years of her debut, Kitty's brilliant comic and singing talents had saved the Drury Lane Theatre from bankruptcy. From then on the 'Queen of Drury Lane' worked successfully with some of the great names of the London theatre, including Colley Cibber and David Garrick. By twenty she had married a barrister, George Clive, and retained her husband's name after the marriage ended. In later years she wrote several plays, one of which, *The Rehearsal* (1753), was published. Kitty was on friendly terms with many of the great literary figures of her day, including Samuel Johnson,

Oliver Goldsmith, and especially Sir Horace Walpole who granted her a pension. Her popularity remained until she made her final appearance - opposite Garrick - at Drury Lane. She was noted for her generosity; her moral character was held to have been above reproach and it was said that she introduced virtue into the theatre of her time. After Kitty Clive's retirement in 1769 she lived at Strawberry Hill, Surrey, in a house presented to her by Walpole, where she died in 1785.

COLUM, MARY MARGARET, née MAGUIRE (1884 - 1957), woman of letters, literary critic and writer. Born Collooney, Co. Sligo, June 13, 1884. She became a teacher in Dublin and was involved in the Irish Literary Revival, associating with all its leading personalities. Mary also joined the women's revolutionary organisation, Cumann na mBan and, in 1918, when Patrick Pearse founded his bilingual school, Scoil Éanna, she obtained a teaching post there. In her pamphlet, *St. Enda's School Rathfarnham*, she explained the ethos, ideal, and methods, of that extraordinary experiment. She contributed to the *Irish Review* and, in 1912, married one of its founders, Padraic Colum, a prominent playwright in the early Abbey Theatre and a poet of the Revival. They went to America in 1914 and spent the rest of their lives there. Both became lecturers in comparative literature at Columbia University, New York. Mary was a member of the Poetry Society and contributed trenchant articles to many important journals, including *Dial, The Freeman, Scribner's Magazine* and *Forum and Century*. For her literary criticisms she received the Guggenheim Fellowship in 1930 and 1938. In 1934 she was awarded the John Ryder Gold Medal for Distinction in Literature by Georgetown University, Washington D.C. She published *From These Roots*, essays in modern literature, in 1937. From her autobiog-

raphy, *Life and the Dream* (1947), a picture emerges of an unusually spirited and forceful 'incorrigibly Irish' young woman. Mary Colum was elected to the American National Institute of Arts and Letters some years before her death in New York on October 22, 1957. *Our Friend James Joyce*, written in conjunction with her husband, was published posthumously.

COMERFORD, MARIE (1893-1982), republican. Born in Wicklow. Her father, who had been a close friend of Charles Stewart Parnell, was a wealthy mill-owner and her mother was from an affluent Roman Catholic Unionist family from Wexford. Marie was sent to a protestant school in London where she was taunted for being Irish. She retaliated by studying Irish history and became so well-informed that she was employed as personal secretary to the eminent historian, ALICE STOPFORD GREEN. Inspired by the events of 1916 Marie joined Cumann na mBan, the radically republican women's association. Soon she was involved in its anti-conscription campaign, its support of the Volunteers during the War of Independence, and especially the organising and distribution of relief funds on behalf of the White Cross to families in need as a result of the war. In November 1920 Marie was part of a team sent to collect evidence of army and police atrocities in Tipperary and North Cork for the British Labour Party Commission of Inquiry into the war situation in Ireland. She was an organiser for Sinn Féin in the north of Ireland during the 1921 elections and for the anti-Treatyites in Wexford in the 1922 elections. Accordingly she took the Republican side in the Treaty controversy and, when their Dublin headquarters in the Four Courts came under artillery attack by pro-Treaty forces, acted as a bicycle courier between the fighters in the besieged building and other battalions of the Dublin Brigade. At the surrender she could have escaped by claiming to be part of the Red Cross as she had also been involved in nursing duties, but choose to march out with the male prisoners, wheeling her bike; however, she escaped in the ensuing confusion. While on the run she was involved in the plot to kill W.T. Cosgrave, Prime Minister of the Free State Government, but was recognised and lodged in Mountjoy Jail where, for protesting against overcrowding, she was removed to the criminal section and given three months hard labour. Marie was shot and wounded, while on hunger-strike, as she waved from her window at her fellow prisoners. She escaped, was recaptured, went on hunger-strike again in protest against the government's determination to continue the war after the Republicans had offered to surrender. She was eventually released from jail on a stretcher. Marie was again an organiser for Sinn Féin in the 1923 elections and was later sent to the USA to raise funds for their continuing constitutional struggle. Finding it impossible to obtain work because of her republican activities, she set up a small poultry farm in Co. Wexford. In 1926 she was elected to the executive of Sinn Féin, then a greatly weakened organisation, and was jailed again, this time for trying to influence a jury. Marie found employment with the *Irish Press*, the Fianna Fáil party organ, when it was set up in 1932 and remained with it for the next thirty years. In 1939 she oversaw the printing of the IRA journal *War News*, and, in the 1940s, actively campaigned with KATHLEEN CLARKE against the treatment of Republican prisoners by the Fianna Fail government. In 1947, when Fianna Fáil were the opposition party in the government, Marie took part in the ineffective Anti-Partition League. At the age of eighty, she was arrested for speaking at a public meeting organised by Nora Connolly O'Brien on behalf of republican prisoners. Her short but important account of the struggle for independence, *The First Dáil*, was published in 1969 but her autobiography remains unpublished. Marie Comerford died in Dublin on December 15, 1982.

CONCANNON, HELENA, née WALSH (1878-1952), author, historian and politician. Born Co. Derry. Went to live in Salthill, Co. Galway, in 1906, after her marriage to Tomás Ó Concheanainn, a prominent figure in the Gaelic League as organiser, teacher and writer. Helena was a prolific writer who contributed to many nationalist magazines and religious journals such as the *Irish Messenger*; she also wrote many books of popular history and religious biography. One of her best known works, *Defenders of the Ford* (1925), subtitled 'Pages from the Annals of the Boys of Ireland from the Earliest Ages down to 1798', contains an enormous amount of readable, though uncritically presented, material. Her *Irish Nuns in Penal Days* (1931) is still a valuable source book. Though Helena Concannon's books are criticised for their romantic nationalist and Roman Catholic bias, they have, until recently, remained among the very few attempts to highlight the role of women in Irish history. She achieved this in books such as *Women of Ninety Eight*, dealing with the 1798 Rebellion, and *Daughters of Banba*, which recounts the story of Irish women from the earliest times. In conjunction with her husband Helena wrote several Irish-language textbooks including *Inis Fail* (1926) and *Eamhain Macha* (1926). In 1935 *Blessed Oliver Plunkett*, a biography of the 17th century martyr, was published. She was elected to Dáil Éireann for Fianna Fáil in 1933. In the Dáil she continually promoted the idea of rural domestic economy schools based on the contemporary Belgian example but remained silent on most radical women's issues. Helena incurred the wrath of many women for supporting de Valera in the controversy over the proposed Constitution of

1937, some articles of which were deemed regressive in relation to women's rights. Speaking for the Bill, though it was vociferously opposed by the Irish Women's Graduates Association of which she was a member, Helena declared, "I sincerely hope that not a comma of this noble declaration will be altered". She was made a senator in 1938. Helena Concannon died in 1952 and a collection of her verse, *Poems,* was published posthumously.

COSGRAVE, MOTHER MARY ANNE (1864-1900), nun and Rhodesian pioneer. Born May 22, 1864, and lived at Summerhill, Co. Meath, where her father was a policeman. Following the death of her parents from tuberculosis Mary Anne was reared in Ballinary, Co. Wexford, and educated at Loreto Convent, Enniscorthy. She began work in a draper's shop in Wexford at seventeen. When, in 1880, the Wexford-born bishop of South Africa's Cape Province called for postulants for the recently established Dominican Convent in Kingwilliamstown she joined the order and taught for eight years in colonist schools in East London and Potchefstroom. Cecil Rhodes' British Africa Company had already begun mining in southern Africa and, in transgression of the permission granted by King Lobengula, the company planned to exploit the mineral resources of Matabeleland and Mashonaland (now Zimbabwe). The first invading 'pioneer column' set out on the thousand-mile trek to Salisbury and, answering a call for volunteer nurses, Mary Anne and four other Dominican nuns, under the supervision of a Jesuit priest, set off to join it in February 1890. Travelling by Cape-cart and train from East London to Mafeking (now in Botswana), they made the four-hundred-mile journey to Macloutsie Camp in an ox-wagon, carrying medical supplies. They set up a hospital at the camp and, following the rainy season, the nuns reached the final *laager* and fort of Salisbury on June 5 1891, the first white women in the area. Cecil Rhodes had a brick hospital built at their request and the following year, as the first British colonist families arrived, the nuns opened the first European-type school in Mashonaland. Mary Anne and another nun later accompanied Rhodes' relieving force to aid the settlers of Gwelo and Bulawayo when war broke out between the colonists and the Ndebele people. When the desperate resistance to colonialism had collapsed and relative calm restored she travelled to Germany and successfully sought new postulants for her order. On her return she was appointed Prioress General of the Dominican Community in what was the British colony of Rhodesia. In 1900 Mother Mary Anne Cosgrave was conferred with the Royal Order of the Red Cross in Salisbury but her health declined rapidly and she died on July 31, 1900. A Celtic cross marks her grave in Harare. Since then her order has established more than forty foundations in Zimbabwe and in Zambia, including schools, orphanages, hospitals, sanitoria and clinics, 'for the benefit of native Africans and coloureds as well as whites'.

COSTELLO, LOUISA STUART (1799-1870), travel writer, illustrator and novelist. Daughter of an Irish officer in the British army, who had earlier served under the French monarchy. At the age of fifteen she was taken to Paris by her widowed mother. There she studied painting and became the breadwinner of the family, especially through her work as a miniaturist, enabling her younger brother Dudley to train as an army officer at Sandhurst Academy in England. After he left the army in 1828, Louisa and Dudley worked in partnership, particularily as book illustrators. They became specialists in the copying of illuminations and illustrations from mediaeval manuscripts. Their work attracted attention in fashionable circles in both France and Britain and influenced the vogue for mediaeval subjects and decoration in art and design. After moving to London Louisa published a volume of verse which sold so well that she turned to full-time writing, producing historical novels, often with a French background, and essays of some historical worth such as *Memoirs of Eminent Englishwomen* (1844). Today she is remembered as the first professional woman travel writer. In the 1840s she began to publish illustrated accounts of her travels. Among the more successful of these were *A Pilgrimage to Auvergne from Picardy to le Velay* (1842), *Bearn and the Pyrenees* (1844), *The Rose Garden of Persia* (1845) and *A Tour to and from Venice* (1846). She was an adviser to Thomas Cook when he organised his first Continental tours in 1855. With tourism becoming fashionable among the upper classes, she supplied guide books for the travelling public. Dudley also became a writer of popular travel books and worked as foreign correspondent for the London *Daily News*. Louisa Costello spent her final years in France and died in Boulogne on April 24, 1870.

COSTELLO, MRS. (ELLEN). See under UÍ CHOISDEAILBH, EIBHLÍN.

COUSINS, MARGARET (GRETTA), née **GILLESPIE** (1878-1954), women's rights campaigner in Ireland and India, theosophist, educator, writer. Born November 7, 1878, at the Crescent, Boyle, Co. Roscommon into a prosperous Methodist family with Ulster connections. After attending a local national school, she won a scholarship to the Victoria High School, Derry. Later she studied in Dublin at the Royal Irish Academy of Music and graduated in music from the Royal University of Ireland. She was teaching music part-time when,

at twenty-five, she married James Cousins, a Belfast-born, self-educated clerk, who was developing a reputation as a playwright. After attending a women's franchise meeting in Manchester Gretta was fired with an evangelical zeal in pursuit of women's rights which was to last her entire life. In 1908 she became treasurer of the Irish Women's Franchise League and was one of six Irish delegates to the Parliament of Women in London in 1910. She was involved in organising a lecture tour for Christabel Pankhurst in Dublin and Cork and was jailed for a month in Tullamore following an act of civil disobedience - breaking windows in Dublin Castle. In 1910 she was sentenced to six months imprisonment for throwing stones at 10 Downing Street, London. With her husband, Gretta had earlier joined the Theosophical Society under the influence of George Russell (AE) and W.B. Yeats. In 1915 the couple went to India where her husband had been given the position of sub-editor on the *New India*, a journal published by the theosophists. Both of them were inextricably connected with the theosophical movement from this time on. Gretta found work as a teacher and became the first non-Indian member of the Indian Women's University at Poona. In 1917 she helped found the Indian Women's Association which, four years later, was instrumental in having members of the Madras legislature support women's suffrage. Involving herself in social and other philanthropic work she became founder and headmistress of the National Girl's School in Mangalore and, in 1923, was the first woman magistrate to be appointed in India. In 1926 she was a co-founder of the All India Women's Conference, a women's rights movement which has 200,000 members today and is active in many areas of social as well as political life. She was imprisoned for a year in 1932 for having addressed a public meeting in Madras to protest

THE IRISH
CITIZEN

For Men and Women Equally
The Rights of Citizenship;
From Men and Women Equally
The Duties of Citizenship.

Printed in
Ireland
on
Irish Paper.

Weekly
One Penny.
Annual
Subscription
6s. 6d. post free.

Vol. 1.   JUNE 15th, 1912.   No. 4.

"UNITED IRISHWOMEN."
NATIONALIST AND UNIONIST, MILITANT AND NON-MILITANT.

Chairman and Delegates at Historic Mass Meeting.

Mary Strangman, T.C.
(Waterford).

Mrs. Gibson
(Limerick).

Mrs. Sheehy-Skeffington,
M.A. (Dublin).

Senator Mary Hayden,
M.A. (Chairman).

Mrs. Cousins,
Mus.Bac. (Dublin).

Miss Geraldine Lennox
(London).

Mrs. Chambers
(Belfast).

[Reproduced from " The Weekly Irish Times" by kind permission of the Editor].

Advertising the Mass Meeting.   **A Proof of Earnestness.**

UNANIMOUS DEMAND FOR POLITICAL FREEDOM.
WHAT IS THE GOVERNMENT'S ANSWER?

*9. Title page of 'The Irish Citizen', June 15, 1912, showing **Margaret Cousins** et al.*

against an emergency powers act. As a dedicated theosophist, Gretta wrote many articles, books, and pamphlets on philosophy, education, and art, from her specific spiritual point of view and in 1928 was awarded the Founder's Silver Medal for her work for the Theosophical Society. She and her husband published a joint autobiography, *We Two Together*, in 1950. When a stroke left her paralysed at the age of sixty-five she received generous donations from the Indian Government and from friends. Gretta Cousins died on March 11, 1954, in Adyar, Tamil Nadu.

CRAIG, MAY (*c.* 1889-1972), actress. Born Dublin. She first came to prominence in the original production of Synge's *Playboy of the Western World* in 1907, playing Honor Blake. After her marriage, in 1916, May began a lifelong association with Dublin's Abbey Theatre and became synonymous with some great roles. As Mrs. Tancred in O'Casey's *Juno and the Paycock*, her great monologue was unforgettable; her interpretation of the part of the medium, Mrs. Henderson, in Yeats' play *The Words Upon the Window Pane* had a startling power to it and prompted Yeats to say 'When May Craig leaves her dressing room, she locks her door and leaves May Craig inside and becomes Mrs. Henderson'. She toured the USA on many occasions and, with her friend, SIOBHÁN McKENNA, was considered one of the great leading ladies of the Abbey Theatre. May Craig died in a Dublin nursing home on February 8, 1972.

CRANWELL, MIA (1880-1972), design artist, gold and silversmith. Born in north Dublin, March 1880, where her parents had settled after leaving St. Louis, Missouri, USA. Mia claimed to be a Wexford woman even though the family had moved to Manchester, England, when she was fifteen. She studied art and the gold and silversmith's crafts in Salford and Manchester Schools

of Art. She did not return to Ireland until she was thirty-seven: the date, a year after the 1916 Rising, is possibly of some significance as she was actively sympathetic to the nationalist cause during the War of Independence (1919-1921). She set up her first workshop in Suffolk Street, Dublin. Her jewellery in gold and silver, overtly 'Celtic' in inspiration and using enamelling to great effect, soon began to attract attention. By the early 1920s Mia was exhibiting widely, not only in Ireland (at the Royal Dublin Society and

*10. **May Craig** in the ' Plough and the Stars' by Sean O'Casey, Abbey Theatre, Dublin, 1972.*

at the Arts and Crafts Society) and Britain, but also in France. It was not only the exceptional craftmanship and the Irishness of her pieces that made her work outstanding but also the symbolic themes which she drew from early Irish myths and literature or from the poems of friends such as W.B. Yeats and AE (George Russell). In 1924 she was commisioned by Senator ALICE STOPFORD GREEN to make a casket to hold the velllum roll of the first Free State Senate; the casket, in gold, silver, and enamel, on a copper foundation, received unanimous praise. Mia was also commissioned by the Free State Army to design the standards for the first, second and fourth Brigades. Although an agnostic, she received important commissions for Roman Catholic churches. In 1926 she crafted a tabernacle door that is recognised as one of the finest pieces produced during the Celtic Revival. It was made for St. Michael's at Ballinasloe, Co. Galway, a church which, as a whole, is a showpiece for Irish craft work of all kinds. The tabernacle door was made in gold, silver and enamel, its decoration reminiscent of early Irish Christian artwork and its figures stylised in the same mode while bearing the artist's own unique and individual stamp. Perhaps her greatest achievement and personal triumph was a set of ecclesiastical works she completed for St. Patrick's Church in San Francisco, California, USA, after more than twelve years of labour. These included a tabernacle, sanctuary lamp, candlesticks and a monstrance, hand-wrought in solid silver and platinum and decorated with tracery and enamels. The monstrance in particular was described as containing 'something of the faith that renews itself through sorrow and loss in the Ireland that she loves.' Mia's commissions were many and varied. They included a pectoral cross for the tenor Count John McCormack, an episcopal ring for the Bishop of Clonfert, and jewellery based on Theosophical beliefs for George Russell (AE). She became a member of the Theosophical Society and a follower of AE. Decades of metal work had impaired her health so, in her sixties, Mia took to weaving designs on a hand loom. In her seventies she turned to illus-trating books for the then prestigious Dolmen Press. In her eighties she moved from her cottage at Druim Coibhneann, Killiney, Co. Dublin, where she had had her workshop for four decades and spent the last ten years of her long life at Alexandra Guild House in Dublin. Mia Cranwell died there on October 20, 1972.

CRAWFORD, EMILY, née JOHNSTONE (*c.* 1840-1915), journalist. Born Corboy, Co. Longford. Her father, once a wealthy country gentleman, got into severe financial difficulties and died when she was in her mid-teens. Her American mother took Emily to Paris where she attended the Sorbonne University and broke into journalism by accident when the editor of the *Scotch Quarterly* saw a letter she had written to a friend in England describing the social and political life of Paris. He invited her to send him material which was an immediate success. Emily began working freelance for other journals and was soon earning the very substantial sum of four hundred pounds a year. In her mid-twenties she married George Morland Crawford, Paris correspondent of the British *Daily News*. Emily and her husband reported from the city during the 1870 siege of Paris and the following year, when the communists captured the city, she got her first 'big story' by crossing the barricades in the middle of the fighting and obtaining an interview with the leaders of the attempted coup d'état. Just over a month later she made one of the great 'scoops' in the history of journalism by gaining admission to the Versailles Conference, her report being the first and fullest to reach the English press. She gradually replaced her husband, now an elderly man, as Paris correspondent. After his death in 1885 she took over the post officially and also wrote for the *New York Tribune*. Early in the First World War, aged and ailing, she was brought from France to Bristol, England, by her son and died there on

December 30, 1915. She once advised that no woman should think of becoming a professional journalist unless, in addition to special aptitude, she had "dauntless courage, exceptional health and powers of physical endurance, and a considerable amount of reserve force." Emily Crawford is now recognised as one of the most distinguished figures in the history of early modern journalism.

CREED, SAINT. See under CRIDA, SAINT.

CRIDA (CREDA, CRÉDE), SAINT (7th century). Very little is known about this woman who was to become the patron saint of Creed in Cornwall which is named after her. She is said to have been the daughter of a king of Leinster, Senach Rón. Having moved to a hermitage to lead a contemplative life she was raped by a brigand. As a consequence she gave birth to a child who was to become the future Saint Boethin, abbot of Clonmacnoise. She continued in the religious life and set up communities in the upper part of the kingdom of Ossary (now generally comprising counties Kilkenny and Laois) notably Kilcredy, the church which bears her name. It is not known for certain when she went to Cornwall. There were two Irish missions or religious *exodi* to south-west Britain in the early Christian period which included many holy women. It is likely that Crida went at the later period which is associated with Saint Finnbarr. An ancient fresco of her is still extant (if over-much restored) in the church at Laniver, about ten miles from her main foundation at Creed. Her feast-day is observed in Cornwall on 'the Sunday nearest November 30.'

CRILLEY, MARGARET (1888-1961), painter. Born Newry, Co. Down. At seventeen Margaret entered the Metropolitan School of Art, Dublin, and studied with William Orpen. Orpen invited her to become his assistant and, by the age of twenty-one, she was making her name as a painter. In 1911 and 1912 she won Board of Education medals. She met and painted with Harry Clarke, then a student at the School of Art and already winning awards for stained glass design, and they were married in 1914. Margaret made her début at the Royal Hibernian Academy, Dublin, in 1913, was an annual exhibitor from then on, and became an elected member in 1927. Besides the many portraits she painted of prominent Irish personalities in the 1920s and 1930s, she also produced large canvases, many of which were allegorical, as well as those of landscapes, flowers and various subjects. In 1929 her work was shown in the first Exhibition of Contemporary Irish Art in New York, held at the Helen Hackett Gallery, along with that of Harry, Charles Lamb and Dermod O'Brien. Her husband established the Harry Clarke Studios at 33 North Frederick Street, Dublin, in 1930 and, after his death the following year, Margaret ran the studios with her daughter and son while continuing to paint. In 1939 she held her only solo exhibition, at the Dublin Painters' Gallery, and, always in contact with avant garde artists, joined MAINIE JELLETT, EVIE HONE, Louis le Brocquy and others to establish the Irish Exhibition of Living Art in 1943. Margaret Crilly's output, in her own academic and realistic manner, continued uninterrupted up to her death in 1961 and her work is represented in most of the prominent Irish art galleries.

CROTTY, ELIZABETH (LIZZIE), née MARKHAM (1885-1960), traditional musician. Born December 6, 1885, in Gower, Cooraclare, in south west Clare. Her family were small farmers and she grew up in a house filled with traditional music. The women musicians and singers in Ireland at that time were restricted to

*11. 'A girl's head', drawing, 1909, by **Margaret Crilly**.*

performing in their own homes or that of neighbours, taking down their instruments only to entertain at house dances, weddings, christenings and 'American wakes' within walking distance. Although Elizabeth's mother was an excellent fiddle player, having learned the instrument from a travelling blind fiddler named Schooner Breen, the child followed her older sister Maggie by playing the Anglo concertina. She perfected her style while playing at local house dances with her mother and sister. In 1914 Elizabeth married Miko Crotty who owned a

12. **Elizabeth Crotty,** *(second row centre), at the first Comhaltas meeting in Clare 1954.*

public house in Kilrush. Over the years she achieved a local reputation for her playing but it was not until the 1940s and 1950s that her fame began to spread outside of west Clare as the Crotty public house attracted the cream of musicians from around the country. Like many other traditional musicians of the time Elizabeth was elderly before she became widely known. After the founding of Comhaltas Ceoltóirí Éireann, the national organisation of traditional musicians, she became active in the Clare branch during the 1950s and was elected its first president. Mrs. Crotty (as she was always known outside her home area) began to make appearances at the newly-instituted *fleadhanna ceoil,* the music competitions and gatherings organised throughout the country by the Comhaltas, although she did not take part in competitions or

adjudication. Neither did she make commercial recordings. Her playing was recorded by folk music collectors, notably by Ciarán Mac Mathúna, and broadcast on radio. Thus she earned nation-wide recognition as a virtuoso on her Lachenal concertina. Elizabeth Crotty died at the height of her fame on December 27, 1960.

CUMMINS, GERALDINE DOROTHY (G.D. CUMMINS) (1890-1969), author and psychic. Born in Cork and educated privately. Geraldine was involved in the suffrage movement in Cork and collaborated with a friend, Suzanne R. Day, on three plays; *Broken Faith* (1913), *The Way of the World* (1914) and *Fox and Geese* (1917), produced at the Abbey Theatre, Dublin. These comedies were based on life among the Cork peasantry; a background that also provided material for the fiction Geraldine produced after Suzanne moved to London: the novels *The Land they Loved* (1919), *Fire of Beltane* (1936), and a collection of short stories, *Variety Show* (1959). A biography of her close friend EDITH SOMERVILLE, *Dr. E. OE Somerville*, was published in 1952. She married the poet Austin Clarke in 1920 but the couple separated after ten days. Geraldine was also a well-known psychic and wrote several books on psychical research and related material which, she claimed, had been dictated to her while in trance with a spirit presence: *Beyond Human Personality* (1935), *Childhood of Jesus* (1937), *The Fate of Colonel Fawcett* (1952) and *Swan on a Black Sea* (1965). Her *Scripts of Cleophas* was the subject of a famous law case to determine whether copyright belongs to the medium or the spirit. The judge ruled for the medium. G.D. Cummins died in Cork in 1969.

CURRAN, SARAH (1782-1808), sweetheart of Robert Emmet. Born Rathfarnham, Dublin, youngest daughter of John Philpott Curran, lawyer and nationalist, whose family seat was in Newmarket, Co. Cork. Curran, a protestant, was an MP who opposed the union with Britain and defended Wolfe Tone and others involved in the 1798 Rebellion. Her mother was a member of the once prominently Roman Catholic Creagh family in Munster. Sarah's youth was unhappy owing to parental discord and the death of her sister. After her mother eloped with a clergyman she was sent to live with the Crawford family in Lismore, Co. Waterford. She returned to Dublin and met Robert Emmet on her début, at sixteen, at a ball in Wicklow. After the failure of the 1798 Rebellion, Emmet went to the Continent to canvass support for another rising. He returned to Rathfarnham in October 1802 and began organising to that end. Sarah met him at her father's house, which Emmet frequented, and joined in discussions on politics and national aspirations. They became secretly engaged. After the rebellion of 1803 and Emmet's execution her father, who had not been in sympathy with the rebellion, came under suspicion because of Sarah's attachment to the rebel leader. He forced her to leave home and she took refuge with the Penrose family, near Cork city, with whom her sister had been living. By now her health had seriously declined but, in 1805, she met and married Captain R.H. Sturgeon of the Royal Staff Corps and went to Sicily with him. Forced to leave because of anti-British unrest, she gave birth to a stillborn child aboard ship. Sarah died of consumption on May 5, 1808, at home in Hythe, Kent, England. Because her father refused her burial beside her beloved sister in Dublin, Sturgeon had her body interred at the family seat in Newmarket, Co. Cork. Her ill-starred love affair and early death emotionally affected the nationalists of the period and of later times. The mood was captured by Thomas Moore in his melody 'She is far from the Land'.

CUSACK, MARGARET ANNE (SISTER MARY FRANCIS CLARE) (1829-1899), the 'Nun of Kenmare', social activist, feminist, writer and founder of the St. Joseph's Sisters of Peace. Born in Dublin. Daughter of an Episcopalian doctor who practised in Coolock where he was especially concerned with the poor. When her father became ill the family broke up and Margaret and her brother were taken by their mother to live with a rich relation in England. She joined an Anglican Sisterhood in London after her fiancé died. Frustrated in her efforts to work with the poor in East London, she converted to Roman Catholicism and, in 1860, joined the Irish Poor Clares in Newry, Co. Down, to work with homeless girls. The following year Sr. Mary Francis was sent to Kenmare in Co. Kerry, at the request of the parish priest, to open a branch of the order there. She remained in

13. Margaret Anne Cusack, c. 1880.

the name of M.S. Cusack, Sr. Mary Francis gave all profits to her order and once even wrote a detective story to raise funds. In 1872 she set up a fund for relief of the poor in the famine conditions which then prevailed and raised fifteen thousand pounds. In the following year she published, in Ireland and in the United States, her most controversial pamphlet attacking landlordism and supporting the Land League and the Home Rule movement. This incurred the wrath of the Roman Catholic hierarchy and Sr. Mary Francis was publicly attacked by Archbishop McCabe of Dublin. With ecclesiastical permission she left her convent in Kenmare in 1881, following protracted conflict with her community, and attempted to open a new convent at Knock, Co. Mayo, but the church authorities refused consent. In 1884 she secured episcopal support to start a new order in Nottingham, England, intended to undertake work among the poor in that city; her ally, the local Bishop Bagshawe, was especially concerned with the Irish immigrants in the area. Sr. Mary Francis then went to Rome to expound her case. After four months of negotiations she was publicly cleared by the Vatican of the accusations levelled against her in Ireland, including those made by her community in Kenmare. She was then given personal approval by Pope Leo XIII to found the Sisters of Peace, whose apostolate was to assist working girls by providing lodgings and refuges as well as training, especially for domestic work. The order opened its first house on June 12, 1884, in Nottingham and its first school in the same year. Bishop Bagshawe sent Sr. Mary Francis to America to raise funds for the Nottingham diocese. Soon she had established a convent and a home for working girls in Jersey city and an orphanage in Newark, New Jersey. In America she again found herself and her work opposed by many bishops with the result that the work

Kenmare for twenty years during which time her activities brought her into escalating conflict with the Roman Catholic religious authorities. She first became known for her writings; in all she produced some fifty books and pamphlets, including biographies of Irish saints, small histories of Ireland and Kerry, and biographies of national figures such as Daniel O'Connell and Fr. Mathew. Her pamphlets on the position of women in modern society, which she wrote in support of equal rights, equal pay, and suitable education, caused her to be looked upon with suspicion by her peers. In 1872, concerned as always with the situation which applied to young poor girls, she wrote *Advice to Irish Girls in America* which sold 10,000 copies. Writing under and growth of her order was inhibited. Ill health eventually forced Sr. Mary Francis to retire from her order and, after some time spent lecturing and writing, she returned to England in 1891. She appears, by this time, to have reverted to her former Episcopalian faith. In 1898 Margaret published her autobiography, *The Story of my Life*, in which she made a bitter, if justifiable, attack on the Roman Catholic authorities but, at its conclusion, the book lapsed into an almost paranoiac tirade that blunted its message. Margaret Cusack died on June 5, 1899, in Leamingston, Warwickshire; there is some cause for supposing that she was restored to the Roman Catholic faith on her death-bed. Rome had requested her order to change its name and efface all memory of the founder but in 1970, seventy-five years after her death, it reverted to Margaret's original choice, 'The St. Joseph's Sisters of Peace,' at a General Chapter held in Nottingham, England. Today the order flourishes in Britain, the USA, and Canada.

CZIRA, SYDNEY née GIFFORD (1889-1974). republican and journalist. Born Rathmines, Dublin, the youngest of twelve children of an affluent Roman Catholic solicitor and his protestant Anglo-Irish wife. Sydney's mother was a niece of the painter, Sir Frederick Burton. Her parents were conservative and Unionist. Their six Roman Catholic sons remained respectably middle class while the six protestant daughters became either socialists or Sinn Féiners. Sydney was educated at Alexandra College, Dublin, and almost immediately became involved in the national movement, following her sisters Muriel and GRACE GIFFORD, both of whom were to marry leaders of the 1916 Rebellion. She joined Inghinidhe na hÉireann and, in 1906, was one of five women voted on to the executive council of Sinn Féin. After leaving college Sydney began contributing to national journals under the name 'John Brennan', feeling that a male name would lend her articles more authority. She used this pseudonym for the greater part of her long journalistic career and, from 1910 onwards, contributed as Sorcha Ní Hanlon to *Bean na hÉireann*, the organ of the Inghinidhe. While in many of her articles Sydney discussed questions of nationalism she also wrote about the appalling working conditions of nurses and women in factories. She took part in many pageants with COUNTESS MARKIEVICZ while fundraising for Cumann na mBan. In 1910 she was involved in the Inghinidhe scheme to supply meals to school children. In 1914 she went to the USA, expecting it to be easier for a woman to work as a journalist, and married a Hungarian emigré who soon returned to his native country; they had one son. Sydney continued to write and campaign for Irish independence, contributing mainly to the *New York Sun*, before working with John Devoy and Clan na Gael, the influential Fenian propagandising and fund-raising society which had two papers, the *Irish Nation* and the *Gaelic American*. In 1920, following the split in the umbrella organisation, Friends of Irish Freedom, over policy regarding the use of money raised in their Victory Fund, she joined the faction headed by Joseph McGarrity, one of the Clan na Gael leaders who favoured using the fund in Ireland for Irish purposes alone and wholeheartedly supported the flotation of the Dáil Éireann External Loan. Thereafter, Sydney worked for McGarrity's *Irish Press*, a paper founded in Philadelphia in 1918 specifically to combat anti-Sinn Féin propaganda in the USA by the British, that also backed the Dáil Loan. British authorities had refused Sydney admission to Ireland for several years but, in 1922, using an illicit passport, she was able to return with her son. She was soon involved with the Women's

Prisoners' Defence League, founded by MAUD GONNE and CHARLOTTE DESPARD to protest against the prison conditions and executions of republican prisoners during the Civil War; she remained an active member of the League until the late 1930s. Madame Czira, as she became known, continued to work as a journalist, contributing to all the daily and republican newspapers, and also as a broadcaster with RTÉ, particularly aiming to perpetuate the memory of republicans she had known and events she had witnessed before she emigrated. Following the Second World War she was involved with DOROTHY MACARDLE in bringing German children refugees to Ireland. Madame Sydney Czira died September 15, 1974. Her recollections, *The Years Flew By*, were published posthumously.

DAVIES, CHRISTIAN. See under CAVANAGH (KIT), CHRISTIAN.

DAVYS, MARY (1674-1732), novelist. Born in Dublin. She married the Reverend Peter Davys, head-master of the Free School attached to St. Patrick's Cathedral, in Dublin. Mary was one of the earliest published Irish women writers in the English language. It is unlikely she and her husband were friends of Swift's, as is often stated, because Rev. Davys died within a few years of marriage, in 1698, and she had moved to England some twenty years before Swift was given the deanery of St. Patrick's. Mary remained in England for the rest of her life, running a coffee-house in Cambridge, and writing plays, novels and her memoirs. Her best-known novel was *Familiar Letters Betwixt a Gentleman and a Lady* (1725). Her writings, aimed at female readers, appear to have been popular for a collection, *The Works of Mary Davys: Consisting of Plays, Novels, Poems and Familial Letters*, was published in 1725, a few years before she died.

DE BARRA, LESLIE, née PRICE (1893-1984), revolutionary and Red Cross official. Born and reared in Dublin. After qualifying as a teacher in Belfast, she joined the revolutionary women's movement, Cumann na mBan, in Dublin and carried despatches during the 1916 Easter Rebellion. Resigning her teaching post, she became Cumann na mBan's director of organising after the 1917 convention. Leslie was instrumental in the rapid increase of the number of branches, from one hundred to six hundred, and in establishing a communications network. When sent to Cork she met and married the guerrilla leader, General Tom Barry, in 1921; Michael Collins and de Valera were guests at the wedding. The couple sided with the republicans in the Civil War and Tom Barry was imprisoned in the Curragh. Meanwhile, Leslie worked untiringly for Cumann na mBan, now as director of training. After the cessation of hostilities the couple settled in Cork where he joined the Harbour Commissioners and she continued her long and active association with Connradh na Gaeilge. In 1939 Leslie's life took a different direction with the founding of the Red Cross Society and, for the next four decades, her name was linked with the Society's activities, both national and international. She became chairperson of the Society in 1950. For her services to the International Red Cross during and in the aftermath of the Second World War she was decorated by the West German and Italian Governments and, in 1978, was awarded the prestigious Henri Dunant Medal by the International Committee of the Red Cross. She was also the national president of Gorta, the state organisation for famine relief, from its inception until she resigned the position in 1968. She died on April 9, 1984.

DE BURGO or BURKE, SISTER HONORIA (1575-1653), victim of religious persecution. Born in 1575, a daughter of the house of MacWilliam Burke of Mayo (possibly of Risteard an Iarainn, who later married GRÁINNE UÍ MHÁILLE). Few names have been recorded of the countless Roman Catholic women who suffered religious persecution to the point of martyrdom at the hands of the English authorities from the time of the 'Reformation Parliament' in 1536 until the Restoration of Charles II in 1680. Among the exceptions is that of Honoria de Burgo, probably due to the fact that not only was she of noble blood but also had a reputation for sanctity. At the time of her birth her family were rapidly losing their lordship in Mayo to the Elizabethans. She received the habit of the Third Order of Saint Catherine of Sienna at the age of fourteen during a period of fierce warfare and religious persecution when many of her kinspeople were murdered. Sr. Honoria later erected 'a residence or small monastery' close to the Dominican convent of Burrishole, near Newport, Co. Mayo, which was then under the protection of Gráinne Uí Mháille and her son, Tibbot-na-Long de Burgo. Here she 'led a sanctified life during the reigns of Elizabeth, James I and Charles I, devoting herself to holy works'. She survived wars, famines and further religious persecutions 'till the decrepitude of old age.' In February 1653, during the Cromwellian persecutions when Burrishole convent came under threat she, an attendant lay-sister, and a young tertiary Honoria Magan or Magean, took refuge on a *crannóg* or island, probably on nearby Lough Feeagh, 'whither they were pursued by the fanatics, seized, and despoiled of their garments (i.e. religious habits) and left in this state in the depth of winter.' The young Sr. Magan ran naked into the forest to escape rape and died of exposure. Sr. Honoria was carried by her attendant back to the ruined chapel in Burrishole convent where she died.

DEEVY, TERESA (*c.* 1894-1963), playwright. Born Kilkenny, January 21, 1894, and reared in Waterford where her mother encouraged her to write from a young age. She attended the Ursuline Convent, Waterford, and entered University College Dublin, with the intention of becoming a teacher but developed complete deafness when Menieres disease, a hearing problem present from childhood, deteriorated. When Teresa did graduate it was from University College Cork. She then went to London to study lip-reading and became interested in the theatre, particularly in the work of Chekhov and Shaw. Back in Ireland, in 1919, she joined Cumann na mBan but her handicap made fully active participation impossible. About this time she began to submit scripts to the Abbey Theatre but had no success for ten years. Then, between 1930 and 1936, she wrote a series of outstanding plays. Most of these were staged by the Abbey, proved highly popular, and were regularly revived by amateur companies over the next four decades. *The Reapers* (1930) was followed by a one-act comedy *A Disciple* (1931), *Temporal Powers* (1932), and *In Search of Valour* (1934). Her best known piece, the one-act *King of Spain's Daughter* (1935), was followed by *Katie Roche*, in the same year. The latter caused a stir by its honest exploration of a marriage situation in rural Ireland. *The Wild Goose* (1936) was less successful as a dramatic piece. Two of her plays were produced by pre-war BBC television. Deevy's favourite theme was that of high-spirited romantic young women trapped in marriage to less-than-heroic husbands. She turned from the stage to writing passable scripts for radio, although one, *Within a Marble City*, was considered a masterpiece and another, *Going Beyond Alma's Glory*, was successfully adapted for the stage in 1951, She returned to her original medium in 1948 with the one-act *Light Falling*. Her last stage play, *Wife to James Whelan*, came two years later. She was elected to the Irish Academy of Letters in 1954. There is little doubt that Teresa Deevy's talent as a playwright was stunted in the conservative atmosphere of the 1930s and 1940s and her most potentially fruitful years were spent in writing radio scripts and convent school pieces. She died in Waterford in 1963. The script of *Wife to James Whelan*, considered her best play, has remained unpublished.

DERVILLA (DERBHILEDH, DERBILED), SAINT (6th century), hermit. There is mention of two contemporaneous saints of this name in the different ancient religious calendars. Dervilla of the royal race of Connaught and Dervilla of Erris (in north-west Connaught); though they have been assigned different feast days, most modern commentators believe that they were one and the same person. There is little account of Dervilla of Connaught. Dervilla of Erris was the daughter of Cormac, great-grandson of Fiach, ancestor of the chiefs of Uí Fiachra, which comprised very much of modern Mayo; she was also great-grand-daughter of the powerful Daithi, high king of Ireland, who was killed by lightening in the Alps while leading his army into the heart of the Roman Empire. This princess became an anchorite on the Mullet peninsula in the barony of Erris, the most remote part of Uí Fiachra territory, where she appears to have spent the whole of her religious life. The ruin of a church near the site of her hermitage, believed to date from her time, indicates that Dervilla attracted followers as would have been quite usual in the Early Christian period. Her significance, despite the reclusive nature of her life, may be judged from the fact she took part in the Synod of Ballysodare in 585. This synod, presided over by Saint Columcille, took place immediately following the famous political council known as the Convention of Drumceat

and can be judged of major ecclesiastical importance. It brought together many abbots, bishops, priests and women religious, as well as eminent laymen. The recording by the annalists of Dervilla's participation is an indication of her status. The saint probably died about the turn of the century and was buried in the cemetery attached to her foundation. Her feast day is August 3, the 'other' Dervilla being venerated on October 16 .

DERVORGILLA, (DEARBHORGAILL) (1108-1193), in tradition, the cause of the Norman invasion of Ireland. Daughter of Muirchertach mac Floinn, king of Meath, and sister of the future king, Mael Sechnaill. She was married at a young age (*c.* 1125) to Tigernán Ua Ruairc, king of Breifne, as part of a political settlement following the division of the Meath kingdom as Toirdhealbhach Ua Conchobhair established himself virtual king of Ireland. She doubtlessly resented her marriage to the man who had been the main ally of the king of Connaught in the destruction of her ancestral kingdom. During this period Ireland was 'a trembling sod' from the endless wars waged between the principal kingdoms to achieve the high kingship and Dervorgilla's husband was continually involved in these power struggles. Diarmait Mac Murchadh, nominal king of Leinster since 1121, allied himself with Mac Lochlainn of Ailech, helping the latter to become high king in 1139 and, in return, receiving a third of the Meath kingdom when it was partitioned. Now at the height of his power Diarmait joined forces with Dervorgilla's husband and the king of Connaught to smash the Uí Briain of Munster at the battle of Móin Mór (1151). In the following year, when her husband was away on pilgrimage, Dervorgilla sent a message to Diarmait to come for her. Her reasons for this remain uncertain. She was in her mid-forties and

Diarmait was recorded in the *Annals of the Four Masters* as being sixty-two (although some modern historians assert that he was two years younger than Dervorgilla). Diarmait's secretary, Maurice Regan, wrote that she was 'a fair and lovely lady, entirely beloved of Dermot' (Diarmait). Whatever mutual attraction was involved it is plain that there were political advantages, with regard to the kingdom of Meath, to be gained by both parties from the liason. Dervorgilla was certainly acting under the advice of her brother, king of depleted Meath and lately an ally of Diarmait's. Furthermore the 'abduction' may have been carried out with the connivance of the king of Connaught, Dervorgilla's brother-in-law, who was threatened by the rising power of his ally Ua Ruairc. Keating's *History* states that Diarmait 'went quickly to meet the lady, accompanied by a band of mounted men . . . the woman wept and screamed in defense, as if Diarmait was carrying her off by force.' Brehon law would have allowed for divorce and remarriage in the circumstances had not the couple departed with 'her cattle and furniture' i.e the dowry which Ua Ruairc was then entitled, by law and custom, to recover by force. The following year Ua Ruairc and Ua Conchobhair marched on Diarmait and recovered Dervorgilla, although fourteen years were to pass before Diarmait was forced to pay 100 ounces of gold in reparation for the abduction. Having recovered his wife, Ua Ruairc then repudiated her. Dervorgilla took refuge in the almost-completed Cistercian Abbey of Mellifont, Co. Louth, then being built as part of a campaign for church reform. Perhaps the 60 ounces of gold she bestowed on the abbey in 1157 as a royal gift was part of a settlement that decreed she live out the rest of her life there. She was to witness the king of Connaught first defeat the high king and then, joining forces with Ua Ruairc who was implacable in his desire for revenge, defeat and drive out Diarmait Mac Murchadh who in turn brought in the Norman-Welsh war-lords. The disunity of the Irish chieftains allowed the latter to overrun the country and, in 1175, the high king of Ireland was forced to recognise Henry II, king of England, as overlord and accept all of Ireland being pledged to pay tribute. Dervorgilla outlived Mac Murchadh, Ua Ruairc and Strongbow the Norman king of Leinster, the province she may have hoped to control after her elopement. Three years before her death, at eighty-five, Dervorgilla had the Church of the Nuns built at Clonmacnoise. All traditions hold that she spent the last forty years of her life in penance, 'lamenting that she had brought so many evils on her country.'

DESPARD, CHARLOTTE, née FRENCH (1844-1939), radical, civil rights activist, socialist and suffragist. Born Kent, England, of a minor Co. Roscommon branch of the noted Connaught Roman Catholic landed family, the Frenches of Monivea. Her father, a naval commander, died when she was nine; she was the elder sister of the future Lord French, Field Marshal and Commander in Chief of British Forces during World War One, and Lord Lieutenant of Ireland during the War of Independence. Her mother's family were merchant Presbyterian Scots. Charlotte was educated privately and from her early years was non-conformist in outlook and supportive of suffragists. She married Maximillian Despard, a wealthy Irish merchant with an estate in Kent, and lived with him in the Far East for some years. In 1890, after her husband's death, Charlotte moved from Kent to the slum district of Nine Elms in London's East End where, now an active socialist, she joined the independent Labour Party and addressed many meetings. She served on Poor Law and Education Committees, founded a working

14. *Charlotte Despard in Grafton Street, 1921.*

man's club, and one of the first child care centres. She was also active in the militant Women's Social and Political Union, founded by Emmeline Pankhurst but, in 1907, in reaction to the Pankhurst's autocracy, she formed and became first president of the Women's Freedom League. She was especially concerned for a time with the issue of 'no taxation without represen-

tation.' She came to Ireland to address public meetings at the request of the Irish Women's Franchise League, the militant suffrage association set up in 1908 by HANNA SHEEHY SKEFFINGTON, MARGARET COUSINS and others. She was a close friend of MAUD GONNE MACBRIDE who described her as 'a most remarkable woman and intensely Irish in feeling.' Charlotte was to divide her time between Ireland and England for the next twenty years. During the 1913 labour unrest in Dublin she financially supported the locked-out workers and was active in feeding their children. During the War of Independence she publicly supported Sinn Féin and the IRA, thus irrevocably estranging her brother, the Lord Lieutenant, who was implacably hostile to Irish independence. She continued her socialist activities and founded the Irish Workers' College at her home in Eccles Street, Dublin, for the political education of workers. Although Charlotte had stood unsuccessfully as a candidate for Battersea, in the 1919 general elections, she tirelessly campaigned throughout Britain until equal suffrage was achieved in 1928. In November 1920 she toured Ireland as a member of the British Labour Party Commission of Inquiry. Together with Maud Gonne MacBride, she collected first-hand evidence of army and police atrocities in Cork and Kerry, making good use of the incongruous fact that she was the Viceroy's sister. During the Civil War she acted as president of the Women's Prisoners' Defence League, founded by Maud Gonne MacBride, to support republican prisoners. After the Coercion Act became law, the women continued their vehement protest through the People's Rights Association. The enraged Minister for Justice once openly threatened 'Mrs. Despard and Mrs. MacBride and those who were trying to bring in Soviet conditions . . . if it is necessary, we are going to execute them.' In 1930 as secretary of the Friends of Soviet Russia, she and Hanna Sheehy Skeffington made a six week tour of Russia and, on their return, lectured extensively on conditions there. In her late eighties and early nineties Charlotte was still addressing public demonstrations in Hyde Park, and other venues, against General Franco and the Fascist movement in general. After her Workers' College in Dublin had been ransacked by a right wing Roman Catholic mob she handed it over to the Friend's of Soviet Russia and moved, at ninety years of age, to riot-torn Belfast in an attempt to unite protestant and Roman Catholic workers; here her house was burned down by a protestant mob. Not surprisingly she was declared bankrupt shortly before her death in 1929. Influenced by Theosophist ideas, at least for a time, Charlotte Despard's ideal was a Christian-based communism. In the graveside oration, her friend Maud Gonne likened her to 'a white flame in the defence of prisoners and the oppressed.'

DE VALERA, SINÉAD, née FLANAGAN (1879-1975), author and wife of President Éamon de Valera. Born Balbriggan, Co. Dublin. Having trained as a national teacher she was working in Dorset Street, Dublin, when she developed a life-long interest in the Gaelic League. Sinéad taught Irish part-time in the Leinster College in Parnell Square, where one of her pupils was Éamon de Valera, then a teacher of mathematics at Carysfort Teacher Training College, Dublin. They married on January 8, 1910. She did not become involved in public life and in the decade following the 1916 Rising, when her husband served prison terms in English jails and spent long periods in America working for the republican cause, Sinéad devoted herself to her family of five sons and two daughters. She did not begin to write for children until her family was almost grown. In 1934 she published *Buaidhirt agus Bród*, the first of some fifteen plays she was to write for children in the Irish language. Several of these were based on historical heroes. Sinéad is best known for her retellings in English of Irish fairy and folk tales, including *Fairy Tales of Ireland* (1967) and *More Irish Fairy Tales* (1979). She was seventy-eight

MIDNIGHT ASSASSINS.
RAID ON
MRS Eamon de VALeRA.

15. *Sinéad De Valera and children, drawing by Countess Markeivicz.*

when she wrote the first of these and ultimately published ten such collections. Her only outside interests were Gaelic League functions and children's drama competitions. Sinéad de Valera died in a Dublin Nursing Home on January 7, 1975, predeceasing her husband by eight months.

DEVLIN, ANNE (*c.* 1778-1851), revolutionary. Born Cronebeg, Rathdrum, Co. Wicklow. Her father was a prosperous tenant farmer and United Irishman. Michael Dwyer, insurgent leader in the '98 Rising and subsequent guerrilla, was a first cousin on her mother's side. Her father was held without trial for two and a half years after the rebellion. Upon his release he brought his family to Rathfarnham, then on the outskirts of Dublin city, where he appears to have set up a thriving dairy and horse-hire business. Robert Emmet, planning a new insurrection, moved into nearby Butterfield Lane under an assumed name and Anne, working in his house, acted as messenger between him and fellow conspirators in the city. After the ill-fated rebellion of 1803, while Emmet was in hiding in the Dublin mountains, Anne and her sister were tortured by yeomen looking for information. They were later imprisoned in Kilmainham Jail, with all their family, where she refused a five hundred pound bribe from Major Sirr and again underwent torture rather than betray the rebel leaders. She was released in 1806. Anne then worked as a domestic servant and washerwoman in Dublin and, broken by imprisonment and eviction, spent the rest of her life in poverty. She married a man named Campbell and had two children who, it appears, predeceased her. At some earlier time she had dictated an account of her prison experiences to a Carmelite brother named Cullen and was contacted by Dr Richard Madden for material for his *History of the United Irishmen: their Lives and Times* (1843-1846). Dr. Madden raised a subscription for her. After the death of her husband, in 1845, Anne lived in ill health and near-blindness in the slum area of Elbow Lane, The Coombe, Dublin, where she died on September 18, 1851. Dr Madden, who had continued to help her financially, arranged her burial in Glasnevin Cemetery where he erected a monument over her grave. Anne Devlin's story was made into a film, *Anne Devlin,* in 1984.

DILLON, EILÍS (1920-1994), novelist and woman of letters. Born Co. Galway into a branch of an old Connaught family which produced several noteworthy nationalist figures in the last century. Her maternal grandfather, Count Plunkett, was a minister in the first Dáil Éireann and a poet, while her mother's brother, also a poet, was executed for his part in the 1916 Rising. Her immediate family was intensely republican, and her father, a professor at University College Galway, was jailed for his Sinn Féin activities. This background greatly influenced her writing when she drew on family history to recreate the nation's past and the traumas of the country's march to nationhood. She was an outstanding student at the Ursuline Convent, Sligo, but Victorian family attitudes prevented her from attending university. Ironically, her husbands in two marriages were both professors of literature, to whose publications she made huge contributions, and both her children became noted academics. Eilís began her literary career as a writer of children's books in the Irish language but soon switched to English. In all she wrote more than forty books and plays for both children and adults and her work has appeared in twelve languages. Her books for children published in the 1950s were of such high standard that they resurrected this genre from the critical neglect to which it had fallen. These earlier books included *The Children of Bath, Lost Island, The Island of Horses, San Sebastian, The House on the Shore, Plover Hill, The Singing Cave, The Fort of Gold, Bold John Henbry,* published for the most part between 1950 and 1965. In 1973 her most famous book, *Across the Bitter Sea,* an historical novel dealing with the traumatic events of Ireland in the last century, was acclaimed by the *Sunday Times* as 'a quite remarkable novel . . . of which Zola might have felt proud.' *Blood Relations* (1977) is based on the period of the War of Independence while *Wild Geese* (1981) and *Citizen Burke* (1984), considered her finest achievement, were set in 18th century France. Eilís Dillon was also a short story writer, poet, critic, autobiographer, dramatist, scholar and an excellent translator of Irish poetry. In 1979 she was elected Fellow of the British Royal Society of Literature. She lived for a period in America where she taught Irish; she lectured in Japan and the continent of Europe. She was involved with the setting up of the Irish Children's Book Trust, of Aos Dána (Arts Council scheme for the promotion of the arts and artists) and the Roman Catholic Church's commission for liturgy reform after the Second Vatican Council. Eilís Dillon was a most generous advocate of artists and writers and was chairperson of the Irish Writers Union and Centre until ill health forced her to retire the year before her death on July 19, 1994. Her first husband was Cormac Ó Cuilleanáin, professor of literature at UCG. Their daughter, Eiléan Ní Chuilleanáin, has become one of the foremost Irish women poets of her time. After her first husband's death Eilís married Vivian Mercier, critic and professor of literature, whose final volume of essays she prepared for publication in the last few months of her life. She is buried with him in Clara, Co. Offaly.

DIX, RACHAEL McCLINTOCK. See under UÍ DHIOSCA, ÚNA BEAN.

DOBBS, MARGARET EMMELINE CONWAY (1871-1962), historian and Gaelic Leaguer. Born Dublin, November 19, 1871, into an upper-class Unionist family who had originally settled in Co. Antrim during the Ulster plantations. Her father was High Sheriff in Carrickfergus, Co. Antrim and later, in Co. Louth; her mother was a member of the Belfast family of Mulholland. A brother later became Governor of North Carolina, USA. When Margaret was still very young a Scots governess interested her in the Gaelic languages. After the death of her father, in 1898, the family returned to Glenariff, near Cushendall, Co. Antrim, and Margaret learned Irish from a Gaelic League teacher. Although she never became a nationalist like some of her contemporary Ulster Protestants, Margaret did undoubtedly come under the influence of the centenary commemorations of the 1798 Rebellion. She joined one of the most unusual of all Gaelic League branches, known as the 'Glens' group, the leading figures of which were mostly from protestant Unionist backgrounds. Her house at Portmagolan was the nerve-centre of League activities as members naturally gravitated to the Glens of Antrim where there were still many Gaelic-speakers. She was present (with her two close friends, the revolutionaries Roger Casement and Denis McCullough) at the inaugural Feis na nGleann ('The Glens Festival') held in Waterfoot in 1904. Margaret became secretary of the literary section of the Feis and for many years organised a scholarship scheme whereby children were sent to Coláiste Uladh, a summer school in the Donegal Gaeltacht of which she was treasurer and ÚNA NÍ FHAIRCHEALLAIGH was president. The extraordinary character of the Glens group is attested to by its ability to bridge the growing divide between nationalists and unionists within its ranks until about 1916. Although Margaret's brother, James, took part in the Larne gun-running of 1914 by the Ulster Volunteers in order to fight the granting of Home Rule, she contributed towards the costs of Roger Casement's trial after his abortive Banna Strand gun-running for the nationalists. She publicly defended Casement's reputation over the years. Along with Pádraig Mac Cormaic, the only surviving member of the original committee, she revived Feis na nGleann in 1931 and worked loyally to keep it alive for the next thirty years. In mid-life, Margaret had acquainted herself so much with Old Irish and Celtic studies that she began to contribute (from 1910 onwards) articles on history, archaeology and other areas of antiquarian interest to important journals such as *Revue Celtique, Zeitschrift Für Celtische Philologie, Éiriú, Scots Gaelic Studies, Journal of the Royal Society of Antiquaries, Irish Genealogist* as well as *An Claidheamh Solais,* the official Gaelic League organ. She died on January 2, 1962. Margaret Dobbs was a staunch propagandist for the language all her life, believing that 'to those who do not know her language . . . (Ireland's) treasures are as hidden as a book unopened.'

DRUMM, MÁIRE, née McATEER (1919-1976), republican. Born November 22, 1919, the eldest of four children in Killean, Newry, Co. Armagh. Máire came from a family with a strong republican background, her mother having been active in the War of Independence and Civil War. She went to the local national school and to a convent grammar school in Newry. In 1940 she moved to Dublin to seek employment. There she joined Sinn Féin which, at that time, was at a low ebb following its return to militarism in the late 1930s. This had resulted in a politically unproductive IRA bombing campaign in England and internment of many of its members by the Irish and British Governments for the duration of the Second World War. Máire went on to Liverpool where she was active in the Gaelic League. Two years later she returned to Ireland and worked as a grocery assistant in Belfast. Interested in Gaelic games, especially in camogie (the women's form of hurling), she began an enduring involvement in an administrative capacity with her club, Gael Uladh, and the Camogie Association of Ireland, of whose Ulster Council she later became chairperson. In Belfast, too, she first became actively involved in the republican movement. While visiting Republican internees in Belfast Prison she met Jimmy Drumm whom she married in 1946 after his release, and set up house in Belfast. Her husband was again interned, without trial, in

Belfast Prison between 1957 and 1961 - at a time when the IRA had begun a new armed attempt to force an end to the partition of Ireland and overthrow British control of the Six Counties (Northern Ireland). During this period, Máire, while fending for her family of five children, maintained links with the National Graves Association and the republican movement. In the late 1960s a Civil Rights campaign to end discrimination against Roman Catholics and nationalists within Northern Ireland was ruthlessly opposed by extreme Unionists and the constabulary. Rioting in the Roman Catholic districts of Belfast in 1969 was followed by sectarian violence between the two communities, protestant and Roman Catholic. Máire Drumm, as a member of Sinn Féin, was actively involved in re-housing evacuees forced to leave their homes because of loyalist intimidation. From the end of 1970 there were armed clashes between the British army and the IRA, internment was re-introduced in 1971, and the IRA began bombing civilian targets. The following year, after British soldiers fired on a Civil Rights march in Derry and killed thirteen men, the British prime minister dissolved the Stormont Parliament and ruled the six Ulster counties directly from Westminster. Máire quickly came to the fore as a dynamic speaker at rallies and protest meetings, was elected to the Ard-Chomhairle (Supreme Council) of Sinn Féin, later became its vice-president and, for a time, acting president. At one stage she had talks with loyalist paramilitaries in an effort to bring sectarian murders to an end. As an uncompromising republican who greatly influenced the ordinary Roman Catholic and nationalist people Máire underwent continuous harassment from the British army and police. Because of the involvement of her immediate family in the Republican movement (her husband and son were interned together in Long Kesh), her house was constantly raided. She was jailed twice (once with her daughter) for 'seditious speeches' and lived under the threat of assassination by both loyalist paramilitaries and the British Secret Service. Her health broke down under the strain and she was admitted to the Mater Hospital in Belfast where, on the night of October 28, 1976, loyalist gunmen shot her dead. In one of the most-quoted excerpts from Máire Drumm's speeches, she asserted that "the only people worthy of freedom are those who are prepared to go out and fight for it every day, and die if necessary."

DRURY, SUSANNA (*c*. 1710-*c*. 1776), artist. Born, most likely in Dublin, into a well-established Anglo-Irish family of soldiers and clerics and also with an artistic strain. Along with LETITIA BUSHE and Miss Forster, the painter of miniatures, Susanna is one of the earliest recorded Irish women artists and among the first of that generation of native-born artists who were encouraged by the premiums for painting and sculpture awarded by the Dublin Society from 1731 onwards. Lack of opportunity for women to train formally meant that 18th century women artists usually followed the footsteps of a father or brother and Susanna's brother, Franklin, was a professional painter of miniatures. She may have received some training from Continental painters visiting Ireland or from a Dublin artist, Joseph Tudor. The little surviving evidence of her work suggests Susanna painted in the topographical tradition of the time and, like many later women painters, probably led a somewhat peripatetic existence, moving from big house to big house, painting families and estates and teaching art. Susanna won a twenty-five pound premium from the Dublin Society for two pictures of the Giant's Causeway, Co. Antrim, in 1740. Mrs. Delaney, wife of the Dean of Down, recorded in 1758 that the artist, when making her gouaches of the Giant's Causeway, 'lived three months near the place and went almost every day.' Some of her views of the Causeway were engraved in London and sold throughout Europe, providing the French geologist, Demarest, with evidence to support

16. East Prospect of the Giant's Causeway, *c.1739, by* **Susanna Drury.**

his theories about the origin of basalt. Her only dated work is 'A View of London from One-Tree Hill', painted in 1773. Susanna Drury may have spent the latter half of her life in London and, quite probably, died there.

DUFFERIN, LADY HELEN SELINA BLACKWOOD, née SHERIDAN (1807-1867), songwriter and author. Born Dublin into the literary and theatrical Sheridan family. Richard Brinsley Sheridan, playwright, MP and owner/director of Drury Lane Theatre, London, was Helen's grandfather. His theatre burnt down shortly after her birth and the Sheridan fortunes decayed. After her father's death the family was left in great poverty. However, through the influence of his friends and Sheridan admirers, her mother was allowed to raise her large family in a 'grace and favour' apartment in London's Hampton Court, the heart of the city's fashionable society. It was here Helen met and married Captain Price Blackwood, later the Marquis of Dufferin, with whom she had one son. She divided her time between Hampton Court, Italy, and her husband's estate at Clandeboyne, Co. Down. After his death she married Lord Gifford. In 1863, following her explorer son Frederick's account of voyaging in northern latitudes, *Letters from High Latitudes*, she wrote and illustrated the hilarious and well-received parody on the contemporary vogue for travel books, *Lispings from Low Latitudes*. She did not live to see Frederick become Governor-General of both Canada and India. He edited and published his mother's *Songs, Poems and Verses* (1894) that included two evergreen ballads which had already gained widespread popularity and were to remain popular for a century after her death, 'Terence's Farewell to Kathleen' and 'Lament of the Irish Emigrant'. The following lines are taken from the latter:

I'm biddin' you a long farewell
My Mary - kind and true!
But I'll not forget you, darling,
In the land I'm going to;
They say there's bread and work for all,
And the sun shines always there -
But I'll not forget old Ireland,
Were it fifty times as fair!

And often in those grand old woods
I'll sit, and shut my eyes,
And my heart will travel back again
To the place where Mary lies;
And I'll think I see the little stile
Where we sat side by side:
And the springin' corn, and the bright May morn,
When first you were my bride.

DUFFY, LOUISE GAVAN (1884-1969), educator and revolutionary. Born Nice, France. Her father, Sir Charles, had been one of the foremost figures in the Young Ireland movement and an MP before becoming Prime Minister of Victoria, Australia. He retired to Nice where Louise and her brother George were born and reared. She came to Ireland for the first time in 1903 for her father's funeral and immediately resolved to become part of the independence movement. She learned Irish and was one of the first women to attend University College Dublin, in 1911. Under the auspices of Patrick Pearse, future Commander-in-Chief of the Republican forces in the 1916 Rising, she managed and taught in Scoil Íde (St. Íde's School), the girls' equivalent of the more famous Scoil Éanna (St. Enda's School), a bilingual educational institution founded by him in 1908 to advance the ideal of a free and Gaelic Ireland. In 1914 she joined the revolutionary women's organisation, Cumann na mBan, and was elected to its executive. During the 1916 Rising, although disapproving of it, she joined the rebels in their General Post Office headquarters where she acted as a cook during the four days bombardment. When ordered to leave in the final evacuation Louise helped take the wounded to hospital before escaping capture. In 1917 she was co-founder of Scoil Bhríghde, an Irish-language secondary school for girls, run on Pearse's educational principles. She was re-elected in 1917 to the executive of Cumann na mBan and, more determined than before the Rising, organised a new recruiting drive in South Armagh the following year. Although one of the most dedicated members of that organisation, Louise reluctantly resigned in 1922 when the Cumann voted to reject the Anglo-Irish Treaty, to which her brother George had been the last and most unwilling signatory. Half-heartedly, she joined Cumann na Saoirse, the women's organisation formed in support of the Treaty and the Free State Government after the split in Cumann na mBan. Disillusioned by the ensuing Civil War Louise directed her energies, from then on, to the education of girls in a Gaelic cultural milieu and her school subsequently prospered. She received an honorary doctorate from the National University of Ireland for her pioneering work in education. Louise Gavan Duffy died in Dublin on October 12, 1969.

DWYER, MARY, née DOYLE (*c.* 1780-1861), wife of insurgent leader Michael Dwyer. Born on a prosperous farm in Co. Wicklow, near the Glen of Imaal, she eloped with Michael Dwyer after he became an outlaw following the rising of 1798 and remained with him and his band for five years on the run in the Wicklow mountains. It is said that the local landlord, one Huntley, apprehended her when she was on a visit home and demanded not only information on her husband's whereabouts but also his *droit de seigneur*. She tricked him into meeting her husband at night and the affair ended in Huntley's death. After the failure of the Emmet rebellion, in 1803, Michael Dwyer evaded the British forces for five months before surrendering voluntarily. He was sentenced to transportation to New South Wales, Australia. Mary subsequently followed with her two children and experienced a remarkable change in fortune: her husband, released from the prison colony, became a policeman and, rising through the ranks, was appointed High Constable of Sydney in 1815. When she died in 1861, a widow for thirty-five years, the *Sydney Freeman's Journal* reported that 'all her wishes in life were accomplished before her eyes closed in death' and added that her two grandchildren had entered the religious life. The romantic story of her runaway marriage and support of her husband became the subject of a recitation which was extremely popular in Wicklow nationalist circles up to recent times:

Mary came out in her beauty
The loveliest maid in Imale:
The loveliest flower that blossomed
In all the wild haunts of the vale,
Arrayed in an emerald habit
And the green and the white in her hair.
They led out a horse on the heather:
She patted his neck with her hand
Then sprang on his back like a feather
And stood in the midst of the band.
Away dashed the cavalcade fleetly,
By beauty and chivalry led,
With their carbines aflash in the sunlight
And the saucy cockades on their heads!

DYMPNA (DAMNAT, DAMHNAIT, DYMPHNA) OF GEEL, SAINT (5th or 6th century), christian martyr, patron of the mentally ill. Dympna, patron saint of Geel, in the Flanders area of Belgium, is often associated with Saint Damnat of Slieve Beagh and the early Christian settlement, Tedavnet, in Co. Monaghan, which is named after her. According to Irish tradition Damnat was a grand-daughter of Milcho for whom St. Patrick herded swine as a slave. A crozier known as the Bachall Damhnait, in the National Museum, is considered to be a relic of hers. In Belgium the tradition of Dympna goes back to the murder of a contemporary Irish princess. An account of the saint's life by Petrus of Cambray, *De Vita Sanctae Dimpnae* (written some seven centuries after the event), relates that she, with her priest and servants, set up quarters at Zimmel near present-day Geel. She was fleeing from her insane heathen father who saw in his daughter the image of his dead Christian wife and had an incestuous desire to marry her. An innkeeper, who had recognised the currency with which she paid him, led her father and his retinue to her. Dympna vowed that she, as a Christian, would never marry him and he personally beheaded her and her priest. Some modern experts believe that the father's actions can be explained in the context of some Dionysian-type cult. Irish missionaries to Liege in the 9th and 10th century may have promoted devotion to her. Records show that her body was re-interred in the 12th century and, at least from this on, she was venerated as a patron of the insane. In 1286 a hospital was built at the site of her supposed martyrdom. In 1349 a new church and hospital were constructed and later a 'sicke chamber' was added to accomodate the 'possessed and foolish'. Because of overcrowding, due to increasing numbers of pilgrims, villagers welcomed the mentally ill into their homes. Since then caring for the mentally ill has been part of daily life for people in the locality and, to this day, more than half the families take in patients in a scheme known officially as Foster Family Care. From the time of the French Revolution this system, as well as the running of the town's hospitals, has been

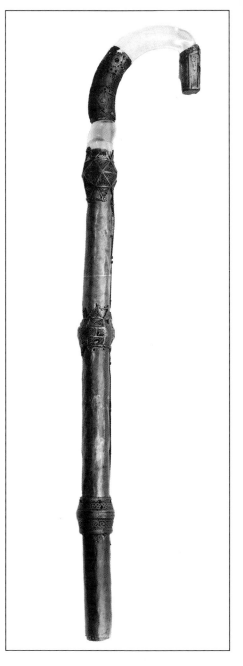

17. A 10th c. crozier attributed to **St. Dympna.**

organised by the state rather than the clergy. The people of Geel celebrate St. Dympna's feast day on May 15, while Damhnat of Tedavnet's is June 13. Cardinal Ó Fiaich, an authority on the Irish presence on the Continent in the mediaeval period, has expressed his doubts as to whether the two Dympnas were one and the same person; but neither has any evidence to the contrary been produced to refute the earlier assumption. Other tantalising references in the ancient calendars mention a contemporary St. Damnoda who was named 'the fugitive'. It is not beyond the bounds of possibility that all three 'Dympnas' were one and the same person.

EARLY, BIDDY (*c.* 1798-1874), *bean feasa* ('wise woman'), healer and clairvoyant. Born in Faha near Kilanena, Co. Clare, as Brigid O'Connor or Connors. Although she is widely remembered in folklore and people who knew her personally were alive up to the 1950s, details of Biddy's life are vague and conflicting. Some say she was employed as a young serving girl in the house of Dr. Dunne at Ayle, near Kilbarron, and as a parlour maid in Affick House, Tulla. Other traditions tell of her paying rent for her own property at a young age and foretelling the death of the bailiff who was to evict her. This was when her reputation as a clairvoyant began. She married the first of several husbands while living in Carraroe, east Clare, moving later to Kilbarron near Feakle. For more than sixty years she was credited with healing thousands of people from the mid-west region, through herbal medicines as well as through her mystical or occult powers. Biddy was famed for the 'dark bottle' which she used as other clairvoyants use a crystal ball and she was not at all adverse to the belief she was in league with the fairies. She was accused of witchcraft in 1865 and appeared in an Ennis court but the affair came to nothing. She had at least one son and some accounts tell of a daughter.

Although she did not drink herself, all Biddy's husbands, according to tradition, died from alcohol abuse. In 1869, when she was about seventy years old, she married for the last time. Her husband was a young man from Co. Limerick known variously as O'Brien or Meaney. Many stories are still told of her clairvoyant and telepathic powers which she reputedly never used for an evil purpose or direct monetary gain. Biddy Early died in poverty at her home in Kilbarron, Co. Clare, on April 22, 1874.

EDGEWORTH, MARIA (1767-1849), novelist and educator. Born January 1, 1767, at Black Bourton, Oxfordshire, England, on the Elers estate, her mother's family home. Her father, Richard Lovell Edgeworth, was an absentee landlord with estates in Edgeworthstown, Co. Longford, where his ancestors had been granted six hundred acres in 1610. The marriage of Maria's parents was unhappy. Her father remarried after her mother's death and brought the family back to Edgeworthstown. The young Maria, a difficult child, was sent to boarding school in England. In 1782, at fifteen, she returned home following her father's third marriage to take care of the younger children. Eventually Maria had eighteen siblings - the offspring from four marriages - to look after. Her father became a progressive landlord and responsible MP in the Irish Parliament where he took an anti-Unionist position, advocating reforms and emancipation for Roman Catholics. Although well-known for his inventions it was his ideas on education which proved more important and influential. Through Maria he saw his ideas put into practice in his own family and inculcated in her a lifelong interest in moral education and a sense of duty and responsibility with which her later novels were imbued. She began to write moral tales for children under his direction. In 1795 Maria published *Letters to Literary Ladies*, obviously influenced by her father's ideas on women's education, and in the following year *The Parent's Assistant*, a book of moral tales for children. In 1798 she published *Practical Education* in collaboration with her father. These popular books proved to be influential in England and America. She began her first novel while on holiday with her cousin in Navan, Co. Meath, writing for her own amusement, 'without any idea of publishing.' This was the story of a dissolute landed Anglo-Irish family destined for bankruptcy and the ruin of all concerned - a subject to which she would return repeatedly believing, as she did, that the profligate life of the gentry was at the bottom of all the evils in Irish society. The novel *Castlerackrent*, published anonymously in 1800, proved an immediate success. It was subsequently acclaimed as the first regional novel in English. Another novel, *Belinda*, was published in 1801 along with *Moral Tales for Young People*, followed in 1802 by *Essays in Irish Bulls*, a light, somewhat satirical collection of unique humour at the expense of the landed gentry. Maria had been her father's chief assistant in running the family property which prospered through their progressive methods and this, coupled with her royalties, enabled her to visit Brussels and Paris. Here she refused, although not without regret, a proposal of marriage from a Swedish count. On her return to Ireland she continued to write. Books such as the novel *Leonara*, six volumes of *Tales of Fashionable Life* (1809-1812) and another novel *Ennui* (1809), sold well and further enhanced her reputation. *The Absentee* (1809) again explored the life of the Anglo-Irish ascendancy and was both a moral tale and realistic fiction. Maria Edgeworth was now a figure of distinction. At home in Edgeworthstown and during time spent in England she was visited by such literary personalities as Scott, Byron and Wordsworth.

Another novel, *Patronage*, was published in 1814 and her most ambitious work, *Ormonde*, in which she attempted to explore and reconcile the foreign and native cultures in Ireland, appeared in 1817. Her father who had collaborated in much of her work died in the same year. Maria prepared his *Memoirs* for publication and then turned to managing the estate for her somewhat inept brother. She wrote one more novel, *Helen* (1834), which has an English setting. Maria's work had an immense influence on the English novel, through Scott in particular, and also on the later French and Russian realists. She spent the latter years of her life in the endeavours characteristic of the responsible land-owner exemplified in her novels of Irish life. She had a market house built in Edgeworthstown, promoted the education of children of the estate, and protected the tenants from the typical harshness of the landlord system. During the years of the Great Famine, although approaching eighty, she worked conscientiously in organising relief. Maria Edgeworth died on May 22, 1849.

EIRC (EARCA), (5th and 6th century), ancestor of royal dynasties and grandmother of St. Columcille. Daughter of Loarn, son of Erc, 5th century king of Dal Riada (the Antrim kingdom which was to extend to Argyll in Scotland) and fifth in line of descent from Conaire Mac Nessa, king of Ulster in the Táin period. Very few details of Eirc's life are known but the fact that a woman of the period was recorded in the genealogies and remembered by the ancient historians implies that she was of most unusual character and importance. Not alone was Eirc an ancestor of royal dynasties in Ireland and Scotland but also of several saints and the hereditary abbots of Iona and Kells. She was wife to Muiredach, king of Aillech, son of Eógan, son of the great high king Niall Naígiallach ('Niall of the Nine Hostages'). Their son Muirchertach reigned as high king from 512 - *c.* 534. From Eirc, through this son, the dynastic family Cenél Eógan (from whom Co. Tyrone is named) were descended. Muirchertach was said to have been the first Christian king of Ireland. After his death Eirc married her first cousin, Fergus, known as Long Head, son of the king of Tír Chonaill (Donegal). One of her sons by this marriage, Fergus Mór, conquered the Picts of Scotland and became king of the Scots in that country. Another son, Sétna, was the ancestor of the great O'Donnell dynasty of Tír Chonaill. Her grandson, St. Columcille, was the apostle of Scotland and with Patrick and Brigid, patron of Ireland.

ELLIOT-LYNN, SOPHIE. See under HEATH, LADY MARY.

ERCNAT, SAINT (5th century), virgin saint. Born possibly about the time St. Patrick brought Christianity to Ireland (*c.* 432). She was a daughter of Daire Derga, chief of the Uí Niéllain, whose people and territory surrounded most of the shores of Lough Neagh and included northern Armagh. The fortress of Dún-dá-én in Dal-Araidhe, now Duneane, Co Antrim, appears to have been her home for her memory was venerated there up until the early twentieth century. It has been said she was one of the first women to take the veil from Patrick but this is open to question. She did take the veil from him but it was probably later at the time when her father, at her instigation, gave the land of Drom Sailech to Patrick to build a church. (The Church of Armagh, the principal See of Ireland, grew from this foundation). It appears that Ercnat, with Patrick's sister Lupait, and at least one other woman Cruimeris, travelled in his retinue on many of his journeys. But the function recorded of these ladies, making altar cloths and

vestments, would surely have required a more settled existence, perhaps at the convent Lupait founded at Na Fearta in Co. Armagh. Ercnat fell in love with Benignus, who had been following Patrick since the age of seven, and she fell ill as a result; but, as O'Hanlon wrote in *Lives of the Saints* (1875-1903), the pining nun was 'rescued from a temporal and spiritual death, through the instrumentality of St. Patrick and St. Benignus,' and 'bewailed with abundance of tears in after-life the frailty of a short time.' It is thought she moved to a hermitage at Tamlachta-Bó (Tamlacht), a townland in Eglish, west of Armagh. She died here after 'her closing years were rendered illustrious by signs and miracles.' Two feast days were assigned to her honour. January 8 is regarded as the most important date to observe while October 30 may mark the removal of her relics or some important event in her life.

'EVA OF THE NATION,' pen-name of MARY EVA KELLY (1826-1910), poet. Born Headford, Co. Galway, and educated privately. At a young age she was contributing verse of a patriotic nature to nationalist journals such as the *Irish Tribune* and especially the *Nation* under the pen-names of 'Fionnuala' and 'Eva.' Her writings for the latter journal were so well received that she became known and romanticized as 'Eva of the Nation.' In 1849, when visiting Young Ireland revolutionaries in prison, she met and fell in love with Kevin Izod O'Doherty, a young medical student awaiting trial on a charge of treason-felony. He was convicted and sentenced to ten years transportation to Van Diemen's Land (Tasmania). When he was pardoned and returned to Dublin in 1854 Eva married him the day after he landed at Dún Laoghaire. In 1857 Kevin qualified as a doctor and, three years later, the couple emigrated with their children to Brisbane, Australia, where he began a successful practice. Both became active in Irish-Australian affairs and Kevin entered politics. In 1877, the year he ran successfully for election in the Queensland legislative assembly, Eva's *Poems* were published - in San Francisco, because of their nationalist content. Two years later the couple spearheaded fundraising of twelve thousand pounds in Queensland for Irish famine relief. Eva and Kevin returned to Dublin to support Parnell and the National League in the general election of 1885, in which Kevin was elected MP for North County Meath. However, in 1888 after the defeat of the Home Rule Bill, they returned to Australia but Kevin was unable to successfully revive his practice and eventually went blind. The couple spent their final years in increasing poverty and obscurity. In 1909 Eva's *Poems* were reprinted in Dublin at a time of growing nationalist fervour. She died in Brisbane shortly afterwards having outlived her husband by five years.

FANCHEA (FAINCHE, FUINCHE), SAINT (died c. 500), virgin saint. Born in Rathmore, celebrated fortress of the kings of Oirghialla (Oriel), near Clogher, Co. Tyrone, according to the earliest traditions, a daughter of the king, Conall Dearg, and of a noblewoman of the Dal Riada people. Her grandfather may have been converted by St. Patrick. Choosing celibacy, Fanchea avoided marriage to Aengus, king of Munster, by arranging his match with her sister before setting up her hermitage at Ros Airthir (Rossary) on the shores of Lough Erne, not far from Enniskillen, Co. Fermanagh. Here she was joined by a number of women of royal birth. Tradition referred to a journey or sojourn made by Fanchea and some of her followers to Britain, probably to Scotland, as her mother was of the race of the Gaelic colonists there. There are interesting aspects to the story of her other foundation, at Killary in Co. Louth, then also part of Oirghialla. Early hagiographies hold that she was the elder sister of St. Enda, although some modern scholars dispute this; he may, however, have been a half-brother or first cousin. As a young man he had taken over the kingship after his father had been killed and ruthlessly avenged the killing. When Enda came to Ros Airthir, demanding to be given one of Fanchea's postulants with whom he was in love, she refused and reproved him for his earlier act of revenge. The postulant providentially died and Fanchea, converting Enda, sent him to the famous monastery of Candida Casa in Scotland. According to another tradition St. Fanchea died after a visit to Rome, where she had gone to convince Enda that his vocation lay in Ireland. Consequently, he went to Inis Mór, Aran Islands, and became the founder of Irish monasticism in the strictest sense. Fanchea's feast day is on January 1. Over the centuries her memory in the folk mind was intermingled with that of the Oriel war-goddess Fuinche Garb(h). Possibly it was to counteract such a trend that, as the *Annals of the Four Masters* record, an abbey dedicated to her was built on the site of her Ros Airthir convent some five centuries after her death.

FARREN, ELIZABETH, COUNTESS OF DERBY (c. 1759-1829), actress. Born in Cork. When her father, an apothecary and surgeon, died from alcohol-related illness her mother, a former actress, was forced to return to the stage. She joined a touring company in the English provinces thus introducing her three daughters to the stage. Elizabeth made her first appearance in London, at eighteen, in the mature part of Mrs. Hardcastle in Goldsmith's *She Stoops to Conquer*. After moderate success her talents blossomed and she was, for twenty years, a leading lady in the Drury Lane and Haymarket Theatres. Renowned for her elegance and wit, Elizabeth was popular in society and took part in many

18. Elizabeth Farren, c.1790, by Ozias Humphry.

private theatricals in the great houses of London. Unusually for an actress of the period her private life was notably free from scandal; she was befriended by Lord Derby whom she married after the death of his wife in 1798. The couple had three children. Elizabeth, Countess of Derby, died on April 29, 1829, at Knowsley Park, Lancashire, England.

FITZGERALD, BRIDGET (*c.* 1588-*c.* 1650), Countess of Tyrconnell and Viscountess Kingsland. Daughter of Henry, twelfth Earl of Kildare, she was probably born at Maynooth Castle, Co. Kildare, principal seat of the family. In 1604 she married Rory O'Donnell (Rudhraighe Ó Domhnaill), Earl of Tyrconnell. O'Donnell had fought a valiant rearguard action after the disastrous defeat of the Gaelic forces by the English at Kinsale (1601) and had submitted to the Lord Deputy. He was created Earl in 1603 having been well received in London by the new king, James I. It is highly likely that the marriage

of Bridget and Rory was arranged at the same time and was part of a politically acceptable situation to help perpetuate the once powerful houses of Kildare and Tyrconnell while ensuring their loyalty to the English throne. However, when the greed of the English colonists drove O'Donnell and other northern chiefs into plotting rebellion, Bridget appears to have favoured compromise. She was with her mother in Maynooth, perhaps for reasons of political expediency, when her husband and the Earl of Tyrone and their followers made their flight to Spain, taking with them her year-old son Aodh (Hugh). Secret arrangements were made for Bridget to follow her husband but, choosing to remain, she perhaps hoped for the future restoration of the earldom to her son. When interrogated by the authorities she denied all knowledge of her husband's treasonable activities, condemned them publicly and, though still remaining under suspicion, saved herself. In 1608 Rory died in Italy. Many believed his death was due to either fever or poisoning by an English agent. Bridget went to the court of King James in London to proclaim her loyalty and plead for the restoration of the Earl's confiscated estates. Although failing in the latter claim she was granted a pension of three hundred pounds per annum and, on her return to Ireland, married Sir Nicholas Barnwell, Viscount Kingsland, of the house of Trimleston, an Old English family who had in previous decades proven their unqualified loyalty to the Crown. It is unlikely that Bridget ever saw her son Aodh again: he was reared mainly in Louvain and attained to a high position in the Spanish army before dying in 1642. Mary Stuart, her daughter by Rory O'Donnell, had a curious history: as a pawn in the political machinations of the period she eventually escaped to Flanders, where her brother was in service, and married an O'Gallagher who was yet another claimant to the chieftaincy of Tyrconnell. Married to one of the 'lords of the Pale,' Bridget would have enjoyed relative security during the period of the early Stuart monarchy; one of the thirteen children of her second family married Luke Plunkett, Earl of Fingal. However, the Roman Catholic lords of the Pale, having been reluctantly induced to join in the rebellion against the government in 1641, meant Bridget may have been 'transplanted' to Connaught in her old age following the re-conquest of Ireland by Oliver Cromwell and the puritan army in 1649. But it is more likely that she was one of those granted dispensation 'in regard to their great age and infirmity of body.' More could be deduced of Bridget Fitzgerald's role in the politics of her time if the date and circumstances of a remarkable poetic exchange between herself and Cuchonnacht Óg Maguire, chieftain of Fermanagh, were known. The conventional love poem that Maguire addressed to her confessing that he will die if she refuses him her love, and her reply, were in fact an allegorical exchange in which she appears to have rejected a request to ally the Fitzgeralds with the rebellious northern chiefs.

FITZGERALD, LADY ELEANOR (*b.* 1495), protector of the young Earl of Kildare. Daughter of the Great Earl of Kildare and probably born in their principal castle of Maynooth. In 1513 Eleanor was married to the young Domhnall Mac Carthaigh Riabhach (MacCarthy Reagh), Prince of Carbery, Co. Cork, as part of the network of marriage alliances made by the Earl between his twelve children and his Gaelic and Norman-Irish allies. The marriage treaty, which not only gave Eleanor one half of Mac Carthaigh's land but also a veto on his 'officers and officials' and the right to dismiss his gallow-glasses (mercenary soldiers) if they refused to obey her, reflects her father's trust in her as his representative in the south-west. Mac Carthaigh

died within a few years and the childless Eleanor continued to live in Carbery, in her castle at Kilbritten, Co. Cork. In 1537 when her five brothers and a nephew, Silken Thomas Fitzgerald, were executed in England after an ill-fated revolt and her father died in despair in the Tower of London, the power of the once mighty Kildares was shattered. All hope for the future rested in the twelve-year-old heir, Gerald, who was smuggled out of Leinster to his aunt's castle in Kilbritten where Eleanor was politically concerned with the restoration of the Fitzgeralds as Earls of Kildare in the person of her nephew. At the same time Mánus Ó Domhnaill (Manus O'Donnell), Lord of Tyrconnell (Donegal), was masterminding the great alliance of Irish chief-tains in what was to become known as the first Geraldine League. Marriage between Eleanor and Mánus was a diplomatic necessity not only to cement the League but to end the traditional enmity between the houses of O'Donnell and O'Neill who was married to Eleanor's sister. With a bodyguard of twenty-four horsemen she brought young Gerald from Cork to Donegal, under the protection of the League, and married Mánus in May 1538. This union ensured that O'Neill and O'Donnell were 'bound and sworn together to take one part with the said Gerald against the Englishry.' Lack of aid from France and the defeat and death of their ally, James IV of Scotland, two years later led to the disintegration of the League. Mánus, fearful of an English attack, smuggled Gerald to the French Court without Eleanor's consent, opened negotiations with England, and became one of the first Gaelic lords to commit himself to the Crown's new policy of 'surrender and regrant.' Eleanor returned to Kildare in outrage. The irony is that Gerald, who had survived so many adventures in Ireland and the Continent, returned to England in 1548 where his sister had married Sir Anthony Brown, the new king's Master of the

Horse. He married Brown's daughter by an earlier marriage and eventually had much of his Irish estates and the Earldom of Kildare restored to him. It is doubtful if Eleanor lived to see the restoration of her nephew to the Earldom. Whether she would have approved of his absolute loyalty to the English monarchy is open to question. Ó Domhnaill, often looked upon as the traitor and coward he was branded by Eleanor, may have rightly suspected that the remaining Fitzgeralds in Leinster could not be relied upon to continue to oppose the English. Two hundred and fifty years passed before the Kildare Fitzgeralds produced another patriot name in the person of Lord Edward Fitzgerald. It is not known when or where Eleanor died but it may be presumed that she passed the remainder of her life in the relative security of the Fitzgerald stronghold of Maynooth.

FITZGERALD, COUNTESS KATHERINE (LADY CATTELYN OR CAITILIN), (1464-1604), the 'Old Countess of Desmond'. Her chief claim to fame is that she lived for one hundred and forty years which, incredible though it may seem, was attested to by several of her later contemporaries including Sir Walter Raleigh. She is believed to have been born in the Castle of Dromana in Co. Waterford, the daughter of Sir Thomas Fitzgerald, Lord of Decies, and of Ellen Fitzgerald, daughter of the White Knight. In 1483 Katherine became the second wife of her kinsman, Thomas Fitzgerald, younger brother of James, ninth Earl of Desmond. The marriage took place in London and the Earl of Gloucester, afterwards King Richard III, danced with the bride. As part of the marriage settlement, her husband granted her, 'besides the manor of Inchiquin, Co. Cork, an annual rent of thirty-three marks in Kerry'. In 1529 Thomas, known in Irish as Tomás Maol, succeeded to the earldom at the age of seventy-six when his wife, the new

countess, was sixty-five. The Earl died a few years later, at the time of the rebellion of Silken Thomas and the Fitzgeralds of Kildare in 1537. Katherine survived the wars of succession following her husband's death in which her step-grandson, the rightful heir, was murdered. After the failed Desmond rebellion of 1583 the Desmond estates were declared forfeit to the crown. However, in 1591 the new grantee, Sir Walter Raleigh, informed Queen Elizabeth that all south-east Cork had been let out to English settlers except for 'an old castle and demayne, which are yet in occupation of the Old Countess of Desmond for her joynture.' This tenuous occupancy came to an end when Raleigh's estates changed hands; faced with absolute ruin, the Countess and her very elderly daughter undertook the journey from Youghal, Co. Cork, via Bristol, to the court in London to make a personal plea to King James. According to Sir Robert Sydney, second Earl of Leicester, 'Shee came on foote to London; being then soe olde that her daughter was decrepit, and not able to come with her, but was brought in a little cart, their poverty not allowing them better provision of means.' Katherine secured some measure of redress from the king and returned home where she died shortly afterwards. By all accounts the death of the 'Old Countess of Desmond' was not due to old age but to an accident while picking fruit. She was probably buried with her husband, the late Earl of Desmond, in the Franciscan Friary in Youghal. While in London, although being so reduced in circumstances, Katherine had her portrait painted; it was in the possession of Colonel Herbert of Muckross House, Killarney, Co. Kerry, in this century.

FITZGIBBON, THEODORA, née ROSLING (1916-1991), cookery expert and writer. Born in London the only child of Irish parents. Theodora's father, who spent most of his life in

India, was from a landed family settled in Ballymackay, Co. Tipperary, for three hundred years. Her youth was spent in Tipperary and Clare for irregular periods, in convent schools, and with her Cornish grandmother in London. She later attended schools in Brussels and Paris. Theodora worked as an actress on stage and film, and as a photographer's model, in London before going to Paris prior to World War Two. There she met and lived with English painter and photographer, Peter Rose Pulham, and was drawn into the bohemian life of that city. She and Pulham, escaping back to London ahead of the Nazi invasion, spent the war years in the bohemian world of Chelsea. Dylan and Caitlin Thomas, Augustus John and Donald Maclean were among her friends. Eventually she married the future novelist Constantine Fitzgibbon. These years were recounted with gusto by Theodora forty years later, in *With Love* (1982), the first of her two books of autobiography. She travelled widely before and after her marriage, living in India, America, France and Italy, as well as in England and Ireland, where she spent the latter part of her life. For many years she was cookery editor of *Image* magazine and the *Irish Times* and was a widely known contributor to many journals such as *Homes and Gardens*, and *Harper's Bazaar*. She wrote more than two dozen books. *Flight of the Kingfisher*, which was success-fully adapted as a play for television, was her only novel. Theodora is best known for her outstandingly successful cookery books. Three of these were awarded Bronze Medals at the Frankfurt International Food Fair and another won a special Glenfiddich Gold Medal Award. In 1968 she wrote *A Taste of Ireland*, first of the cookery books which were to make her a household name in Ireland and Britain. This book was instantly popular and has been reprinted many times. In her youth Theodora had been taught to appreciate local cooking by her father, a connoisseur of good food, and she single-handedly brought recognition to the existence of an Irish cookery tradition by highlighting native dishes, often from 19th century and even 18th century, family papers that had never before been published. She must be credited with introducing native Irish 'cuisine' to international tables. She followed her first cookbook with *A Taste of Wales*, and *A Taste of Scotland*, both of which also attained wide international success. Some of her other acclaimed cookery books are *The Food of the Western World* (1976), and *Irish Traditional Food* (1983). Theodora's second book of memoirs, *Love Lies a Loss*, appeared in 1985. After her second marriage to George Morrison, photographic archivist and film-maker, she made her home in Dalkey, Co. Dublin, where she died in 1991. Theodora Fitzgibbon wrote, 'the best food of a country is the traditional food which has been tried and tested over the centuries ... The food of a country is part of its history and civilization, and, ideally, the past and the present should be combined, so that traditional food is not lost under a pile of tins or packages.'

FOX, CHARLOTTE MILLIGAN (1864-1916), folk music collector and author. Born March 17, 1864, in Omagh, Co. Tyrone. Her father was a wealthy protestant businessman, Seaton F. Milligan, who was an antiquary and member of the Royal Irish Academy. Her younger sister was ALICE MILLIGAN the writer who played an important role in the early days of the Gaelic League and Sinn Féin. Although her family belonged to the protestant and British elite, young Charlotte was not only introduced to Irish history by her father but was also exposed to Irish language and music on visits to her mother's family in Omagh, Co. Tyrone. Her musical gifts were recognised early and she was sent to the Conservatoire in Frankfurt, the Royal College of Music in London

19. Charlotte Fox.

and the Conservatoire in Milan. Although she wrote original songs Charlotte is mainly remembered today as one of the first folk song collectors of the Irish Revival period. She founded, in 1904, the Irish Folk Song Society with her sister Alice as a member of its publications committee. Charlotte and her two sisters composed new lyrics in English to the Gaelic airs; she noted many airs from traditional singers and was one of the first collectors to use a recording machine. In 1911 she published the influential *Annals of the Irish Harpers* based on her study of the papers of Edward Bunting, an Armagh musician who, a century earlier, had collected more than one hundred and fifty airs from the remnants of traditional exponents of the Irish harp. As a result she went on a lecture tour in the USA but the onset of ill health prevented further work in this area. Charlotte Fox died on March 25, 1916, in London where she lived after her marriage to a solicitor.

FOX, DAME EVELYN EMILY MARION (1874-1955), pioneer of modern service for the mentally handicapped. Born at Fox Hall in Co. Longford, a descendant of the 18th century English Whig politician, Charles Fox. First educated at home, Evelyn attended school in Switzerland and Somerville College, Oxford, where she worked in the Women's University Settlement, a voluntary charity organisation. This involvement grew into a lifetime of service to improve the lot of the mentally handicapped in Britain. The passing of the Mental Deficiency Act in 1913 was due in great part to Evelyn's efforts. In the same year she was instrumental in founding the Central Association for Mental Welfare, of which she was honorary secretary and moral force for three decades. The Association, which was active in providing facilities and services on a national basis for the mentally-impaired and promoting better training for those working with them, saw the culmination of its efforts with the provisions for the care of the mentally-ill contained in the National Health Service (established 1946). Dame Evelyn Fox was also the first secretary of the Child Guidance Council which played a central role in the formation of the British National Association for Mental Health.

GAFFNEY, MARGARET. See under HAUGHREY, MARGARET.

GAHAN, MURIEL (1897-1995), promoter of rural crafts and produce. Born in Co. Mayo where her protestant father was a senior inspector with the Congested Districts Board but spent most of her life in Shankill, Co. Dublin. Her father's work in deprived areas of the west led to Muriel's commitment to improve conditions for rural women and to promote rural crafts. She was asked, in 1929, to help paint a stand at the RDS Spring Show for the United Irishwomen. This group, formed twenty years before at a time of emerging co-operative movements, was intended to assist rural awakening through social action at a local level. Contact with the group opened the way for her life's work. The following year, under the auspices of the United Irishwomen, Muriel opened the Country Shop in a basement in St. Stephen's Green, Dublin. This depot and outlet for country crafts and home-made produce became an institution in the life of the city although the organisation behind it had reached a very low ebb following divisions caused by the civil war and the earlier World War. Muriel Gahan played a major role in helping Lucy Franks reform it into the new Irish Countrywomen's Association (ICA). She was also a driving force behind the Homespun Society and Irish Country Markets, co-operative associations retailing rural produce. She became an important figure in rural Ireland, travelling widely in her car to discover and encourage male and female craft workers. Muriel was the first woman vice-president of the RDS and initiated crafts exhibitions at their shows. Always interested in education, she was instrumental in obtaining the necessary finance from the Kellogg Foundation to establish the ICA residential college, An Grianán, in Termonfeckin, Co. Louth. Eventually her dream, regarding the potential role of craft workers in Irish life, foundered on the rock of the capitalist enterprise system as did the co-operative ideal. But Muriel's efforts, particularly for the ICA, brought her several national awards including an honorary doctorate from Trinity College Dublin. She had an enduring interest in the arts - her office above the Country Shop was a noted meeting place for painters and writers for years - and she was a founder member of the Arts Council. Muriel Gahan died in St. Mary's Home, Dublin, on July 12, 1995, aged ninety-eight.

GARSON, GREER (1903-1996), film actress and Oscar award winner. Born on September 29, 1903, in Co. Down; as a baby she was taken to London after the death of her father. Graduating from London University she worked for a time in an advertising agency before making her acting début with the Birmingham Repertory Theatre. Greer's apprenticeship was a relatively long one and she was an experienced actress in her mid-thirties when she became a star in the theatres of London's West End, appearing in plays such as Shakespeare's *Twelfth Night* and Sheridan's *School for Scandal* and, opposite Laurence Olivier, in *Golden Arrow*. In 1938 she was 'spotted' by Louis B. Meyer, one of the great Hollywood directors, who was struck by her archetypal 'English' beauty and demeanour. She went to California on the then huge contract of five hundred dollars a week, but, disappointed that no suitable role was available, returned to England. The following year Greer took what was considered to be the minor part of Kathy in the film *Goodbye, Mr. Chips* but made so much of the role that she was nominated for the Oscar award for best actress. From then until the 1960s she was one of Hollywood's leading ladies. In 1940 she starred with Olivier in the screen version of Jane Austen's *Pride and Prejudice*. The following year she appeared in *Blossoms in the Dust*, the first of eight films in which she co-starred with Walter Pigeon, a performance which earned Greer a second Oscar nomination for best actress. Her portrayal of a courageously forbearant woman in a time of great trial was to become her hallmark and used to good effect for propaganda purposes, by the Americans and

British, for the duration of the Second World War. Her performance in a similar role, *Mrs. Miniver*, a film set set in London during the blitz, won her the Oscar for Best Actress in 1942. She made many other notable films including *Random House* and *That Forsythe Woman* and was nominated for Oscars for her performances in *Madam Curie* (1943), the *Valley of Decision* (1945) (in which, at the age of forty-two, she played a romantic part opposite the young Gregory Peck) and one of her last films, *Sunrise at Campobello* (1960). Greer Garson died on April 6, 1996.

GEDDES, WILHELMINA MARGARET (1887-1955), stained glass artist. Born in Drumreilly, Co. Leitrim, into a Methodist family from Belfast; she spent most of her youth in that city and attended the Methodist College and the School of Art. She was 'discovered' by SARAH PURSER when exhibiting a water-colour at the 1910 Arts and Crafts Society of Ireland exhibition in Dublin and was soon designing for stained glass. A travelling scholarship from the Belfast art school enabled Wilhelmina to study in the British Museum. In 1911, she attended the Dublin Metropolitan School of Art, where William Orpen, then already a successful portrait painter, was her mentor. Working in Purser's An Tur Gloine studios in Dublin, she revealed a highly original talent in the stained glass medium and her first public commissions, for two protestant churches in Fermanagh, followed. Throughout Wilhelmina's career the Church of Ireland, especially in Ulster, proved to be a consistent and loyal patron. In 1914, a tour of the great French mediaeval cathedrals in the company of Purser and CATHERINE O'BRIEN indelibly influenced her work and confirmed her belief in the importance of 'strength in design and intensity of colour.' Commissions followed in Dublin, Belfast, and in New Zealand (Karori Crematorium, Wellington). In 1919 the *Memorial*

20. The leaves of the trees for the healing of nations', *design for stained glass window by* **Wilhelmina Margaret Geddes.**

to the War Dead, a large three-light window at St. Bartholomew's Church, Ottawa, Canada, won her international acclaim. At this period, Wilhelmina transferred her originality of design and talent for powerfully expressive drawing to graphics and needlework, and produced striking book illustrations, banners and linocuts. In 1922, having completed notable works such as the window at St. John's, Malone Road, Belfast, and the five-light *Crucifixion* for St. Luke's, Wallsend-on-Tyne, Northumberland, England, poor health interrupted her output. Three years later Wilhelmina rented a studio at the Lowndes and Drury Glasshouse in Fulham, London, and began a new phase in her career which brought her unqualified recognition as 'the greatest stained glass artist of the century.' Two outstanding works date from this period, *The Fate of the Children of Lir*, an eight-panelled window for the Belfast Museum and Art Gallery (1929) and the *Memorial to the King of the Belgiums* in the restored Cathedral of Ypres (1934). The latter work, which took four years to complete, was a vast rose window, twenty-five feet in diameter, incorporating over eighty sections and including some fifty figures. Although in chronic ill health, Wilhelmina Geddess continued to work up to her death, in 1955.

GERMANA, SAINT. See under GRIMONIA, SAINT.

GIFFORD, GRACE (1888 - 1955), republican and cartoonist. Born Rathmines, Dublin, one of twelve children of an affluent Roman Catholic solicitor. Her mother, an Anglo-Irish protestant, was a niece of the painter, Sir Frederick Burton. Although the parents were conservative Unionists, their six daughters were strongly nationalist and some were socialist. Her sister Muriel married Thomas McDonagh, the 1916 revolutionary leader, and her youngest sister, Sydney, became the republican journalist MADAME CZIRA. Grace was educated at Alexandra College, Dublin, and was Orpen's pupil at the Metropolitan School of Art; she later attended the Slade School in London. She came under the influence of COUNTESS MARKIEVICZ and joined Sinn Fein, the United Arts Club, Inghinide na hÉireann and, later, the Irish Trades Council. Grace gained a reputation for her cartoons of writers, artists and actors when these were published in such newspapers as *The Irish Citizen* and the *Irish Review* (of which her future husband, Joseph Plunkett, was co-founder). In 1910, with Sydney and Muriel, she participated in the ultimately successful attempt by the Inghinide to force local authorities to accept responsibility for supplying meals to poor children. Although not as radical as her sister Nellie who was a member of the Irish Citizen Army and took part in the fighting in St. Stephen's Green during the 1916 Rising, Grace supported the republican movement and, like Muriel, fell in love with one of the revolutionary leaders. She and Joseph Mary Plunkett planned to marry on Easter Sunday, 1916, but instead her fiancé took his place in the General Post Office during the Rising. After the surrender a court-martial sentenced him to death. On May 4 Grace married Plunkett in his cell at Kilmainham Jail a few hours before his execution. Her brother-in-law, Thomas McDonagh, had been executed the previous day. At the Sinn Fein Convention of October 1917, Grace was included with Countess Markievicz, KATHLEEN LYNN, and KATHLEEN CLARKE on the new twenty-four member executive although she did not have the same political experience as the other women or had ever been a committed activist. She promoted the cause through her artistic talent by designing posters, banners, and the cover of Doyle's *Women in Ancient and Modern Ireland* which was a battle cry for women to take their

21. Cartoon from 'The Irish Citizen', *May 17th 1913, by* **Grace Gifford.**

place in 'the new Ireland which is dawning on us.' Grace opposed the Treaty, as did all the wives of the 1916 leaders, and wrote an influential article in *The Republic* (March 1922). In 1923, during protests by the Women's Prisoners Defence League against the ill-treatment and execution of Republican prisoners in Free State jails, Grace was arrested and held without charge at Kilmainham Jail with many other Republican women including MAUD GONNE. With pencil and water-colours she painted her 'Kilmainham Madonna' on the wall of her cell and this act almost became as much part of republican symbolism as her wedding. After the Civil War she was never so politically active again but willingly lent her name, over the years, to a variety of republican organisations. Grace is recorded in art histories for the three published collections of her caricatures, the best known of which being *To hold as 'twere* (1919). Her 'Kilmainham Madonna,' already dilapidated, was destroyed when the jail was restored as a museum but the near-facsimile that replaced it is now one of the more poignant exhibits.

GIFFORD, SYDNEY. See under CZIRA, SYDNEY.

GILBERT, LADY. See under MULHOLLAND, ROSA.

GILBERT, MARIE DOLORES ELIZA ROSANNA. See under MONTEZ, LOLA.

GLEESON, EVELYN (1855-1944), designer, founder of the Dun Emer Guild. Born in Knutsford, Cheshire, England, daughter of an Irish doctor from Tipperary. At fifteen she moved with her parents to Athlone, Co. Westmeath, where her father, motivated by philanthropical ideas, founded the Athlone Woollen Mills to give local employment. Evelyn inherited her father's practical patriotism. She studied portraiture in the Ludovici Atelier in London, design under Alexander Miller, and also studied painting in Paris. At this time she made several designs for the prestigious Templeton carpets. In London, she was involved in the suffrage movement, the Irish Literary Society and in the Gaelic League. Having become friendly with SUSAN MARY and ELIZABETH YEATS, daughters of the painter John B. Yeats both of whom had a background in art and design, Evelyn proposed her plan for founding a craftwork enterprise in Ireland where a remarkable arts and crafts movement was springing up as part of a general cultural and political renaissance. In 1902 the three women set up the Dun Emer Guild in a house in Dundrum, then on the outskirts of Dublin, and recruited several trainees. The enterprise and the Yeats' salaries were financed from Evelyn's private income and by a friend, Augustine Henry, the botanist and linguist. Evelyn took charge of the tapestry and carpet-making department. An enormous variety of craft work was produced during the early years of the Guild, including the famous Dun Emer Press of which W.B. Yeats, poet and brother of Susan Mary and Elizabeth, was editor. The Guild attracted many artists, including another brother, Jack B. Yeats, and George Russell, to produce designs and one of its early outstanding successes was a series of banners and vestments for the newly-built Loughrea Cathedral in Co. Galway. Through its preference for Celtic designs and use of Irish materials, as well as associations with other artists and designers, the Guild made an exceptional contribution to the Irish revival movement. Guild members exhibited regularly at the RDS and Oireachtas in Dublin; they also showed at the St. Louis World Fair (1904) and were silver medalists at the Italian International Exhibition in Milan (1906). Financial and personality problems led to the departure of the Yeats sisters who then set up Cuala Press in Churchtown. But Evelyn Gleeson, assisted by two exceptional designers, May Kerley and Katherine MacCormack (who was Evelyn's niece), continued at Dundrum and later in Harcourt Street, Dublin, fulfilling many

22. **St. Gobnait**, *Holy well at Dún Chaoin, Co. Kerry, stone carving by Cliona Cussen.*

notable commissions for the greater part in Celtic design. These included embroidered furnishings for the Honan Chapel in Cork and carpets for Leinster House, seat of the newly-formed Free State Government. As Evelyn moved into semi-retirement, in the late 1920s, Katherine MacCormack took over as designer and continued to successfully work in the Celtic style introduced by the founder, but in a more 'La Tène' mode; examples may be seen in the Mansion House and Dáil Éireann. At the end of her life Evelyn Gleeson witnessed the interest in design in Ireland lapse in the general cultural malaise of the 1930s and 1940s which forced the Dun Emer Guild to close not long after her death in 1944.

GOBNAIT (GOBNET), SAINT (6th century), patron saint of Muskerry, Co. Cork. Most likely born in north Clare and, according to some of the ancient calendars, a descendant of Conaire the Great, king of Ireland. It is said her first hermitage was near the Cliffs of Moher, before she was driven out to Inis Oírr, the smallest of the Aran Islands, where there is an 11th century church, Cill Ghobnait, which bears her name. She later journeyed to Ballyvourney, at the foot of the Derrynasagart mountains, between Cork and Kerry. When a monk was given a grant of land in the area and wished to found a convent he asked Gobnait to be the abbess. She agreed and may have stayed in Ballyvourney for the rest of her life. She and St. ITA have remained the most popular of the early holy women of Munster. Several ancient church sites in the province, including Kilgobnet in Kerry, bear her name. St. Gobnait is inextricably connected with beekeeping: tradition tells that she routed an invading army with her bees and, indeed, for many centuries her beehive was a special relic kept in the possession of the O'Herlihys, the ruling family of that west Cork area. St. Gobnait is venerated in both Aran and Ballyvourney on her feast day, February 11. The pilgrimage to her church and well at the latter was approved by indulgences issued by the papacy in 1601.

GONNE, MAUD (1865-1953), revolutionary. Born December 20, 1865, in Aldershot, England, daughter of a wealthy British army colonel. Her mother was English, her father of Irish descent. After her mother's early death Maud was educated by a governess in France and when her father was posted to Dublin Castle, in 1882, she joined him there. Her father died in 1886, leaving her financially independent. Back in France, following a tubercular haemorrhage, she fell in love with the politician and journalist Lucien Millevoye. The lovers agreed to work together for the nationalist causes of France and Ireland. It was difficult for a woman to find a place in Irish nationalist activities at that time, but in the end Tim Harrington of the National League (the more moderate successor to the Land League) recognised her propaganda value and sent her to Donegal where mass evictions were taking place. Maud followed the example of the Ladies Land League, organising the building of huts, fund-raising, nursing the evicted sick and writing to the press. About to be arrested, she escaped to France in early 1890, where she gave birth to Millevoye's child. After the death of her baby she returned to Ireland the same year and worked for famine relief. In 1891 Maud helped Yeats to set up the National Literary Society of

London but refused his proposal of marriage, returning to Millevoye and France, where she bore their second child, Iseult. In Paris she published a newsheet, *L'Irlande Libre* to promote the Irish cause. Maud ceaselessly continued her nationalist activities, lecturing and collecting funds, in America as well as France, and during the centenary commemorations of the 1798 rebellion she made a lecture tour of the west of Ireland. By this time she was established as an inspirational force in Irish nationalism. Maud travelled to France, broke off her relationship with Millevoye, and returned to Ireland where she co-founded the Transvaal Committee which supported the Afrikaners in the Boer War. In 1900, realising that if women wished to have political impact they must form their own organisations, she was foremost in founding Inghinidhe na hÉireann (Daughters of Erin), the revolutionary women's society of which she was first president. The Inghinidhe produced the influential monthly journal *Bean na hÉireann* (The Irish Woman) for which Maud wrote many articles on feminist and political topics including the need to alleviate poverty. The Inghinidhe indirectly led to the formation of the Abbey Theatre, having provided the impetus through its propagandist pageants. Maud Gonne, with whom W.B. Yeats had been in love since meeting her in 1899, inspired and played the leading role in his influential *Kathleen Ní Houlihan* (1902). At about this time she joined the Roman Catholic Church. In Paris, in 1903, she married John MacBride, a major in the Irish Brigade which had fought with the Boers. The marriage soon broke up and MacBride went to Dublin. Maud, afraid of losing custody if she returned to Ireland, lived in Paris with her son, Seán, until 1917. However, in 1910 she was involved with the Inghinidhe in inaugurating a scheme to feed poor children in Dublin which eventually forced the British Government to extend to Ireland the act enabling

*40. **Maud Gonne Macbride** (second from left) supporting hunger strike at Mountjoy prison in 1922.*

local authorities to provide meals for school-children. During the First World War Maud took part in Red Cross work in France. After her husband was executed for his part in the 1916 Rebellion she returned to Ireland and, in 1918, was interned in Holloway Jail for six months with KATHLEEN CLARKE, COUNTESS MARKIEVICZ, HANNA SHEEHY SKEFFINGTON and others. This was supposedly for being part of the 'German Plot' but, in reality, was for leading the anti-conscription campaign.

Soon after her release Maud began working with the White Cross for the relief of victims of the War of Independence and their dependants.

During the occupation of the Four Courts building by the Republicans, who rejected the treaty with Britain, Maud Gonne led a group representing women's organisations in a 'supreme attempt' to prevent civil war but they were unsuccessful. Subsequently, she rejected the Treaty and, together with CHARLOTTE DESPARD, established the Women's Prisoners Defence League to help Republican prisoners and their families. During one of their rallies in O'Connell Street, government troops opened fire on the crowd, wounding fourteen. In 1923 she was imprisoned without charge by the Free State Government and was one of ninety-one women who went on hunger strike. In 1935, when the

Fianna Fáil Government began to jail Republicans, the Women's Prisoners Defence League, with Maud to the fore, again went into action. In the following year Seán was made Chief-of-Staff of the IRA. In 1938 she wrote *A Servant of the Queen*, an account of her activities up to 1903. In her old age she saw her son become Minister for External Affairs as head of Clann na Poblachta but she did not live to see him awarded the Nobel Prize for Peace in 1974. Maud Gonne died at Roebuck, Clonskeagh, Dublin, on April 27, 1953. She is buried in the Republican Plot in Glasnevin Cemetery, Dublin.

GORE-BOOTH, CONSTANCE. See under MARKIEVICZ, COUNTESS.

GORE-BOOTH, EVA (1870-1928), poet, trade unionist, feminist. Born May 22, 1870, in Lissadell, Co. Sligo, into a wealthy family of the Anglo-Irish landed gentry. Her sister Constance was to become the revolutionary leader COUNTESS MARKIEVICZ. The sisters were educated by governesses and presented at the Court of Queen Victoria. Both were keenly interested in the arts and drama. The young W.B. Yeats was a frequent visitor to the house and many years later, in one of his great poems, 'In Memory of Eva Gore-Booth and Con Markievicz', he presented the sisters, and the house at Lissadell, as an image of the end of the Anglo-Irish and landlord era which had produced them. Eva was involved in suffrage activities when she met Esther Roper, secretary of the Manchester National Society for Women's Suffrage, on an Italian holiday in 1896 and the pair became life-long friends and co-workers. Inspired by Roper, Eva moved to Manchester and became active in trade union organising for women, appearing regularly on suffrage platforms. She used her literary talents to write propaganda pamphlets and edit the *Women's Labour News*. She was also a noted platform speaker for the Independent Labour Party. While heading a group of radical socialists Eva worked tirelessly to improve conditions for the barmaids and mill-girls of Lancashire and became secretary of the Barmaids Political Defence League. In 1903 she and Roper founded the Lancashire and Cheshire Women Textile Workers Representation Committee, which was quickly given recognition by the wider trade union movement. In 1908 Constance joined them for a time and her general election campaign in north-west Manchester, when she unsuccessfully opposed Winston Churchill, was organised by Eva and Esther. Some short time later Eva went back to London and, although concentrating on her literary work, found time to take

23. Eva Gore-Booth.

up the cause of marginalised women such as flower sellers and circus performers, and used her own finances to aid victims of the Great War. Between 1904 and 1918 she published ten volumes of poetry, including the verse dramas *Unseen Kings* (1904) and *Death of Fionavar* (1916). The latter was dedicated to 'the Many who died for Freedom, and the One who died for Peace,' the 'One' being pacifist Francis Sheehy Skeffington who was killed by British soldiers during the 1916 Rebellion in Dublin. Although her poetry was overly influenced by the 'Celtic Twilight' fashion of the time, a few pieces, especially 'The Little Waves of Breffny,' remain evergreen. Although long overshadowed by Constance, Eva Gore-Booth is now being recognised for her social and feminist work and, ironically, for her pacifism. She died June 30, 1926, at Hampstead, London. Esther Roper posthumously prepared a collection of her work, *Poems*, (1929).

GORMLAITH (GORMFHLAITH) (*c.* 880-947), poet and queen of Munster, Leinster and all-Ireland. Daughter (or step-daughter) of Flann Sionna, king of Tara and high king of Ireland of the long standing Uí Néill dynasty; her mother was Maelmhuire, daughter of Kenneth, king of the Scots and the Picts. Gormlaith's father, having succeeded to the high kingship and subduing both his native Irish and Scandinavian enemies, made a political alliance with Cormac Mac Cuilleannáin, king of Cashel, and arranged his daughter's marriage to him. Although she thus became queen of Munster the marriage was never consummated due to Cormac's adherence to his vow of celibacy as Bishop of Cashel. The marriage appears to have been free of rancour for its short duration but Cormac returned his wife and her dowry to Flann when his advisers advocated the secession of Munster from the control of the high kingship. Flann Sionna

immediately married Gormlaith to Cerball Mac Muireacáin, king of Leinster, to redress the political imbalance. In 906, the Munster army under Cormac invaded Leinster but was defeated and Cormac killed by Cerball's forces at Bealach Mughna on the border of what is now Kildare and Carlow. Cerball, jealous of her former husband, ill-treated his queen so much that she sought refuge with Niall Glún Dubh, king of Ailleach, son of Flann, and thus her stepbrother and, possibly, cousin. Niall married her after Cerball died from wounds in 906. In 915 Niall Glún Dubh succeeded to the high kingship with Gormlaith as his queen and had to contend with invasions of Norsemen through Waterford and Dublin. When he was killed and the Gaelic armies routed at the battle of Islandbridge, near Dublin, Gormlaith was left a widow and ex-queen for the third time. She appears to have had two sons by Niall. In 920 Niall's son Donnchadh stopped the advancing Norse tide for a time but, while he was engaged in a civil war with another brother, the Scandinavians gained control over all the southern parts of Ireland. However, a third son, Muircheartach na gClóca Leathair, successfully contained and finally reduced the power of the Scandinavians over the next twenty years. Although the *Annals of Clonmacnoise* many centuries later recorded that, after the death of Niall, Gormlaith 'begged from door to door, forsaken of all her friends and allies and glad to have been relieved by her inferiors,' this can only have been relatively true up to the death of Muircheartach, in battle against the Norse, in the year 940. In the terrible wars of succession which followed, Gormlaith's position must indeed have been precarious. It appears that, in the end, she took refuge in a convent where she died in the year 947. A romantic tale or cycle of tales and poems, *Triamhuin Ghormlaithe* ('The Tragedy of Gormlaith'), one of the great mediaeval romances, has been lost for many centuries but several of the 'pittifull and learned dittyes' attributed to Gormlaith, lamenting the death of Niall and the disasters that followed, are still extant. An edition and translation of these by Osborn Bergin, taken from the O'Gara MS, 'Poems attributed to Gormlaith', were published in *Miscellany presented to Kuno Meyer* (1912), and since then some of the texts have been frequently anthologised, both in the original and in English translations:

Aisceadh bháis iaraim anocht
ar Mhac Dé do dhealbh gach corp
cidh bé ionad a bhfuil Niall
go rabhar-sa is é ar énrian.

The gift of death I ask this night
from the son of God who made man,
whatever place that Niall now be,
that I and he were there as one.

GORMLAITH (*c.* 955-1042), queen of Dublin, Munster, and all- Ireland, recorded in the *Annals of the Four Masters* (1636) as taking 'the three leaps which a woman shall never take: a leap at Dublin, a leap at Tara, and a leap at Cashel of the goblets.' Born most probably at the family seat in Naas, Co. Kildare. Her father was Murchadh whose Uí Dhúnlaing ancestors had been overlords of North Leinster for the previous two hundred years. When Gormlaith arrived at a marriageable age, the Norse were reaching the zenith of their power in Ireland and, in a political alliance between North Leinster and the Viking capital of Dublin, she became the last wife of the elderly king of Dublin, Olaf Cuarán. Olaf seemed likely to become the greatest power in Ireland when (backed by his Gaelic allies in Leinster) he defeated the high king and subjugated Meath, in 977. Three years later, however, the new king of Meath, Mael Sechnaill Mór (Malachy), surprisingly defeated the Scandanavians; Olaf was

forced to surrender Dublin. He sailed to Iona, in Scotland, but Gormlaith remained behind. Probably due, at least in part, to her stratagems North Leinster and Dublin assisted Mael Sechnaill as he forcibly gained the high kingship. To cement the alliance the new high king married Gormlaith and installed her son by Olaf, Sitric Silkbeard, as king of Dublin in 994. At the same time, Brian Ború, king of Munster, became so powerful that he forced Mael Sechnaill to divide Ireland between them and to grant him the vassalage of the Norse towns, including Dublin. With her husband in a weakened position Gormlaith appears to have urged her brother, Mael Mordha, to ally with Sitric and reclaim full control of their kingdoms. Mael Sechnaill and Brian reacted swiftly by uniting and routing the combined Norse and Leinster forces under Sitric and Mael Mordha. Sudden changes, in the balance of political power, then forced Brian to seek the support of both the defeated Norse and Leinster men. Taking Gormlaith as his wife, Brian restored her brother to the kingdom of Leinster, and her son Sitric to the kingdom of Dublin. By 1003, with their help, Brian had forced Mael Sechnaill to surrender the high kingship to him. He continued to exact heavy tribute from Sitric and Mael Mordha over the next decade and, after his forces plundered Leinster, Gormlaith is said to have incited her son and brother to rebel. In 1013 Brian and Mael Sechnaill, brought together once more by a common enemy, overran Leinster and besieged Dublin. Gormlaith, now repudiated by Brian, was in the city during the siege. Sitric approached the Earl of Orkney, Sigurd the Stout, with a promise of marriage to Gormlaith and the chance to conquer all Ireland with the help of Leinster and the Scandinavian Irish. The same offer was made to Broudar, captain of a vast fleet of Viking marauders on the west coast of Britain. Both parties joined the Norse alliance which was, nonetheless, defeated by the Gaelic alliance at the battle of Clontarf in 1014. Despite the death of Brian this battle ended all threat of a Scandanavian conquest of Ireland. As the balance of power swung once more, following the death of the high king, Gormlaith saw Sitric restored to a much-reduced kingdom of Dublin where he reigned for many decades. It was he who, in 1040, had Christ Church Cathedral built in the city. On the other hand Donnchadh, believed to be her son by Brian Ború, lost his life in an attempt to gain the high kingship. Gormlaith died in 1042. Although Irish history has portrayed her as a vindictive background figure it seems more likely, in retrospect, that she was a prime mover in the momentous events of her time and, in fact, the Norse sagas (which refer to her as 'Kormlada') imply as much. The somewhat scathing reference in the *Annals* to her 'three leaps' relates to her attempts to take control of the kingdoms of Dublin, Meath and Munster. The Icelandic *Saga of Burnt Njal* describes her in bitter terms: 'Fairest and best-gifted in every thing that was not in her own power, but it was the talk of men that she did all things ill over which she had any power.'

GRAY, BETSY (d. 1798), insurgent heroine. There is little documentary evidence regarding this heroine of the United Irishmen Rebellion apart from a letter by MARY ANN McCRACKEN, sister of the insurgent leader Henry Joy McCracken to Dr. Madden, the historian of the rebellion. According to some sources Betsy was born at Killinchy, about twelve miles south east of Belfast, while others give Granshaw, between Newtownards and Donaghadee, as her native place. Tradition says that her father, a prosperous Presbyterian farmer, was a member of the United Irishmen and that, at the time of the insurrection, Betsy was engaged to a local farmer and United Irishman, Willie Boal. The 1798 Rebellion was disjointed and sporadic. After coercion by government forces the call to arms by the insurgent commander for Co. Down, Henry Munroe, brought a thousand men to his side at Ednavaddy, near Ballinahinch. Willie Boal and George Gray, Betsy's brother, having rescued a Colonel Bryson from Newtownards Jail, proceeded to the insurgent camp. Here they were joined by Betsy who, on June 13, 1798, rode at General Munroe's side carrying a green flag, in the attack against the government forces at Ballinahinch and fought alongside her lover and her brother. At the point of victory the untrained rebels became confused and were overwhelmed by government reinforcements. In the ensuing flight Willie and George would not desert her and all three were overtaken and killed by the yeomanry. Betsy Gray's memory remains alive in song and in story.

GRAY, EILEEN (1879-1976), interior designer and architect. Born August 8, 1879, at Brownswood Manor near Enniscorthy, Co. Wexford, into a wealthy aristocratic, Scots-Irish family. Her father, an amateur artist, brought Eileen to Italy on painting expeditions. She was educated by governesses and in private schools in England and on the Continent before persuading her mother to allow her to study at the Slade School of Art in London. While studying at the Académie Julian in Paris in 1905, she found a mentor in Sugawara, a famous exponent of traditional Japanese art and design, who specialised in lacquer. In 1911 she exhibited at the Salon de la Société des Artistes Décorateurs and established her name as a professional designer of modernist furniture. A prestiguous commission followed - to design the entire apartment of the famous couturier Jacques Doucet. The First World War interrupted her career but in 1919, with Paris again the centre of the cultural world,

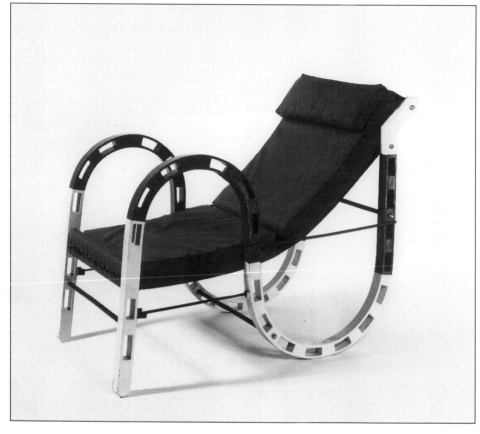

24. *Folding hammock chair, designed 1938, by* **Eileen Gray.**

she opened a gallery, the Jean Désert, at 217 Faubourg St. Honore. Working with simplified geometric forms echoing Cubism, Eileen was recognised as a pioneer of modernist furniture and produced some of the best lacquer work ever made in Europe. She was now commissioned to create total environments for expensive apartments and exhibited an entire room at the Salon des Artistes Décorateurs exhibition in 1923. Turning naturally to architecture she designed two houses, which are now famous, at Roquebrune with Jean Badovici, a pioneer of modern architecture. She also designed her own house at Castellar, recognised as an influential masterpiece. Although leading journals of architecture and design, such as *Wendwigen* and *Architecture Vivante*, featured her work Eileen remained largely unknown outside a specialist circle of artists, architects and rich patrons, until her late eighties. In 1972, when an auction of her work brought Eileen's talent to the fore, she was showered with honours including the Honorary Fellowship of the Royal Institute of Architects of Ireland, 1975. Some of her furniture is on display at the Pompidou Centre, Paris; other items form part of a permanent collection at the Victoria and

Albert Museum in London where she first became fascinated with furniture design and the technique of lacquer work almost three quarters of a century earlier. Eileen Gray died in her apartment in the Rue de Bonaparte, Paris, on October 31, 1976, and was buried at Père Lachaise cemetery.

GREEN, ALICE STOPFORD (1847-1929), historian and nationalist. Born May 31, 1847, in Kells, Co. Meath, where her father was Archdeacon. Alice was educated at home, learned Greek to assist her father in his biblical studies, and was one of the first women to attend the College of Science. Following his death, when she was twenty-seven, Alice's family moved to London. Three years later she married John Richard Green, author of the famous *Short History of the English People*. As he was in ill health she collaborated with him in finishing and revising his works, thus adopting mediaeval history as her special field. *The Conquest of England* was completed in 1883, the year of her husband's death, and her first independent work, *Henry II*, in 1888. Her two volumes of *Townlife in the Fifteenth Century* (1894) established her reputation as a historian. As a result of her mediaeval studies Alice had begun to research Irish history and recognised a need to redress the bias of British propagandists and historians against Ireland: "There is no more pious duty to all of Ireland birth than to help in recovering from centuries of obloquy the memory of noble men, Irish and Anglo-Irish, who built up the civilization that once adorned their country." She published *The Making of Ireland and its Undoing*, in 1908. This uncovered little-known facts about the period 1200-1600, including the attempted 'English extirpation of Irish society,' and was violently attacked by English reviewers. In 1911 *Irish Nationality* made an even greater impact. Her earlier Home Rule

sympathies developed into a more active nationalism and in 1913, with her friend Roger Casement, Alice addressed a meeting of protestant nationalists at Ballymoney, Co. Antrim. In 1914 she was chairperson of the London Committee, which included Casement, Mrs. Childers and MARY SPRING RICE, set up to raise money and organise what became known as the 'Howth gun-running' from Germany for the Irish Volunteers. She disapproved of the Easter Rising. Deciding her place was in Ireland, Alice moved from her London house where she had conducted one of the most notable contemporary salons to 90 St. Stephen's Green, Dublin, which in turn became an intellectual centre. The following year she spear-headed, with ÚNA NÍ FHAIRCHEALLAIGH, the women's protest against the Conscription act; once supported by Cumann na mBan, the campaign proved successful and the British Government abandoned the idea of conscription in Ireland. In the same year her pamphlet, *Ourselves Alone in Ulster*, attacked Carson's policy to permanently exclude the six north-eastern counties from any Home Rule settlement. She supported the Treaty wholeheartedly and, after Cumann na mBan rejected it in 1922, joined the break-away women's nationalist organisation Cumann na Saoirse (League of Freedom) with WYSE POWER, GAVAN DUFFY and others who supported the establishment of the new state. She and Wyse Power were members of the organising body of the new pro-Treaty political party, Cumann na nGael, and thus, at seventy-five, Alice was nominated to the first Irish Senate, one of four women members. In 1925 she supported W.B. Yeats in the Senate, favouring the retention of the existing right to divorce. She published her last book, *History of the Irish State to 1014*, in the same year. Alice Stopford Green died on May 28, 1929, in Dublin.

GREGORY, LADY (ISABELLA) AUGUSTA, née PERSSE (1852-1932), playwright and art patron. Born March 1852, at Roxborough House near Loughrea, Co. Galway, to a family of protestant landed gentry and prominent unionists. She was educated privately. At the age of twenty-eight she married Sir William Gregory, a widower of nearby Coole Park, who was thirty-five years older. He had been both a Conservative and Liberal MP and Governor of Ceylon before retiring to the estate at Coole Park. After his death in 1892 his widow edited his *Autobiography* (1894), and *Mr. Gregory's Letter Box* (1898), the correspondence of Sir William's grandfather as Irish under-secretary. Lady Augusta had gradually become converted to Home Rule ("I defy anyone to study Irish history without getting a dislike and distrust of England"); her acquaintance with W.B. Yeats, whom she met in London in 1889, and her friendship with Edward Martyn, a Roman Catholic landowner and near neighbour, made her even more responsive to the emerging new Ireland of the time. Having been influenced as a child by her Irish-speaking nurse Lady Augusta was already sympathetic to the rural Roman Catholic poor and, encouraged by Yeats, began to collect folklore. This was to form the basis for many of her plays and books. Having met Douglas Hyde, she formed a branch of the Gaelic League in the Coole district. The idea of a national theatre came about when leading figures of the Irish Literary Renaissance, including Yeats and Martyn, discussed the project and Lady Gregory offered to collect the initial money required. The first production of the new Irish Literary Theatre, in May 1899, was Yeats' *The Countess Kathleen*. The Abbey Theatre opened in Dublin in 1904. Lady Gregory was co-director with Yeats and Synge and devoted her administrative talents to the company for the rest of her life. In her book *Our Irish Theatre* (1914), she described the early years of the Irish

25. **Lady Augusta Gregory,** *Irish postal stamp issued 1996.*

Literary Renaissance and its ideals. She was not only guide and patron to many playwrights from Synge to O'Casey but also became a popular playwright herself. She wrote twenty-seven plays, mostly comedy, and invented a particular form of Hiberno-English for the stage based on the dialect in her local Kiltartan area and on her knowledge of Irish. Although slightingly referred to as 'Kiltartanese,' this style influenced Synge and numerous other playwrights and poets since then. *Spreading the News* (1904), *The Rising of the Moon* (1907), *The Workhouse Ward* (1908) were among her more successful plays and have often been revived. The longer plays she wrote later were less successful but a relatively high income as a professional playwright buttressed Lady Gregory's uncertain financial state. Under the influence of Yeats and Douglas Hyde she produced books based on Kiltartan lore and on early Gaelic literature; notably *Cuchulain of Muirthemne* (1902), and *Gods and Fighting Men* (1904). Other such books were *Poets and Dreamers* (1903), *Kiltartan History Book* (1909) and *Kiltartan Poetry Book* (1918). Lady Gregory suffered two great personal losses during the First World War; her son Robert, the landscape painter, was killed in action and her nephew, Sir Hugh Lane, was drowned aboard the Lusitania in 1915. For many years she campaigned vigorously to have Lane's important collection of modern paintings returned to Dublin from the English National Gallery and also for a gallery to house them. Her old home at Roxborough was burned down in the Civil War and financial problems forced her to sell Coole Park to the Irish Land Commission in 1927. She remained in occupation of the house and garden, however, until her death from cancer on May 22, 1932. Not long afterwards the house at Coole Park was demolished. In recent years Coole Park estate was turned into a National Park.

GRIERSON, CONSTANTIA (1706-1733), classical scholar and poet. Little is known of her background except that she was born in Kilkenny into comparatively poor circumstances and probably lived in Dublin after her marriage to a printer and publisher. It is generally accepted that Constantia was entirely self-taught in the classics though she may have been educated by a relative. She was virtually unknown during her short lifetime even though, between the ages of eighteen and twenty-four, she produced scholarly editions of the classical authors Virgil, Terence, and Tacitus. These were published by her husband's press in Dublin. Not unusual for the period, the editor's name was not included. As these works became highly regarded, and sold well in pocket-editions, their origin became known and seems to have won Constantia entry to Dublin literati circles. After the young woman's death in 1732, a member of these circles, MARY BARBER, included some of Constantia's verse in her anthology, *Poems on Several Occasions*. Barber said of her: 'She was too learned to be vain, too wise to be conceited, too knowing and clear-sighted to be irreligious.' Her reputation increased enough posthumously to warrant her inclusion in Ballard's *Memoirs of*

Several Ladies of Great Britain, who have been celebrated for their writings or skill in the learned Languages, Arts and Sciences (1752). Some of her poems also appeared three years later in an anthology, *Poems of Eminent Ladies.*

GRIMONIA (GERMANA), SAINT (4th or 5th century), Christian martyr. Little is known about this pre-Patrician martyr who was one of the earliest Irish saints. She fled from Ireland to what is now the border area of France and Belgium, then Celtic territory, to escape her pagan father. She was martyred in the forest of Thierache with her Irish companion Proba (Preuve) who may have been her confessor. This tradition contains a remarkable resemblance to that of another saint, DYMPNA, who was martyred near Geel less than a hundred miles to the east, two centuries later. The town of La Chapelle developed around St. Grimonia's burial place as a church built at her grave became famous for miracles. Her relics were enshrined at Lesquilles in the 13th century and removed in the 16th century to the Abbey of the Cannons Regular at Henin-Lietard near Douai. She is venerated in the diocese of Soissans and her feast day is on September 24.

GRIMSHAW, (ETHEL) BEATRICE (1871-1953), traveller, writer, and sportswoman. Born Cloona, Co. Antrim, into a wealthy, upper-class family. Educated in Belfast, London, and Normandy. In her twenties Beatrice moved to Dublin to work as a journalist and, as an emancipated woman, broke the world's twenty-four hour woman's cycling record, in 1892. This feat got her a job as sub-editor of a sporting paper. From that position she graduated to being editor of a social journal but, growing bored after four years, Beatrice moved to London and published her first novel, *Breakaway*, in 1897. She then had the idea of offering press coverage to shipping companies in exchange for free passage. In this way Beatrice travelled to Tahiti and, bitten by the travel-bug, spent the next thirty years of her life exploring the Pacific Islands, especially Papua New Guinea, which she had first visited when commissioned by the Australian Government to publicise the resources of the area. She lived by her writing, which included some ten travel books, thirty novels, articles for *Wide World* and other adventure magazines, and for the more prestigious *National Geographic*, as well as much publicity material commissioned by shipping companies and others. The flavour of her subjects and style of her novels is conveyed by some of their titles: *When the Red Gods Call* (1910), *My South Sea Sweetheart* (1921), *Conn of the Coral Seas* (1922), *Mystery of the Tumbling Reef* (1932), *South Sea Sarah* (1940). Her travel books were full of practical advice as well as vivid description of exotic places and hair-raising circumstances presented in a highly readable style. Best known of her travel books were *In the Strange Seas* (1907), *From Fiji to the Cannibal Isles* (1907) and *The New Guinea* (1910). Beatrice was an extraordinary traveller and faced continual danger in the wild head-hunting areas of Fiji, New Hebrides, Solomon Islands, Moluccas, Tonga, Samoa and Papua New Guinea, where she settled for some eighteen years. She once sailed in a three-masted topsail trading schooner among the outer islands of the Cook group. She is often credited with being the first white woman to travel up the Sepik and Fly rivers in New Guinea but this is probably erroneous. She was recognised as an authority on the resources and colonisation of these areas. In 1930 she published her autobiography, *Isles of Adventure*. Circumstances forced her to leave her home in Papua New Guinea, in 1939, and move to Australia. Though she continued to write novels Beatrice Grimshaw slipped into obscurity even before her death thirteen years later.

GUINNESS, MAY CATHERINE (1863-1955), painter. Born at Tibradden House, Rathfarnham, Dublin, an elder child of a wealthy solicitor and landowner, Thomas Hosea Guinness. She was educated by governesses and remained at home to assist in looking after the younger children and their education. When May was twenty-five her father died and, for about fifteen years more, was preoccupied with family responsibilities. This explains to some extent why she was a late developer as an artist. She began to visit Paris annually from about 1910 and studied there with Van Dongen and André Lhote, the first of several important Irish women painters to work with the latter. She was prominent in the unsuccessful effort in 1912 and 1913 to have the Hugh Lane collection of modern paintings housed in a gallery in Dublin. Her career was interrupted by the First World War when she became a French Army nurse; for her bravery she was awarded the Croix de Guerre. She lived in Dublin after the war but regularly returned to Paris, continually working at her painting. In 1925, at the age of sixty-two, feeling she had completed her studies and experimentations, May announced her first solo exhibition in Paris. She was greatly influenced by Cubism and Fauvism while attempting to work out her own individual mode of expression, with the result her style always varied a great deal. As an avid traveller she also painted in Greece and Sicily, often depicting scenes of traditional life in those countries, as well as in Brittany and Belgium. Up to the Second World War she staged several exhibitions in Paris (at the Salon des Indèpendents and other galleries), in London and Dublin, where she showed at the Irish Exhibition of Living Art. May Guinness continued to paint into her very old age. A retrospective exhibition was held at the Dawson Hall, Dublin, in 1956, and her work is represented in the Hugh Lane Municipal Gallery, Dublin, and other major Irish galleries.

26. 'The cathederal of Diest', *by May Guinness.*

HALL, ANNA MARIA, née FIELDING (1800-1881), travel writer, author and philanthropist. Born January 6, 1800, at Anne Street, Dublin, into a prosperous protestant family and reared in Bannow, Co. Wexford. Although often thought of as English, Anna Maria did not go to that

*27. **Anna Maria Hall**, 1851, by G. de Latre.*

country until she was fifteen. At an early age she began to write novels and contributed to the *Amulet* and the *Art Journal*. In 1824 she married the editor of these journals, Samuel Carter Hall. Throughout their long life together the Halls wrote incessantly and often collaborated, especially so on their famous books about Ireland and its people. With the publication of *Mabel's Curse* (1825), Anna Maria's popularity as a writer was assured in Britain for the rest of her life. In 1829 she published the first of her descriptions of life in Ireland, *Sketches of Irish Character*, which did so well that she followed it almost immediately with *Further Sketches*. Besides her novels, including *St. Pierre the Refugee* (1837), and *The Whiteboy* (1845), Anna Maria published sketches, plays, burlettas, operas, verse, children's books and religious tracts. It is said that she wrote or collaborated in more than five hundred publications. Her best-known play, *The Groves of Blarney*, had the outstanding William Tyrone Power - great-grandfather of the Hollywood actor - play the lead for the entire run, at the Adelphi Theatre, London, for the whole theatrical season in 1838. Despite their contemporary popularity none of Anna Maria's writings stood the test of time apart from her descriptions of Ireland and its people which are invaluable to researches in Irish social history and character. She completed her *Lights and Shadows of Irish Life* in 1838. The Halls travelled so extensively in Ireland between 1839 and 1844 that Anna Maria's husband claimed in his reminiscences they 'posted on the common car - the time honoured but nearly obsolete jaunting-car - six thousand miles'. The result of these travels was an extraordinarily comprehensive description of the social life of ordinary people just before the Great Famine. It was published, with many valuable illustrations, in twenty-seven monthly parts before being issued in book form as *Ireland, its Scenery, Characters, etc.* (1840). *Stories of the Irish Peasantry* was published in 1850. The Halls' writings on Ireland have often been denigrated by Irish commentators and Anna Maria's fiction did not attain anything like the same popularity in this country as it did in Britain. Much of this antipathy was said to be due to her active support of protestant proselytism. In 1868 she was given a government pension of one hundred pounds per annum. By using her personal wealth she founded a hospital for consumptives, a governesses' institute, a 'Home for Decayed Gentlewomen' and the Nightingale Fund to further the work of the nursing pioneer Florence Nightingale. It is little known that she was also an early campaigner for women's rights and that she actively supported the Temperance Movement. Survived by her husband, Anna Maria Hall died in East Moulsey, England, in 1881.

HAMILTON, LETITIA MARION (1878-1964), painter. Born Hammond, Dunboyne, Co. Meath. Her father was a wealthy land agent and her mother a sister of Sir George Brooke: ROSE BARTON the painter, and Erskine Childers the revolutionary, were cousins. Letitia was educated at Alexandra College, Dublin. She and her younger sister Eva, who was to become a well-known portraitist and landscape artist in her own right, studied with William Orpen at the Metropolitan School of Art, Dublin. Letitia went on to study at the London Polytechnic with Frank Brangwyn. She first exhibited at the British Royal Academy in 1909 and, in 1912, was awarded a silver medal in the Board of Education National Competition. Like many young women of her class, Letitia travelled widely on the Continent, and many of her early works were painted in Italy. She came under the influence of Paul Henry, already established as a painter of Irish landscape, on her return to Ireland and joined him in 1920 to found the Dublin Painters' Society to provide an alternative to the exclusive and hidebound Royal Hibernian Academy. The group, which also included Grace Henry, Harry Clarke, MAINIE JELLETT and Charles Lambe, attracted a majority of women members; the Society held its first exhibition in the same year. Letitia took part in the Irish Exhibition in Paris in 1922. Although she visited the Continent regularly and was much influenced by painters such as Dufy, Marquet, and Roderic O'Connor, her primary subject matter was to be the landscape and country life of Ireland's west and midlands. With the Henrys and Lambe she must be included among the outstanding painters who discovered the west of Ireland at this period. While she learned much from Henry her work is richer in colour and tends more towards the impressionistic; her landscapes are peopled by figures often dwarfed by the rugged mountainy country they inhabit. Letitia was made a member of the Royal Irish Academy in 1944. In 1947 she went to live in a Regency house in Lucan, Co. Dublin, with Eva and two male friends. It became a meeting place for artists and friends and the house and its occupants were often painted by the sisters. Letitia Hamilton painted continually for the next two decades, winning a bronze medal in the Sport in Art section of the 1948 Olympic Games and holding regular exhibitions in Dublin, mostly at the Dawson and Waddington galleries, until her death at eighty-six.

HANLEY, ELLEN (*c.* 1804-1819), the 'Colleen Bawn' murder victim. Birthplace unknown but reared by an aunt at the Commons in Ballingarry parish, Co. Limerick. Her father lived at nearby Ballyelean. At the time of her murder, she was living in the house of an uncle in Ballycahane near the village of Croom, Co. Limerick. Ellen disappeared from her home on June 29, 1819, not yet sixteen years old, and took with her a hundred and twelve pounds belonging to her uncle, considered a surprisingly large amount for a man of his class to have amassed. Her body, bound with a rope, was washed up at Carndoite near Moneypoint, Co. Clare, on September 6. Circumstantial evidence pointed to John Scanlan of Ballycahane Castle House, Croom, Co. Limerick and his man-servant, Stephen Sullivan, as the girl's murderers. A local landowner, Peter O'Connell (uncle of the Liberator), gave permission for Ellen's remains to be buried in his family plot in nearby Burrane churchyard. It emerged later that Scanlan, a lieutenant in the British Navy and son of a Roman Catholic 'strong' farmer, had eloped with the girl and gone through a form of marriage in Limerick before taking her on the Shannon estuary in his boat, ostensibly to live with him in Glin. Scanlan was brought to trial seven months later and, although ably defended by Daniel O'Connell and protesting his innocence, was found guilty and hanged. Sullivan was subsequently caught and hanged after admitting to his part in the crime. The case received much publicity and provided the plot for Gerald Griffin's novel *The Collegians*, Dion Boucicault's play *The Colleen Bawn*, and Julius Benedict's opera *The Lily of Killarney*. The story acquired the status of myth, possibly because of the youth of the victim and her innocent belief that a son of the local gentry could persuade his people to accept her as a future mistress of the house.

HARRISON, SARAH CECILIA (CELIA) (1863-1941), artist and social reformer. Born Holywood, Co. Down, daughter of Letitia and Henry Harrison JP. She was a great grand-niece of MARY ANN McCRACKEN and of Henry Joy McCracken, the executed United Irishman leader. Sarah moved to London with her family after her father's death, when she was ten, and later attended the Slade School of Art for several years. She returned to Ireland in her mid-twenties, made Dublin her home, and spent some time painting in Brittany and other parts of France. From 1889 she was a regular exhibitor with the Royal Hibernian Academy (RHA) and the Royal Ulster Academy. It is as a successful portrait painter that she is best remembered today but, for some thirty years, Sarah was involved in social reform and women's rights. In 1909, as secretary of the City Labour Yard, she attempted to highlight the appalling number of unemployed in Dublin. As a close friend of Sir Hugh Lane, Governor and Director of the National Gallery, she became enthusiastically involved in the campaign to found a modern gallery to house the collection of pictures Lane had wished to present to the Irish people. In 1912 Sarah was the first woman to be elected to Dublin City Council; working in association with Alderman Alfie Byrne she was able to achieve a

28. *Sarah Cecilia Harrison, a self-portrait, c.1910.*

great deal for the city poor including an extension of poor relief to the able-bodied unemployed. She ran an advice centre for the impoverished from her home and supplied financial assistance, often from her own pocket. Sarah's work for women's rights was recognised by her prominent place in the suffrage victory procession, escorting ANNA HASLAM, the pioneer suffragist, to vote in William Street Courthouse, Dublin, in the 1918 General Elections. She never lost her interest in social reform and in politics (she was an ardent nationalist), yet continued to paint and exhibited at the RHA and other galleries until a few years before her death. Sarah Harrison died on July 23, 1941. Her work is represented today in the Ulster Museum, the National Gallery of Ireland and, appropriately, in the Hugh Lane Municipal Gallery, Dublin.

HASLAM, ANNA MARIA, née FISHER (1829-1922), pioneer suffragist. She was born, one of seventeen children, in April 1829 at Youghal, Co. Cork, into a prosperous flour milling Quaker family; her mother was Welsh. Anna was educated at Quaker boarding schools in Co. Waterford and in Yorkshire, England, until she was sixteen. For some years she worked in famine relief in Youghal. In 1854 Anna married a teacher, Thomas Haslam, who was already active in the feminist cause. They settled in Dublin where, over the next twenty years, she was a co-worker with ANNE JELLICOE and Isabella Tod in advancing women's education. In 1866, her husband's health having failed, Anna set up a stationery business which provided their main source of income thereafter. While taking part in other campaigns on women's issues, such as the repeal of the Contagious Diseases Act, she became increasingly involved in the suffrage movement from 1866 onwards. During the six decades of their married life Thomas backed Anna by publishing many important pamphlets and papers on women's rights and the political means to achieve them. She founded the Dublin Women's Suffrage Association (DWSA) in 1876, the first suffrage organisation in Ireland to have long-lasting impact, and remained secretary of the organisation until 1913. Although the DWSA was primarily a small middle-class group Anna was instrumental in bringing it to actively support trade unionism for women and, in return, getting union support for the suffrage cause. The suffrage issue in Ireland was complicated by the confrontation of nationalists and unionists. For a time Anna became immersed in unionist politics, taking part in the anti-Home Rule campaign with the Women's Liberal Unionist Association and the Central Unionist Committee. When the Women Poor Law Guardian Act (1896) and the Local Government (Ireland) Act (1898) gave women all local government franchises on the same footing as men, the DWSA vigorously encouraged women to participate in public political life. Before the end of the century the DWSA had spread from Dublin to other parts of the country and evolved into the Irish Women's Suffrage and Local Government Association (IWSLGA). From 1908 onwards this was superceded to a great extent by the more militant (and nationalist) Irish Women's Franchise League (IWFL), founded by HANNA SHEEHY SKEFFINGTON and MARGARET COUSINS. In 1911 the combined suffragist movement gained another victory when women were made eligible for election as county councillors. Two years later Anna resigned as secretary from the IWSLGA, but remained on as life-president. In 1918, at the first general election which afforded a measure of female suffrage, she was given a central position in the victorious procession of suffrage groups when, at the age of eighty-nine, she was allowed to vote for the first time; Thomas had died the year previously. Anna Haslam died on November 22, 1922, the year when the newly-constituted Irish Free State gave the franchise to all women and men above twenty-one years of age.

HAUGHREY, MARGARET, née GAFFNEY (c. 1813-1882), philanthropist and business woman, the 'Bread Woman of New Orleans'. Born Killashandra, Co. Cavan. As a child she was brought by her parents to Baltimore, Maryland, in the USA, with two other members of the family. Margaret was orphaned at nine when her parents died of yellow fever and was looked after by a Welsh woman they had first met on the voyage to America. She received no schooling and never learned to read or write. In her early twenties she married an Irishman, Charles Haughrey, and the couple moved with their infant daughter to New Orleans where she found herself alone once more after the deaths of her husband and child. She worked as a laundress for a time and began to help in an orphanage which had been recently set up by the Sisters of Charity. Margaret managed to buy some cows from her savings, set up a small dairy, and peddle milk in the city. Within a handful of years she owned a herd of forty cows and was able to finance the founding of a second orphanage for the nuns. Later she took over a small bakery and, in time, built it into one of the biggest businesses of its kind in the southern states. She gave so much of her produce to the poor that she became known as the 'Bread Woman of New Orleans'. One of the first and most successful self-made business women of her time in America, Margaret Haughrey is estimated to have made profits of at least half a million dollars from her enterprises, most of which she gave away, especially to support orphanages, and not only those of her own religion but protestant and Jewish institutions as well; it was said she established eleven orphanages in all. Her charity also extended to victims of the numerous floods and yellow fever epidemics that intermittently swept the city; she piloted her own raft to relieve and rescue poor families in times of flood and nursed the sick in times of fever. After Margaret Haughrey's death in New Orleans on February 9, 1882, a square in the city, Margaret Place, was named after her and a statue erected in her honour.

HAYDEN, MARY or NÍ AODÁIN, MÁIRE

(1882-1942), historian, campaigner for women's rights. Born May 19, 1862, in Dublin where her father was a professor in the Roman Catholic University. Educated at Alexandra College and the Royal University of Ireland, Dublin, she took an MA in 1887. Mary first came to prominence as a feminist when her name headed the list of those who signed 'The Case of the Roman Catholic Lady Students of the Royal University of Ireland Stated.' She joined the staff of the Royal University in 1895 and with ÚNA NÍ FHAIRCHEALLAIGH was foremost in the campaign for women's rights in the universities. In 1903 she was co-founder and vice-president of the Irish Association of Women Graduates, having been refused a professorship the previous year because she was a woman. From 1909 she served on the Senate of the National University of Ireland for a period of fifteen years and, in 1911, was appointed the first Professor of History in University College Dublin, a post she retained for twenty-seven years. Mary was an early convert to the ideals of the Gaelic League and sat on its executive council. She was a colleague and close friend of Patrick Pearse, one of the leaders of the 1916 Rising. However, eschewing violence, she did not approve of the Rising, and, though an important member of the Irish Women's Suffrage and Local Government Association, refused to back COUNTESS MARKIEVICZ in her bid to become the first woman MP in 1917. In 1921, together with George Moonan, Mary published *A Short History of the Irish People, From the Earliest Times to 1920*, which, popularly known as 'Hayden and Moonan', became a standard text for the next forty years. In the 1930s when women believed that their rights to work were being undermined by Fianna Fáil with the Conditions of Employment Bill of 1935 and the 1937 Constitution, She represented the National Council of Women in Ireland and the Women's Graduates Association in their protest against the reactionary economic and social policies of the government stating, "what is proposed by the new Constitution is not a return to the mid-ages, it is something much worse." Mary Hayden died on July 12, 1942.

HAYES, CATHERINE (1825-1861), opera singer. Born October 29, 1825, at 4 Patrick Street, Limerick. Her father, a bandmaster in the city milita, abandoned his family to extreme poverty. Catherine was discovered by the protestant Bishop of Limerick, Dr. Edward Knox who, it is said, heard the young girl singing while milking in the yard of the Earl of Limerick's town house where her mother worked as a servant. The bishop raised funds to enable the girl to study in Dublin with Antonio Sapio. She sang in concert in Limerick at the age of fifteen and was soon one of the chief soprano concert singers in Dublin. With the money she had earned, and assistance from patrons, Catherine went to Paris to study with Manuel Garcia (who also trained Jenny Lind) and, eighteen months later, to Milan where she was taught by Felici Ronconi. Signora Grassini, a prima donna, took a motherly interest in her career and arranged Catherine's first public operatic appearance in Marseilles, in May 1845, where she sang the part of Elvira in *I Puritani*. Despite an outstanding reception and offers of further engagements she returned to Milan where, in the same year, she became the youngest prima donna ever to appear in La Scala Opera House. From the beginning Catherine was extraordinarily well received by Italian audiences who named her 'La Perla del Teatro'. She went on to Venice to appear in an opera especially composed for her and, in 1849, performed in London where she was engaged for Covent Garden at the remarkable salary of one thousand and three hundred pounds. Catherine sang for Queen Victoria at a private concert before returning home to appear in Limerick, Dublin and Cork. After an engagement in Paris she began a world tour, lasting five years, which took her to North and South America, Australia, India, Java, and the Sandwich Islands. By now Catherine was known in the USA as the 'Irish Nightingale', and so immensely popular that more than one thousand dollars were paid for single tickets to one of her concerts in California. In 1856 she sang in Dublin and Limerick with the Royal Italian Opera Company. She married her manager, Avery Bushnell, in London in 1857 but ill health overtook them both and he died the following year in Biarritz. Catherine Hayes died three years later at Sydenham, Kent, England, on August 11, 1861, aged 36.

HEATH, LADY MARY, née PIERCE (SOPHIE CATHERINE), also known as SOPHIE ELLIOT-LYNN (1896-1939), pioneer aviator and athlete. Born November 10, 1896, at Knockaderry House, near Newcastlewest, Co. Limerick. Her unstable father, son of a doctor, had inherited a large farm but a family tragedy resulted in Sophie being taken as a baby to Newcastlewest, where she was reared by aunts. She attended boarding school in Dublin. After the outbreak of World War One, she went to Britain and became a despatch rider for a unit attached to the Royal Flying Corps. Sophie married an army officer, William Elliot-Lynn, after the war and took a degree in agriculture at the Dublin College of Science in preparation for farming in Africa, where her husband had gone. Working for a period in Aberdeen University, she was able to develop her interest in women's athletics, helping to found the British Women's Amateur Athletic Association in 1922. She became its vice-president before breaking records for the World high jump and British javelin the following year. She joined her husband on their coffee farm in Kenya but the marriage broke up after two years. On her return to England, Sophie resumed her promotion of women's athletics, wrote *Athletics for Women and Girls* (a coaching manual which remained a standard work for decades) and, as

29. **Lady Mary Heath** *at the peak of her flying career, 1928.*

a British representative to meetings of the Olympic Council, was instrumental in the decision to allow women to compete in the Olympic Games. In 1925 she became interested in flying and, as the first female member of the London Light Aeroplane Club, made her maiden flight in August of that year. In 1926 Sophie became the first woman in Britain to hold a Commercial Pilot's Licence and to make a parachute jump. Touring as a professional pilot she took part in flying demonstrations and races in Britain, Ireland, and the Continent. After her husband's death and re-marriage, in 1927, to Sir James Heath, a wealthy English businessman, she began a series of record-breaking aviation feats. Between February 12 and May 17, 1928, Lady Mary Heath (as Sophie Pierce Elliot-Lynn was now known) completed the first solo flight from Cape Town, South Africa, to London (via Cairo). She also broke the Women's seaplane altitude record and the light aircraft altitude record. In 1929, her second marriage over, she began a long tour of the USA giving flying demonstrations and lectures. Although seriously injured in a plane crash in Cleveland, Ohio, in August 1929, she took to the air again, in partnership with her third husband, a professional aviator, and continued to give exhibitions and lectures. Back in Ireland in 1931, Lady Heath took an active interest in the growing aviation business and bought the newly-formed Iona National Airways (originally a flying school for which she had been working as an instructor); the venture, renamed Dublin Air Ferries, failed in the cut-throat situation which preceded the founding of a national airline. She returned to England in search of work. By this time, her third marriage had ended, her health had deteriorated and she had a serious drink problem. In May 1939 Lady Mary Heath died from injuries received from a fall in a public bus.

HECK, BARBARA, née RUCKLE (1734-1804), founder of Methodism in Canada. Born into a German- and Irish-speaking Palatine community in East Limerick. The Palatines were Protestants from the Palatinate region of Germany who had sought refuge in Britain and whom the British authorities sent as colonists to parts of Limerick, Clare and Kerry. The Irish Palatines were converted to Methodism through the evangelising of John Wesley and in the early 18th century some emigrated to the New World including Barbara and Paul Heck, her husband of a few weeks. They landed in New York in the autumn of 1760, with friends from Rathkeale, Paul and Mary Embury. Years later when more Palatines arrived from Ireland, her brother and brother-in-law among them, Barbara was appalled to find the newcomers gambling and determined to convert them back to strict Methodism. The Hecks and the Emburys held their first meeting in the Embury home and arranged a weekly 'class' meeting. So many people attended that soon the hired rooms and lofts proved inadequate. Barbara was instrumental in buying a site and building a stone chapel, opened October 30, 1788, in what is now the heart of New York City. Two years later the Hecks and Emburys travelled along the Hudson river, evangelising as they went. During the American Revolution the Palatines, recalling how Britain had come to their rescue a century previously, chose to stay loyal. They set out for Canada and, after a strenuous and dangerous trek, eventually arrived in Montreal. Barbara and her husband settled with other Palatines in the new township of Augusta, near Maitland; there they established a religious community based on the Methodist ideal which became known as the Heck Settlement. The way was thus prepared for the mission of the future itinerant preachers in Canada, the first of whom was to arrive in 1790 at the Heck Settlement which, as an evangelising base, was possibly the most important centre for the Methodist faith in Canada. Barbara Heck survived her husband by six years and died in the home of her son, Samuel, in 1804. She was buried in the community graveyard, 'the Old Blue Churchyard' between Maitland and Prescott. By this time the first Methodist house in 'Upper' Canada had been built by her followers in Hay Bay, Adolphustown. Today, the Methodist Church is one of the major denominations in Canada with some 650,000 adherents of that faith in the eastern half of the country where the Hecks and Emburys first introduced it.

HERLIHY, NORA (1910-1988), founder of the Irish Credit Union. Born February 27, 1910, in Ballydesmond, Co. Cork, where her father was a principal teacher. Although he died relatively young, all nine children got secondary school education. Four of them, including Nora, qualified as national teachers. She taught in underprivileged areas of Dublin for twelve years before joining the teaching staff of the Orthopaedic Hospital for Children in Clontarf, Dublin, in 1948. Having already obtained a BA degree and a diploma in liberal art studies Nora qualified in the Montessori system of teaching. In 1955 she was appointed principal of St. Joseph's Girls School in West Liffey Street, a deprived city centre area, where she remained until retirement twenty years later. She had become attracted to the ideas of the cooperative movement and to the principle of cooperative credit and with the help of Seán Forde and Séamus MacEoin, who were to be her associates for the following twenty years, she set up an exploratory group, the Credit Union Extension Services, in her house at Phibsboro and encouraged a group of neighbours to form Ireland's first Credit Union in Donore Avenue, Dublin. In 1960 a federation of the four existing credit unions was established, the Credit Union League of Ireland, with Nora as

first secretary and later as managing director. She was given leave of absence from teaching to accept an invitation by the Credit Union National Association (CUNA) in the USA to study the movement there and, on her return, an all-out organising effort resulted in a total of eighteen Credit Unions being opened throughout the country by the end of 1962. Through the influence of Jim Girvan, an Armagh-born promoter of credit unionism in the USA, five American Credit Union Leagues voted one thousand dollars each to the Irish League, which resolved initial financial problems especially with regard to insurance. After persistent lobbying of government ministers, the Credit Union Act was passed in 1966, the realization of almost twenty years of hard organising. However, following an internal struggle, Nora was removed from her position as managing director and appointed life director of the League without voting rights. From then until 1980 she served on the Credit Union Advisory Committee to the government. She retired from teaching in 1975 but occasionally lectured on the credit union ideal. Nora Herlihy's death, on the February 7, 1988, went almost unnoticed in Ireland. However, the World Council of Credit Unions officially honoured her memory by circulating a 'Resolution in Memoriam' to all its members world-wide. At the time of Nora's death the Credit Union in Ireland had approximately one million members in more than five hundred branches.

HERON, HILARY (1923-1977), sculptor. Born in Dublin to a protestant family. She was reared in Wexford and Coleraine, Co. Derry. After a mostly private education Hilary attended the National College of Art, Dublin, where she was recognised as a brilliant student and awarded three Royal Dublin Society Taylor Art scholarships in a row. At twenty she was involved in the founding of the Exhibition of Living Art, although very much a background figure to the older avant-garde artists who had begun this 'alternative' annual exhibition in opposition to those held by the strictly academic Royal Irish Academy. In 1947 she was awarded the first Mainie Jellett Travelling Scholarship, through which she was able to study Italian and French Romanesque and Renaissance carvings. Much of Hilary's earlier work was in wood though she also sculpted in limestone and marble, showing strength and simplicity in an academic style, and often choosing religious themes. Influenced by the work of Picasso, Moore, and by African and Sumerian carving, she was considered as the most modern and innovative Irish sculptor of her time, especially when she began to work in welded metal in the 1950s. Hilary held several one-woman shows at the Victor Waddington Galleries, Dublin, from 1956 onwards, and was one of Ireland's two representatives at the Venice Biennale in 1956. She travelled widely in the USA, USSR and China, absorbing the varied influences. Her style and themes changed in the 1960s to a more whimsical and humorous mode. In the 1970s she served as a member of the RTÉ Authority. Hilary Heron was married to Professor David Greene, outstanding Irish scholar and much-loved personality in the Irish-language milieu, whom she predeceased on April 28, 1977.

HONE, EVIE (1894-1955), artist and stained glass maker. Born April 22, 1894, in Roebuck, Co. Dublin. Her father, a wealthy businessman and director of the Bank of Ireland, was a member of the famous artistic family of that name and a direct descendant of the 18th century portrait painter, Nathaniel Hone. Contracting poliomyelitis in her youth left Evie physically handicapped. In 1914 she began to study art in London with Walter Sickert, Meninsky and

Byam Shaw, together with her devoted friend MAINIE JELLETT. On a visit to Italy she saw the works of Giotto and Fra Angelico which had a lasting influence on her. Between 1920 and 1930 she and Jellet made prolonged visits to Paris where they were pupils at the academy of Andre Lhotè and later, of Albert Gleizes, both disciples of Braque and Picasso. The two women held a joint exhibition in Dublin in 1924 which, while shocking a conservative viewing public by its Cubist content, had a liberating effect on the Irish art world. In 1925 Evie spent a short period with an Anglican religious community in Cornwall: later she converted to Roman Catholicism. Her faith was to become the main inspiration for her work. Although she maintained close artistic links with Jellett her development took her into the different forms of

30. 'St. Martin of Tours dividing his cloak', *c.1945 by* **Evie Hone.**

stained glass where, further influenced by the work of El Greco and Georges Rouault, she turned to representational religious art. She assisted Jellett and other avant-garde artists to found the Irish Exhibition of Living Art in 1943. At this time Evie was already best-known among the second generation of the century's outstanding Irish stained glass makers. In 1934 she had joined SARAH PURSER's famous co-operative glass and mosaic works, An Túr Gloine ('The Glass Tower'), where she applied her Cubist style with wonderful effect. Despite ill health she produced over one hundred and fifty small stained glass panels (much of the original cartoons in goache remain extant) besides her larger works which include *My Four Green Fields* for the CIE (national transport system) offices in Dublin and her *Last Supper* and *Crucifixion* for the east window in the chapel at Eton College, England, a major work by any standards. Evie Hone died on March 13, 1955 at Rathfarnham, Dublin. Her works may be seen in churches throughout Ireland and Britain and in principal Irish galleries, including the National Gallery, Dublin; among her own favourites is the two-light *Christ and Apostles* (1948) at Kingscourt church, Co. Cavan.

HOUSTON, MARY GALWAY (1871-c. 1948), craftswoman and designer. Born Coleraine, Co. Derry, where her father was headmaster of the Academical Institution. At nineteen Mary came to Dublin to study at the Metropolitan School of Art and, for the next six years, demonstrated her versatility and sense of design by exhibiting and winning many prizes for lace, crochet, leather-work, metal-work and drawing. She moved to London and attended the South Kensington School of Art to study wood-carving. Within five years Mary had established herself as one of the most talented craftswomen in the British Isles. In 1898 she won a gold medal, for her leather book cover for the Kelmscott Chaucer, in a national competition run annually by the South Kensington school. She also embossed and modelled leather panels which were exhibited at the Royal Academy and the English Arts and Crafts Society. By this time she was also famous for her repoussé metal work, particularily in silver, and examples of this was sent to the Paris Exhibition in 1900. Up to this Mary's style was very much in keeping with both the contemporary English and art nouveau manner but, in quick succession, she also produced many outstandingly ornamented pieces in the Celtic style. In an effort to improve design nationally *Studion* magazine commissioned her to design two silver cups; she based one of these on the ancient Irish three-handled 'mether' to produce a strikingly bold 'loving-cup'. Another impressive piece of Celtic design, her silver-plated casket derived from the early mediaeval Irish reliquaries, was shown at the Cork Exhibition of 1902. When Mary became a teacher at the Camberwell School of Art, London, she showed an increasing interest, from 1902 onwards, in costume design and history. In the 1920s and 1930s she published three books on the history of dress. She rarely exhibited in the later part of her life and slipped from the public eye. The time and place of her death are uncertain.

HULL, ELEANOR or NIC CHOILL, EIBHLÍN (1860-1935), author, Celtic scholar, folklorist. Born January 15, 1860, in Manchester and reared in Dublin where her father was Professor of Geology at the Royal College of Science. Eleanor's mother was from Cheltenham, England. The Hulls were a County Down family with protestant clerical antecedents. Eleanor was educated at Alexandra College, Dublin, and the Royal College of Science. She went to London in her early twenties and came under the influence

31. *A silver-plated casket, shown at the Cork Exhibition in 1902, by* **Mary Houston.**

of the scholar Standish Hayes O'Grady who taught her Irish and interested her in early Irish history and literature. She became a member of the London Irish Literary Society and the Gaelic League. Her formal Celtic studies were under the direction of great scholars such as Meyer, Pedersen and Flower and, in 1898, Eleanor published her first work, *The Cuchulain Saga in Early Irish Literature*. She founded the Irish Texts Society to 'advance public education by promoting the study of Irish literature and to publish texts in the Irish language,' and acted as honorary secretary for thirty years. In 1904 the Society published her *Pagan Ireland* and *Early Christian Ireland*. During the following nine years she produced *A Textbook of Irish Literature*, in two volumes, (1906-1908), *The Poem Book of the Gael* (1912) and *Northman in Britain* (1913). Eleanor also contributed to the principal journals of Irish and Celtic studies of her time. She was a council member of the Folklore Commission and published *Folklore of the British Isles* in 1928. A devout protestant, she translated some hymns from the Old Irish, including 'Be thou my Vision' (*Irish Hymnal, No. 322*), and edited a series of publications, *Lives of the Celtic Saints*. Her last major publication was her two-volume *History of Ireland and Her People* (1926-1931). Eleanor Hull died in London on January 13, 1935.

HUTCHINS, ELLEN (1785-1815), botanist and painter. Born Ballylickey, west Cork, and educated in Dublin. Ellen required medical care as a teenager and was treated by Dr. Whitley Stokes, who, among other distinctions, was a foremost naturalist of the period. He got her interested in botany and she began a study of cryptograms, especially seaweeds and lichens, in the Bantry Bay area. Even though in chronic ill health and caring for an elderly mother and invalid brother she achieved much in her field during her short lifetime. Through Dr. Stokes'

introductions Ellen came into contact with many eminent naturalists, including James Townsend Mackay, curator of the newly-established Trinity College Botanic Gardens (1806), Dawson Turner and J.E. Smith, all of whom she provided with fundamental new research material. She also supplied drawings and paintings for scientific publications such as Mackay's *Flora Hibernica*, Smith's *English Botany*, and Dawson Turner's *Historia Fuci*. Ellen Hutchins died at home on February 10, 1815, in Ardnagashel House, Bantry, Co. Cork. The importance of her pioneering work, particularily in the study of algae, is reflected in the remarkably high number of plants named after her, including an Alpine cress *Hutchinsia alpina* and a native liverwort *Jungermannia hutchinsiae*. Some of her water-colours are still on exhibition in such distinguished institutions as the Royal Botanic Gardens, Kew, England.

INGHEAN DUBH. See under MacDONNELL, FIONNGHUALA.

ITA (ÍDE, ÍTE, MÍDE), SAINT (*c.* 488 - c. 570), virgin saint. Born of royal blood near Drum, in the Decies kingdom, now Co. Waterford. When her father wanted her to marry she fasted until allowed to enter a Christian community, possibly at Ardmore in the same region. She was originally named Deirdre but on becoming a contemplative took, or was given, the name Íte which means 'thirst', and referred to her extraordinary desire for God. Her main convent, one of the earliest monasteries for women in Ireland, was near Newcastlewest, Co. Limerick, at what has since been named Cill Íde or Killeedy, 'Ita's Church'. She gained a wide reputation for her asceticism but in popular tradition is best remembered as the '(St.) Brigid of Munster,' or the 'foster-mother of saints,' the latter because it seems she kept a school or novitiate for boys many of whom became important religious figures. Among her charges were St. Brendan the Navigator (who, according to the *Navigatio*, consulted her before making his most famous voyage), St. Cummian, reformer of the Irish Church, and St. Mochaemóg, her nephew. Ita died at her foundation, at a very old age, in about 570 and is buried within the ruins of a Romanesque church on the site. She was venerated for many centuries in Cornwall, England, as well as in west Limerick where devotion to her is still practised, especially on her feast day, January 15. Ita's name appears in several ancient Continental litanies and in the poem on the Irish saints composed by Alcuin of York at the court of Charlemagne in the 8th century. Of the many stories about her, perhaps the one that appeals most to the modern mind is her charitable care for one of her nuns who became pregnant and whose child, a girl, she reared as her own. Tradition ascribes to Ita the authorship of the powerfully passionate poem to the Christ child, 'Isucán';

Isucán
alar lium im dísiúrtán;
cia beth cléirech co lín sét
is bréc uile acht Isucán.

JACOB, ROSAMUND (1888-1960), suffragist, nationalist and author. Born Waterford into a Quaker family. Her religious beliefs motivated her involvement in the political struggle for women's rights and Irish independence. Little is known of Rosamund's earlier years but she could not have been considered a typical nationalist when she joined the Irish Women's Franchise League, the most militant suffrage group of the period, and began, in 1912, to contribute articles to the suffragist paper, *Irish Citizen*, then under the editorship of Francis Sheehy Skeffington. Yet, in the heated contro-

versy of 1914 as to whether one could give loyalty to both the nationalist and feminist ideal at that time, Rosamund took the *Irish Citizen* to task for advocating that 'we nationalists should abandon for an indefinite time, and even oppose, the cause of national liberty for the chance of getting the vote a few years earlier than we might otherwise get it'; on the other hand, she called on Cumann na mBan to oppose the Irish Party on the grounds of its leader John Redmond's hostility to women's suffrage. As a confirmed supporter of Sinn Féin Rosamund was the Waterford delegate to the momentous Sinn Féin Convention of 1917 where she was instrumental not only in getting the organisation to accept the principle of women's equality but in ensuring that women would be given an active role in shaping the future Dáil Éireann. At the onset of the Civil War, she was a member of the women's committee under MAUD GONNE MACBRIDE which unsuccessfully attempted to bring about peace talks. She was one of the honorary secretaries of the Irish section of the Women's International League for Peace and Freedom which hosted the League's first Congress in Dublin in 1926. Rosamund's first novel, *Callaghan*, was published in 1920 (under the pseudonym of F. Winthorpe) and she continued to write, although not prolifically, to the end of her life. Other books included a novel, *The Troubled House* (1938), and a children's story, *Raven's Glen* (1960). *The Rebel's Wife* (1957) is based on the life of Matilda Tone, wife of the United Irishman leader, Wolfe Tone. Generally accepted as an accomplished novelist, if of minor popularity, Rosamund Jacob's most ambitious work was her history, *The Rise of the United Irishmen*, published in 1937 in an attempt to heal the wounds of the Civil War and the resulting splits in contemporary Irish life.

JAMESON, ANNA BROWNELL, née MURPHY (1794-1860), author, travel writer, art historian and reformer. Born Dublin, the eldest of five girls. Her mother was English and her father, a painter of miniatures, was involved in the United Irishmen. Because of his involvement in the 1798 and 1803 Rebellions, the family moved to Cumberland about 1808 and later to London. Educated at home Anna was governess, at the age of sixteen, to the Marquis of Winchester. In 1821, while still a governess, she became engaged to Robert Jameson, a lawyer. Breaking with him she travelled as a governess with a family making the fashionable Continental tour. On her return Anna resumed the relationship and married Jameson but the couple were soon estranged. During this period she published her first book, *A Mother's First Dictionary*. The following year she wrote a semi-fictional account of her time on the Continent and published it anonymously as *The Diary of an Ennuyée*. The success of this book encouraged her to produce, in quick succession, *Memoirs of the Loves of the Poets* (1829), *Memoirs of Celebrated Sovereigns* (1831) and, in 1832, *Characteristics of Women* - a study of women in Shakespearean plays that entered the canon of Shakespearean criticism - and a reprint of the *Diary* under her own name. Anna supported herself, mother, sister and niece from her writing, and continued to do so for many years. She belonged to a circle of progressive women including Fanny Kemble, Elizabeth Browning, Ottiline von Goethe and Lady Byron. In 1837, she went to Canada to rejoin her husband, supporting him in his successful attempt to become vice-chancellor there. She made two tours, one on her own by public stage-coach visiting Toronto and Detroit among other places, and the second through Chippewa Indian territory in North Michigan. She had several adventurous journeys by canoe that included shooting the rapids at St. Mary's Fall between Lake Superior and Lake Huron. These adventures, unique for a woman and particularily one of her class, provided the basis for *Winter Studies and Summer Rambles In Canada* (1838). This book is remarkable not least for its sympathetic observations of Indian life and critical moral judgements of so-called Christian and civilised living. In 1840 she was commissioned to write guide books for public and private art galleries in London and contributed articles on art to *The Athenaeum*. Her *Companion to the Public Picture Galleries of London* (1842), followed by *Memoirs and Essays on Art, Literature and Social Morals* (1846), established Anna as being the first woman art historian and earned her the appellation of 'mother of art criticism'. All her writings were imbued with a strong moral sense and focused strongly on the role and rights of women and on the contribution of women to art and society. In 1855 and 1856 her lectures, *Sisters of Charity* (on the social work of the order of that name, including their work in Ireland during the Great Famine), and *The Communion of Labour,* were published. She was a founder member of The Society for the Promotion of Employment of Women and spoke on the role of women as educators and social reformers at the Social Science Association Congress in 1859. From 1848 onwards she had undertaken a massive work on *Sacred and Legendary Art* in six volumes, which was finally completed by Lady Eastlake after Anna Jameson's death in 1860.

JELLETT, MAINIE (1897-1944), artist. Born Fitzwilliam Square, Dublin, into an affluent protestant background. Her father was a barrister and her mother, Jane Stokes, an accomplished musician. ELIZABETH YEATS and William Orpen were among Mainie's earliest art instructors. After attending the National College of Art she went to London, with devoted friend and fellow student EVIE HONE, to attend the Westminster School and study art with Walter

32. 'The Virgin of Eire', *painted 1943 by* **Mainie Jellett.**

Sickert. In 1920 the women made the first of many extended visits to Paris where they were pupils of Albert Gleizes and André Lhote, both moderate disciples of Braque and Picasso. They spent the next ten years alternating between Paris and Dublin, "seeking inner principles and not outside appearance." Working in oil and gouache they mastered pure Cubism. Although Jellett's work was greeted with hostility in Dublin she and Hone held a joint exhibition there in 1924. Their work, though shocking to the public, had a strong influence on the country's art. Mainie is considered one of the great innovators in modern Irish painting whose introduction of Cubism and later, Expressionism, was to have a liberating effect on the Irish art world. She also lectured, broadcasted, and wrote articles, in an attempt to create an appreciative public for non-representational art. While most of her work ranked between Cubism and total abstraction, Mainie regularly returned to realism and semi-abstract work. She designed textiles and carpets, sets and costumes, for the innovative Gate Theatre of Edwards and MacLiammóir. Much of her later non-representational work was based on Christian religious subjects, for example, 'Deposition', one of her best-known works. In 1943, along with Hone, le Brocquy, NORAH McGUINNESS and others, she founded the Irish Exhibition of Living Art in rebellion against the autocratic and hidebound Royal Hibernian Academy. Soon afterwards she became ill with cancer and died in Dublin early the following year. Her work is included in all major Irish collections and her striking murals, commissioned by the Irish Government for the Irish Pavilion at the Glasgow Fair, are now in the National Gallery of Ireland, Dublin.

JELLICOE, ANNE, née MULLIN (1823-1880), educator, co-founder of Alexandra College, Dublin. Born into a prosperous Quaker community in Mountmellick, Co. Laois. Although her father, a schoolmaster, died when she was three the family never were unduly poor. Anne was probably taught by a governess, yet many of her later educational ideas were rooted in the Quaker school tradition. Her mother died when she was seventeen and she may have worked as an embroiderer before marrying John Jellicoe in 1848. Her husband set up a successful flour-milling business in Clara, Co. Offaly, where Anne ran embroidery and lace-making projects to provide employment for destitute women. After 1858, having moved to Harold's Cross, Dublin, as her husband's business expanded, she opened a small school and, by giving lectures, attempted to better the lot of working class women in the city's 'sweatshop' factories. Having joined The National Association for the Promotion of Social Science, her ideas on education developed considerably, especially with regard to the necessity of educating middle-class women for employment. In 1861 she co-founded a society for the latter purpose which became known as the Queen's Institute. However, she found she could only cater for 'distressed gentle-women' to be trained as scriveners, sewers and telegraph clerks, as their existing educational standards were so low. Becoming a wealthy woman after her husband died in 1862 and, being childless, Anne devoted the rest of her life to providing a sound liberal education for young middle-class women. She prevailed on Dr. Trench, Church of Ireland Archbishop of Dublin, and on Trinity College professors to found a college offering education for women, and so Alexandra College in Earlsfort Terrace was opened in October 1886, the first of its kind in Ireland. Anne Jellicoe, who was not allowed to be a member of the all-male Council or Committee of Education, was appointed Lady Superintendent or Principal. In 1867 she set up the Governess Association of Ireland to raise funds for teacher training, especially through scholarships and bursaries. She also organised a registry of employment and persuaded Trinity College to provide the certificated examinations for women which were introduced in 1870. In 1873 she established Alexandra School, a preparatary 'feeder' school for the College, as so many pupils of the latter had never received a proper elementary education. She was able to staff this school with gradutes of the College. Anne Jellicoe died suddenly on October 18, 1880, while on a visit to her brother's house in Birmingham, England. Although by constraint her pioneering educational establishments catered for protestant 'gentle-women' only, she and her fellow reformers provided the stimulus for the huge growth nationwide of Roman Catholic convent secondary schools in the last decades of the 19th century. Alexandra College itself was and remains an exemplar for the liberal education for women.

JONES, MARY, née HARRIS or MOTHER JONES (*c.* 1837-1930), American labour organiser. Born Cork city between 1830 and 1837 into impoverished circumstances. She was to boast that her people 'for generations had fought for Ireland's freedom.' The family emigrated to North America when Mary was five years old and her father worked as a labourer in railroad construction in Toronto. She attended Toronto Normal and became a teacher in a Roman Catholic convent in Monroe, Michigan, but shortly after turned to dressmaking. In 1864 in Memphis, Tennessee, she married George Jones, an iron-moulder and later organiser of the Iron Moulder's Union. Mary and her young family followed her husband to the southern coal fields where she gained her first experience of labour agitation and organisation. George and their four children died in the yellow fever epidemic which swept Memphis in 1867; having buried the last of her family, she got a permit to nurse fever victims in the city. She later ran a successful dress-making business in Chicago which was destroyed along with her home in the great fire of 1871. Deciding to dedicate her life to fighting industrial slavery, Mary joined the Knights of Labour, a secret society which was organising textile workers in Chicago. Her rousing speeches at strike meetings made such an impact that she was soon called upon by labour organisers outside of the textile industry to support their agitation. Thus she came to play a prominent role in the Baltimore and Ohio railroad strike of 1877, campaigning from New York to Pittsburgh. From 1880 onwards she was a full-time agitator, working unceasingly for oppressed workers, especially miners, in an era when unionisation was normally suppressed by police, federal troops, armed militia and hired gunmen, the latter often supplied by the Pinkerton Agency. For more than four decades Mary took part in disputes in Alabama, Tennessee, Maryland, Colorado, New York, Michigan, Arizona, Kansas, New Jersey and, above all, West Virginia. Known affectionately as Mother Jones, she had gained a reputation for extraordinary courage, once putting her hand over the muzzle of a militia gun that threatened a group of strikers. In 1899 she mobilised the miners' women folk at a crucial point in the United Mine Workers' strike in Pennsylvania, a pattern of action she was to use successfully throughout her fifty years of campaigning. Mary began to write for labour and socialist papers and was instrumental in founding the influential socialist weekly *Appeal to Reason* in 1895. In 1903 she organised the March of the Mill

Children during the strike of seventy-five thousand textile workers in Kensington, Pennsylvania; although President Roosevelt refused to meet her and her child labourers in New York, and the strike was lost, the publicity was such that a child labour law was passed by the Pennsylvania legislature. A pioneer socialist, she helped found the Industrial Workers of the World (IWW) in 1905, known as 'The Wobblies', which became possibly the most influential labour agitation force in American history. A legend in her own lifetime, Mary also worked on behalf of jailed labour activists, lobbied presidents and state governors, and campaigned for sympathetic candidates in Senate elections. When more than eighty years of age she visited Mexico City to address the Pan-American Federation of Labour and, in 1924, was involved in her last labour dispute - fittingly a dress-maker's strike in Chicago where she had joined the Textile Worker's Association more than forty years previously. In the same year Mary published her autobiography. Despite her commitment to non-violent methods of agitation she was jailed on several occasions; a military court sentenced her to twenty years penal servitude when she was close to eighty years of age for her part in a coal-strike (the sentence was revoked). The last year of Mary Jones' life was spent with a farming family in Maryland where she died on November 30, 1930. She was buried in the Union Miners' Cemetery in Mount Oliver, Illinois, where a large monument commemorates her inspiring life. Motivated by her intense Christian faith and concern for the oppressed, Mother Jones' credo was, "Pray for the dead but fight like hell for the living!". She was noted for her scathing wit, telling crowds such parables as that of her meeting a man in prison for stealing a pair of shoes: "I told him if he had stolen a railroad he would be a United States Senator."

JOYCE, NORA. See under BARNACLE, NORA.

KAVANAGH, JULIA (1824-1877), novelist. Born Thurles, Co. Tipperary, only child of Morgan Kavanagh, philologist and novelist. The family moved to France when she was young and Julia lived in Paris and Normandy. She was educated at home. At twenty she and her invalid mother left her father in France and moved to London where Julia turned to writing to support herself and her mother. Initially she wrote stories for journals and children's books. Her first novel, *The Montyon Prizes*, published when she was twenty-two, was extremely popular in Britain. So too were the many other books she produced over the following three decades even though they reflected her very strong Roman Catholic faith. In many of her books she also drew from her French experiences. Much of their popularity may have been due to their featuring capable and independent-minded women at a time when most upper-class women, especially in the country, were still expected to be subordinate to their men folk and confined to the domestic sphere. Among the better known of these novels were *Madeleine* (1848), *Nathalie* (1851), *Daisy Burns* (1853) - translated into French after her death, *Adele* (1858), *Bessie* (1872), and *Two Lilies* (1877). All published in two or more volumes. Julia's travels in Italy were the basis for *A Summer and Winter in two Sicilies*. Her three collections of biographical and historical essays on notable women were considered to be of more lasting importance: *Women in France in the Eighteenth Century* (1850), *French Women of Letters* (1861), and *English Women of Letters* (1863). In 1857 she was drawn into an unpleasant public dispute with her estranged father over the authorship of her books; it appears that he attempted to trade in her established name. Julia Kavanagh moved to Nice after the death of her mother and died there in 1877.

KEARNEY, TERESA (MOTHER KEVIN) (1875-1957), 'Mama Kevina', missionary to Uganda and founder of the Franciscan Missionary Sisters for Africa. Born after the death of her father on April 28, 1875, on a small tenant farm at Knockenrahan, Co. Wicklow, and orphaned at ten, Teresa went to live with a grandmother in nearby Arklow. Her only education was at a convent national school in Arklow. Until she was twenty she worked as a monitor or assistant teacher and as a child-minder in various convent schools or institutions in Wicklow and Dublin. Rejecting a proposal of marriage, she went to teach in Essex, England, and shortly afterwards entered the convent of the Franciscan Sisters of Mary's Abbey, Mill Hill, London, as a choir sister. Professed in 1898, she took the name 'Kevin'. Having volunteered for missionary work, she arrived in East Africa with five other Sisters in early 1903. Travelling west to Uganda, the women were passengers on the first train to successfully complete the journey from

33. *Julia Kavanagh, c. 1875, by Henri Chanet.*

Mombasa to Kisumu. The nuns quickly set up their first dispensary, an open-air one, at Nsambya, Bugunda. Some years later Sister Kevin was put in charge of a tiny foundation at Nakifuma and, later again, following her superior's illness, was given responsibility for the entire mission. In 1913 she opened their first foundation outside Bugunda, in Busoga, an extremely poor area, plagued with sicknesses. The original foundation at Nsambya, now a hospital, was used throughout World War One to attend to native carrying corps in the British forces. Realizing that midwifery training was a priority Sr. Kevin found, on a visit to England after the War, that church rules still prohibited religious from practising maternity work; surreptiously, she attended a course in obstetrics. On her return to Uganda in 1921, she was officially appointed superior of the fourteen Franciscan sisters there. As Mother Kevin she established, with the aid of a trained volunteer from Ireland, a school for nurses and midwives in Nsambya. In time this provided a widespread nursing and midwifery service. Following a visit by a group of tribal girls who wished to become nuns, she founded an African congregation, the Little Sisters of St. Francis; beginning with eight postulants in 1923, the African sisterhood today has several hundred nuns working in Uganda. In the ensuing thirty years, Mother Kevin directed the founding of some fifty religious centres in Uganda and neighbouring Kenya which ran primary, secondary, teacher-training, nursing schools and schools for the blind, orphanages, general clinics and hospitals, as well as two villages for lepers. Exhausted by 1943, Mother Kevin asked to be relieved of her duties as superior. After nine years as an 'ordinary' nun, she was appointed Superior-General of the newly-constituted Franciscan Missionary Sisters (a congregation which had evolved from her own order) and directed the opening of new foundations in East Africa and South Africa. At eighty, her second request to retire from leadership was granted, but two years later her order sent her to America (she had set up a novitiate in Boston some years previously) to promote awareness of the missionary role of the church and to raise funds. She never returned to Africa, dying on October 17, 1957, at her convent base in Brighton, Massachusetts. After Mother Kevin's burial in Ireland, a swift nationwide effort by the Ugandan people brought her body back to Uganda, for burial at Nkokonjeru, where her funeral was possibly the biggest ever seen in East Africa. Mother Kevin was awarded an MBE in 1919 for her services to British army sick and wounded during World War One and a CBE in 1955 in recognition of her life's work in Africa. It is said that among the pupils of her schools were the first native East African woman to qualify as a doctor and the first native holder of a Bachelor of Science degree. Named 'Flame-in-the-Bush' by Bugandan tribespeople in their own language, Mother Kevin's English name passed into Ugandan languages when 'Kevina' came to mean a hospital or school or any charitable institute.

KEARNS, LINDA (1888-1951), republican activist and nurse. Born July 1888 into comfortable circumstances in Dromard, Co. Sligo. She was educated in Belgium after attending the local national school and qualified as a nurse at Baggot Street Hospital, Dublin. She joined Cumann na mBan and was associated in particular with COUNTESS MARKIEVICZ and HANNA SHEEHY SKEFFINGTON. Linda distinguished herself in the 1916 Rising by first setting up a Red Cross field-hospital in North Great Georges Street and then, refusing to comply with the British military's demand to attend British personnel only, acting as despatch-carrier and nurse for the rebels. From the earliest days of the War of Independence she was a despatch-carrier and arms smuggler, mostly in the Sligo area, and had many daring escapes from detection. She nursed in Achill for a short time during the influenza epidemic of 1918 and afterwards opened a nursing home in Gardiner Place, Dublin, which became a 'safe house' for Volunteers on the run. In November 1920, while driving three Volunteers and a consignment of explosives from Sligo to Ballymote, she was arrested by a Black and Tan patrol and sent to Belfast with the others for trial. She claimed full responsibility in an unsuccessful attempt to save the men and was sentenced to ten years penal servitude. She was sent to Walton Prison, Liverpool, as a common criminal but protests and lobbying succeeded in having her transferred back to Mountjoy Prison in Dublin. From there she and two other republican women, with the help of a female warder, escaped by rope-ladder to an IRA camp at Duggett's Grove, Co. Carlow. Linda resumed active service with the Republicans when the Civil War began. During the bombardment of the Republican garrison in Hammom's Hotel, O'Connell Street, Dublin, on July 5, 1922, she remained with the besieged and tended the dying commander, Cathal Brugha. She was imprisoned again and, on her release in 1923, immediately went to the USA, at Éamon de Valera's request, to raise support for the Republican cause. Linda also toured Australia before returning home to become a founder member of Fianna Fáil. She was one of five women elected to the executive. Although a staunch supporter of de Valera she joined with the National Council of Women to fight for women's equality when Fianna Fáil introduced the discriminatory Conditions of Employment Bill in 1935 and the Constitution in 1937. In 1938, now Mrs. Linda Kearns MacWhinney, she became a Senator on the nomination of the Women's Industrial Development Association, of which she had been a founder member. She was honorary secretary of the Irish Nurses Association for many years and, in 1945, set up a nursing home at Kilrock, Howth, Dublin. Linda Kearns died here on June 5, 1951, shortly after being presented with the Florence Nightingale Medal by the International Committee of the Red Cross for her work on behalf of the nursing profession.

KELLY, MARY EVA. See under EVA OF THE NATION.

KENTIGERNA (CAÍNTIGERN, CAOINTIARN), SAINT (8th century), anchorite of Loch Lomond, Scotland. Daughter of the royal house of Leinster and sister to St. Comgán of Tureff and St. Conchennia (whose death in 738 is recorded in the *Annals of the Four Masters*). Scots and Irish sources indicate that her father was named Kellanus (i.e. Ceallach) and so may be identified with Ceallach Cualann, son of Gerrtide, king of Leinster, who died in 713. Kentigerna (as the Scots know her) married an Ulster chieftain, Feradach, and raised a large family renowned for their religious fervour. Her son, Foilan, abbot of Cluain-Mhaoscna, Co. Westmeath, is the most celebrated and also venerated among the saints of Scotland. Another son, Mundus, is also recorded in the martyrologies and the 'daughters of Feradach' were assigned a feast day on the March 23. After the death of her husband Kentigerna went to Scotland (where her brother, St. Comgán, was already evangelising in Argyll) and made her hermitage on the island of Inchelroiche, in Loch Lomond, Dunbarton, where she lived in notable austerity and sanctity. Here Kentigerna died, according to the Scots and Irish calendars, in 728 or 734. Many miracles were attributed to her during her lifetime and afterwards. Her feast day is on

January 7, the date of her death. (She is not to be confused with the male Kentigern, better known as St. Mungo, the 7th century Bishop of Glasgow.)

KNOTT, (PHILIPPA MARIE) ELEANOR (*c.* 1886-1975), Gaelic Irish scholar and lexicographer. Daughter of a surgeon from Kingsland, Co. Roscommon, and an English mother from Hull. It is not known where Eleanor was born but the family were living in Dublin in the first decade of this century. Her father, John Freeman Knott, wrote extensively on scientific and technical subjects but it was mostly through her mother, who had Cornish connections and an interest in the Celtic language of Cornwall, that she became interested in Celtic languages, especially in Old Irish. She was probably educated at home by her parents and governesses. It is a mystery how Eleanor got the basis of her knowledge of spoken Irish and what the circumstances were that gained her a place on the staff of the recently-founded School of Irish Learning in Dublin were she came under the influence of the great Celtic scholar Richard Irving Best. She published *Foclóir d'Eisirt*, a glossary on the ancient tale of *Eisirt*, in 1910. The following year she began work on the monumental *Dictionary of the Irish Language* for the Royal Irish Academy (RIA) as an assistant to Karl Marstrander; after his departure she was its 'living embodiment' for the next forty years, producing three fasciculi, with Maud Joynt, which have been acknowledged as among the most exact of all the lexicographic works published by the Academy. In 1911, she began to study the work of 15th century bardic poet Tadhg Dall Ó hUiginn, the two volumes of which were completed by 1926 and acclaimed as 'the most valuable of all those (publications) issued by the Society of Irish Manuscripts'. Later books were an *Introduction to Irish Syllabic Poetry of the Period 1200-1600* (1928),

Tógáil Bruidne de Derga (1936), *Irish Classical Poetry* (1937), a book still consulted by probably every student of Irish at university level, and *Early Irish Literature* (1966) in conjunction with Gerard Murphy. She also wrote numerous articles for all the learned Irish journals of the time. Although long recognised as an outstanding scholar, and employed for years as a lecturer in Trinity College Dublin, Eleanor did not take an MA degree until her forty-sixth year. Some years later a professorship of Old Irish was instituted in Trinity College to make use of her special talents and, in 1947, she was the first woman to be elected to the RIA. By this time, she was already going blind and, though still at the height of her capabilities, could no longer work by 1955. Eleanor Knott died on January 4, 1975, in the Molyneaux Home for the Blind and was buried in Mount Jerome Cemetery, Dublin. She was a very private person and is possibly the least remembered of all the great Irish scholars of this century. With regard to the history of the modern language movement, it is seldom remembered that she edited several works of Canon Peadar Ó Laoghaire and was one of those scholars who assisted Shán Ó Cuív in his efforts to introduce the system of simplified spelling into modern Irish.

KYTELER or KETTLE, DAME ALICE (*c.* 1280-1325), reputed witch and heretic. Ireland's most notorious witch lived in the rapacious feudal world of Norman conquest in Kilkenny in the first part of the 14th century. Probably the richest woman in Kilkenny, she was an English or Norman colonial, possibly English-born. Prior to 1302 she married her first husband, William Outlaw of Kilkenny, a wealthy banker and moneylender, and had at least one son, also William, who was to be accused of involvement in her alleged sorceries. Before 1324 Alice had married and buried three other rich and powerful men, le Blond, de Val and de Poer, and her son William had become a great land pirate in this era prior to the Gaelic resurgence and the Geraldine supremacy. Holinshed's *Chronicle of Ireland* (1577) relates that, in 1325, she and two accomplices were accused by Richard le Drede, Bishop of Ossory, of holding 'nightly conference with a spirit named Robert Artisson and taking part in a witches' sabbath,' among other charges. Two members of the Kyteler household, Petronella de Mida and her daughter Basilla, were accused as accomplices. They were abjured, possibly through the power of Alice's in-laws, the de Poers, and did public penance. However, within a short period they were charged again and this time Petronella was burned at the stake in Kilkenny. Before dying she accused Alice's son, William, of having been privy to her sorceries and he was jailed forthwith. Arnold de Poer, Seneschal of Kilkenny, freed him and imprisoned the bishop for three months. Little is known about either Kyteler or the other accused after these events. It is generally thought that Alice went to England. However, Friar John Clyn, a contemporary chronicler who was in Kilkenny during the period, recorded she was in fact executed for heresy rather than witchcraft and this was the first instance of such in Ireland. The case has several postscripts. De Poer was subsequently imprisoned in Dublin Castle for his treatment of le Drede and a relation of Kyteler's first husband, the Prior of Kilmainham, was accused of heresy. De Poer was exonerated in 1328 but died in prison before receiving his pardon. Bishop le Drede was, in turn, charged with heresy and some twenty-five years went by before he was restored to his cathedral. These circumstances indicate the Kyteler affair was part of a power struggle which had begun in England between the supporters of King Edward and those of the Earl of March. The King's side was taken by the de Poers and the Outlaws while the Earl's side was supported not only by the Butlers and Geraldines, now rapidly growing in power, but also by Bishop le Drede who had initially charged Dame Alice Kyteler with witchcraft.

LARKIN, DELIA (1878-1949), trade unionist. Born in a Liverpool slum to impoverished Irish emigrants of Co. Down origin; younger sister of the future labour leaders, James ('Big Jim') and Peter Larkin. She may have spent some of her childhood years with her grandparents in Newry, Co. Down. Delia's father died young of tuberculosis and her brother James became a father-figure to the family. Delia worked as a nursing sister in Liverpool before coming to Dublin in 1911 to help James found the Irish Women Workers Union (IWWU), which had some one thousand members when it affiliated with the Trades Union Congress soon after. A good organiser and public speaker, Delia acted as secretary for the IWWU and edited a women's column in *The Irish Worker*, organ of the Irish Transport and General Workers Union. She was also involved in the suffragist movement and, in 1912, spoke at a women's mass meeting in Dublin to demand the inclusion of female suffrage in the proposed Home Rule Bill. At the same time she organised the Transport Union's social programme, founded the Irish Workers' Choir and ran dance, drama, and Irish language classes, in Liberty Hall, the Trade Union headquarters in Dublin. She was also elected that year to represent women workers of Dublin on the Irish Trades Board. With COUNTESS MARKIEVICZ she was in charge of the soup kitchen in Liberty Hall during the 1913 Dublin Lock Out, a lengthy labour dispute in which employers attempted to break the unions. Delia favoured the controversial plan, countered by the Roman Catholic hierachy, to send the children of 'locked out' workers to homes in

*34. Members of the Irish Women Worker's Union with **Delia Larkin** (centre) c.1913.*

Britain. She travelled England and Ireland with her Irish Workers Dramatic Company to organise support and raise funds for victims of the conflict. Her attempts to set up workers co-operatives for women made redundant as a result of employers' intransigence were ultimately unsuccessful. After her brother James went to the USA Delia got involved in internal disputes with less militant officials of the Transport Union and failed, through lack of union support, as a Labour Party candidate in the Poor Law Elections. She was forced to go to Liverpool to earn a living and so was not involved during the period from the formation of the Citizen Army to the 1916 Rebellion. She returned to Dublin in 1918 to take part in the growing dispute in the Transport Union

between the radical 'Larkinites' and followers of the relatively conservative William O'Brien. She edited the short-lived weekly *The Red Hand,* until James, finding it too divisive, ordered it to be discontinued. Not least because of her informal associations with the embryo Communist Party of Ireland, Delia was refused re-entry into her old union, the IWWU. When James was sentenced to ten years penal servitude in the USA for 'criminal syndicalism' (i.e. trade unionism) in 1920, she organised support on his behalf. On his unexpected release three years later he returned to Ireland to attempt to heal the breach in Irish trade unionism. He suddenly broke off a national tour in the cause of unity when, in the light of the O'Brienites plan to secede and form an independent organisation,

Delia advised him to confront his opponents. Defeat and expulsion from the union followed. In 1925 Delia backed Peter in founding the radically left wing Workers Union of Ireland, but, although 'Big Jim' was elected to the Dáil three times between 1927 and 1944, the power of the socialist element was steadily eroded. Trade unionism and the labour movement had gone into serious decline. From the time of her marriage in about 1930 to Pat Colgan, a member of the executive committee of the Workers Union of Ireland, Delia had retired from active work in the labour movement. She and her husband looked after 'Big Jim' for the last decade of his life in their house at 41 Wellington Road, Ballsbridge, Dublin. She outlived her brother by two years.

LAVERTY, MAURA, née KELLY (1907-1966), novelist and cookery writer. Born Rathangan, Co. Kildare and reared by her grandmother at Derrymore House. Maura received some teacher training at the Brigidine Convent, Carlow but, due to economic circumstances on the death of her grandmother, was required to find work. She went to Spain as a governess at the age of nineteen. Although only there for two years, Maura also worked as secretary to a Spanish princess, and as a foreign correspondent and freelance journalist in Madrid. In 1928 she was back in Dublin working as a journalist and as a broadcaster with the recently-founded Radio Éireann. Her first novel, *Never No More* (1942), received an enthusiastic reception by critics such as Seán O'Faolain. Her *Touched by Thorn* was published the following year and, although banned by Irish censorship, received the Irish Women's Writers award. It was republished as *Alone we Embark* in 1943. Other novels followed; *No More than Human* (1944), *Lift Up Your Gates* (1946) - republished in 1947 as *Liffey Lane* - and *Green Orchard* (1949). Her themes for the most

part were drawn from experiences in her own life: childhood and adolescence in the rural Ireland of the 1930s, family friction, life as a governess. She also wrote a play, books for children and cookery books, in particular *Full and Plenty* (1960), which made her a much beloved national figure. The most popular Irish TV serial of the 1960s, *Tolka Row*, was based on her novel *Liffey Lane*. She died in Dublin in 1966.

LAVIN, MARY (1912-1996), short story writer and novelist. Born June 11, 1912, to Irish parents in East Walpole, Massachusetts, USA, and returned, as a child, to her mother's middle class home in Athenry, Co. Galway. Eventually Mary and her mother went to live in Dublin where she attended Loreto Convent, Stephen's Green. She regularly visited her father in Bective, Co. Meath, where he worked as a farm manager. Mary drew on memories of her happy childhood when she came to write but the tensions and frustrations of 'normal' family life were also explored in her stories. She studied history and French at University College Dublin. While preparing a thesis on Virginia Woolf she was inspired to write her first short story, published in *Dublin Magazine*, in 1938. Within two years her work appeared in prestigious international journals such as *Atlantic Monthly*. Her first volume of short stories, *Tales from Bective Bridge* (1942), found immediate acclaim and won the James Tait Black memorial prize. Two novels, a novella and two further collections of stories followed in the twelve years of Mary's marriage to William Walsh, a Dublin solicitor, He died in 1954, leaving her with three children to support. On the strength of her published works she obtained a contract from the *New Yorker* and produced two more collections within two years. This consolidated her reputation internationally as one of the greatest Irish writers in the field of the short story which, up to then, was dominated by the male trio of O'Connor, O'Flaherty and O'Faolain. Her *Selected Short Stories* appeared in 1959 and *The Short Stories of Mary Lavin* in 1964. While much of her earlier work grew out of the experiences of her youth, the work of this period reflects the loneliness of her widowhood. *In the Middle of the Fields* (1967), for example, has been described as one of the most moving studies of vulnerability and isolation. Mary married again in 1969, to Michael MacDonald Scott, and their home in Dublin became a meeting place for the new wave of young writers of the time. She continued to write, always examining 'the vagaries and the contraries' of the human psyche, and five more volumes of stories came from her pen. Her life's work reflects not only her own experiences but that of Irish society in the six decades following independence. Her thirteenth and last collection, *A Family Likeness,* appeared when she was seventy-three. Incapacitated by illness in her final years, Mary Lavin died on March 25, 1996, in a Dublin nursing home. During her career she was awarded many honours including several Guggenheim Fellowships and the Gregory Medal; she was president of the Irish Academy of Letters from 1972 to 1974.

LAWLESS, EMILY (1845-1913), novelist, poet, historian and biographer. Born June 17, 1845, at Lyons Castle, Celbridge, Co. Kildare to a wealthy land-owning Anglo-Irish family with strong Irish sympathies. Some of Emily's ancestors had fought with the Jacobite leader, Patrick Sarsfield, and followed him into exile; her grandfather fiercely opposed the Act of Union and was imprisoned in the Tower of London for his sympathies with the United Irishmen revolutionaries. Her father, third Lord Cloncurry, committed suicide and Emily was reared by her mother's family, the Kirwans of Castlehacket, Co. Galway, where she came in contact with the peasantry and learned to speak Irish. Her youth was spent in relative isolation and eccentricity, marred by other family tragedies, including the suicides of two of her sisters. In later life she had close ties with several important figures in the political and literary world, particularly with Sir Horace Plunkett, pioneer of agricultural cooperation in Ireland. When Emily was forty-one she published the novel *Hurrish* (1886), by which she may be acclaimed as the first novelist of the Irish Literary Renaissance. The book, dealing with the topical subject of Home Rule activities among small tenant farmers in Co. Clare, was generally well received and praised by Gladstone, the British prime minister who became a friend and correspondent. Emily's next novel, *Grania* (1842), a tragic romance set in the Aran Islands, won her recognition as one of the foremost Irish writers of the time. Always interested in history, she published historical studies and romances such as, *The Story of Ireland* (1887), *With Essex in Ireland* (1890), *Maelcho* (1894). She is best remembered for her poetry, particularily the moving 'After Aughrim' and 'Clare Coast', inspired by the vicissitudes that befell her family in the Jacobite period. These appeared in the volume *With the Wild Geese* (1902). Three other books of verse followed including *The Inalienable Heritage* (1914). All her work shows a passionate love of Ireland but she believed in keeping the connection with Britain. This probably accounts for the decline in the popularity of her writings and in the appreciation of her achievement. She also wrote short stories and historical essays. Her last book, the biography *Maria Edgeworth*, appeared in 1904. She was conferred with an Hon. D. Litt. by Trinity College Dublin, in 1905. In later life Emily Lawless moved, for health reasons, to Gomshall, Surrey, in the south of England where she died in seclusion on October 19, 1913.

LEADBEATER, MARY, née SHACKLETON (1758-1826), writer. Born Ballitore, Co. Kildare, into a Quaker family of school teachers; the Shackletons have been prominent in Irish history over several generations. Mary grew up in the environment of the small but influential Quaker network of communities of the period in the Midlands. Her father took her to London for a time where she was introduced to Edmund Burke (who had been taught by her grandfather), Sir Joshua Reynolds and MARIA EDGEWORTH, with all of whom she kept in correspondence. Mary married a neighbouring landowner, William Leadbeater, in 1791, and from then on ran the post office in the nearby village. She did not begin to publish until her fiftieth year, when her *Poems* appeared. This was followed by *Cottage Dialogues* (1811), *The Landlord's Friend* (1813), and *Tales for Cottagers* (1814), collections of moral tales written to instruct both peasantry and landlord. *Cottage Biography being a Collection of Lives of the Irish Peasantry* (1822) was, as the title indicates, a remarkable endeavour for its time. Her work is important as social commentary. Her *Annals of Ballitore*, better known as *The Leadbeater Papers*, were not published until 1862. The two volumes, reminiscing on sixty years of her life, contain much local history and an eye-witness account of the 1798 Rebellion as well as biographical material. Mary Leadbeater died in Ballitore on June 27, 1826.

LEESON, MARGARET (1727-1797), brothel keeper. Born Margaret (Peg) Plunkett at Killough, Co. Westmeath, one of twenty-two children into a prosperous landed family. Abused by a brother and abandoned by several lovers, she turned to prostitution in Dublin. Margaret was sought-after by wealthy gentlemen and soon became a woman of means. She adopted the name Leeson as a badge of respectability after a liaison with a wealthy Dublin merchant of that name. 'Mrs. Leeson' soon became the most fashionable and wealthy brothel keeper in Ireland. She ran several establishments which catered for the wealthy, including the Governor of the Bank of Ireland, and for the politically powerful, as well as for lawyers, journalists and theatre folk. She married the son of Lord Avonmore and then accepted five hundred guineas from his father to give him up. Mrs. Leeson was at the 'very zenith of (her) glory, the reigning vice queen of the Paphian goddess', in the decade following 1784. She moved her brothel to Pitt Street, the site now occupied by the Westbury Hotel and, having imported girls from the Covent Garden and Drury Lane Theatres in London, won the seal of social approval when the Duke of Rutland became a client. By her own account Mrs. Leeson's career was one of extraordinary flamboyance and exhibitionism. After retirement her large collection of IOUs became valueless, her house was plundered, and she attempted suicide; she recovered only to be sent to the debtors prison which, fortunately for her, was run by a former client. From her retirement quarters in Blackrock, Co. Dublin, she wrote her memoirs motivated by the need of money and a wish for revenge. She claimed to have made some six hundred guineas from the first two volumes, having sent copies to various well-known people from whom she extracted 'patronage' obviously under threat of exposure. The third volume, it appears, was written after her repentance and conversion to the Roman Catholic faith, probably the religion of her youth. This was apparently written under the guidance of Mrs. Leeson's confessor but was still unpublished when, at seventy, she was attacked and gang-raped thus, ironically, contracting the venereal disease which was to kill her. She died in abject poverty. *The Memoirs of Mrs. Leeson* have recently been republished from the single copy that remained extant. They are an important social record of the period especially as historians such as Lecky tended to portray the Anglo-Irish ascendancy of the period as the exemplar of moral rectitude.

LELIA (LILE), SAINT (5th or 6th century). Little detail is known of the life of this woman. She was a sister of St. Mainchín (Munchin), patron of Limerick, whose dating is also uncertain although some sources state he met St. Patrick as a youth. Their genealogy, however, was thoroughly recorded. Lelia and Mainchín were of the race of Dal gCais, children of Sédna, one of the thirteen sons of Cas, who was fifth in descent from Olioll Olum, king of Munster; in the *Leabhar Uí Máine* (c. 1400), Sédna is listed as the father of Mainchín and 'the Daughters who are in Cell na nInghin'. The fact that these 'Daughters' were mentioned at all in secular genealogy is a testament to their importance. Lelia's church was in Kileely, later to become the North Liberties of Limerick city and part of the barony of Bunratty, Co. Clare. Her name is also closely connected with the church at Killilagh, Doolin, west of the Burren in Co. Clare. At least one other church, Kileely, near Kiltartan, Co. Galway, on the eastern approach to the Burren, may also have been a daughter-house of Lelia's foundation. The latter two centres, which were outside immediate Dal gCais control, may have been part of her *paruchia* (a network of religious centres under the authority of a mother-house). Doubtlessly, Lelia had close links with the religious centres in Kilrush in west Clare, founded by her sister, Ros, and Fidh-Inis in the Fergus estuary of south Clare, founded by her brother but taken over by Brigid, a blood-relation, if not another sister. Her *paruchia* may have extended into the dioceses of Limerick and Kerry where there is at least one other ancient church, Killilee near Killarney,

dedicated to her. As far away as Co. Wexford, the church of Killila, Ballaghkeon, is tenously associated with her. Some of the ancient references to St. Mac Creiche and other early church-builders in north Clare state that they were 'friends of Mainchín' and that the latter was given grants of land for church-building in association with them by Baoith Brónach, a king of Corcomroe in the sixth century. It is likely that Lelia played an important role in the extraordinary spate of church building and religious foundations in Co. Clare and the rest of Thomond (North Munster) in the fifth and early sixth centuries. There is some intriguing evidence to indicate that Lelia and her contemporary Christians in Thomond may have been outside, or even preceded, the Patrician mission *per se*. Her feast is on August 11.

LÍADAIN (7th century), *ollamh* or master poet. Born Corca Dhuibhne, West Kerry, into a family of hereditary poets. She is one of the few female *ollamhna* or master poets on record and is the heroine of a mediaeval romance. When Líadain went to Connaught, as part of her poet's circuit, she and the arch-poet Cuirithir fell in love at the ale feast he had prepared for her and her retinue. Having committed herself to marriage she continued her circuit and returned to Corca Dhuibhne. Assailed by doubts, and perhaps due to Cuirithir's delay in coming for her, she took a religious vow of chastity. When he eventually arrived she left with him and he, too, took a vow of chastity. They placed themselves under the direction of a holy man, Cuimmíne Fata of Clonfert in east Galway. On his advice, they chose to be allowed to communicate without seeing each other and, for a time, were even permitted a form of celibate cohabitation. But eventually Cuimmine commanded Cuirithir to leave. This he did in great rage until he repented and joined another monastery in Deise territory, probably in Limerick. In several poems attributed to her Líadain lamented the fate of the lovers and, according to tradition, she died in the Clonfert hermitage while still a young woman.

Joyless the bargain I made:
The one I loved I tortured.

Joyfully, except God came between us,
would I have done his pleasure . . .

The forest sang for me by Cuirithir's side
In harmony with the blue sea's sighing . . .

A blast of flame has pierced my heart:
I cannot live without him.

LINDON or NIC GHIOLLA FHIONDÁIN or NIC a' LIONDÁIN, MOLLY, (mid-18th century), Gaelic scribe and poet. Born Creaggan, near Crossmaglen, Co. Armagh. Her father, Pádraig Mac a' Liondáin, was a farmer of comfortable means and a well-known Gaelic scribe and scholar. He kept a school or 'Court of Poetry' for scribes in his house and perhaps at Cnoc Chéin Mhic Cáinte, closer to Dundalk. Her mother, also a scribe and poet, was a Macardle from a family noted for scribal output in southeast Ulster and Meath. Molly earned acceptance as a *file* (a person versed in the lore of the Gaelic poet) by the Gaelic literati who frequented her home, among them Ó Doirnín, Mac Cubhaigh and O'Carolan the harper. She was regarded as superior to her brother, Pádraig Óg, who also practised as a *file* and one of whose manuscripts is in the British Library. Very little of Molly's poetry has come down to us; a small portion of her once-popular poetic disputation with Peadar Ó Doirnín (1704-1769) is extant. Although many of the 18th and 19th century scribes were descended, through their mothers, from families with hereditary associations with Gaelic schol-

arship, Molly Lindon is one of the very few women of her period who was recorded as being connected, in a learned capacity, with the production of Gaelic manuscripts.

*35. **Kitty Linnane** at the 85th anniversary of the Kilfenora Ceili Band in July 1992.*

LINNANE, KITTY, née O'DEA (1922-1993), musician, secretary of the Kilfenora Céilí Band. Born into a farming family at Ballygannor, Kilfenora, in north Co. Clare. Her mother, Lily Lynch, had inherited a long tradition of Irish music from the well-known Lynch family of Clogher, Co. Clare, and has been credited with composing many of the typical north Clare dance tunes widely played today. Kitty's uncle, John Joe Lynch, was the main force behind the original Kilfenora Céilí Band, a group of 'house musicians' who came together in the first decade of the century to play in public on special occasions. While at the local national school Kitty took piano lessons from the principal, Molly Conole. She began playing for the band while still a pupil at Seamount College, Kinvara.

The band had regrouped in the 1930s and became known outside Co. Clare from broadcasting with 2RN, the new national radio station. However, social and economic changes in the 1940s brought about the band's demise. In 1943 Kitty married a local man, Tommy Linnane, with whom she had six children. After the founding of Comhaltas Ceoltóirí Éireann (the national organisation of traditional musicians) in Clare in 1953, she and her cousin, P.J. Lynch, revived the band. Most of the members were related with several being first cousins. The following year they won their first all-Ireland championship at Cavan Fleadh Ceoil (a music festival organised by the Comhaltas) and repeated the feat in 1955 and 1956. By this time, with Kitty as secretary holding together some twelve individualistic musicians and playing piano, the band was a household name and played two or three times a week, especially at marquee dances, throughout Ireland. They also made many trips to England. In 1961 Kitty led the Kilfenora Céilí Band to another all-Ireland title. When the *céilí* dances began to die out in the mid 1970s, she kept a small contingent of the band together. Kitty Linnane continued playing almost up to her death, on March 15, 1993, and had an input in the revived band of the 1990s which again began taking first places in *Fleadhanna Ceoil*. In July 1992 she was given pride of place on the stage in the Square of Kilfenora when the band celebrated eighty-five years 'on the go' with a live broadcast. Besides being the driving force behind the band for some forty years Kitty was also known locally for her charity to the old and lonely and her fund-raising for Roman Catholic missions abroad.

LONSDALE, DAME KATHLEEN née YARDLEY (1903-1971), crystallographer, physicist, chemist. Born January 28, 1903, Newbridge, Co. Kildare where her father was postmaster. She was the youngest in a large family which moved to England while she was still a child. Through scholarships she was, at sixteen, able to enter Bedford College, London, to study mathematics and physics. In spite of her youth Kathleen had a brilliant record as a student and joined the research team of physicist W.H. Bragg. Her wide-ranging research contributed greatly to many advances in the field of crystallography, including notable discoveries made through X-ray techniques which she developed. Her work was carried out at University College London, and Leeds University. Always concerned with the idea that science should be used wisely and for the benefit of mankind, Kathleen also applied crystallography techniques to the study of medical problems. She married a fellow scientist, Thomas Lonsdale, in 1927 and raised three children while also travelling widely in her academic capacity. In 1945 she was the first woman Fellow of the Royal Society of London (Physical Sciences), and later made a vice-president. She was also president of the International Union of Crystallography and, in 1968, first woman president of the British Association. She received the Davy Medal of the Royal Society in 1957 and was created a DBE. In 1935 she and her husband joined the Society of Friends (Quakers), in the affairs of which she took an active part. She was jailed for a month in 1943 as a conscientious objector and thereafter agitated for penal reform. Dame Kathleen Lonsdale died in London on April 1, 1971.

LYNCH, SISTER CONCEPTA (1874-1939), illuminator in the Celtic style. Born Lilly Lynch in Dublin. Daughter of Thomas Joseph Lynch, an illuminator who specialised in producing presentation addresses which were fashionable in the 19th century. The growth of

36. **Kathleen Lonsdale** *in the research department at the University College, London, in 1948.*

national consciousness had led to a revival of illumination in the Celtic style and Lynch had evolved his own system. His eleven-page vellum address to Cardinal Newman, in 1880, was recognised as a 'perfect renovation of ancient Irish (as) has never yet been produced'. He imparted these skills to his daughter so well that on his death, while she was still attending the Dominican Convent, Dún Laoghaire, Co. Dublin, she could take over the studio in Griffith Street, Dublin, and run it to his high standards. At the age of twenty-two Lilly joined the Dominican Sisters in the Dún Laoghaire convent where she had gone to school. After her profession in 1898, she mainly taught art in the convent boarding school. Her own talent found an outlet in

designing illuminated addresses for other convents and the clergy. When a small plain oratory was built in the convent grounds, in 1919, a statue of Christ was brought from France to commemorate the Dún Laoghaire soldiers who were killed in Flanders in the First World War and Sr. Concepta was asked to decorate the niche. She later received permission from the prioress to decorate the entire interior. In 1920 she began the work which is acclaimed as a masterpiece of Celtic design. The decoration was planned as a single unit; the walls and ceiling are covered in Celtic interlacing and zoomorphic ornament developed, with great originality, from the art of illuminated manuscripts such as the Book of Kells. The work took sixteen years and

*37. Frescoes by Sister **Concepta Lynch** and stained glass windows by Harry Clarke in the 'Oratory of the Sacred Heart'.*

eventually the onset of illness prevented Sr. Concepta from completing it. She died on April 30, 1939, and is remembered for this one monumental achievement which has been described as 'the chef-d'oeuvre' of the school of stricter traditional Celtic art (as opposed to that influenced by art nouveau). *The Lynch method of Celtic Art* was published posthumously by the Dominican Sisters. The convent in Dún Laoghaire has since given way to a shopping centre but the tiny oratory (the interior measures 5.85m by 3.66m) remains. It is now under state care and a 'peace garden' is planned for the immediate surrounding area. The entire conservation project has been made possible by an EU funding award.

LYNCH, MADAME ELIZA (1835-1886), adventurer and Regent of Paraguay. Born at Dundanion, Blackrock, Co. Cork, of (as she wrote) 'highly respectable parents, members of an old Anglo-Irish family.' On the Lynch side she claimed kinship 'to several worthy bishops and more than sixty magistrates' and, on the distaff side, to 'a Vice-Admiral who together with his two brothers fought with Nelson at the Battle of Trafalgar.' Other commentators propose more humble origins for the later Regent of Paraguay, but, given the history of Ireland over the previous two and a half centuries, such would not necessarily have been incompatible with her own story. When Eliza was ten the family, driven by poverty, emigrated to Paris where they probably had family connections. Matters did not improve there and Eliza, age fourteen, married a French army veterinary surgeon and went to Algiers with him. Within two years she returned alone to Paris where, after several liaisons, she became the mistress of Don Francisco Solano Lopez, eldest son of the President of Paraguay, who had been sent to Europe to be educated. The twenty-year-old, now styling herself as Madame Lynch, joined her lover on his return to Paraguay in 1855. Seven years later, after the death of his father, Lopez became Marshal-President and Madame Lynch lived openly as his consort and adviser. The new regime began extremely well and Paraguay flourished, having concluded treaties of commerce with the USA, Britain and France. However the ambitions of the President and Madame Lynch, and resulting jealousy of neighbouring states, led Paraguay into a rash and ultimately disastrous war with Brazil, Uruguay and Argentina, in 1864. After initial successes the war turned against Paraguay with its tiny population of one million. Women fought alongside men in the Paraguayan ranks and Madame Lynch is said to have commanded a female regiment of the native Guarani people who, unable to pronounce her name, knew her as 'Lavinge'. Lopez made her Regent of Paraguay to give her control of state affairs while he commanded the army. After five years of fighting and with circumstances becoming desperate, she and their four children joined him as his army was beaten back to Cerro in the north-west, distinguishing herself in battle with her women soldiers. Lopez was killed in 1870 when they were surprised by Brazilian forces and Madame Lynch tried to escape with her children and remaining possessions; this attempt caused mutiny among her followers, the death of her eldest son, and her capture by the Brazilians. It is said she and her surviving sons, with their bare hands, buried both her lover and son in the same grave. She eventually managed to return to Europe where her latter years were uneventful and she gradually slipped back into poverty. Eliza Lynch died on July 25, 1886, and was buried at public expense in Père Lachaise in Paris. In 1932, after Paraguay had been victorious in a war against Bolivia for the northern Gran Chaco territory, she was declared a national hero. Madame Lynch's body was transported from Paris and re-interred in the Panthene de Los Heroes in the capital of Paraguay, Ascuncion.

LYNCH, HANNAH (1862-1904), travel writer, novelist and Land Leaguer. Born Dublin into a family of comfortable means. She received a Continental convent school education and travelled widely as a governess. Hannah was only nineteen when she was elected to the Executive Council of the Ladies Land League at its inauguration on February 4, 1881, and, acting as one of its secretaries, was one of the signatories of its first address to its countrywomen to unite and challenge the landlord system. At one stage she managed to distribute 30,000 copies of the Land League paper, *United Ireland,* after the leading male Leaguers had been imprisoned. When the printers were also imprisoned Hannah, and other members of the Ladies Land League, rushed to Paris and had the paper illicitly printed there. Having remained on the Continent in political exile after the collapse of the Ladies Land League, and the break-down of her friend and leader ANNA PARNELL, she worked as Paris correspondent for the English literary journal, *Academy.* She wrote novels in English, including *Prince of the Glades,* and *Clare Monroe,* while also producing fiction in French. Several books on European culture and customs, including *Toledo, the story of an old Spanish Capital* (1898) and *French Life in Town and Country* (1900), resulted from her travels. The latter was written in Ireland and contains asides on the character of the Irish bourgeoisie and trades people: 'I felt like Rip Van Winkle, as I walked in my native land, and found everyone gone mad with pride and pretension.' She also wrote a study of George Meredith who was recognised as one of the greatest English novelists of his day. Hanna Lynch died in Paris at the age of 42.

LYNCH, PATRICIA NORA (1898-1972), journalist and author. Born Sunday's Well, Cork, into a comfortably-off Fenian family where her grandfather was a teacher. On the early death of Patricia's father, her mother moved the small family to England where they lived in different places before settling in London. Patricia attended schools in England, Scotland and Belgium before becoming a journalist. She was active in the women's franchise movement and was sent to Ireland by Sylvia Pankhurst to cover the 1916 Rebellion for the *Worker's Dreadnought.* This was described as the first reasonably objective account presented to the British public, published as the pamphlet, *Rebel Ireland,* and

PATRICIA LYNCH

THE TURF-CUTTER'S DONKEY

38. Book cover of 'The Turf-Cutter's Donkey' by **Patricia Lynch,** *drawing by J.B. Yeats.*

circulated widely in Britain, the USA, and Europe. Patricia settled in Dublin in 1918 and, two years later, married the writer R.M. Fox. Her husband was a left-wing English journalist who became involved in the Irish labour and nationalist movement and, from that point of view, wrote extensively on the chief figures and events of the period. Patricia Lynch's first book, *The Cobbler's Apprentice,* appeared in 1932, winning the Tailteann Games silver medal for literature. She was to write more than fifty books, all reprinted many times in Britain and America and translated into most European languages, and gained recognition as one of the world's finest writers of children's books. Her most famous creation, *The Turf Cutter's Donkey* (1934), illustrated by Jack B. Yeats, was chosen as a Junior Book Club selection. The novel *The Grey Goose of Kilnevin* was a Cardinal Hughes Literature Committee choice as one of the best one hundred books, junior or adult, published in

the USA in 1941. Among her other better-known books are *Long Ears* (1943), *Fiona Leaps the Bonfire* (1957), *Kerry Caravan* (1967) and her semi-fictional biography, *Storyteller's Holiday* (1947). The much-loved Brogeen, a character who appeared in a series of books, was successfully translated to television as a cartoon. Patricia Lynch died in Dublin on September 1, 1972.

LYNN, KATHLEEN (1874-1955), doctor, feminist and revolutionary. Born Cong, Co. Mayo, daughter of the Anglican rector and also with clerical antecedents on her mother's side. COUNTESS MARKIEVICZ and EVA GORE BOOTH were distant cousins. During her youth in Mayo Kathleen witnessed widespread malnutrition and other diseases caused by poverty and, at sixteen, took the bold decision to become a doctor. She graduated from the Royal University, Dublin, in 1899 as one of the first women to achieve a degree in medicine but had difficulty getting a position. After a refusal from the Adelaide Hospital she set up in general practice in Rathmines. Kathleen first came to prominence in Dublin, in 1912, when she tended jailed and hunger-striking suffragists and spoke from public platforms on their behalf. During the labour troubles of 1913 she used her medical skills to help locked-out workers. She was the only female doctor of the era with active nationalist sympathies. As a member of the women's section of the Irish Citizen Army she gave first aid classes to the Citizen Army and the Irish Volunteers. During the 1916 Rising she was medical officer to Countess Markievicz's battalion in the College of Surgeons, St. Stephen's Green. At the time of surrender Kathleen, then attending to the dying Seán Connolly in City Hall, was the only officer present. To the consternation of her captors, whose code of conduct did not allow for women officers, she took the surrender, was arrested and taken to

*39. **Dr. Kathleen Lynn** and Madeline Ffrench-Mullen.*

colleague, Madeleine ffrench-Mullen, who had been with her in the ambulance corps of the Irish Citizen Army. This was the first hospital in Ireland to care specifically for children. The women started with a capital of less than one hundred pounds and two cots at the time of the great 'flu and tuberculosis epidemics. Kathleen continued her involvement in politics and, in 1920, was made a member of the Sinn Féin executive. She sided with the republicans in the Civil War and when elected to the Dáil for Dublin north, in 1923, refused to take her seat in accordance with her party's policy. Disappointed in Sinn Féin's failure to embrace social reform in 1926 she dedicated the rest of her life to the children of St. Ultan's and attended her clinic until the spring of 1955 when she was eighty-one years of age. A devoted Anglican, Kathleen Lynn died in the care of St. Mary's Anglican Home, Ballsbridge, Dublin, on September 14, 1955.

MACARDLE, DOROTHY (1889-1958), teacher, historian, republican, activist, writer. Born into a strongly Unionist family, owners of Macardle Breweries of Dundalk, Co. Louth, her father was Sir Thomas Macardle KBE, DL. After graduating from University College Dublin, she became a teacher at Alexandra College, Dublin. Aspiring to be a writer, she published her first play *Atonement,* in 1918. Dorothy had already been attracted to the republican movement through the example of MAUD GONNE MACBRIDE, and acted as a Sinn Féin publicist during the War of Independence. She took the republican side during the Civil War and, as an active member of the Women's Prisoners' Defence League, demonstrated against the Free State Government, particularly in relation to the detention of MARY MacSWINEY. She was twice imprisoned, the second time in 1922 when she was arrested in Maud Gonne's house and held without charge in Kilmainham Jail, Dublin. In

Kilmainham Jail with Countess Markievicz. In 1917 she was one of four women members of the executive of reformed Sinn Féin. The others were the Countess, KATHLEEN CLARKE and GRACE PLUNKETT. In 1919, representing the League of Women Delegates, Kathleen was part of the united front of women's organisations who urged their sisters in other countries to demand an international committee of enquiry be formed to look into the conditions of Irish political prisoners. That year Kathleen founded St. Ultan's Infant Hospital with her friend and the absence of judicial mechanism to protect the prisoners from harsh treatment and appalling conditions she and ninety other women went on hunger strike. After her release, seven days later, she returned to her teaching position in Alexandra College. In 1924 Dorothy published *Earthbound*, a collection of short stories concerned with the military struggle and its effect on women. When the Roman Catholic Church excommunicated all republicans, she publicly renounced her religion in protest. Always an admirer of de Valera, she joined the newly-formed Fianna Fáil political party in 1926 and was a member of the first executive. Between 1918 and 1931 Dorothy had written four plays, and become drama critic for the *Irish Press*, the Fianna Fáil organ, in the early 1930s. As a journalist for the paper, she covered sessions of the League of Nations in Geneva during de Valera's presidency of the League in 1938. At his request she produced her most important work, *The Irish Republic* (1937), a detailed account of the War of Independence and Civil War which is still a standard reference book. Although showing great independence of mind in opposing the Conditions of Employment Bill (1935) and in becoming vice-chairperson of the National Council of Women (1936) in opposition to Fianna Fáil legislation affecting women, Dorothy Macardle's history of the 'Troubles' is totally uncritical of de Valera, weighted against the Free Staters and neglects to a remarkable degree the role of women in the republican movement. She wrote several novels, mostly concerned with the occult and extra sensory perception: *Uneasy Freehold* (1942), *The Seed was Kind* (1944), *Fantastic Summer* (1948) and *Dark Enchantment* (1953). *Uneasy Freehold* was made into the film, *The Uninvited*, in the USA. She also wrote plays for children. Two further accounts of the republican struggle were *Without Fanfares* (1944), and *Tragedies of Kerry* (1946). During and after the Second World War she worked on behalf of refugee children, and in 1949 wrote a 'Study of the Children of Liberated Countries,' *Children of Europe*. She became president of the Irish Association of Civil Liberties in 1951. Dorothy Macardle died in December, 1958.

McAULEY, CATHERINE (1778-1841), founder of the Sisters of Mercy. Born September 29, 1778, into a wealthy, upper middle-class, Roman Catholic family at Stormanstown House, Drumcondra, Co. Dublin. Despite her mother's disapproval Catherine's father was a benefactor of the poor and even had them instructed in the Roman Catholic faith in his own house. After his early death her brother and sister, encouraged by their mother, converted to protestantism. Her mother died when Catherine was eleven; the child was made a ward of a maternal relation, a surgeon named Conway, also a member of a Roman Catholic family who had converted to protestantism. When she was eighteen other wealthy relations, Mr. and Mrs. Callaghan, returned from India, bought Coolock House and demense, and, being childless, adopted her. These were Quakers and not as anti-Catholic as her other relations. Catherine secretly contacted Archbishop Murray of Dublin and was restored to the Roman Catholic practice. She began charitable work among the rural poor of the area. Both Callaghans became Roman Catholics and, when they died, left her sole heiress of Coolock House with a fortune of thirty thousand pounds and six hundred pounds a year in perpetuity. In July 1824 Catherine bought a site in one of the most fashionable areas of Dublin, Lower Baggot Street. This may have been in anticipation of Catholic Emancipation but also to challenge the protestant Society of Proselytisers in neighbouring Kildare Street. She had a fine Georgian building erected on the site and, assisted by a few friends of her own social class, made it a home for unemployed servant girls, homeless children and the sick and dying It was named 'House of Our Blessed Lady of Mercy' but there was no intention of forming a religious order at first. In 1825 the group answered Archbishop Murray's call for volunteers during a cholera epidemic and after it subsided Catherine set about raising funds for the families of victims. She audaciously petitioned the Duchess of Kent by letter to support a bazaar that had, in consequence, unusual financial success. When Catholic Emancipation was granted the Archbishop advised her, and two companions, to enter the novitiate at Presentation Convent, George's Hill, Dublin. They took simple vows on December 12, 1831, and Catherine was appointed superior of the new order of the Sisters of Mercy at their Baggot Street premises. When applying for papal approval she stated that "the principal purpose of this Congregation is to educate poor little girls, to lodge and maintain poor young ladies who are in danger, that they may be provided for in a proper manner, and to visit the sick poor". Once the approval was conferred so many novices of good family flocked to joined the order that Archbishop Murray joked, "Catherine is the greatest enemy the fashionable world has." The orphanage came into being when she found a child alone in a cellar with its dead parents and took it back to Baggot Street. As Roman Catholic religious were not welcome in hospitals she dressed as a gentlewoman and arrived by carriage when she had occasion to visit the sick. In 1835 the Sisters opened a school in a neglected area near Dún Laoghaire, Co. Dublin. Two years later they set up a new house in Carlow. In 1839 the Vicar Apostolate of the London District invited them to work in Bermondsey, London, and the

following year another institution opened in Birmingham. Mother Catherine was planning foundations in Newfoundland, when she took ill and died on November 10, 1841. In 1936, centenary of the founding of the order, it was calculated that there were then some twenty thousand Sisters, in one thousand five hundred convents, between Ireland, England, North America and the Antipodes, running elementary and high schools, hospitals, homes and orphanages. Their congregation was considered to be the largest in the world. The process for the canonisation of Catherine McAuley is well advanced.

MacBRIDE, MAUD GONNE. See under GONNE, MAUD.

McCRACKEN, MARY ANN (1770-1866), patriot and philanthropist. Born Belfast, July 8, 1770, into a Scots Presbyterian family. Her father was a sea-captain with a rope-making business, and her mother's family, the Joys, owned a large cotton factory and a successful newspaper. The McCrackens were of strongly independent Calvinist stock, separated from the protestant ascendancy by their culture and history, and smarting under the penal laws of the period. Mary Ann attended a co-educational school in Belfast run by David Manson who was noted for his advanced ideas on education for 'young gentlewomen.' While still in her late teens she broke the accepted stereotype for women by setting up a small muslin business, with her sister Margaret, which was to operate for a decade. She was associated with the renaissance of Irish harp music from the beginning; the famous collector of Irish traditional music Edward Bunting being a member of her father's household and a life-long friend. She and her brother John remained patrons to Bunting and his assistants, Lynch and Balfour, until his death in 1843. The McCrackens were the driving force in the founding of the Belfast Harp Society of which Mary Ann was one of the original members. She was drawn into the revolutionary movement through her brother Henry Joy McCracken who, with Wolfe Tone and others, established the Society of United Irishmen in October 1791. She was intimately connected with radical politics for the following twelve years and appears to have contributed much to her brother's ideology with regard to social reform. She faithfully supported and visited her two brothers, Henry Joy and William, when they were jailed in Kilmainham, Dublin for their part in the organising of the United Irishmen, assisted in running the family business in their absence and nursed them on their release. When Henry was sentenced to death for his role in the insurrection of 1798 Mary Ann lobbied the authorities on his behalf. She also made arrangements to aid his escape but the attempt failed and she accompanied her brother on the way to his execution. She had known (and possibly hoped to marry) Thomas Russell since 1792 when he had made the first of many visits to Belfast as an organiser of the insurgents. She visited him in Kilmainham when he was arrested and sentenced to death for his part in the 1803 Rising, supported him financially, and also pleaded with the authorities on his behalf. After his execution she withdrew from radical politics and concentrated on her muslin business until economic depression, caused by the war in America, forced her to close down in 1813. Mary Ann was in her late fifties before she emerged into prominence again. Influenced by the English reformer, Elizabeth Fry, she became a force in the Ladies Committee of the Belfast Poorhouse of which she remained secretary for more than twenty-five years, being especially concerned with the education of destitute children. She was also active in the Society for the Relief of the Destitute Sick and in the Belfast Ladies Clothing Society. She campaigned on behalf of child chimney sweeps and factory workers and for the anti-slavery movement. For twenty years she corresponded with the Irish historian Dr. Madden, thus contributing greatly to his seven-volume history of the United Irishmen. Concerned with her social work to the end, Mary Ann McCracken died on July 26, 1866, at the age of ninety-six.

MacDERMOTT, ÚNA BHÁN (17th century), tragic lover, said to have been the inspiration of the famous and enigmatic song 'Úna Bhán'. Daughter of the house of the MacDermotts of Caisleán na Carraige who, for centuries, was one of the most important families in Connaught. The second Act of Settlement passed by the all-protestant Irish Parliament in 1662 divided the Gaelic lords more than ever: while some, among them the MacDermotts, had their former lands restored to a greater or lesser degree, others were excluded from all grace and turned to guerrilla warfare as 'Tories' or 'Rapparees'. Úna fell in love with Tomás Láidir Mac Coisdealbha (Costello) whose immediate branch of the Costello family had been excluded from the benefits of the Act. Tomás' elder brother, Dudley (Dubhaltach Caoch), had become leader of a band of Tories determined to drive off the Dillons, the new proprietors of confiscated Costello territory and allies of the MacDermotts. In 1667 the Dillons ambushed and killed Dudley. The O'Rourkes, former princes of Breffni, Lords of Leitrim, and enemies of both the MacDermotts and Dillons, attempted to make a marriage alliance with Tomás. At the same time MacDermott hoped to consolidate his ties with the British colonists by marrying Úna Bhán to one of them. A banquet was arranged for this purpose and Tomás was among the guests probably because he had saved the life of Úna's brother a little earlier. Úna, asked by her father to toast her proposed husband, toasted Tomás who was then driven from the house. Her health then went into a decline and, as a last desperate measure, MacDermott invited Tomás to return. The girl recovered following his visit but her father delayed in agreeing to their marriage and Tomás left in despair. When MacDermott finally relented, it was too late: Tomás had cast in his lot with the O'Rourkes. The death of Úna followed. Tomás is said to have lain on her tomb until her ghost bade him not to come again. There is some evidence that he later married O'Rourke's daughter. All that remains are two songs said to have been composed by him, 'Úna Bhán' and 'Tá mé sínte ar do Thuama' ('I am stretched on your Grave'). Tomás was buried beside Úna on the island of Lough Key and it is said that between their graves a rose bush grew entwined in the shape of a heart. Some modern commentators on the song (of which at least fifty verses have been recorded from traditional singers) believe that, whatever parts of it may have been composed by Tomás Láidir Mac Coisdealbha and refer to a real-life Úna Bhán, the extant material contains one or more of the allegorical political poems characteristic of that early modern period.

MacDONNELL, FIONNGHUALA (INGHEAN DUBH) (born *c.* 1555), mother of Red Hugh O'Donnell and Rory, first Earl of Tyrconnell; 'the head of advice and the counsel of Cenél Conaill'. Born either at Glenshesk, north Co. Antrim, or on the island of Islay in the North Channel between Ireland and Scotland, daughter of James MacDonnell, Lord of the Isles, whose territory included Islay, Rathlin and most of Antrim. Fionnghuala's mother was Lady Agnes Campbell of Kintyre, a Scottish peninsula that reaches to within a dozen miles of the Antrim coast. The Antrim Scots posed a threat to Shane O'Neill, then the most powerful Ulster leader,

who attacked the MacDonnells, defeated them at Ballycastle, and killed James. Lady Agnes subsequently married Turlough Luineach O'Neill, Shane's successor in Tyrone, bringing with her a dowry of one thousand two hundred Scots soldiers (*gall-óglaigh* or 'gallowglasses'). Fionnghuala most likely accompanied her mother to Tyrone. About 1570 she became the third wife of the ageing Sir Hugh O'Donnell (Aodh Dubh Ó Domhnaill), lord of Tyrconnell, an area which roughly comprised County Donegal of today. Like her mother, Fionnghuala, now known as Inghean Dubh, brought as many as a thousand gallowglasses to bolster O'Donnell's army; in turn, her husband gave her strategically important lands and castles on the coast of Lough Foyle. Under Brehon law Inghean Dubh was able to play an active part in the political and military affairs of her husband's territory and is recorded by the annalists as being 'the head of advice and the counsel of Cenél Conaill'. By 1587, so strong was the alliance between the O'Donnells, O'Neills and MacDonnells that the English Lord Deputy had Inghean Dubh's young son Aodh Rua (best known to history as Red Hugh O'Donnell) kidnapped and held as hostage with other sons of the Ulster nobility in Dublin Castle. In 1588, when Aodh Ó Gallchubhair, from the most ancient and royal family of Tyrconnell, attempted to take over the territory she had him ambushed and killed by her Scots, gaining revenge for the death of her brother at the hands of the former. The English then incited her stepson, Donnell, to take over Tyrconnell with a promise of earldom but Inghean Dubh mustered her troops and 'all the Cenél Conaill who were obedient to her husband,' and killed Donnell at the battle of Doire Leathan, Donegal, in 1590. After Red Hugh escaped, and the English moved against her, Inghean Dubh persuaded her husband to abdicate and succeeded in having

Red Hugh inaugurated chief of the O'Donnells in 1592. Through this she made an enemy of his cousin, Niall Garbh O'Donnell, who had a better claim to the title. To appease him, she gave Niall her daughter Nuala in marriage and thus temporarily retained his loyalty. Red Hugh expelled the English from southern Tyrconnell and bought time to retrench by going to Dublin to submit to the Lord Deputy and Queen of England. He later seized Sligo, overran Connaught, and joined forces with Hugh O'Neill to inflict a heavy defeat on the English at the battle of the Yellow Ford (1598). For two years there was hope that, with Spanish aid, the English might be driven out of Ireland but all was lost at the battle of Kinsale (1601) and Red Hugh went to Spain for further aid. He died the following year; his death suspected of being caused by poison administered by a British agent. Inghean Dubh's second son Rory, after duly submitting to the new king, James I, was made Earl of Tyrconnell. In 1607 he was forced to take refuge on the Continent with his younger brother, his sister NUALA O'DONNELL, and several of Inghean Dubh's grandchildren as part of the exodus of the Ulster nobility known to history as 'The Flight of the Earls'. Within a year Inghean Dubh's sons were dead either from fever or poison. To some extent the change in O'Donnell fortunes could be attributed to Inghean Dubh's son-in-law Niall Garbh who, by going over to the English side, had caused havoc in Tyrconnell for years. In 1608, he was accused of conspiring in the rebellion of Cahir O'Doherty and sent to the Tower of London, with his son, where he died eighteen years later: the information which condemned him was furnished by Inghean Dubh. It appears that, as part of the deal, she got a grant of lands from the English at Kilmacrenan, the ancient inauguration place of the O'Donnell chiefs, and remained in residence and relative security there until her death.

McGROARTY, SISTER JULIA (1827-1901), educator and founder of Trinity College, Washington D.C., USA. Born Inver, Co. Donegal, February 13, 1827, into a poor family, one of ten children. The future Sr. Julia emigrated to Cincinnatti, Ohio, with her family when she was four years old. At twenty-one she made her profession with the Sisters of Notre Dame de Namur, a teaching order, and was posted to the Academy of Notre Dame in Roxbury, Massachusetts. After twelve years she was transferred to Philadelphia where she founded a school for black children. An able administrator, Sr. Julia was appointed superior of her order's foundations east of the Rockies in 1886 and later for those in the state of California. She greatly developed the curriculum and established standardised examination systems throughout all the convent schools under her jurisdiction. Entrance to universities for women was limited at the time and Sr. Julia determined to found a university college for women, especially because of the reluctance of the Roman Catholic University in Washington D.C. to increase its intake of women. However, with support from within the university authorities, she was able to overcome resistance to the incorporation of a women's college with full authority to grant degrees, and saw her plans fulfilled when Trinity College was opened in Washington in 1900. Trinity offers a liberal arts programme for women to BA standard and has grown from an initial intake of twenty-two students to more than a thousand. Sr. Julia died, almost exactly a year later, at Peabody, Massachusetts, on November 12, 1901.

McGUINNESS, NORAH (1903-1980), painter. Born in Derry, daughter of a ship owner and coal merchant. She was educated at Victoria High School and Derry Technical School where she received her first art training. She studied under

41. 'Dublin Bay', lithograph by **Norah McGuinness.**

Patrick Tuohy at the Metropolitan School of Art in Dublin and began to work for Harry Clarke, the stained glass artist, who not only helped her to get commissions for book illustrations but imparted a decorative quality to her style. In 1923, while studying at the Polytechnic in Chelsea, England, Norah married the poet, Jeoffrey Phibbs. Having settled in Wicklow, in 1925, she began to design sets for the Abbey and Peacock Theatres in Dublin and continued to illustrate books. When the marriage failed she went to study in Paris under André Lhote on the advice of MAINIE JELLETT. In the early 1930s Norah travelled widely in Europe and visited Egypt and India. In 1933 she held her first solo exhibition in London, where she was based for a time and produced some of her best work, much of it in a Fauvist style. Four years later she went to New York where she exhibited in the Sullivan and Reinhardt Galleries and, following the

example of Salvador Dali, took to designing windows for leading department stores. Back in Ireland, before the outbreak of the Second World War, she settled in Dublin. Her first exhibition at the Royal Hibernian Academy was held in 1940 and, returning naturally to the circle of modernists such as Jellett, EVIE HONE and le Brocquy, she was among those who assisted Jellett in founding the Irish Exhibition of Living Art, of which she became president in 1944, a position she held for many years. Up to this period Norah's main theme had been landscape, with water colour as her preferred medium, but there followed a sustained switch to oils and a step into a semi-abstract style which kept her abreast of the main-stream of European and British painting. In 1950, along with NANO REID, she represented Ireland at the Venice Biennale and later showed in London and Paris. In 1957 she was elected to the Royal Hibernian

Academy. During this period, while she continued to illustrate, design stage sets and shop window displays, Norah's painting took a step further. In the early 1960s the industrial landscape of Dublin Bay and port, presented in her subtly expressionist manner, became the theme which is now often deemed to typify her work. In 1973 she was given an Honorary D. Litt. by Trinity College Dublin. A major retrospective of her work was held in the Douglas Hyde Gallery, Dublin, in 1968. Norah McGuinness died in November 1980.

McKENNA, SIOBHÁN (1922-1986), actress. Born July 24, 1922, Clonard, West Belfast; her father was from Cork and her mother from Co. Longford. She attended a Montessori school in Belfast and was reared in an Irish-speaking home. When Siobhán was eight her father was appointed Professor of Mathematics at Galway University and the family moved to Shantalla, Galway. She continued her education in the Dominican Convent, Galway, St. Louis Convent, Monaghan, and University College Galway, where she captained the University camogie team. While still a student Siobhán began to act in the Irish-language theatre, An Taibhdhearc, playing leading roles and translating Shaw and Barrie into Irish. While studying for an MA in Dublin in 1944, without any ambition to be a professional actress, she was brought into the Abbey Theatre initially to take part in Irish-language plays. Ernest Blyth was Director of the Theatre at the time. But soon she was a full-time actress, working with such 'greats' as MAY CRAIG and F.J McCormick. Siobhán married a fellow Abbey actor twenty years her senior, Denis O'Dea, in 1946. The following year her London debut at the Embassy Theatre in Paul Vincent Carroll's *The White Steed* impressed the critics. She won instant acclaim in a Paramount film, the melodramatic *Daughter of Darkness*, and,

after the birth of her only child Donnacha, in 1948, she made two films in London. Two years work on the English stage with indifferent results led to Siobhán's return to the Taibhdhearc to play the lead in her own Irish translation of Shaw's *St. Joan*. Its production was an outstanding success in Galway and in Dublin's Gaiety. In 1951, under the direction of SHELAH RICHARDS, she first played Pegeen Mike in Synge's *Playboy of the Western World*, one of the roles for which she will be especially remembered. In 1954, playing Shaw's *St. Joan* at the

42. *Siobhan McKenna.*

London Arts Festival, Siobhán took the city by storm and critics prophesied that she might 'become one of the greatest actresses alive.' In 1956 she and Denis starred simultaneously in separate Broadway shows. In America Siobhán was hailed as the 'greatest Joan of our generation' and 'one of the greatest living actresses'. In 1958 the *Evening Standard* (London) named her 'Actress of the year'. By the end of the 1960s, however, her career had gone into decline but she revived it with a one-woman show, *Here are Ladies*, which she had devised from excerpts of Irish poetry, novels and plays. Delighting in the role of *reacaire* (traditional Irish story-teller) as she termed it, Siobhán opened in London, again to ecstatic reviews, and began a four-year worldwide solo marathon which ended with her return to Dublin in 1974 as the most celebrated Irish actress of the modern era. She toured with the Abbey in the US and made several successful visits to the Continent before her final appearance for the Abbey Theatre in 1984 directing and acting in her own production of Merriman's *Cúirt a' Mheán Oíche* in the original Irish. Her last, and possibly greatest, triumph was as Mamo in Tom Murphy's *Bailegangaire*, written especially for her and for Galway's Druid Theatre, where it was played until Siobhán's last stage performance on May 24, 1986. In the same year, on November 16, she died of lung cancer and was buried at Rahoon, Galway.

Siobhan McKenna received many honours in recognition of her services to the arts. Several universities in Ireland and America granted her honorary degrees. She campaigned against internment without trial in Northern Ireland, for the hunger-striking Price sisters and Bobby Sands, for the wrongly imprisoned Nicky Kelly, against apartheid, and against the destruction of the archaeologically important Wood Quay area in Dublin. Despite her involvement in such controversies, the President of Ireland, Dr. Cearbhall Ó Dálaigh, invited her to serve on the Council of State, the first artist to do so. She is generally considered to have been the foremost of all Irish actresses, able to bear comparison to such internationally acclaimed artistes as Ellen Terry and Sarah Bernhardt.

McLOUGHLIN, KATHERINE (mid-17th century), Quaker evangelist. Born Coleraine, Co. Antrim, of 'Irish parents of account, and sent to Londonderry for education'. At sixteen, she went to Barbados, easternmost island of the West Indies, where she married a man named Norton. Hearing George Fox, the founder of the Society of Friends (Quakers), preach there, Katherine was 'convinced' and became a preacher. In 1678 she returned to Ireland where the Quaker movement had been taking root since the Cromwellian conquest. At a time when Quakers were undergoing severe persecution from the British authorities and the established church, she held meetings in houses and market places all over Ulster. Although the vast majority of Quakers in Ireland were English or Scottish, it is recorded that she preached in Irish at the Lurgan marketplace. According to Anthony Sharpe, a contemporary Quaker personality, 'she stayed in the north, for some time and was of great service here, and some were convinced by her and we had very large meetings.'

MacMANUS, ANNA. See under CARBERY, ETHNA.

MacNEILL, MÁIRE (1904-1987), folklorist. Born in Dublin of northern Ireland parentage. Her father, Eoin MacNeill, a clerk in the Dublin law courts and a founder member of the Gaelic League (1893), was to become Professor of Early Irish History at UCD four years after her birth; chief-of-staff of the Irish Volunteers in the approach to the 1916 Rebellion and Minister for Education in the first Free State Government, he was appointed chairman of the Irish Manuscripts Commission in 1927. Máire's mother, Agnes Moore, was from Belfast and novelist Brian Moore was a cousin. Being reared in a bilingual household, holidaying in the Omeath (Co. Down) *breac-Ghaeltacht* (where her father ran a Gaelic Summer College) and taking part in Gaelic League activities gave Máire a grounding in Gaelic culture and language that was unusual for a child growing up in metropolitan Dublin. When her father was sentenced to penal servitude for life (he was released after a year in the general amnesty), Máire was sent for a time to live in the Irish-speaking Aran Islands in Galway Bay; during the War of Independence she was sent to boarding-school in Dublin. Máire graduated with a BA degree in Celtic studies from UCD in 1923 and, finding no suitable outlet for her talents, worked as a journalist, sub-editor, and secretary, for a decade. Then, in 1935, she was invited to join the staff of the recently-founded Cumann Béaloideasa Éireann (Irish Folklore Commission), financed by the government to record living folklore from the oral tradition which was on the verge of extinction. Under the direction and inspiration of the great Antrim-born folklorist, Séamus Ó Duilearga, Máire spent fourteen years as part of a team of dedicated workers who, in endeavouring to preserve a priceless heritage for the Irish nation, gathered one of the world's greatest stores of folklore. She married John L. Sweeney, a Harvard University academic, poet, and art collector, in 1949, and moved to Boston, Massachusetts, USA, where she was attached to the Department of Celtic Studies at Harvard University. In 1962 she published *The Festival of Lughnasa*, a deep and wide-ranging study of the Irish 'Garland Sunday' harvest festival and its mythological origins; the result of many years research, the book is recognised as being one of the most important explorations of its kind. Máire and her husband made their home in Co. Clare when they retired in 1965. She continued with her researches and writings in folklore and history and published three other books: *Fairy Legends from Donegal* (1977), *Seán Ó Conaill's Book* (1981),

both translations of collections of folktales published in Irish by Seán Ó hEochaigh and Séamus Ó Duilearga, respectively, and *Máire Rua, Lady of Leamaneh* (1990), a study of the famous seventeenth century Clare aristocrat, MÁIRE RUA O'BRIEN. Máire MacNeill died on May 15, 1987, and left, to the National Gallery of Ireland, a collection of modern art worth some ten million pounds known as the Sweeney Bequest.

MacSWINEY, MARY (MÁIRE NIC SHUIBHNE) (1872-1942), republican. Born in Surrey, England, on March 27, 1872, of a Cork father and an English mother, both teachers. She was reared in Cork to which her father had returned to start a tobacco factory. When this venture failed he emigrated to Australia where he soon died. Her mother, assisted by Mary who was the eldest of seven children, opened a shop in Cork city. At twenty Mary obtained a loan from a student's aid society and was admitted to a teacher-training programme normally reserved for men, in Cambridge University, England. She taught in London for some time then returned to Cork, on the death of her mother, to look after the younger members of the family and found employment there as a teacher. Increasingly influenced, both culturally and politically, by her revolutionary younger brother, Terence, she joined the Gaelic League, the Irish-language revival movement, and Inghinidhe na hÉireann, the radical nationalist women's organisation later to form the basis of Cumann na mBan. She was also an active member of the Munster Women's Franchise League up to 1914 when she left the suffrage movement because it appeared to support the British war effort. She was a member of the Executive of Cumann na mBan when it was formed, in 1914, to advance the cause of Irish liberty through armed resistance and was arrested in her classroom during the

1916 Rising. The Bishop of Cork effected an early release for women prisoners; Mary, however, was dismissed from her teaching post. Borrowing two hundred pounds, she established her own school with the help of her sister. This school, St. Ita's, was located in her home and modelled on the famous St. Enda's boys school founded by Patrick Pearse in Dublin. As an active Sinn Féin member Mary campaigned for Terence when he was elected to the first Dáil Éireann in 1918 and, in 1920, supported his fatal hunger strike in Brixton Prison, England. She then visited the USA to give evidence before the American Commission on Conditions in Ireland. For nine months she and Terence's widow, Muriel, toured America lecturing and giving interviews, providing invaluable publicity to the republican cause. In the General Elections of May 1921, as president of Cumann na mBan, Mary MacSwiney was one of the Sinn Féin candidates swept to victory in a wave of support for the party. During the Dáil debates which followed the Treaty negotiations Mary and the other five women TDs (members of the Irish Parliament) remained committed to the political goal of an Irish Republic and irrevocably opposed any compromise on total independence from Britain. Her speeches were among the longest and most bitter, calling on the Dail not to commit, "the one unforgivable crime that has ever been committed by the representatives of the people of Ireland" by accepting a treaty which required an oath of allegiance to the British monarchy. After the Treaty was ratified Cumann na mBan, following a resolution by Mary, was the first national organisation to reject the formation of the Free State. She was elected again to the third Dáil which, owing to the outbreak of the Civil War, was never to sit. In July 1922 she was imprisoned by the Free State authorities, went on hunger strike, and was released. She then toured the country on behalf of the Republicans and ran the Republican headquarters in Cork until she was jailed again. She was released after twenty-one days on hunger-strike.

After the ceasefire, she retained her seat in the General Election of 1923 but, in common with the other Republican deputies, refused to take the oath of allegiance required under the constitution of the Free State. She also refused to join with Éamon de Valera when he broke with Sinn Féin in 1926 to form a new Republican party, Fianna Fáil, which would partake in institutional politics within the Free State; subsequently, in 1927, Mary suffered her first election defeat. At this time she was still vice-president of Sinn Féin and Cumann na mBan but both organisations were now spent forces, inhibited by their policy of 'principled abstensionism' from the Dáil on the one hand and their rejection of radical social reform on the other. She continued to advocate militant opposition to the Free State and witnessed the remnants of Sinn Féin turn to a new and desperate militarism in 1939 with an IRA bombing campaign in England. Mary MacSwiney died on March 8, 1942, at her home in Cork. Her stance both before and after the Treaty may be summed up by her statement that "a rebel is one who opposes lawfully constituted authority and that I have never done".

MAEVE, QUEEN. See under MEDB, QUEEN.

MARKIEVICZ, COUNTESS CONSTANCE, née GORE-BOOTH, (1868-1927), revolutionary, labour activist and politician. Born February 4, 1868, at Buckingham Gate, London, daughter of Sir Henry Gore-Booth, explorer and philanthropist, and heir to extensive estates in Lissadell, Co. Sligo. The Gore-Booths, recognised as model landlords, were descended from 18th century planters and boasted of antecedents in

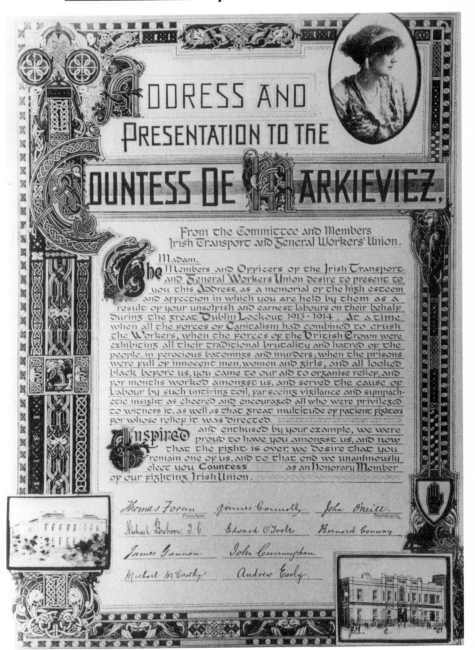

43. *Address and presentation to* **Countess Constance Markievicz** *from the Irish Transport and General Workers Union, 1913.*

Ireland since Tudor times. When Sir Henry inherited his estates the family settled in Lissadell, where Constance and her younger sister, EVA GORE-BOOTH, were educated by governesses. The young W.B Yeats was a frequent visitor. Constance, who had a reputation as a horsewoman and a crack shot, was presented at the court of Queen Victoria when she was nineteen and took her place in society. She intended to be an artist and, in 1893, went to London to study at the Slade School and to Paris, in 1898, to the Julian School. Here she met her future husband, Count Casimir Dunin Markievicz, a practising artist from a wealthy land-owning family of Polish extraction in the Ukraine. The couple settled in Dublin in 1903. They had one daughter, Maeve, born in Lissadell in 1901, who was reared by her grandparents and became estranged from her mother. Constance and her husband soon became part of the artistic and social life of the capital. She began to make a name as a landscape artist. (Her work is represented in the Municipal Gallery, Dublin.) Together with the Count and Ellen Duncan she founded the United Arts Club in 1905 to 'crystallize the renaissance then going on in Dublin'. Constance, sharing her husband's growing interest in the theatre, acted in several plays he wrote for the Abbey Theatre. However, increasingly frustrated by what she considered a frivolous existence, and demanding that 'nature should provide me with something to live for, something to die for', she was drawn into the rapidly-developing political and social events of the time. Influenced by Eva, her suffragist sister in England, Constance joined forces with her and stood for election in Manchester in 1908, unsuccessfully opposing Winston Churchill. She had already been somewhat involved with Inghinidhe na hÉireann, the radical women's organisation founded by MAUD GONNE. In 1909 she founded Fianna Éireann, an organi-

sation of boy scouts and effectively the youth movement of the Irish Republican Brotherhood without which, according to Patrick Pearse, 'the Volunteers of 1913 would not have arisen.' By 1911 she was an executive member of both Inghinidhe and Sinn Féin, and in that year was arrested with HELENA MOLONEY for her part in demonstrations against the visit of the British monarch, George V. Increasingly concerned with issues of social justice, Constance supported labour leaders Larkin and Connolly, and took part in the successful campaign to force the authorities to accept responsibility for the welfare of poor Irish children by extending the Provision of Meals Act to Ireland. She organised a soup kitchen in Liberty Hall during the lockout of unionised workers in 1913 following which she was elected honorary treasurer of the Irish Citizen Army. She was instrumental in bringing the Inghinidhe into the militant women's organisation, Cumann na mBan, founded to support the Irish Volunteers. About this time her husband went to the Balkans as a war correspondent and later served as a cavalry officer in the Russian Imperial Army. In the 1916 Rising, Constance was initially a member of the Citizen Army Ambulance Corps but, appointed second in command to Michael Mallin in St. Stephen's Green, she took part in the actual fighting. At her trial she pleaded guilty saying, "I did what I thought was right and I stand by it." Her death sentence was commuted to penal servitude for life on account of her sex. In the General Amnesty of 1917 she was released to a heroine's welcome in Dublin and was made a freeman of Sligo. Her experiences in prison hastened Constance's conversion to Roman Catholicism. In the same year, when Sinn Féin became unequivocally republican, she was elected to its executive. Shortly afterwards, she was jailed again for her part in the anti-conscription campaign.

In the General Election of December 1918, while still in prison in England, she successfully stood as a Sinn Féin candidate for St. Patrick's, a working class division in Dublin. She was the first woman in history to be elected to the British House of Commons but refused to take her seat in accordance with party policy; two months later she was elected to the first Dáil Éireann, the Irish parliament convened in defiance of the British government. As its first Minister of Labour she had to go on the run, like her fellow ministers, and was jailed twice during her period of office. After the Truce she was given early release to take part in the Treaty debates. During the debates, only she and Liam Mellows spoke for the working class interests; she attacked the 'deliberate attempt to set up a privileged class' contrary to the ideal envisioned in the 1916 Republican Proclamation. Under her leadership Cumann na mBan rejected the Treaty, the first national organisation to do so. In the General Elections that followed she lost her parliamentary seat. During the Civil War, the Countess took part in the fighting in Moran's Hotel in the centre of Dublin; later she toured the US to enlist support for the repubiican cause. After the unconditional surrender of the Republicans in 1923, she regained her seat in the Dáil. She was again arrested while campaigning for the release of political prisoners, but, joining in a mass hunger-strike, she was freed after a month. Without consideration for her failing health, she attempted to get Cumann na mBan to regroup in a further campaign to establish a republic. However, when Eámon de Valera broke with Sinn Féin in 1926 to form Fianna Fáil, she presided over the public launching of the new republican party and was elected for it to the Dáil in 1927. On July 15 of the same year Constance died after a short illness in a public ward in Sir Patrick Dunn's Hospital, Dublin, with her husband and daughter at her side. She was given a huge funeral, her coffin followed by eight lorryloads of flowers from the ordinary citizens of Dublin who lined the streets in their thousands. Countess Markievicz was buried in Glasnevin Cemetery, Dublin.

MARTIN, MOTHER MARY (1892-1975), founder of the Medical Missionaries of Mary. Born Glenageary, Co. Dublin. Her father, a wealthy timber merchant, was a member of a noted Dublin business family. She was educated at the Sacred Heart Convent, Leeson Street, Dublin, and the Holy Child College, Harrowgate, Yorkshire. As a young woman during the First World War she was a Voluntary Aid Nurse and saw service in Malta and France as well as in England. Convinced that her vocation in life lay in the service of the sick, she returned to Dublin after the armistice and trained as a midwife in the National Maternity Hospital, Holles Street, Dublin. In 1921 she went to Calabar, Nigeria, following a call for volunteer workers by the Roman Catholic missionary, Bishop Shanahan. Working in appalling conditions, she conceived the idea of forming an order of nuns who would devote themselves to medical work, especially in the area of obstetrics and surgery; at that time Rome forbid its women religious from engaging in these areas of medicine. On Shanahan's advice she returned to Ireland after two years and entered a religious order as a novice, only to leave again on the advice of her spiritual director. She suffered a long period of ill health but continued to work towards the realization of her dream, building up a small network of followers. Offered the position of matron at a new Benedictine school at Glenstal Abbey, Co. Limerick, she accepted on condition that she and her colleagues would receive spiritual guidance from the monks. After three years, following a relaxation of the papal rule regarding women religious and medical work she set up, at the age of forty-five, her embryonic medical order in the basement of her mother's home in Monkstown, Co. Dublin before answering a request from Bishop Mynagh of Calabar, to go with her companions to the Southern Nigerian town of Anua. Although extremely ill with malaria and a subsequent heart attack, Mother Mary received her vows from Dr. Moynagh in Port Harcourt Hospital in April 1937 and the Medical Missionaries of Mary was canonically erected as a religious congregation. Almost immediately she was sent back to Ireland for medical treatment. From her hospital bed, the nun recruited novices, directed their religious and medical training, and organised fund-raising. As the order flourished in Africa, a student house was opened in Booterstown, Co. Dublin, a novitiate at Collon, Co. Louth, and a maternity hospital in Drogheda, Co. Louth. The International Missionary Training Hospital was established in Drogheda in 1957. Today, as well as running hospitals throughout much of Africa, the Medical Missionaries of Mary are active in Italy, Spain and in the USA. Mother Mary Martin received many honours, including the Florence Nightingale Medal of the International Red Cross (1963), and was the first woman to be made an honorary Fellow of the Royal College of Surgeons in Ireland (1966), in recognition of her 'singular achievements in the field of medical missions.' After forty-five years suffering from a serious heart condition, she died on January 27, 1975, in the training hospital she had founded in Drogheda. Possibly Mother Mary's greatest achievement lay in paving the way for Roman Catholic women religious to undertake comprehensive medical study and practice, going beyond the nursing work to which they had previously been restricted.

MARTIN, MARY LETITIA (1815-1850), 'Princess of Connemara', novelist. Born August 28, 1815, at Ballinahinch Castle, Co. Galway, seat of a branch of the landowning Martin family who, although Roman Catholics in the early 18th century, had been exempted from much of the Penal Laws. Originally a Norman family who were one of the 'Tribes of Galway', the Martins of Ballinahinch were known as the 'Princes of Connemara'. The novelist's grandfather, 'Humanity' Dick, foremost in founding the Royal Society for the Prevention of Cruelty to Animals, was noted for his generosity as much as for the 200,000 acres of his estate. Mary Letitia published her first book, *St. Etienne, a Tale of the Vendean War*, in 1845. During the Famine, she assisted her father, Thomas Barnewell Martin, MP, who spent vast sums of money to feed and clothe tenants and provide relief work for hundreds of labourers. In 1847 she married a penniless gentleman, Arthur Gonne Bell, Brookside, Co. Mayo. In the same year her father died and she discovered he had mortgaged her inheritance. She was unable to meet the repayments in the aftermath of the Famine and lost the entire property in the Encumbered Estates Court. The couple went to Fontaine L'Évêque in Belgium to escape their creditors. She turned to writing novels to support herself and her family. *Julia Howard, a Romance* appeared in 1850; it is notable for its autobiographical content in the Famine context. The author, with her husband and family, sailed to New York in 1850 hoping to improve their situation but, contracting childbed fever, she died on reaching New York on November 7, 1850.

MARTIN, VIOLET FLORENCE. See under ROSS, MARTIN.

MAUDE, CAITLÍN (1941-1982), poet, actress, singer, political campaigner. Born May 22, 1941, in Na Doiriú, Casla, in the Gaeltacht of Conamara. Her father was a land owner in nearby Cillbhriocáin, Rosmuc, and her mother taught in the local national school. Her maternal grandmother had a reputation as a poet and a song maker and Caitlín began to write poetry at secondary school in Spiddal, Co. Galway, and Mountmellick, Co. Laois. While studying for a BA degree at University College Galway, she gained recognition as a *sean-nós* singer and actress. After qualifying Caitlín caused a stir in the greater Irish-language world, not only because of the passionate quality of her acting and singing, but because she epitomised in her lifestyle and in her outspoken views the 'liberated' young woman of the sixties. In 1964, the vitality of her acting in the lead role of Mairéad Ní Ghráda's *An Triail,* in the Halla Damer, Dublin, caused a sensation but Caitlín was unable to capitalise on this triumph as the Irish-language theatre of the day could offer little scope for her talents. She taught in several vocational schools throughout the country, while furthering her reputation as a singer and promising poet, but was even more in the news for her involvement in language and political controversies. Before the 1969 General Election Caitlín canvassed for Cearta Sibhialta na Gaeltachta (the civil rights movement for Irish-speaking areas) and later was involved in the campaign to keep Ireland out of the Common Market. She was also a prominent sympathiser with the hunger strikers in Long Kesh prison, Northern Ireland, in 1981, during which ten republican prisoners died while seeking to be granted political status. Caitlín and her husband, Cathal Ó Luain, whom she had married in 1969, were involved in setting up one of the first Gael-Scoileanna (all-Irish schools), in Tallaght, Dublin. In 1975 *Caitlín,* a recording of her *sean-nós* singing, was released under the Gael-Linn label; it contained traditional singing of an outstanding quality. She wrote one drama, *An Lasair Choille,* (in conjunction with the poet Michael Hartnett), and the complete collection of her poems *Caitlín Maude: Dánta* was published

two years after her death from cancer on June 6, 1982. Her collected prose works *Dramaíocht agus Prós, Caitlín Maude,* were published in 1988.

MAURE and BRIGIDA (BRITTA) (*c.* 5th or 6th century), twin martyrs, venerated in Beauvais, France. The original names of these twin sisters were probably Mór and Brigit and various ancient martyrologies and other sources, including the reference by St. Gregory of Tours in *De Gloria Confessorum,* indicate they were Irish. It is possible, however, that they belonged to a Gaelic colony in north Britain. Their father, Alell or Ella (Ailill?), was 'king of Scotia' but was also recorded as king of the Northumbrian area, which was never an Irish colony. Evidently determined on a life of exile for religious reasons, the sisters and a brother, Hispadus or Espian, travelled through England to France and from there to Rome and to the Holy Land before returning to the north-west of France. There is a church dedicated to Maure in Touraine. Early hagiographical writings refer to many wonderful events and miracles associated with the trio. Having arrived at Balagny near Beauvais they were put to death, along with a widow and her son, by a party of barbarian raiders. As early as the mid-sixth century Maure and Brigida were venerated as martyrs. When their relics were being removed to a newly-built monastery, in the ninth century, the oxen were said to have turned away at a crossing still known as Croix de Sainte Maure and so the burial took place at Nugent. In 1185 Pope Urban III directed that the relics be enshrined and granted indulgences for pilgrimage. A century later St. Louis, king of France, had the remains removed to shrines at Beauvais. For several more centuries they were the subject of great veneration, 'especially invoked during the periods of prevailing epidemics and pest.' Their feast day is assigned to July 13 although the old Gallic breviaries and martyrologies, which name them Maria and Brigidona, give January 5. There is much uncertainty, however, in regard to their life with some authorities doubting that the saints venerated in Tours can be equated with those in Beauvais.

MAXWELL, CONSTANTIA (1886-1962), historian, first woman professor at Trinity College Dublin. Born Dublin, and educated at St. Leonard's School, St. Andrew's, Trinity College Dublin, and Bedford College, London. In 1909 she joined the History Department in Trinity College Dublin, and in 1914 published her *Short History of Ireland*. In 1923 she published *Irish History from Contemporary Sources (1509-1610)*, and her edition of Arthur Young's *Tour of Ireland* appeared in 1925. *The English Traveller in France* followed in 1932 and her acclaimed works on the Georgian period, *Dublin Under the Georges* and *Town and Country in Ireland under the Georges*, were produced in 1936 and 1940 respectively. As Professor of Economic History, from 1939 to 1945, she was the first woman to be appointed to a Chair in Trinity College since its foundation in 1592. From 1945 until her retirement in 1951 she was Professor of Modern History and published *History of Trinity College* (1946), and *The Stranger in Ireland from the reign of Elizabeth to the Great Famine*, in 1954. She was, for years, considered the doyenne of Irish historians. Her histories, especially of the Georgian period, constituted a watershed in historical writing, incorporating a broader social perspective. Much of her work has been reprinted since her death. Constantia Maxwell died at Pembury, Kent, England, in February 1962.

MEDB (MEADHBH, MAEVE), (3rd century?), Queen of Connaught, anti-heroine of the saga *Táin Bó Cúailgne*. The name 'Medb' was originally that of a triune goddess of sovereignty and most modern historians have considered the fabled Medb, Queen of Connaught, to have been a typically Gaelic 'incarnation' of the goddess Medb of Cruachain. Cruachain was the place of inauguration for the ancient kings of Connaught: to gain possession of Medb (through a ritual marriage ceremony) was to gain possession of the kingship. It has been shown that in both oral and literary traditions, the story of female rulers tended to become entwined with that of the territorial earth goddess, two outstanding late examples being those of GRÁINNE UÍ MHÁILLE and MÁIRE RUA O'BRIEN. From this perspective, two distinct figures emerge in the case of Medb. Attempts to dismiss the existence of a historical Queen Medb of Connaught are not convincing, especially when one accepts that early traditions reflect historical situations. *Táin Bó Cúailgne*, the main but not the only source of information with regard to Medb, was compiled in the 7th century; the historical Medb possibly belonged to an era some four centuries earlier. She was said to have been the daughter of Eochaid, king of Connaught, and, according to the 11th century *Lebor na hUidhre*, of his chief wife's handmaid who may have been a princess of a sub-people such as the Cruithne or Gailni. After her brothers had been killed in battle, her father set Medb up as Queen of Connaught despite the fact that she was among the younger of his celebrated daughters. Under Brehon Law women were not allowed to inherit land but were entitled to acquire a life interest in their father's property if they had no brothers. The wars depicted in the *Táin*, attributed by tradition to Medb's pride, probably arose as she strove (successfully it seems) to retain full control of her kingdom while also, perhaps, attempting to establish a form of matriarchial succession as practised by the Cruithne people. She was first married to Conor Mac Nessa, king of Ulster, but left him when hostilities broke out between the two provinces. Medb then married Ailill, possibly king of an earlier Lagunian settlement in north Connaught and, after his early death and that of her father, she was left in a position of power. As a mature woman she made a 'royal progress' into neighbouring kingdoms in search of a husband and chose the teenager Ailill, younger son of Rossruadh, king of Leinster, wedding him under the Brehon marriage contract called *Lánamnas Fir For Bantinacur* which set 'the woman in the place of the man'. While their two daughters Findabar and Linabar, may also be merely 'incarnated' goddesses their stories could represent attempts by their mother to establish a matriarchal dynasty. Stories of Medb's numerous other offspring by different lovers, notably by Fergus Mac Róich, the Ulster god-king, most likely originated with the perception of her as a goddess. All traditions of her refer to her pride and ambition and blame her for wars against the Ulster and Leinster provinces but these accounts have come from the enemies of Connaught. While leading her armies in the manner of a Boadicea (the British queen who for a time repulsed the Roman advance) they were not successful overall outside Connaught but neither was her kingdom overwhelmed in her lifetime. Medb is said to have lived to a great age (the Annals of the Four Masters claim one hundred and twenty). She was killed by an assassin's sling shot while taking her daily bath at a spring on her island residence at Inis Clothran. Archaeology has shown that the tradition of her burial under the cairn on Knocknarea, in Co. Sligo, is not a fact but must instead be connected, in some way, with Medb the goddess.

MEREDITH, SUSANNA, née LLOYD (1823-1901), pioneer welfare worker, especially with women criminals. Born in Cork, the daughter of the governor of the county jail. Married at seventeen to a young doctor she was widowed and childless at twenty-four. Subjugating her grief, Susanna engaged in charitable work for unemployed girls such as involving herself in the running of a lace-making industrial school in Cork. At thirty-seven, after her father's death, she moved to London with her mother and started to promote women's rights and needs. She became editor of *The Alexandra*, a journal calling for the improvement of opportunities for women and, through this, highlighted the problem of female unemployment. A chance suggestion led Susanna to take an interest in women prisoners, the pariahs of society. Having obtained permission from the Home Secretary to visit Brixton Prison she was shocked at the conditions but her efforts to improve them were thwarted by prison regulations. She took the practical step of renting a small house opposite the gates of Tothill Fields Prison from where she provided food, moral support, and advice, for the women on their release; soon this service was extended to the provision of some employment, particularily sewing and dressmaking. Susanna set out to raise funds to develop the project but failed to obtain public backing for some time. However, with the support of influential acquaintances, she eventually succeeded in purchasing a large house in South London and a laundry that supplied at least temporary employment for women released from prison. Realizing the plight of the children of women criminals, she pioneered a revolutionary approach to the care of such children by accomodating them in small village-type residential centres, each separate unit having its own house-mother, and with a school, hospital and church as part of the complex. After a successful appeal to have the laws concerning guardianship amended, Susanna opened her first village-home for the children of convicted criminals at Addlestone, Surrey, in 1871. At the same time she continued, as best she could under the regulations, to improve the spiritual and physical welfare of women prisoners. In 1881 she published two books intended to raise public awareness of the situation, A Book about Criminals and Saved Rahab!, which told the story of her own endeavours. Her evidence before the Gladstone Committee on prisons led to some measure of prison reform. Susanna Meredith died at Addlestone in 1901.

MILLIGAN, ALICE (1866-1953), writer, nationalist and Irish revivalist. Born September 14, 1886, at Gortmore, near Omagh, Co. Tyrone, into a wealthy Methodist family. Her father, a commercial traveller and company director, was a member of the Royal Irish Academy, an acknowledged antiquarian and local historian. Her elder sister, CHARLOTTE MILLIGAN FOX, became an important folksong collector. Alice was educated at the Methodist College, Belfast, and King's College, London, before being employed as a governess in the Ladies Collegiate School in Derry. Having made a decision to devote her life to 'Irish-Ireland' ideals she went to Dublin to learn Irish and met Michael Davitt, W.B. Yeats and others who would take part in the Irish Renaissance in general. Alice had been contributing poems to various periodicals and now attempted to make her living as an author, co-writing with her father Glimpses of Erin, a guide book, and writing two novels, A Royal Democrat (1892), and Daughter of Donagh, serialised in United Ireland (1903). She developed a reputation as one of the foremost of Ireland's 'young school of writers' with Return of Lugh Lámhfhada (1893), a long heroic poem, published in United Ireland. Alice was an enthusiastic member of the National Literary Society and the Gaelic League. She co-founded the Henry Joy McCracken Literary Society in Belfast and, under its auspices, she and ETHNA CARBERY

founded and edited the Northern Patriot, a nationalist monthly journal; Alice and Carbery later founded and edited the more radical and widely influential Shan Van Vocht (1896-1899), which advocated separatism and social reform. They published, for example, the earliest writings of James Connolly. In 1898, influenced by William Rooney and MAUD GONNE, Alice became organising secretary for the 1798 centenary commemorations in Ulster and toured the country giving lectures on the United Irishmen. In the same year her Life of Wolfe Tone was published and subsequently her writing, including the poetry, did much to stimulate the early Sinn Féin movement. In 1900 Alice became associated with Inghinidhe na hÉireann and she and Carbery wrote several plays or tableaux for the society. Her play, The Last Feast of the Fianna (with music composed by her sister Charlotte), was staged by the Irish Literary Theatre, forerunner of the Abbey Theatre, in 1900; she was acclaimed as 'the first playwright to dramatise Celtic legend for an Irish audience'. The Escape of Red Hugh (1904), was also a success from which W.B. Yeats 'came away with (his) head on fire'. In the same year Alice took a full-time position with the Gaelic League as an organiser and travelling teacher, but later had to return home to nurse her mother. Although a collection of patriotic verse, Hero Lays, was well-received when published in 1909 Alice gradually receded from the public eye. The Civil War deeply upset her and resulted in her last important poem on a public issue, Till Ferdia Came. She spent many years caring for relatives in Ireland and England before returning, in 1932, to Omagh to live in genteel poverty. In 1938 she was a signatory of a leaflet issued by the Northern Council for Unity protesting against partition. She received an honorary D. Litt. from the National University of Ireland in 1941. Alice Milligan died, poor and lonely, on April 13, 1953, at Tyrcur, Omagh. Bigots have attempted to destroy her headstone in nearby Drumragh churchyard which bears the inscription, Níor car fód eile ac Éirinn ('She loved no other land but Ireland'). Her most famous poem,'When I was a Little Girl' through its vivid evocation of a childhood experience symbolised the conversion of many from Unionist backgrounds to nationalism:

Then the wind-shaken pane
Sounded like drumming;
'Oh!' they cried, 'tuck us in,
The Fenians are coming!'

But one little rebel there,
Watching all with laughter,
Thought, 'When the Fenians come
I'll rise and go after!'

MISSET, MADAME, née GILAGH (c. 1700-c. 1750), one of the party of 'rescuers' of Princess Maria Clementina Sobieski. The daughter of a captain in Count Arthur Dillon's Irish regiment in the service of France, she was 'a gentle woman of Irish birth and extraction, but bred in France'. She was married to a Captain Misset of the same regiment, said to have been an Irish officer but more likely to have been Franco-Irish. Sir Charles Wogan, the Jacobite soldier of fortune from Kildare, was selected by the exiled 'King James III', the Old Pretender, to win him the hand of Princess Clementina Sobieski of Poland. When the Princess was subsequently detained for political reasons in a castle at Innsbruck, Austria, Wogan included Captain Misset and two other Irish officers of Dillon's regiment in the rescue party. To successfully accomplish the mission a chaperone was required for the Princess and Madame Misset, although pregnant, volunteered to act in that capacity. She brought her maid, Janiton, when the party journeyed from France

disguised as merchants. They succeeded in making secret contact with the Princess in Innsbruck and conveyed her in disguise to safety in Italy. Three days later, on September 2, 1719 the royal pair were married. Shortly afterwards, Madame Misset gave birth but the infant did not survive. She does not appear to have had any other children. In December of that year Sir Charles Wogan and Captain Misset went to Spain where they became colonels in the Spanish army. Misset was later made Governor of Oran in North Africa where he died in 1733, and it is presumed that his wife accompanied him throughout his career. She was still alive in 1745 when Wogan wrote an account of the adventure for Marie Leczinsky, Queen of France. Madame Misset was then living in Barcelona where she had retired with her faithful maid, Janiton. It is not known where or when she died.

MITCHELL, SUSAN LANGSTAFF (1888-1926), journalist and poet. Born Carrick-on-Shannon, Co. Leitrim, where her father was a bank manager. After his early death she was sent to live in Dublin with aunts who sent her to a private school in Morehampton Road, Dublin. At intervals she stayed with her mother in Co. Sligo and there became friends with W.B. Yeats. From 1901 she was assistant editor to George Russell (AE) of the *Irish Homestead*, organ of the Irish Agricultural Organisation Society, a co-operative movement founded by Horace Plunkett. Susan played an important role in the life of this influential magazine by contributing many essays and book reviews. AE, her life-long friend, included some of her verses in an anthology and this encouraged her to publish, in 1908, *The Living Chalice* which contained mostly spiritual poetry and *Aids to Immortality of Certain Persons in Ireland*, a collection of witty verse. The latter poked fun at notables in the intellectual and public life of Dublin, especially members of the

44. **Susan Mitchell**, *drawing by George William Russell, c.1920.*

United Arts Club of which she herself was a prominent member. Another collection, *Frankincense and Myrrh,* was published in 1912 and '*Aids*' proved popular enough to merit reprinting in 1913. Susan produced an unflattering study of the novelist George Moore in 1916 and more witty lampoons, *Secret Springs of Dublin Song* in 1918. She was well-known in artistic and intellectual circles and counted many of the great names of the Irish Literary Revival among her friends. Despite a protestant middle-class background Susan was a sincere supporter of early Sinn Féin and served on the executive of the United Irishwomen, an organisation representing the women's counterpart of Plunkett's co-operative movement. In 1921 AE choose her to be his assistant editor on *The Irish Statesman* for which she wrote several pieces. She had never enjoyed robust health and died of cancer in Dublin in 1926.

MODWENA (MONINNA), SAINT (7th century), abbess and missionary. Modwena is the Saxon form of Moninna, given to one of the several holy women of the latter name, the details of whose lives are hopelessly confused. In particular, distinction must be made between this Modwena and the earlier saint MONINNA, who is also named Blinne. Modwena was, it appears, an abbess in an unidentified site in Ireland when she received the request from the Saxon King, Aldfrid, who had studied for many years in Ireland, to be the second abbess of Whitby on the death of its founder, Hilda, about 680. The King's sister Elfeda entered the convent and trained under Modwena until such time as she could succeed as abbess. Modwena is said to have also founded other convents in Northern Britain: according to *Holingshed's Chronicles* (16th century), 'manie monasteries she builded both in England and Scotland, as at Striveling, Edenbrough, and in Ireland at Celisline and elsewhere.' Some authorities hold that she is the Modwena whose remains were removed to Burton-on-Trent when an abbey was founded there in 1004; if that is so, then she was the saint who was recorded as having her hermitage on an island in the river Trent for seven years. Modwena's feast day is on July 8.

MOLONEY, HELENA (1884-1967), socialist, republican and trade unionist. Born Dublin. Helen was strongly nationalist-minded while still in her teens and rushed to support MAUD GONNE'S 'black petticoat' protest on the occasion of a visit to the Irish capital by King Edward VII. Shortly afterwards, in 1903, she joined Maud Gonne's radical women's organisation Inghinidhe na hÉireann (Daughters of Erin), acting as secretary for a time. In 1908 she was co-founder and editor of the association's journal *Bean na hÉireann*, which advocated 'militancy, separatism, feminism' and was the first women's newspaper ever in Ireland. Her growing interest in the labour movement was reflected in the paper's advocacy of social reform and socialist ideas. In 1909 Helena joined the Abbey Theatre Company but her acting career over the following decade was to be interrupted and finally ended by her political activities. Also in 1909, she assisted COUNTESS MARKIEVICZ to set up Na Fianna, the youth movement of the Irish Republican Brotherhood, and took part in the ultimately successful Inghinidhe campaign to force Dublin Corporation to provide meals for school children. Helena was closely linked with James Connolly and the Socialist Party of Ireland. She appeared with him at protest rallies against the visit of King George V and was arrested, during a Sinn Féin protest, for throwing a stone at a picture of the monarch. This made her the first woman jailed in Ireland for a political act since the Ladies Land League almost three decades previously. On her release she was almost immediately jailed for a seditious speech and just as quickly released as the authorities feared they would create a *cause célèbre*. During the 1913 Lock Out, when Dublin employers attempted to starve the trade union movement into submisssion, she worked in the soup kitchens set up in Liberty Hall, the union's headquarters, under the supervision of Countess Markievicz. This experience brought Moloney, the Countess and others further into the labour movement. In 1915, at the request of James Connolly, she became secretary of the Irish Women's Workers Union (IWWU). In the fateful year of 1916 she joined the Citizen Army, becoming a commissioned officer and member of the army council. She was one of nine women and ten men who took part in an attack, under the command of her fellow actor and close friend Seán Connolly, on Dublin Castle, the British military headquarters, during the 1916 Rebellion. When the attack failed the unit occupied City Hall where, with Connolly shot dead, Helena organised the area for a commissariat and hospital. Later she got through the British army cordon to ask for reinforcements from the rebels' supreme command in the General Post Office. After the surrender she was imprisoned in Aylesbury Jail, in England, but was released after eight months. In 1917 she was involved in the efforts to unite all the nationalist movements, culminating at the momentous Sinn Féin Ard Fheis (party congress) which committed itself to the republican ideal. During the Civil War she supported the republican side. After the war she continued as organiser of the IWWU and became the first woman to be made president of the Irish Trade Union Congress. In the early 1930s she was much involved in the politics of the far left and was one of the four women on the executive of Saor Éire, a short-lived breakaway republican socialist organisation. Despite the Coercion Acts against republicans in the early 1930s, she campaigned vigorously as a member of the Women's Prisoners' Defense League and People's Rights Association, especially by holding illicit public meetings. Concentrating thereafter on trade union activities she took part in one more political battle, the unsuccessful campaign against the Conditions of Employment Bill, brought in by the newly-elected Fianna Fáil Government in 1935, and regarded by women in general as an attack on their rights. Ill health forced Helena Moloney to retire in 1946. She died on January 28, 1967.

MONINNA (MO-NINNE) or BLINNE (BLÁTHNAIDH), SAINT (5th and 6th century), virgin saint. There is much confusion in the various religious lives and acts between the holy woman of this name and SAINT MODWENA, and perhaps even a third near-contemporary. Moninna, it seems, was one of the numerous holy women of the 5th century baptised by St. Patrick. She was born in the Louth area, almost certainly of noble blood, and became a Christian as a child. Moninna was a term of endearment substituted for her early name Der Erca. Later it appears that she and nine female associates, having first attempted to follow some form of religious rule in seclusion in their homes, transferred to Begerin in Wexford where they lived under the direction of St. Ibar. There was a connection also between Moninna and SAINT BRIGID, apparent in the fact that Moninna founded a convent at Faughart near Dundalk, the area which may have been Brigid's birthplace and has other Brigidine associations. Apparently Moninna moved northwards to the wilderness at Cill Shléibhe (Killeavy), on Sliabh Gullion mountain in Co. Armagh, where she lived a life distinguished by asceticism. Many women joined her hermitage and, through her sanctity and wisdom, she appears to have exerted an enormous influence on events outside her enclosure, contributing greatly to the advance of Christianity in mid-Ulster. Her foundations were the earliest recorded in Ireland after St. Brigid's. 'Blinne' and 'Bláthnaidh' are modern forms of the saint's name and are sometimes anglicised to 'Blanche'. Her feast day is on July 6.

MONTEZ, LOLA, stage-name of MARIE DOLORES ELIZA ROSANNA GILBERT (1818-1861), dancer and courtesan. Born in Limerick where her father, a British army officer, was stationed. She was taken to live in Britain and educated in Scotland and Paris. While still in her teens Marie eloped to Ireland with an army officer. The marriage ended after a few years and she was left almost destitute. In 1843 she appeared in London as 'Lola Montez, the Spanish dancer', evidently with little success; some time later, however, she made a big impact in Dresden and Berlin. Lola danced in St. Petersburg and in Paris where she began a liason with a young republican activist who was killed in a duel. By 1847 she was attracting large audiences in Germany and captivated the ageing King Ludwig I of Bavaria, in Munich. He made her Countess of Landsfeld with an estate of five thousand pounds a year, feudal rights over two thousand people, and gave her one of his magnificent castles. In the prevailing unstable political situation she was used to influence the king into introducing liberal and extravagant changes and opposing the Jesuits. The 1848 Revolution led to the confiscation of her estate and banishment. She married another army officer who died within two years. From 1851 to 1853 Lola toured America as a dancer. She toured Australia next and gained further notoriety for publicly horsewhipping the editor of the *Ballarat Times* who had made her conduct the basis of an editorial on public morality. Back in America, after another short-lived marriage, she toured the country lecturing on such subjects as gallantry, beautiful women, and heroines in history. She also wrote a few minor novels and *The Art of Beauty* (1858), which was translated into French. *Autobiography and Lectures of Lola Montez* also proved popular when it appeared in the same year. In 1859, influenced by the example of a childhood friend, Lola underwent a radical conversion and devoted the last years of her life to the poor and especially to the care of inmates of the Magdalen Asylum, New York. On January 17, 1861, not yet forty-five years of age, she died in poverty at Asteria, New York.

MOONEY, RIA (1904-1973), actress and producer. Born in Dublin. She began her stage career at six and, while still a teenager, made her name in her native city as a promising actress. After playing in Chekov's *Proposal*, Ria was invited to join the Abbey Theatre Company at the age of twenty.

45. **Ria Mooney** *directing in the Abbey Theatre, Dublin, 1951.*

Seán O'Casey's choice of her to play the prostitute, Rosie Redmond, in the first production of *The Plough and the Stars* was vindicated, not only by her memorable performance, but also her defiance of the play's critics in the controversy that followed when even the threat of kidnap hung over her head. Twenty years later she was to back O'Casey again in the controversy which accompanied his *Red Roses for* *Me* which she directed. Ria toured the USA with MOLLY ALLGOOD and remained there for some years as assistant director of the Civic Repertory Theatre in New York. On her return she joined Dublin's Gate Theatre Company and later specialised in the production of verse plays at the Abbey and Peacock for Austin Clarke's Dublin Verse-Speaking Society/Lyric Theatre Company. In 1944 she became director of the

Gaiety Theatre School of Acting. Returning to the Abbey, as its first woman producer, she remained the theatre's resident director for fifteen years. One of the greatest performances of her later years came in O'Neill's *Long Day's Journey into Night* in 1962. Ria Mooney died in January 1973, in Dublin.

MOONEY, ROSE (*c.* 1740-*c.* 1810), harpist. Born in Co. Meath about the time Turlough O'Carolan died. Nothing is known of Rose's background or youth except that she went blind and so was trained to become a musician. Among her teachers was Thady Elliot, a brilliant but unpredictable itinerant harper also from Meath. Although it was not uncommon at the time for women harpers to perform as semi-professionals in the houses of the landed gentry, Rose was possibly unique in that, attended by her maid Mary, she seems to have travelled over a wide area of north Leinster and south Ulster in the manner of the professional itinerant male musicians of the period. In 1781 she took part in the 'Grand Ball' or competition in Granard, Co. Longford, instituted for the encouragement and preservation of harp music by Granard-born James Dungan, a wealthy merchant of Copenhagen. Rose was the only woman of the nine competitors and took third prize. She repeated this feat at the 'Grand Balls' of the following two years. She also participated in the four-day Harper's Festival in Belfast, organised on July 10, 1792, by the 'estimable citizens of Belfast' who had established the Belfast Harp Society the previous year. This festival took place in the Assembly Rooms to an audience of 'Ladies and Gentlemen of the first fashion in Belfast city and its vicinity'. Edward Bunting, stimulated by the festival into embarking on his systematic collection of native music, collected airs from Rose at this time and again in 1800. Some of these were published in Bunting's *General Collection of Ancient Irish Music* (1796) and in its extended edition (1809). What little else is known of Rose Mooney's life is summed up by Captain Francis O'Neill in his monumental work *Irish Music and Musicians* (1913): 'she sacrificed her popularity and, in a sense her life, for conviviality.'

MORGAN, LADY SYDNEY, née OWENSON (*c.* 1776-1859), novelist, travel writer. Said to have been born on the mail boat in the Irish Sea on Christmas Day, 1776. Daughter of an Irish actor-manager, Robert Owenson, and an English mother. Her father, who changed his name from MacOwen for stage purposes, was the product of a run-away marriage between a ne'er-do-well farmer and the daughter of gentry from Tyrawley, Co. Mayo. He had returned to Ireland to make a career on the stage and, for some time, was a notable figure who presented entertainment with a genuine Irish flavour. Sydney's early childhood years were spent in Drumcondra, Dublin; after her mother's death, she and her sister were sent to a Huguenot Academy in Clontarf, Dublin. She published her first volume of poems at the age of fourteen. When her father was bankrupted she became governess in the house of landed gentry in Bracklyn, Co. Westmeath. Sydney developed a reputation as a harpist in the big houses of the area and, in 1805, achieved national prominence with *12 Original Hibernian Melodies*, one of the earliest collections of Irish music. She had published her first novel years earlier and, in 1806, followed it with *The Wild Irish Girl*, which brought her both fame and fortune. The story was based on events in her father's family and the time she had spent with relatives in the west of Ireland. The book was praised by the Roman Catholic faction in Dublin for its 'nationalist sentiments' and by the liberals for its

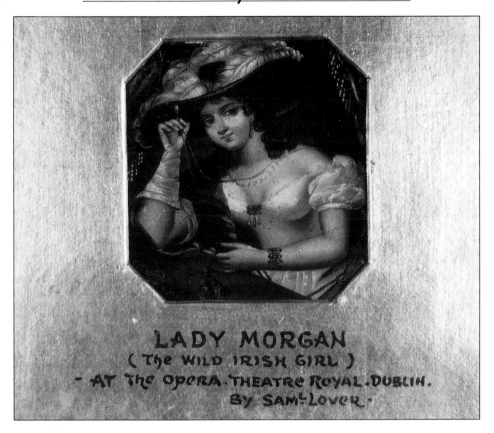

46. Sydney Morgan.

'progressive views'. The vivacious author became known as 'Glorvina' after the heroine in her book and as such was the social rage of Dublin. The cult of the 'Wild Irish Girl' spread to London, where Sydney's various talents made her a star in fashionable society. She accepted the invitation of the Marquis and Marchioness of Abercorn to be their permanent guest and was later persuaded to marry their physician, Thomas Charles Morgan. The Abercorns arranged a knighthood for her husband and the travelling actor's daughter became Lady Morgan. She continued to write and made a considerable fortune from her next book,

O'Donnell - A National Tale, which presented the case for Roman Catholic emancipation. Returning to Dublin, she set up a salon at her house in Kildare Street. In 1816 she published the four-volume *Florence Macarthy: An Irish Tale*, generally accepted as her finest novel. In the same year, the Morgans made an extended visit to the Continent, where, with her liberal and republican views, Sydney made her mark on Parisian society. Her book *France* (1817), rapidly translated into French, caused controversy in both England and France and ran into at least four editions in two years. When offered two thousand pounds by her publisher for a book on

Italy she spent a year in that country before returning to Dublin and publishing *Italy* in 1821. This provoked an even more violent reaction than her earlier book and was banned by the Pope, the Emperor of Austria and King of Sardinia because of its exposure of misrule and corruption. Over the next decade Sydney wrote several other lengthy novels and two non-fiction works, *The Book of Boudoir* (1829) and *Woman and her Master* (1840) but her appeal as an author declined rapidly in this period. Her husband lost his position as physician to the Marshalsea Prison, and, in 1837, she gladly accepted a pension of three hundred pounds a year from the British prime minister, Lord Melbourne, for her services to the world of letters - making her the first woman writer to be so honoured. She and her husband left Dublin in 1839 for Belgravia, London, where her salon again became prominent. Lady Sydney Morgan died in 1859 and was buried in Brompton Cemetry, London. In her will she left considerable sums of money to aid actors and governesses in distress, as well as one hundred pounds for a marble plaque to the memory of Carolan the harper in St. Patrick's Cathedral, Dublin. Much autobiographical material was published in the years following her death.

MORIARITY, JOAN DENISE (*c.* 1920-1992), ballet choreographer and composer, founder of the Irish National Ballet. Born Mallow, Co. Cork. The details of her early life are obscure. She is believed to have been the illegitimate daughter of a Lord Chief Justice of Appeal for Ireland. Joan spent some time in an orphanage in north England before being fostered by relatives in Cork. She studied dance from the age of six, and later trained with Mme. Espinosa and Dame Marie Rambert in London. She made her début in the old Cork Opera House as a teenager and, in the early 1940s, was teaching dance and taking

a small troupe on stage at pantomimes and cinema matinees; she played the Irish war-pipes as a novelty act. In 1945 Joan opened her first ballet school, later to become the Cork Ballet Company, which gave its first performance at the Cork Opera House in 1947. For some time she was a protégée of Aloys Fleischmann, composer and Professor of Music at University College Cork, who was attempting to set up an orchestra in the city; the collaboration of the amateur ballet troupe with the amateur orchestral society and Moriarity's personal relationship with Fleischmann, which was to be life-long, set her on the road to fame. The 1951 ballet Week in the Cork Opera House, their joint production, was a breakthrough for ballet in Ireland. In 1959 Joan founded a professional company but it failed financially within five years. She vowed to get government support to fund a future professional company and spent a decade lobbying for a grant. Finally receiving £40,000, in February 1973, she formed the Irish Ballet Company which began its inaugural season at the Cork Opera House in January 1974. The programme contained her own work *Billy the Music*, set to the music of Seán Ó Riada. Joan worked in conjunction with Ó Riada on many of the ballets she composed with Irish themes. Her first full-length work, a dance version of Synge's *Playboy of the Western World*, was premièred at the Dublin Theatre Festival in 1978 and later played at the City Centre Theatre, New York. It was revived with music by the Chieftains, at the Sadler's Wells Theatre, London, for the 1980 'Sense of Ireland Festival'. When invited by the Taoiseach to create a short work for the Pádraic Pearse Centenary in 1979, Joan choreographed *Diúltú (Renunciation)* to the music of John Buckley. In 1981 her second full length work, *The Táin*, was produced at the Dublin Theatre Festival, and *Reputations* was commissioned by RTÉ. In 1983 her Irish Ballet Company, still Cork-

47. *Joan Denise Moriarty demonstrating in her Cork Dance Studio, 1987.*

based, became the Irish National Ballet, setting the seal on her long battle to establish ballet in Ireland. However, difficulties arose with the Arts Council, the main funding agency, and Joan resigned her position as artistic director in 1985; four years later, the Irish National Ballet had to be disbanded. From 1985 she devoted herself full-time to the amateur Cork Ballet Company and School she had founded some four decades previously. She was awarded an LL.D. from the National University of Ireland in 1979, in recognition of her work for ballet, and the Harvey's of Bristol Award in 1982 for outstanding service to Irish Theatre. Joan Moriarty died in Beaumont Hospital, Dublin, on 25 June 1992.

MORROGH-BERNARD, AGNES (MOTHER MARY JOSEPH ARSENIUS) (1842-1932), founder of Foxford Woollen Mills. Born February 24, 1842, in Cheltenham, England. Her father was from a landed Cork family and her mother was a member of an old English Roman Catholic family. Shortly after her birth the family moved to Cork city and, some years later, to Co. Kerry where her father had inherited the Bernard estates at Sheheree House. Agnes attended Laurel Hill Convent, Limerick, before completing her education in Paris. On her return to Ireland she took her place in south Munster society and gained a reputation as a horsewoman and musician. At twenty-one she entered the noviciate of the Irish Sisters of Charity and was professed as Sr. Mary Joseph Arsenius in 1868. For more than a decade she

48. *Agnes Morrogh-Bernard on the day of her profession, 1866.*

worked in several Dublin schools, mostly in slum areas, and in an orphanage. In the late 1870s she was made Rectoress of the Convent of the Sisters of Charity, Ballaghaderreen, Co. Roscommon. When bad harvests and a depression in Britain - which discouraged immigration - caused extreme economic need in the area the nuns not alone nursed the sick during fever outbreaks but also set up a school, laundry, bakery and pharmacy. They also established an industrial school containing a small textile factory. In 1881 Mother Mary Joseph answered her bishop's request to come to Foxford, Co. Mayo; with four other Sisters she opened a school in an old corn store and began

relief work among the destitute. Noting the potential of the Moy River, and a derelict mill close by, she turned for advice to John Charles Smith, a noted manufacturer of fabrics from his mills in Caledon, Co. Tyrone. Mr. Smith, who first of all asked if she was aware that she had 'written to a protestant and a Free Mason,' joined forces with the nun to establish the Providence Woollen Mills of Foxford. The Congested Districts Board, a government aid body established in 1891, provided a loan of seventeen thousand pounds for the project and one thousand five hundred pounds towards training. Beginning in 1892 with only two hand looms, the industry produced flannels, frieze, tweed, shawls, blankets and clerical cloths. Over the next twenty years it developed into an internationally recognised business which transformed the local economy. At its peak, in the 1930s, the mill employed two hundred and fifty workers. Mother Mary Joseph had houses built for mill employees and then, having formed a choir, brass band, and orchestra, had a hall built for performances. She died on August 21, 1932, and is buried in the Nun's Plot beside the Roman Catholic Church in Foxford. The industry she established was forced into receivership in 1987 but has since been refurbished as a Heritage Centre, attracting tens of thousands of visitors annually; it includes a weaving factory which employs approximately one hundred people.

MULALLY, (MARIA) TERESA (1728-1803), educator. Born Pill Lane, now Chancery Street, in the parish of St. Michan's, Dublin. Little is known of her early life except that her family seem to have been without means or influential relatives and Teresa made her living as a milliner. She was determined to set up Roman Catholic schools for poor girls in her home parish despite the fact that such schools were still outlawed and 'those who engage in them' subject to large fines. For this purpose, with helpers Anne Corballis and Judith Clinch, she rented two rooms in an old three-storey house in St. Mary's Lane, in 1776; there is evidence to suggest that she had been running classes elsewhere for several years previously. Teresa had the support of two Jesuits, one of whom ran a clandestine school for boys in the area. Pupils in St. Mary's Lane were taught Christian doctrine, reading, writing, arithmetic, as well as knitting, needlework, dressmaking and glove making. Finance for the venture evidently came from subscriptions from parishioners and a rich benefactor. In 1771 Teresa was able to set up a small orphanage nearby and desperately attempted to find nuns to help her and her two assistants. For several years she had been in touch with NANO NAGLE, who had been running schools for Roman Catholic children in Cork for fifteen years and who, in 1777, with three companions, took religious vows and founded an order which was to eventually become the Presentation Sisters. Mulally visited 'Mrs. Nagle' in Cork at least twice to discuss the founding of a new order of nuns for the specific purpose of providing schooling for the poor under Penal circumstances. In 1784 Nano Nagle died and Teresa fell gravely ill. Nevertheless, in 1786, with the help of two large bequests and a gift of a thousand pounds she bought a disused glass factory at George's Hill, bordering Mary's Lane, for the (then) considerable sum of one thousand four hundred pounds and began to build a convent school and orphanage. Teresa was a shrewd business woman; she rented out several dwelling houses on the property to obtain revenue for her school. Her loyal assistants went to Cork to train in Nagle's establishment which was maintained by only four nuns at the time; Anne Corballis died soon afterwards. Teresa kept building until, in 1794,

the relatively large George's Hill school and convent were completed. By this time, she was joined by Judith Clinch and two others from Cork's now fast-growing community. Teresa Mulally never entered the order. Her health had deteriorated and, committing her school to the Presentation nuns, returned to her orphanage and ran the entire establishment from her bed until her death nine years later, on February 9, 1803. The original Presentation foundation in Cork and the Dublin community developed autonomously with both multiplying rapidly. By 1825, the George's Hill Sisters had opened a second convent school in Dublin and others in Drogheda, Co. Louth, Rahan, Co. Offaly, Maynooth, Co. Kildare, and Mullingar, Co. Westmeath. Missionaries from these latter convents set up the first Presentation foundation in Madras, India, in 1842.

MULHOLLAND, ROSA, LADY GILBERT (1841-1921), novelist and poet. Born Belfast, daughter of a doctor. She was educated privately before going to London to study art. Rosa soon turned to writing and was fortunate that Charles Dickens liked her work. He published many of her early stories in his periodical *Household Words*. She wrote many novels and three volumes of verse over some fifty years, from *Dumara* (1864) to *The Return of Mary O'Murrough* (1910). Her work, which featured Irish peasant life and was overly romantic and sentimentally religious, achieved great popularity. *The Wild Birds of Kileevy* (1883) and *A Fair Emigrant* (1888) were probably the best known. In late middle age Rosa married the outstanding historian and Celtic scholar Mr. (later Sir) John T. Gilbert. After his death she wrote his biography (1904). Her poetry was published in three volumes: *Vagrant Verses* (1886), *Spirit and Dust* (1908), and *Dream and Realities* (1916). Her sister married Russell of Killowen, Lord Chief Justice of England, in 1894, the first Roman Catholic appointed to this position since the Reformation. Rosa's social position, her successful and prolific output, and her impact on younger contemporary writers, is held to have instigated the literary genre of Irish Roman Catholic fiction. Her writings also had an important role in the late 19th century growth of the phenomenon known as 'Irish Catholicism'. Lady Rosa Gilbert died at her home in Blackrock, Dublin, in April 1921.

MURPHY, DELIA (1902 - 1971), ballad singer. Born Roundfort near Claremorris, Co. Mayo. Delia was said to have learned her first songs from a young traveller boy on the way to national school, among them 'If I were a Blackbird', which she made famous. She went to the Dominican Convent boarding school in Eccles Street, Dublin, where she was taught singing by Mother Clement Burke, along with her contemporary MARGARET BURKE SHERIDAN. While studying for a B. Comm. degree, at UCG, Delia sang at student concerts and, later, at private parties and minor concerts; it wasn't until the late 1930s that she became a figure of note. She had married a civil servant, Dr. T.J. Kiernan, then Secretary of the High Commissioner's office in London, who returned to Dublin on his appointment as Director of Broadcasting in the newly-formed Radio Éireann. It is said that while the celebrated opera singer John McCormack was practising in the studio, prior to a broadcast, Delia corrected his phrasing in a ballad. This was overheard by a representative of HMV records and she was invited to make the first of almost a hundred records for the company. From this time, until the mid 1950s, Delia was the most important if not the only exponent of Irish ballad singing to reach an audience on an international scale. She broadcasted numerous times from Radio Éireann and the BBC, becoming a household name among people starved for Irish music. Altogether she recorded some four hundred songs, the great majority of which were on '78' shellac records. Most of her listeners never realised that their favourite singer, whom they thought of as living in a country cottage or a traveller's caravan, was the wife of an Irish Ambassador. Dr. Kiernan was appointed first to the Court of St. James in London, then to the Vatican, during the Second World War, and later to Australia, Canada, and America. Delia accompanied her husband on all his postings. Unknown to him, she was an accomplice of Monsignor O'Flaherty ('The Scarlet Pimpernel') in smuggling escaped prisoners of war and other allied personnel into Vatican City; it is said that on more than one occasion she used the Legation's car to drive escapees through Fascist check-points. Following the death of her husband, in 1967, Delia returned from America to retire in Co. Dublin. Even at the height of her career, she was always aware of her appeal to ordinary Irish people and delighted in performing in halls, large or small, throughout the country, saying, 'I sing for the real people of the gods'. Once, at a concert in a small rural hall, she ordered all the doors to be opened so that the crowd left outside could hear her. Delia Murphy died at her daughter's home in Lucan, Co. Dublin, on February 12, 1971.

NAGLE, NANO (HONORA) (1728-1784), pioneer educator and founder of the Presentation Order. Born Ballygriffin, Co. Cork, into one of the richest Irish Roman Catholic families during the 'Penal days' following the final conquest of Gaelic and Roman Catholic Ireland (1691). Her immediate family were landed gentry who had made many marriage alliances with protestant colonials. Her uncle, David Nagle, lawyer and financier, was reputed to be the wealthiest Roman Catholic in Ireland and had commercial and financial interests in Continental countries. Nano may have received some schooling from the local hedge-schoolmaster, O'Halloran, who gave Edmund Burke (the future political writer and orator) his first education: she was sent to a French convent at a young age. She and her sister remained in Paris for a decade after schooling and moved in the fashionable circles of the city and St. Germain, including (according to her earliest biographers) the Court of Louis XV. After the death of her father, in 1746, she returned to live in Dublin but soon moved back to Paris, this time to enter a convent. On the advice of her spiritual director, Nano came back to Ireland and, in about the year 1754, opened a school in a mud cabin in Cove Lane, Cork. By 1769, although Roman Catholic schools were illegal at the time, she had used an inheritance from her uncle Joseph to open seven schools for poor children. As her health deteriorated and there were insurmountable difficulties with teachers, she brought Ursuline nuns from France and built a convent for them beside her cottage in Cove Lane. However, because of their strict rule of enclosure, the nuns were unable to carry out the educational and social work among the poor that Nano required. She established a new apostolate with two young assistants and rejected every charitable work that was not totally given over to the care of the poor. Despite a new wave of anti-Roman Catholic feeling among the protestant ascendancy, and opposition from wealthy fellow Roman Catholics, Nano and three companions entered the newly-built convent in 1777. In 1783 she opened an alms house for destitute old women. Nano, who had been in bad health for thirty years, died on April 28, 1784. With only three active members left in the foundation it seemed as if her successor, Angela Collins, had no option but to disband the order which, since Nano's death, had been officially designated the Sisterhood of the Presentation. But, ten years later the community numbered twelve, seven of whom were novices; some of these were being trained for a new foundation in Killarney, Co. Kerry, and others for Dublin where Nano's co-worker, TERESA MULALLY, was setting up similar schools for the poor. A gift of more than two thousand pounds from Nano's brother, in 1813, guaranteed the financial viability of the Presentation Order in the longer term. By 1900 there were some fifty Presentation schools in Ireland and others in Newfoundland, England, USA, Australia, Tasmania, New Zealand and India. Those of the Presentation were the first 'convent schools' in Ireland and gave the impetus to the vast number of such establishments set up by new orders in the 19th century.

NÍ CHEARBHAILL, MÁIGRÉD or O'CARROLL, MARGARET, (c. 1405-1451), 'Máigred an Éinigh', wife of O'Connor Failbhe. Born at the onset of the Gaelic revival in the 15th century, she was daughter of Taig Ó Cearbhaill, chief of Ely (roughly the area where counties Offaly, Laois and Tipperary join). Her mother is believed to have been Joan Butler whose nephew James was the White Earl of Ormond. For some sixty years, since the O'Carroll chief 'slew or expelled . . . the nations of the Brets, Milbornes, and other English and occupied castles', Ely had attained a great degree of independence. This was not unduly disturbed when Máigréd's father, Taig Ó Cearbhaill, was defeated and slain by the White Earl of Desmond in 1407. Máigréd married Calbhach Ó Conchobhair Failbhe (O'Connor Falvy), chief of Offaly, about 1420. Although the O'Connors had also suffered defeat by Ormond and Desmond in 1407, Offaly was still a relatively powerful kingdom and Máigréd's husband enjoyed a reign of growing prosperity. The annalists recorded that Calbhach 'never refused the countenance of man and won

more wealth from his English and Irish enemies than any lord in Leinster.' The annals also note Máigréd's important role in the kingdom and praise her for road, bridge, and church building. Her great hospitality and benefaction earned her the sobriquet 'Máigréd an Éinigh' ('Margaret of the Hospitality'): 'while the world lasts her numerous gifts to the Irish and Scots nations cannot be numbered.' In 1433 she presided over two of the notable assemblies of *filí* (poets) and *ollamhna* (learned men) at Killachy in the plain of Offaly, and at Rathangan, Co. Kildare. Poets and learned men acted as policy makers and advisers in public affairs and such traditional assemblies played an important role in both the external and internal politics of the Gaelic states. Dubhaltach Mac Fir Bisigh stated in his *Chronicum Scotorem* (*c.* 1666) that Máigréd 'proclaimed to and invited . . . all persons, both Irish and Scots, or rather Albaines, to the general feasts of bestowing both meate and moneyes, with all manner of gifts, whereunto gathered to receive these gifts and matter two thousand and seven hundred persons, besides gamesters and poore men . . . viz, the chiefe kins of each family of the Learned Irish . . . And Margerett on the garrotts of the great church of Da Sinchell, clad in cloath of gold, her dearest friends about her, her clergy and judges too. Calwagh himself on horseback by the churche's outward side . . .'. Máigréd Ní Chearbhaill was noted for her piety in a period of religious revival. She took part in the great pilgrimage made by many chieftains and nobles from many parts of Ireland to the shrine of Saint James in Compostella, Spain, in 1445. She was doubtless involved in making political marriage alliances between her only daughter, Finnghuala Ní Chonchobhair, to the O'Donnell of Tyrconnell and, after his death, to O'Neill of Tyrone. Máigréd died, possibly of breast cancer, in 1451, hours before her son Feifhlim, a noted warrior-prince, succumbed to 'leprosy'. Her husband survived her by seven years, her other son by twenty. She had no grandchildren and the line died out of 'the best woman of her time in Ireland.'

NÍ CHONAILL, EIBHLÍN DUBH (*c.* 1748-*c.* 1800), poet. Born Derrynane, Co. Kerry, into the prosperous landed O'Connell family which was to produce O'Connell the Liberator. Her mother, daughter of the Kerry chieftain O'Donoghue of the Glen, was also a poet, according to tradition. Eibhlín first married at fifteen but her elderly husband died not long afterwards. She subsequently married twenty-one-year-old Arthur O'Leary of Rathleigh, Macroom, Co. Cork, against the wishes of her family. The O'Learys (Uí Laoghaire) although landed gentry, had a long record of rebellion and outlawry and Arthur, already a major in the Hungarian Hussars, was notorious for his wild escapades and lack of prudence. He had a price on his head through quarrelling with Abraham Morris, the High Sheriff of Cork, but it appears he stood trial and was acquitted. Morris' hatred, however, was implacable and the pair clashed again. Arthur and one of the Sheriff's henchman were wounded in the struggle. For the next five years, during which time they had three children, Eibhlín and her husband were on constant guard. On at least one occasion their house in Rathleigh came under attack by soldiers and Eibhlín loaded the guns during the siege. In 1773 Arthur's mare, reputed to have been given to him by the Empress Maria Theresa of Austria, won all before her at Macroom races. Morris, under a statute of King William III giving a protestant the right to claim any horse owned by a Roman Catholic on payment of five pounds, forced the issue. When Arthur refused to sell Morris had him proclaimed an outlaw at a meeting of local magistrates. On May 4, 1773, Arthur left his home intent on killing Morris but, due to an informer, instead met a posse of soldiers and was shot dead at Carrig an Ime. When she found his body Eibhlín Dubh began a keen that was eventually to become the magnificent poem of four hundred lines, 'Caoineadh Airt Uí Laoghaire' (The Lament for Art O'Leary). Morris was accused of murder at a Coroner's Court but never stood trial. He was wounded by Arthur's brother in an assassination attempt and died some years later from these wounds. It is said that Eibhlín used influential family connections to have some of the soldiers involved in her husband's killing sent to penal colonies abroad. She and her children went through a period of want as her family, particularly her brother Maurice, would not easily forgive the unsuitable marriage and the dangers in which the O'Connells had been placed but another brother, Count Daniel O'Connell, prevailed on Maurice to come to her aid. Little else is known about Eibhlín and her children who, like those of her O'Connell brothers, became absorbed into the English-speaking world of the Union with Britain (1801). One son appears to have become a doctor and a grandson was a professor in Queen's University, Cork. However, her lament for her husband remained alive in the folk tradition of west Munster until this century and has now been widely published in translation.

NIC SHIUBHLAIGH, MÁIRE (1883-1958), republican and actress. Born Mary Elizabeth (Molly) Walker, on May 8, 1883, at Charlemont Street, Dublin. Her father was a printer and typesetter from Carlow, who had married a Dublin dressmaker. The family was Irish-speaking republican and Máire's father printed much Fenian propaganda and other nationalist material. They moved to High Street, Dublin, and Willie Fay came to lodge in the house. Fay, at the beginning of his career as an actor and producer, taught Máire how to act. In 1900, she joined Connradh na Gaeilge and was one of the twenty-nine women who attended the inaugural meeting of Inghinidhe na hÉireann whose prime aim was the re-establishment of complete independence for Ireland. She first appeared on stage in the tableaux presented by the Inghinidhe as a form of propagandist entertainment for nationalists. On April 2, 1902, Máire took part in the first performance given by the Irish National Theatre Company in St. Teresa's Hall, Clarendon Street, Dublin This was to become the Abbey Theatre. Her four brothers and sisters were also involved in the Abbey during its early years. Máire became its first leading lady and first actor to use the Gaelic form of her name for stage purposes. Some contemporary critics, having watched her performances in the lead role in Yeats' *Kathleen Ní Houlihan* (a drama which greatly roused nationalist fervour), believed she embodied the part even more than MAUD GONNE or SARA ALLGOOD. Máire formed her own company, Cluicheadóirí na hÉireann (Theatre of Ireland), but returned to the Abbey after five years and toured with it in America. While earning her living as a teacher of elocution she was heavily involved in Cumann na mBan for whom she produced many concerts and aeraíochtaí (open-air entertainment). In the confusion of the first day of the 1916 rebellion she and five other women, determined to play their part, went to Jacob's biscuit factory where Thomas MacDonogh was in command. Convincing him that women had a role to perform in the rebellion they remained for the rest of the action and cooked meals under sniper fire. She maintained links with the republican movement after the rising and married Major General Éamonn Price, organising director of the Irish Volunteers during the War of Independence. Her reminiscences of the period, *These Splendid Years,* were published in 1955. Máire Nic Shiubhlaigh died on September 8, 1958.

The Irish National Theatre Society.

PRESIDENT : W. B. YEATS,
VICE-PRESIDENTS : MAUD GONNE,
    DOUGLAS HYDE, GEORGE RUSSELL.
STAGE MANAGER : W. C. FAY.
SECRETARY : FRED. RYAN.

34 Lower Camden Street

Dublin   190

49. **Máire Nic Shiubhlaigh,** *drawn by George Russell during rehearsals at Camden Street, Dublin.*

NÍ DHOCHARTAIGH, RÓIS or O'DOGHERTY, ROSA (*c.* 1582-1660), wife and representative of General Eoghan Rua Ó Néill (Owen Roe O'Neill). Born in Inishowen, in the most northerly part of Donegal where her father was chief. She was great-granddaughter of Seán an Díomais Ó Néill (Shane O'Neill), the most powerful native ruler in Ireland a quarter of a century before her birth. About 1596, Rosa married Cathbharr, younger brother of Aodh Rua Ó Domhnaill (Red Hugh O'Donnell), the recently inaugurated chief of Tyrconnell. The O'Donnells incurred the hostility of her brother, Cathbharr Ó Dochartaigh, shortly afterwards when they supported his uncle against him for the chieftaincy of Inishowen and he went over to the service of the English; Rosa, however, remained loyal to her husband. In 1607, six years after the disastrous defeat of the northern chiefs at Kinsale, and in despair following an abortive rebellion against the English Lord Deputy and his British troops, the Earls Tyrone and Tyrconnell made a hurried escape to the Continent with their families and major supporters. This is known to history as the 'Flight of the Earls'. Rosa travelled with her husband but was forced to leave one of her two sons behind. (Years later this son escaped from imprisonment by the Lord Deputy and joined his mother in Louvain.) A storm drove the refugees ashore at Quillaboeuf on the French coast and, having made their way to Rouen, they were threatened with arrest and extradition to England. Securing a passport to the Spanish Netherlands, the company of thirty-one horsemen, two coaches of women and children, and forty foot soldiers proceeded to Arras in Flanders. Accepting an invitation to asylum by the Pope the political exiles had no alternative in midwinter but to leave the children behind in Louvain in the care of nuns. Although virtual prisoners the party was honorably received in Rome and survived on generous grants from the king of Spain. Before the autumn of 1608, Rosa's husband, his brother the Earl of Tyrconnell, and three other nobles, were dead either from fever or poisoning by English agents. It was 1611 before Rosa and her sister-in-law, NUALA NÍ DHOMHNAILL, were able to return to Louvain; here they both were in receipt of a pension of a hundred and seventy-five crowns per month from the Spanish monarchy. Three years earlier, Rosa's brother, Cathbharr (then Sir Cahir O'Dogherty), was forced into rebellion by the English he had served and was ignominiously killed. Rosa was now the moral head of the O'Dohertys of Inishowen. As widow of the Earl's brother and, with Nuala Ní Dhomhnaill, protector of the young pretender to the Earldom, she held considerable influence with the O'Donnells. Her marriage (arranged in secret to avoid English interference) in about 1612 to Eoghan Rua Ó Néill, nephew of the Earl of Tyrone and an officer of the Irish regiment serving in the Spanish Netherlands, in effect united most of the clans of Ulster. Her house in Brussels became the centre of a new conspiracy to regain ancestral lands and restore religious freedom in Ireland. It was to be almost thirty years before the opportunity arose. In the meantime her husband served Spain with distinction, culminating in his defence of Arras against the French, in 1640. During the time of preparation for renewing the struggle in Ireland, Rosa appears to have been politically and logistically active, both as her husband's representative and his purchasing agent. Their son, Henry Roe, took a major part in plotting the rebellion with the conspirators in Ireland. The rebellion broke out in 1641 and, the following year, Eoghan Rua was chosen as general by the Ulstermen. In 1648 Rosa arrived in Limerick in a small fleet commanded by her son Cathbharr and her husband's nephew, Con Rua. She spent the duration of the war at the Ulster army headquarters in Belturbet, Co. Cavan. Eoghan Rua died, in 1649, on a march south to join with the Irish royalist army in a combined front against the Cromwellians. Subsequently, the war went against the Irish forces. Rosa was in Limerick during the siege of that city and, at the request of the commander Hugh Duff O'Neill, was given safe passage from Ireland at the surrender. Rosa returned to Brussels with her four-year-old grandson, Henry Roe's son. The following year Henry Roe was taken prisoner during the fighting in Donegal and executed by orders of Sir Charles Coote the Puritan general. Rosa spent the last decade of her life in Flanders where she had been given permission to settle again by the Spanish; she had made many petitions to them for her husband's military pension and it is likely she obtained it. Róis Ní Dhochartaigh was buried at the Franciscan College of St. Anthony of Padua, in Louvain, beside her eldest son.

NÍ DHOMHNAILL, NUALA(DHA) or O'DONNELL, NUALA (c. 1575–c. 1650), protector of the heir to the Earldom of Tyrconnell, the 'Woman of the Piercing Wail'.

Daughter of Sir Hugh O'Donnell (Aodh Dubh Ó Domhnaill), Lord of Tyrconnell (now Co. Donegal) and of FIONNGHUALA MACDONNEL ('Inghean Dubh'), the formidable Antrim Scot who played a considerable role in the politics of Ulster during this period. Nuala was a younger sister of Aodh Rua Ó Domhnaill, known to history as Red Hugh O'Donnell who, with O'Neill, Earl of Tyrone, almost brought English control of Ireland to an end. She was also sister of Rory O'Donnell, first Earl of Tyrone. About 1592 she was married to her cousin, Niall Garbh O'Donnell, in an attempt to appease him for the fact that, although he had the greater claim to the chieftainship, her brother

Red Hugh had been inaugurated head of the O'Donnells through the machinations of their mother, Inghean Dubh. Seven years later when Niall Garbh, backed by the English authorities, began to wage war against his cousins, Nuala deserted him but was forced to abandon her two young sons and, possibly, a daughter. Following the battle of Kinsale, which was disastrous for the northern chieftains, Red Hugh died in 1602 at the hands of an English agent in Spain. Rory, having first made his submission to the Lord Deputy, was inaugurated Earl of Tyrconnell (to isolate his former ally O'Neill); he then married BRIGID FITZGERALD, daughter of the Earl of Kildare, who was loyal to the crown. Their son Aodh was born in 1606. The following year as Rory began, in desperation, to plan another rebellion his wife returned to Kildare and the baby was left in Nuala's care. Abandoning hope in 1607 Earls Tyrone and Tyrconnell, their major supporters, womenfolk, and children, made the hurried escape to the Continent known as the 'Flight of the Earls'; with them went Nuala and the eleven-month-old heir. A storm drove the ship ashore at Quillaboeuf on the French coast and the party, making their way to Rouen, came under threat of arrest and extradition to England. Obtaining a passport to the Spanish Netherlands from the king of Spain the company of thirty-one horsemen, two coaches of women and children, and forty foot soldiers proceeded to Arras in Flanders. When offered asylum in Rome by the Pope, and forced to travel in severe winter conditions, they had no alternative but to leave the children in the care of nuns in Louvain. The refugees were honourably received in Rome although, technically, in detention. Before the autumn Earl Rory, his brother, and three other nobles of the party were dead either from fever or, it was suspected, from poisoning by English agents. The Spanish ambassador was sympathetic, writing to King Philip that Rory had left 'a sister and brother and others who were dependant on him,' and that he would continue to grant the Spanish pension the Earl had been receiving, 'as they are in a poor way and would be altogether lost without it'. The king agreed and sent his condolences. In desperation Nuala petitioned King James I, through the English agent in Brussels, to have the young Earl pardoned and restored to his estates in Tyrconnell but she was unsuccessful. It was 1611 before she and her widowed sister-in-law, ROSA O'DOHERTY, managed to return to Louvain to be reunited with the children. Nuala ('Dona Nola O daniel') now had the good fortune to receive a pension of one hundred and seventy-five crowns per month from the Spanish monarchy. She oversaw the education of her nephew, by the Franciscans, until he was old enough to become a page at the Court of the Archdukes in Brussels; he later appears to have entered the Irish Legion in their service and attained to a high position before being drowned at sea in 1642. Nuala's one-time husband, Niall Garbh and a son, probably hers, were accused of treason on the information of her mother, Inghean Dubh, and taken to the Tower of London where they died. Another of her sons by Niall was able to join her in Flanders where he took up service for the Spanish and eventually became a colonel in Owen Roe O'Neill's Confederate army during the wars following the 1641 Insurrection in Ireland, losing his life in the battle of Benburb (1646). Fergal Óg mac a'Bhaird, the O'Donnell poet who had followed his patrons to Louvain indicates, in a poem lamenting the death of Owen Roe (1649), that Nuala was still alive but may have removed from Flanders to either Italy or Spain. It is supposed that she is buried in the Franciscan chapel of Louvain. A patron of the poets (she was doubtless the owner of a poem-book known as the *Book of O'Donnell's Daughter*), Nuala is mentioned in several poems, including mac a' Bhaird's well-known lament for Earl Rory and his brothers; through James Clarence Mangan's translation of one of these, two centuries later, she became known as the 'Woman of the Piercing Wail'. Nuala is often accepted as the author of the moving poem of exile known as *Mairgní Nuala Ní Néill fá chontae Dhún na nGall*:

I am the fish from wave to wave,
I am the ship whose sail is smashed,
I the apple tree whose flower has gone,
And in spite of all I still live on . . .

NÍ FHAIRCHEALLAIGH, ÚNA or O'FARRELLY, AGNES, (1874-1951), Gaelic Leaguer, feminist and writer (pen-name Uan Uladh). Born June 24, 1874, at Raffony, near Virginia, Co. Cavan, onto the large farm of a family who could trace their ancestors back to the Úi Fhaircheallaigh chiefs of west Cavan and had a tradition of Gaelic learning in recent generations. After a convent school education Úna took an MA from the Royal University, Dublin. She first gained prominence, with MARY HAYDEN, in the campaign for women's rights in the universities. She was co-founder, with Hayden, of the Irish Association of Women Graduates in 1903 and took part on its behalf in the Royal Commission on university education. Six years later she was appointed to the first governing body of University College Dublin. She had already thrown herself wholeheartedly into the work of the Gaelic League which she was to serve faithfully for the next half century, not only on its executive, but as the most public and important woman involved during that period. Úna was an especially close friend and loyal supporter of Douglas Hyde, president of the League, and also closely associated with many of the principle national figures of her time including MacNeill and Pearse. In the first two

decades of this century her activities spanned the academic, political and literary fields. From 1909 she lectured in Modern Irish at University College Dublin, until appointed Professor of Modern Irish Poetry in 1932, after Hyde resigned the post. Úna was present at the first meeting of Sinn Féin in 1906 and, pursuing its aim of national self-reliance, was later to become president of the Irish Industrial Association and of the Homespun Society as well as administrator of the John Connor Magee Trust which sought to establish industries in the economically disadvantaged Gaeltacht areas. In 1914 she chaired the meeting and gave the inaugural address at the founding of Cumann na mBan, the radically nationalist women's organisation, in Wynn's Hotel, Dublin. As a constitutional nationalist Úna resigned from that organisation later the same year over the question of military support for Britain in the First World War. She also stood with Hyde in the attempt to keep the Gaelic League non-political and non-sectarian when her friend Patrick Pearse and others were converting it into a force for revolution. She took no active part in the Rising or in the War of Independence. In 1922 when many prominent women, appalled at the thought of a civil war, formed a committee and sent delegations to the military leaders of both sides, Úna Ní Fhaircheallaigh was one of those chosen along with HANNA SHEEHY SKEFFINGTON, MADAME DESPARD, LOUIE BENNETT and ROSAMUND JACOB. In 1932 she was appointed to the Senate. She and Mary Hayden led the Women Graduates Association with the demand for the deletion of those articles from the draft Constitution of 1937 which were seen to be retrogressive in relation to women's rights. Úna's interest in the revival of Irish prompted her to write in that language. She produced two novellas, *Grádh agus Crádh* (1901) and *An Creamhaire* (1902) and two books of poetry, *Out of*

the Depths (1921) and *Áille an Domhain* (1927). In 1903 she edited a commemorative volume on Eugene O' Growney, a leading figure of the language revival movement. Her only specifically scholarly work was a study of the poetry of Seán Ó Neachtain, *Filidheacht Sheghan Uí Neachtain* (1911). She was a long-term president of Cumann Camógaíochta na hÉireann, the association for the women's Gaelic game of camogie. As chairperson of the federation of irish language summer colleges she was actively involved, at various times, in their day-to-day running, especially in that of Cloch Cheannfhaola in Donegal. Úna was strongly in favour of Pan-Celticism and was honorary secretary of various Celtic Congresses but did not participate in the acrimonious debates on that issue within the Gaelic League. She was one of the great figures of the 'Irish Ireland' period, a larger-than-life character who attracted and set out to attract attention from the leading personalities of the period. Her name was a by-word for hospitality and her house, in the Donegal Gaeltacht, a mecca for Gaelgeoirí (Irish revivalists).

NÍ GHRÁDA, MÁIRÉAD (1899-1971), playwright and author. Born on December 23, 1899, in Kilmaley, Co. Clare, where Irish was still widely spoken at the time. Her father, a farmer, county councillor and native speaker of Irish, could recite by heart lengthy Clare poems such as Merriman's 'Cúirt a' Mheán Oíche' ('The Midnight Court'). He was a strong influence on Máiréad's life-long commitment to the revival of the language. She was educated at the Mercy Convent, Ennis, won a scholarship to University College Dublin where she graduated with an MA in Irish and took up a teaching post in a private school. Joining Conradh na Gaeilge (the Gaelic League) she worked as a *timire* (a peripatetic teacher) for the League. She also

50. Máirád Ní Ghráda, by Sadbh Trinseach.

joined Cumann na mBan and was jailed for selling republican flags on a public street. She was secretary to Ernest Blyth during the first Dáil period, when he served as Minister for Trade and Commerce, and during the Civil War when he was Minister for Finance. Máiréad resumed teaching and married Risteard Ó Cíosáin, a civil servant. In 1926 she got a job as an editor and producer on 2RN (later Radio Éireann) where she became the first woman radio announcer in Ireland and Britain. Her first plays were written for her language students; Micheál Mac Liammóir thought enough of one of them, *Uacht*, to produce it at his Gate Theatre, Dublin, in 1935. About this time she was also working as a publisher's editor and becoming a prolific writer of Irish language textbooks for schools. A collection of short stories, *An Bheirt Dearthár agus Scéalta Eile* (1939), was followed by a book of children's stories, *Manannan*. However, Máiréad is mostly remembered for her plays including *Micheál* (1933), which won an Abbey Theatre award, *An Grá agus an Gárda* (1937),

Giolla an tSolais (1945), *Lá Buí Bealtaine* (1953), *Úll Glas Oíche Shamhna* (1955), *Súgán Sneachta* (1959), *Mac uí Rudaí* (1963), and *Stailc Ocrais* (1966). In 1964 her *An Triail* caused a sensation when performed during the Dublin Theatre Festival with CAITLÍN MAUDE in the lead role. It was based on an incident in her home remembered from her youth: the victimisation of a pregnant young single girl while the man involved escaped condemnation. Considering the play was in Irish it was unusually well received by the critics, notably Harold Hobson of the London *Times*. It still ranks with Brendan Behan's *An Giall* as the most successful play in the Irish language. However, with their strong roles for young women and exploring women's issues, her other plays met with no more general approval than did the English-language plays of her contemporary TERESA DEEVY. Máiréad Ní Ghráda died on June 13, 1971.

NÍ LAOGHAIRE, MÁIRE BHUIDHE (1774-c. 1849), poet. Born Túirín na nÉan, Inshigeela, in the west of Cork, on the smallholding of one of the nineteen Ó Laoghaire families from whose patronymic this area 'Iveleary' was named. Máire Bhuí belonged to the branch known as the Clann Bhuí and, though her father was a poor tenant farmer, her ancestors had been castle-owning aristocrats a century and a half previously. The Clann Bhuí had produced several poets in previous generations and Máire had a local reputation for her songs. At eighteen she eloped with de Búrca, a horse dealer, from Skibbereen. The couple settled near Ballingeary where de Búrca bought one hundred and fifty acres of land. They flourished for a time, raising cattle and riding-horses. In 1822 Máire Bhuí's sons were heavily involved in the local Whiteboy resistance to the collection of tithes by the Church of Ireland. The Muskerry Yeomenry was reorganised by the authorities to stamp out this latest insurrection. A pitched battle was fought at Céim an Fhia, near Máire Bhuí's house, ending in the Yeomen's retreat; one of their number and two Whiteboys died in the affray. Subsequently, most of Máire Bhuí's six sons had to go on the run, some of them for several years. The battle was the subject of the song 'Cath Chéim an Fhia,' best known of her compositions and still widely sung. Following the outlawry of her sons, the raising of the rent and the general fall in prices for agricultural produce in the 1830s, Máire Bhuí's family fortunes deteriorated. The de Búrcas were eventually evicted from most of their lands at the height of the Great Famine and Máire Bhuí and her husband went to live with a son at Inse Bheag, their only remaining holding. She died here within a couple of years. Fifteen of her songs are extant, either collected orally or in manuscript. Unlike other women poets of her period, Máire Bhuí's compositions commented on contemporary public events such as the United Irishmen rebellions, the Repeal movement, the miserable state of the tenant farmer and the cottier class; she composed political *aisling* ('vision') poems as well as elegies.

NÍ SCOLAÍ, MÁIRE (1909-1985), singer. Born in Dublin. She received an early foundation at the Central Model School in Dublin, a pilot Irish-language primary school. Summers spent at Ring College in the Waterford Gaeltacht as a teenager made Máire a devotee of traditional singing and dancing. She went to live in Galway in her late teens, set herself up as a teacher of Irish singing and dancing, and played some leading roles in the Irish-language theatre, An Taibhdhearc. Winning awards at the country's leading *Feiseanna* encouraged her to formally study vocal and instrumental music and she became a licentiate of the Trinity College of Music, London. Máire, a mezzo-soprano, combined what she had

51. *Maire Ni Scolaí, 1978.*

learned of *sean-nós* singing in the Gaeltachtaí with her training in classical music and was one of the few singers ever to do so with complete success. Her distinctive style and interpretation appealed to audiences all over Ireland, many of whom would have otherwise been adverse to singing in the Gaelic tradition. She broadcast frequently on Radio Éireann but also on the BBC, Radio Vaticana, Radio Française, and in the USA. She also gave recitals in London's Covent Garden and Queen's Hall and at national festivals of other Celtic countries such as; the Welsh Eisteddfod, the Scots Mod, the Breton Bretagne Celebrations and the Manx Tynwald Assemblies. She married Liam Ó Buachalla who later became Professor of Economics at UCG and Chairman of the Irish Senate. She collected many songs in the Galway and Donegal Gaeltachtaí and, for many years, adjudicated at the country's major *Feiseanna*. Máire Ní Scolaí died on June 29, 1985.

NIVEDITA, BHAGINI, or NOBLE, MARGARET ELIZABETH (1867-1911), Hindu missionary, Indian nationalist and author. Born Dungannon, Co. Tyrone, daughter of a non-conformist clergyman from Rostrevor, Co. Down. From her grandfather, who had been involved in the 1798 Rebellion, and her father, Margaret inherited a strong antipathy to British rule, and a searching religious spirit. She was reared by a grand-mother until she followed her father to Halifax, England, where she was educated in a Congregationalist school. Without the benefit of higher education Margaret became a teacher in Wales at a very young age. Influenced by the approach to education propounded by Froebel and Pestalozzi she put their ideas into practice in her classroom and began to disseminate them among her fellow Congregationalists. As a result she was placed in charge of a new experimental school in London. She was twenty-eight when she made the acquaintance of Swami Vivekananda, founder of the Ramakrishna Mission, which propagated his own form of non-casteist and non-hierarchical Hinduism and involved itself in the type of educational and charitable works more usually associated in India with contemporary Christian missionaries. In 1897, following six years of preparation, Margaret went to Calcutta to join the Ramakrishna Mission, taking the name Nivedita ('the dedicated one'). She threw herself whole-heartedly into the work of the Mission and the fact that it is the largest charitable organisation in India today is due in no little part to her endeavours and her example. She wrote a dozen books on India and the Hindu religion, including *Kali the Master, The Master as I saw Him, Cradle Tales of Hinduism* and *The Web of Indian Life*, the latter considered to be one of the best guides to Hindu society. Nivedita was well-known in intellectual, artistic and scientific circles in Calcutta. She was conspicuously active in the struggle for Indian independence and only the fact that she was a British national and a woman saved her from jail, especially as she supported armed rebellion. Bhagini Nivedita's remarkable career in India was cut short by death from dysentry in Darjeeling in October 1911. A memorial to her in that city is inscribed: 'Here reposes Sister Nivedita, who gave her all to India.' Many books, including her official six-volume biography in Bengali, have been written on her life and work in west Bengal. Among other institutions, the Nivedita Girl's school in Calcutta is named after her.

NOBLE, MARGARET ELIZABETH. See under NIVEDITA BHAGINI.

NOLAN, JULIAN (*c.* 1612-1701) **and LYNCH, MARY** (*c.* 1628-*c.* 1710), Dominican nuns in 'Penal days'. First cousins, both born in Galway. From the mid-sixteenth century on, as the Counter-Reformation gained strength, many attempts were made to set up religious foundations for Roman Catholic women in Ireland. The great majority of these were short-lived in the face of successive waves of religious oppression from English forces over two centuries. The exception is the Dominican Order in Galway which has had a relatively continuous existence since 1643. The lives of Julian Nolan and Mary Lynch epitomise this survival. Julian was born into an affluent family, probably city merchants. Her mother was connected with the Lynchs, one of 'the Tribes' or principal merchant families of that thriving seaport. In 1644 she married a relative, Peter Nolan, but they parted by mutual consent after a year: he to become a Dominican priest, she a Dominican nun, shortly after the 1641 Roman Catholic revolt. The first Dominican foundation, the Convent of Jesus and Mary, was established in Galway in 1643 and a younger cousin of Julian's, Mary Lynch, was among the first to receive the habit, in 1644, while still in her teens. Julian was professed in 1647. In 1652 the city capitulated after ten months siege to the Cromwellian forces and the nuns were dispersed. Their vicar negotiated the reception of fourteen into Spanish monasteries and, in September that year, Julian and Mary joined the Convent of the Incarnation in Bilbao when King Philip IV of Spain granted four thousand reales to the convent for their dowries. They remained for thirty-three years and Mary, at least, taught for some of that period. With the accession of the Roman Catholic King James II to the English throne in 1685, some Galway women wishing to openly practice religious life persuaded Father John Browne, the Dominican Provincial, to re-establish the old convent in the city. He called on Julian and Mary, last survivors of the original foundation, to return. Although initially petitioning to be allowed to remain in Spain, the nuns travelled to Ireland in December 1686. Julian's husband had died three years previously after a continuous ministry as a priest in the city during the Penal era. Julian was appointed Prioress of the refounded Convent of Jesus and Mary at the age of seventy-five and Mary became Sub-Prioress and Mistress of Novices. The rule was one of strict enclosure. By 1688 the first novice had been professed. The community survived the defeat of the Jacobites at Aughrim in 1691, was dispersed under the anti-Roman Catholic laws of 1698, and re-grouped in secret. Julian Nolan died in 1701 and was buried in the Dominican Convent, Claddagh, Galway. When Mary Lynch succeeded her as Prioress in 1702 there were thirteen members in the Community. Although raided and dispersed many times in the first half of the 18th century (the convent was once used as a military barracks), the Community survived in Cross Street until 1845 when it moved to Taylor's Hill where the Dominican Sisters of the Monastery of Jesus and Mary continue to run a school.

O'BRIEN, CATHERINE (KITTY AMELIA) (c. 1881-1963), stained glass and mosaic artist, director of An Túr Gloinne. Born Doora House, Spancil Hill, near Ennis, Co. Clare; her father was protestant landed gentry and Justice of the Peace for County Clare. She studied at the Dublin Metropolitan School of Art, and was taught by A.E. Child and William Orpen. When classes were first set up by Edward Martyn and SARAH PURSER, in 1903, to train young artists in stained glass and mosaic techniques with a distinctly Irish character, Catherine availed of the opportunity. In 1904 she went to work at Purser's newly-founded An Túr Gloinne, a stained glass studio in upper Pembroke Street, Dublin, and thus began an association with the studio that lasted some sixty years. During that period Catherine produced countless designs and hundreds of windows for churches at home and abroad. Her most noted works include: 'The Sower', Church of Ireland, Killoughter, Co. Cavan: 'The Good Samaritan', Church of Ireland, Harold's Cross, Dublin: 'The Angel' and 'Christ and Peter in the Water', Gorey, Co. Wexford: the eastern window, Carrickmines, Co Wicklow: 'Stations of the Cross', Vero Beach Church, Florida. Perhaps her most ambitious project was the memorial she executed to her parents in Drumcliffe Parish Church, Bindon Street, Ennis, consisting of two dozen mosaics, representing apostles and Irish saints, divided by marble columns and occupying the entire length of the reredos of the church. A fine example of her work in opus-sectile (a technique for setting glass in concrete) can be seen over the main and aisle doors of the Franciscan Friary in Athlone, Co. Westmeath. Although the creative days of the twentieth century's first two decades gave way to a period of artistic stagnation after the Free State was first established, An Túr Gloinne remained in operation. When Sarah Purser died in 1943, Catherine took over as Director, a

52. 'The virgin and sleeping child', *design for stained glass window by* **Catherine Amelia O'Brien.**

position she held until her death. One of her last commissions was for two windows in the private chapel of Árus an Uachtaráin, the Irish President's residence, but she died in 1963 before they could be completed and An Túr Gloinne died with her. Catherine O'Brien is commemorated in stained glass, to the design of Patrick Pollen, in the chapel of St. Laurence O'Toole in Christ Church Cathedral, Dublin, where she had been in charge of the floral arrangements and decorations of the sanctuary for forty years.

O'BRIEN, CHARLOTTE GRACE (1845-1909), social reformer, botanist and writer. Born November 23, 1845, at Cahirmoyle, Co. Limerick, into a senior branch of the aristocratic O'Brien family of Clare. Her father, a protestant landlord of a relatively small estate, was an MP before joining the Young Ireland movement and leading the rebellion at Ballingarry, Co. Tipperary, in 1848. Charlotte was three when her father was transported to Tasmania. After his release in 1854, she moved with him to Wales where he died in 1864. She then returned to Ireland to live with her brother at Cahirmoyle. There she took up the study of botany and began to write poetry and fiction. A novel, *Light and Shade*, was published in 1878, *Drama and Lyrics* followed in 1880. By this time she was publishing articles in journals such as the *Nation*, *United Ireland* and the *Nineteenth Century*, supporting the Land League and highlighting the desperate state of the tenant farmers and landless cottiers. She went further than many other nationalists in calling for an extension of the franchise within a Home Rule framework. At the same time she had studied the flora of the Isle of Wight; as a result she published *Wild Flowers of the Undercliffe* (1881). That year she also focused her attention on the appalling conditions of emigrants, especially of women, on the 'coffin ships' to America. The matter was raised in the British Parliament following her exposure of the situation in the *Pall Mall Gazette*, and resulted in a Board of Trade investigation into the practices of the White Star shipping line. Rather than rely on State intervention, Charlotte O'Brien set up lodgings in Queenstown (Cobh) for one hundred

*53. **Charlotte Grace O'Brien** in later life.*

prospective emigrants and, inspecting the ships with a medical officer, exposed the inhumane conditions in the papers. The shipping lines grudgingly began to improve their facilities. In 1882 she went to New York and lived in a tenement for some time to experience the situation of Irish immigrants at first hand. She persuaded the Roman Catholic bishop of New York to set up a care service. Irish bishops failed to respond or provide assistance at the points of exit. Nevertheless, she continued to run her accommodation at Queenstown and, having travelled steerage several times to Britain to check on conditions at sea, she continued her publicity campaign, forcing shipping companies to make further improvements. When the British government began to grant financial inducements to emigrate Charlotte was unjustly attacked by nationalists in Ireland and America for aiding a policy they perceived as a form of ethnic cleansing. She responded with a lecture tour of the USA, calling on Irish Americans to develop and extend the rescue operation established by the Roman Catholic Church in New York. Suffering from progressive deafness and disillusioned with Irish politics, she went back to her gardening and writing at Foynes, Co. Limerick. A volume of poetry, *Lyrics*, was published in 1886. Joining the Gaelic League and sympathetic to the ideas of Sinn Féin, she promoted the Irish language and native industry as well as the new co-operative movement in Limerick and Kerry. Charlotte never lost interest in botany and, in conjunction with her brother Robert Donough, she contributed greatly to Lloyd Praeger's plant records of Ireland; and with the distinguished lichenologist, Matilda Knowles, she undertook a study of the flora of north-west Limerick which led to the publication of *The Flora of the Barony of Shanid* in *The Irish Naturalist* (1907). Charlotte O'Brien was completing an article for *Irish Gardening*, to which she had been a regular contributor, when she died suddenly at her home on June 4, 1909. She had converted to Roman Catholicism some years earlier, following the example of her neighbour and friend, the poet Aubrey de Vere.

O'BRIEN, ELLEN LUCY (NELLIE) or NÍ BHRIAIN, NEILÍ

(1864-1925), Gaelic Leaguer and ecumenist. Born June 4, 1864, on the relatively small Smith O'Brien estate in Cahirmoyle, Co. Limerick. Her grandfather, William Smith O'Brien, best known as the leader of the 1848 Young Ireland Rebellion at Ballingarry, was a patron of the scribes and collector of Irish-language manuscripts. Her aunt CHARLOTTE GRACE O'BRIEN, who raised Ellen after her mother's death, was the social reformer who exposed the appalling conditions endured by emigrants. Her mother's people were a neighbouring landed family, the Spring Rices, Barons Mounteagle of Brandon. Ellen went to school in England and studied art at the Slade School in London, becoming a competent but not prolific painter of miniatures. She returned to Dublin, lived with Charlotte in Clonskeagh and,

through her, got to know Dr. Douglas Hyde whose idea of the Gaelic League as a great educational and unifying force in Irish life deeply impressed her. Ellen's involvement with the Gaelic League was frowned upon by other members of her family; perhaps her brother Dermod's defence of her in a letter to his stepmother reflected her own approach; 'Nell's branch is quite non-political, showing that people who are Unionist and protestant are ready to meet their fellow-countrymen on a common platform.' This appears to have been the motivation which led her to set up her own branch of the League, Craobh na gCúig gCúigí ('Branch of the Five Provinces'). She hosted *aeraíochtaí* (open-air assemblies) organised by the local League at Cahirmoyle House. In 1912, she raised funds (especially from her Spring Rice relations) to set up an Irish-language residential summer-school, Colaiste Eoghain Uí Chomhraí, at Carrigholt, Co. Clare, which is still in existence. In 1914 Ellen went to the USA with Fionán Mac Colum, a Gaelic League official, to raise funds for the League. Unlike her step-brother, Conor, and cousin, MARY SPRING RICE, she never associated herself with the militant aspect of the movement which was such a dynamic force in the 1916 Rising and the War of Independence. In her belief that the League could be a unifying agent Ellen wished to Gaelicise the Church of Ireland by infusing it with the spirituality of the Early Irish Church. To this end she founded *An tEaglaiseach Gaedhalach/The Gaelic Churchman*, a bilingual protestant journal which she funded personally. She was also instrumental in getting regular Irish-language services held in St. Patrick's Cathedral and Christ Church, in Dublin. An ecumenist before her time she had strong, if vague, ideas of uniting all the Christian Churches in Ireland in the spirit of the early Celtic Church. Ellen O'Brien died in her brother Dermod's London house on April 1, 1925.

O'BRIEN, KATE (1897-1974), novelist and dramatist. Born Limerick into a wealthy Irish Roman Catholic bourgeois family. When she was six years of age her mother died and Kate was sent to join her sisters at the convent of a French order of nuns who ran an upper-class primary and secondary school at Laurel Hill, Limerick. A scholarship student, she took a BA degree at University College Dublin. She worked in London as a journalist, teacher and translator, before going to Washington in 1919 as secretary to her uncle, James O'Mara, who was there to organise a Dáil loan for de Valera. A period working in Spain as a governess followed before she returned to London in 1924. She married a Dutch writer but they soon parted. Kate first became known as a playwright: her *Distinguished Villa* ran for three months in London in 1926, followed by *The Bridge* (1927). She established a reputation as an important Irish writer with her first novel, *Without my Cloak* (1931), which won her both the James Tait Black Memorial and the Hawthornden prizes. Although she wrote two more plays, *The Anteroom* (1938) and *The Schoolroom Window* (1937), she now concentrated on novel writing. *Mary Lavelle* (1936) and *Pray for the Wanderer* (1938), were followed by *The Land of Spices* (1941) which brought her undeserved notoriety when banned by the Irish Censorship Board. Work at the Ministry of Information in London during the Second World War did not greatly interrupt her output and her *English Diaries and Journals* and *The Last of Summer* appeared in 1943. Possibly her most popular book, *That Lady*, appeared in 1946. It was dramatised on Broadway sometime later and Kate was refused entry into Spain for ten years because it had an unfavourable portrait of King Philip II. She won the Irish Women Writers' Club prize for *For One Sweet Grape* (1946) and was elected a member of the Irish Academy of Letters the following year. However, she remained

54. Kate O'Brien in 1950.

somewhat suspect to the general Irish public because of some of her themes and characters, especially those portraying female friendships and lesbian heroines, and her irreverent observations of middle-class life. For a few years, she settled in Roundstone, Connemara, where she wrote *Flowers of May* (1953) and *As Music and Splendour* (1958). Having returned to England in 1961 she wrote her last two books there: *My Ireland* (1962) and *Presentation Parlour* (1963). In all, she published a dozen novels, four books of memoirs and travel, and a biography *Teresa of Avila* (1951). Kate O'Brien died in Canterbury on August 13, 1974.

O'BRIEN, MÁIRE RUA (1615-1686), Gaelic aristocrat. Possibly born in her mother's home, Bunratty Castle, Co. Clare. Daughter of Torlach MacMahon, Lord of Clonderlaw, and Máire O'Brien, daughter of the third Earl of Thomond. While still in her teens, Máire Rua married

55. Máire Rua O'Brien, c.1640, artist unknown.

'planted' in Limerick and in Sligo. Her husband thus became the legal owner of Leamaneh. He left the army and, becoming a landowner and speculator in property, was soon very wealthy. Contrary to folklore that gleefully relates how Máire Rua killed her hateful husband, the marriage of convenience lasted, at least from the legal and financial points of view and the couple had one son, Henry. In the 1660s murder charges were brought against Máire Rua by the Cromwellian 'planters' relating to her supposed participation in Conor O'Brien's raiding parties two decades earlier. She suffered considerable distress for two years before being granted a royal pardon on December 31, 1664. Cooper eventually encountered financial difficulties and Leamaneh had to be mortgaged. Máire Rua was possibly living independently of her husband at this stage and her son Henry arranged for her to occupy Dromoland Castle, one of his father's acquisitions, also in Co. Clare, where she spent the rest of her life. Her son by Conor O'Brien, Donough, whom she reared as a protestant, was eventually to become the 'richest commoner in Ireland,' and he moved the family seat permanently from Leamaneh to Dromoland. Today the senior branch of the O'Brien family, the Barons of Inchiquin, trace their ancestry back through him to Máire Rua and Conor O'Brien. Folklore portrays Máire Rua O'Brien as something of an ogre: the usual semi-historical element becoming intermixed with a mythological strand of folklore concerning the local earth goddess, Mór Rua, in which the concept of the goddess lived on as a queen with many lovers and husbands.

Daniel Neylon and went to live in the principal Neylon castle at Dysert O'Dea in north Clare. When Neylon died, leaving their four year old son as heir, she gained control of the estate. In October 1639 Máire Rua married her kinsman, Conor O'Brien of Leamaneh, where she went to live. The couple had eight children. In 1642 Conor O'Brien joined in the rebellion begun the previous year to profit from the divisions of the Civil War in Britain and enemies swore that Máire Rua rode in Conor's raiding parties. Conor was killed in 1651 and Máire Rua, then about thirty-six years old, had to abandon Leamaneh before the invading Cromwellian troops. In 1653, after Cromwellian victory and declaration that all who had been guilty of involvement in the rebellion would forfeit all property rights, she contracted marriage to Cornet John Cooper, a Cromwellian soldier of relatively low rank who had family connections

O'CARROLL, MARGARET. See under NÍ CHEARBHAILL, MÁIGRÉD.

O'CONNELL, MARY (SISTER ANTHONY) (1814-1897), American Civil War nurse and Cincinnati hospital and orphanage director, the

'Florence Nightingale of America'. Born August 15, 1814, in Co. Limerick. Little is known of her early life except that the family emigrated to the USA while Mary was still young enough to attend secondary school and her father prospered in Boston, Massachusetts. After the death of her mother she was sent to be educated at the Ursuline Academy in Charlestown, Mass. Inspired by the work of Mother Mary Seton who had founded the American Sisters of Charity at Emmitsburg, Maryland, to care for the sick poor, Mary entered that convent when she was twenty-one and became Sister Anthony. At twenty-four she was sent as a member of a small mission to take over an orphanage in Cincinnati, Ohio. In 1854 she was largely instrumental in founding a new orphanage, St. Joseph's, of which she became superior. Fourteen years later she founded St. John's Hotel for Invalids which, under her direction, became the fully-fledged hospital of St. John's, staffed by faculty members of the Miami Medical College and the city's first modern hospital. Sr. Anthony, whose religious community had by now become an independent order, the Sisters of Charity of Cincinnati, inaugurated the city's first visiting-nurse service. Shortly after the Civil War broke out, in 1861, the nuns nursed sick soldiers at a military camp outside the city. When the Union Army began to evacuate its wounded from the battlefields of West Virginia by riverboat to Cincinnati, St. John's was taken over as the main military hospital and, returning there, Sr. Anthony trained volunteers as nurses and orderlies. Later the Union forces penetrated as far as Shiloh, Tennessee, but met with stubborn resistance in their advance on Mississippi. Sr. Anthony, with members of the nursing and medical staff of St. John's, answered a general appeal for doctors and nurses to come to the war front. Working as a field nurse and in riverboat hospitals, she earned the soubriquet 'Florence Nightingale of America'. Sr. Anthony and her team became officially attached to the army during the Union penetration of Kentucky and accompanied the advancing troops. The medical team, with Sr. Anthony, were eventually assigned to the military base at Nashville where they worked for the duration of the war. After the ceasefire, in 1865, the army returned St. John's to the Sisters but, when cholera swept the city the following year and facilities there proved scarcely adequate, two philanthropic Protestants bought a former Marine hospital and presented it to Sr. Anthony on her birthday; she managed this, the Good Samaritan Hospital, until her retirement sixteen years later. Realizing the need for a hospital to care for unmarried mothers and abandoned infants she acquired a large building, mainly through the generosity of one of her previous benefactors, and opened St. Joseph's Foundling and Maternity Hospital in 1873. This was the first hospital of its kind in Cincinnati. For reasons that still remain unclear Sr. Anthony retired from her posts of responsibility in 1880 at the instigation of her bishop. The announcement was met with dismay from the general public and led to an unresolved controversy during which the nun herself stayed silent. However, she remained attached to St. Joseph's until her death in Cincinnati on December 8, 1897.

O'DOHERTY, ROSA. See under NÍ DHOCHARTAIGH, RÓIS.

O'DONNELL, NUALA. See under NÍ DHOMHNAILL, NUALADHA.

O'FARRELLY, AGNES. See under NÍ FHAIRCHEALLAIGH, ÚNA.

O'HALLORAN, MAURA 'SOSHIN' (1955-1983), Buddhist nun and saint. Born May 24, 1955, in Boston, Massachusetts, USA. Her father, a civil engineer, came from Co. Kerry and her mother was from Wayne, Maine, in the most north-easterly tip of the USA, where Maura was to make many visits and be greatly influenced by her grandmother. The family moved to Dublin when she was four; seven years later they returned to Boston as her father wished to do post-graduate studies. After he was killed in a road accident her mother brought the six children back to Dublin in 1970. Maura proved herself to be an excellent student at a Loreto convent school and received a Foundation Scholarship at Trinity College, Dublin. While at college she did voluntary social work with drug addicts and retarded children; she also travelled extensively (mostly by hitch-hiking) in Europe and North Africa. In 1977 she graduated with degrees in economics/statistics and sociology. Maura hitch-hiked through Canada, USA, Central America, most of South America. She spent about two years in Boston before setting out to 'discover' the Orient in whose cultures she had a long-standing interest. She arrived in Japan in November 1979 and, growing bored with ordinary life in Tokyo, moved to Toshoji Temple in that city where she was given lodgings in exchange for cleaning work. Already a practitioner of meditation, Maura soon began training in the monastic life, the only foreigner, and female, among the postulants. She was given the name Sohsin ('warm heart' or 'simple mind') in her *Tokudo* (initiation) ceremony. She spent a winter month in Konnonji Temple in Iwate, northern Japan, where she trained in strict *Kan-Shugyo*, which involved begging in the freezing weather, and other exercises, for twenty hours a day and sleeping for three. Initially intending to train for six months only, Soshin now determined to become a Zen master. She reached 'enlightenment' (after a period of *zazem* which incorporated intense meditation) in August 1982. In October of the same year she

received the 'transmission' of her *roshi* (master) and became a Buddhist nun having completed one thousand days continuous Zen practice 'to obtain salvation not only for herself but also for all people.' On her way back to Ireland Soshin O'Halloran was killed, in a bus accident in Thailand, on October 24, 1983. Her Kannon statue has been erected in the grounds of Konnonji monastery, Iwate, indicating her sainthood in that she achieved the 'same heart and mind as the Great Teacher Buddha.' In 1995 her journals and letters home during her training were published under the title *Pure Heart, Enlightened Mind*.

O'LEARY, ELLEN (1831-1889), republican, Land Leaguer, and writer. Born Tipperary, daughter of a prosperous shopkeeper and younger sister of the Fenian, John O'Leary. She and her brother inherited some property in the town which she mortgaged, in 1865, for two hundred pounds to finance the successful escape of the Fenian leader, James Stephens. Ellen was devoted to her older brother and followed him as his nationalist sympathies grew into revolutionary republicanism. Her political sympathies were the driving force behind her composition of verse, much of it in the ballad form she sought to revive. She was a highly respected poet in her day. W.B. Yeats corresponded regularly with Ellen from when he was twenty-three and wrote an article on her poetry for the *Boston Pilot* after her death. Using the pseudonym 'Lenel' on occasion, she contributed poems to the *Nation, Irish Fireside* and other magazines in Ireland and the USA, including the *Boston Pilot*. When Stephens, her brother and other Fenians set up the newspaper, *The Irish People,* to promote the cause of the Fenian movement, Ellen took an active interest and contributed to it. In 1865 her brother was jailed for nine years and afterwards went into political exile in Paris. She continued working for the Fenians from the O'Leary house in Dublin. On January 31, 1881, she became a founder-member of the Ladies Land League and one of its two treasurers. Her name was among those of the executive council who issued the militant call to their countrywomen to attack the whole landlord system on February 4 of that year. John O'Leary returned to Ireland in 1885 and, for many years, their home was noted for its literary and political evenings where the young Yeats was a frequent visitor. Ellen O'Leary died in Cork in 1889. In 1891 T.W. Rolleston edited a collection of her verse, *Lays of Country, Home and Friends* with an introduction by Gavan Duffy, one-time Young Ireland Leader and later Prime Minister of Victoria, Australia.

O'MALLEY, GRACE. See under UÍ MHÁILLE, GRÁINNE.

O'NEILL, ELIZA, LADY BECHER (*c.* 1791-1872), actress. Born in Drogheda, Co. Louth, where her father was stage manager and actor at the local theatre and her mother was an actress in the company. Eliza, receiving little formal schooling, began acting as a child. She was said to have appeared in Shakespearean plays from the age of ten. In her mid teens she was 'spotted' by a theatre manager from Belfast and the entire family joined his company. After two years, the O'Neill's returned to Dublin where Eliza achieved great popularity, making the part of Shakespeare's Juliet her own. In 1814 John Kemble of Covent Garden saw her in that role and subsequently engaged her and her parents for the London Theatre. For five years, Eliza reigned supreme on the London stage, especially as an actress of tragedy in parts such as Juliet, Belvidera (*Venice Preserv'd*), and Mrs. Haller (*The Stranger*). She was almost equally praised in the most popular comic roles of the time. Stories raged about the overwhelming effect of Eliza's

performances on males in her audiences, some of whom were so moved after witnessing one of her tragic performances that they fainted and had to be carried away. Macready, possibly the most distinguished producer and actor of the period, stated that, "in the native eloquence, the feminine sweetness, the unaffected earnestness and gushing passion of Miss O'Neill," a worthy successor had been found to the great Mrs. Siddons, the acclaimed Shakespearean actress of

56. *Eliza O'Neill, c.1815, by Thomas Clement Thompson.*

the previous century. In 1819, while visiting Kilkenny and at the height of her career, Eliza met William Wrixon Becher, MP for Mallow, an 'improving' landlord with considerable estates at Ballygiblin in Co. Cork. She returned to Ireland, in 1820, and made a last stage appearance in Dublin before marrying Becher. She spent the rest of her long life at her husband's home in Ballygiblin, becoming a leading figure of society in north Cork. Her husband was created Baronet in 1831. Lady Becher is said to have visited London for each new theatre season. She died at her home in 1872, a half century after her London triumphs.

O'NEILL, MÁIRE (1887-1952), actress. Born Drumcondra, Dublin. Originally Molly Allgood, sister of SARA ALLGOOD, whom she followed onto the stage of the Abbey Theatre in 1905. The playwright John Synge fell in love with Máire; she played Pegeen Mike on the riotous opening night of his *The Playboy of the Western World*. Synge's last play, *Deirdre of the Sorrows*, was inspired by his love for her but he died before he could see her play it. In 1911, Máire married G.H. Mair, drama critic of the *Manchester Guardian*, with whom she had two children. She successfully continued her career on the English stage for more than a decade. In 1926, after her husband's death, she married Arthur Sinclair, a former Abbey colleague with whom she had formed an acclaimed theatrical partnership. They performed in Ireland, and on tour in America, especially in the plays of Seán O'Casey. This marriage ended in divorce. Máire's career eventually went into decline and, like her sister Sara, she turned to playing bit parts in undistinguished films up to her death in 1952.

57. Máire O'Neill, drawing by Ben 'Bay'.

O'NEILL, MARY, née DEVENPORT (1879-1967), poet and dramatist. Born Loughrea, Co. Galway, daughter of a policeman (RIC). She was educated in Dublin at Eccles Street and the National College of Art. She married Joseph O'Neill, a school inspector, later to become secretary of the Department of Education, a novelist and playwright. The couple ran a famous weekly 'salon' at their Rathgar home which was frequented by many prominent literary and artistic figures. Mary's poems appeared in such magazines as *The Bell* and *Dublin Magazine*. Always interested in verse plays (she composed lyrics for her husband's play *Kingdom Maker* as early as 1917), she wrote two one-act plays for Austin Clarke's Lyric Theatre, Dublin; *Bluebeard (1933)* and *Cain* (1945). One collection of her poetry, *Prometheus and Other Poems* (1929), has been published. *Prometheus,* a long poem in five parts, perhaps her most important published work, has been neglected.

OSMANNA (OSANNA?), SAINT (5th or 6th century), anchorite of Brittany, celebrated in many early French manuscripts and invariably said to have been of royal Irish birth: *'Beata Virgo Osmanna clare stripe ac reguli Hiberniensium progenita.'* The sources tell us her name was Agariarga, that she was born into a pagan family and, according to custom, was matched with a man of her own class. However, wishing to give herself to the Christian God, she took one female servant and made her way to Brittany. Their ship was driven ashore near Saint-Brieuc by a storm. The women set up a hermitage in the forest near the Loire river and were discovered by a hunter who reported miraculous powers. They were baptised by the local bishop, presumably taking Osmanna and Aclitenis as Christian names, who then sent men to prepare a garden and build an oratory for them. The various acts and hagiographies attribute many miracles and wonders to Osmanna including curing the wife and daughter of the king of Spain. It appears that she died in her hermitage in Brittany. As the fame of her miracles grew, and pilgrimage to her grave increased, a church was built there in the ninth century. This was followed by an oratory from which grew the parish of St. Osmanna (Osmane), in the canton of Saint-Calais. Osmanna's remains were transferred first to Jotrum in the province of Bria, near Paris, to save them from desecration at the time of the Norse incursions. In the first half of the 12th century they were brought to the abbey church of St. Denis in Paris and a special chapel was built in the saint's honour. A new shrine erected in the 1300s, was torn down by Calvinists in 1567, restored, and then completely destroyed during the French Revolution. Osmanna was venerated in the dioceses of Paris, Le Mans, and Saint Brieuc, and her feast day is observed on September 9. She is the patron saint of Saint-Creota, a few miles from Le Mans, and an effigy wearing a Benedictine habit in a local church is traditionally assumed to be that of her servant, Aclitenis.

PARNELL, ANNA CATHERINE (1852-1911), co-founder of the Ladies Land League. Born Avondale, Co. Wicklow, into a protestant landed family that had first come to Ireland in 1660 and several of whom had been involved in politics, tending to support the independence of the protestant Irish Parliament. Her mother was a daughter of Admiral Stewart of the US Navy. She was a younger sister of Charles Stewart Parnell, destined to become one of the greatest names in Irish political history, and of FANNY PARNELL, co-founder of the Ladies Land League. When her parents separated, Anna, from the age of three, lived with her mother and some siblings in Paris where she was educated by governesses; after her father's death, in 1859, she returned to Dublin and renewed contact with Avondale. In 1870 she returned to Paris to study painting and later attended art college in London before joining her mother and sister, Fanny, in America, at Bordenstown, New Jersey, where they had settled. Anna was attracted to political and social reform by the example of her brother, Charles, who became the dominant figure in the Irish Party at Westminster in the late 1870s. In 1879, with Fanny and Mrs. Parnell, she was involved in the organisation of famine relief for destitute tenant farmers in Ireland. After the founding of the Irish National Land League, the great agrarian movement of which Charles was president, she began to lecture and write in American journals on its aims and methods and, with her sister, was soon promoting the idea of a women's organisation to support it. On October 15, 1880, the Ladies Land League was founded in New York with Mrs. Parnell as president. A network of branches were quickly formed throughout the USA and large sums of money were raised. With the full support of the Land League's founder, Michael Davitt, Anna returned to Ireland to officially establish the Ladies Land League, on January 31, 1881, with

58. **Anna Parnell** *and Lady Land Leaguers at the Dublin office.*

offices in the Land League headquarters at 39 Upper Sackville Street, (now O'Connell Street) Dublin. Shortly afterwards, in Claremorris, Co. Mayo, she addressed the first of countless public meetings to encourage the role of women in the land revolution. From the beginning she was more radical than Charles and most of the other League leaders, eventually calling for an all-out resistance to the payment of rent. The Ladies Land League, at first confined to aiding evicted families and prisoners' dependents, began to protest where evictions were actually taking place. When the leaders of the Land League were imprisoned, leaving the affairs of the organisation in disarray, the Ladies took over and restored order. Under Anna's guidance the *Book of Kells* was compiled. This was a huge dossier on every estate in Ireland recording the situation with regard to their respective tenantry. In October 1881 the Land League was suppressed and the leaders jailed. In response Anna undertook an exhausting tour of England and Scotland urging huge audiences to take their support from the governing Liberal Party. She found time not only to have the Land League paper, *United Ireland,* distributed but, when the printers were arrested, arranged for its printing in Paris. By mid-1882, because of her continued radicalism, Anna was in direct conflict with Charles who had come to terms with the government in regard to the implementation of land reform policy and was thus attempting to disband the Ladies League. In July her beloved sister and loyal co-worker, Fanny, died suddenly and Anna suffered mental and physical collapse. By the time she had recovered, the Ladies Land League had disappeared off the stage of history, and almost from its pages. Having broken absolutely with her brother, Anna wrote her version of events in *Tale of a Great Sham* but was unable to get it published. Bitterly disillusioned she left Ireland and public life in 1886. Some

years later she took up residence in an artists colony in Cornwall, England, under the assumed name of Cerissa Palmer. Anna Parnell drowned while swimming near Ilfracombe, Devon, on September 20, 1911. There were no members of her family, or representatives of the Irish people, at her funeral.

PARNELL, FANNY (1849-1882), co-founder of the Ladies Land League and poet. Born Avondale, Rathdrum, Co. Wicklow, the seventh of eleven children. Fanny was three years younger than her brother, Charles Stewart Parnell, who was destined to become one of the greatest names in Irish political history, and three years older than her sister, ANNA PARNELL, co-founder of the Ladies Land League. Her father, a protestant landowner farming five thousand acres, was of an Anglo-Irish family who had come to Ireland two hundred years previously and was related by blood to all the leading families in the county. Her paternal ancestors had been prominent in eighteenth century politics; her grandfather was an MP for Co. Wicklow and refused to support the Union. Her mother, daughter of Admiral Charles Stewart of the US Navy whose parents were immigrants from Belfast, was from a wealthy and socially prominent Boston colonial family on the distaff side. Her parents separated and Fanny, from the age of six, lived in Paris with her mother and some siblings and was educated by governesses. After her father's death in 1859 she moved back to Dublin with her mother and renewed contact with Avondale. She attended the trials of the Fenian revolutionaries in 1865 with fervour, especially that of O'Donovan Rossa, and wrote nationalist poetry for the *Irish People* and the *Irishman.* As befitted a young lady of her class, Fanny entered society in Dublin, London and Paris, where she was attending art school. In 1873 she went with her mother to live in America, at Bordenstown, New

Jersey, where, although in failing health, she managed their large house and farm. On holiday in Europe, in 1877, she visited the London House of Commons to witness her brother Charles pursue with success a policy of obstruction. He was soon to take over the leadership of the Irish Party. Back in America she and her sister, Anna, met with prominent Fenians and nationalists, and in 1879 they were organising famine relief funds for destitute farming families in Ireland. In the same year the Irish National Land League, the great agrarian movement of which her brother was president, was founded in Ireland and the Land War ensued. At this time she was writing numerous poems for nationalist papers, especially the *Boston Pilot* and the *Nation*, and was compared to SPERANZA, the muse of nationalism in the 1840s. Although much of this verse has since been dismissed, Fanny's most celebrated poem 'Hold the Harvest' rightfully seized the imagination of Irish nationalists in Ireland and America. Called the 'Marseillaise of the Irish peasant' it caused a sensation when being read by the Attorney General to the court during the state trials of the League leaders in 1881. She also published an emotive pamphlet *Hovels of Ireland* (1880), which ran into several editions. She was an indefatigable correspondent and organiser and had 'full instructions from Parnell about all that had to be done politically in America'. In July 1880, when funds for the Land League had fallen off alarmingly, it occurred to her that 'by setting the women at work, much needed stimulus would be given to the men'. With the support of the League founder Michael Davitt, Fanny and Anna launched an appeal 'to the Irish women of America' and the inaugural meeting of the Ladies Land League took place in the New York Hotel, New York, in the early autumn. Their mother, Mrs. Parnell, was nominated president and fund-raising begun immediately. In spite of rapidly deteriorating

health, Fanny worked with Anna for the Irish cause for at least ten hours daily as branches of the Ladies Land League sprang up throughout the USA. When Anna went to Ireland to organise the Ladies Land League Fanny continued to organise and advise. By now a political celebrity, she toured north eastern Canada collecting money for the League. Although at first she incurred the suspicions of republican American Fenianism, because of her support for Home Rule and advocacy of non-violent resistance, she was instrumental in bringing all shades of Irish nationalism there behind the League. On July 20, 1882, Fanny Parnell died while lying down after dinner.

Nationalists of all kinds wished to have her buried in Ireland where, as Boyle O'Reilly said, 'her dead lips will speak more powerfully than ours living.' Her brother Charles would not allow it (fearing the Ladies Land League had become too radical) and her embalmed remains were eventually brought by train to Boston, stopping at various stages along the way and paid homage to by many thousands. Fanny was buried in the family tomb of her Tudor ancestors at Mount Auburn, Cambridge, Massachusetts, and was a cult figure among Irish-Americans for many years afterwards.

PATTERSON, ANNIE W. (1869-1934), musician, composer, author, co-founder of the Feis Ceoil (Dublin). Born in Lurgan, Co. Armagh, and educated at Alexandra College, Dublin, she studied music at the Royal Irish Academy of Music, Dublin. Annie, a brilliant student, was made an examiner in music for the Academy in her early twenties; she worked for it and for the Irish Intermediate Board of Education in that capacity, and, as a music teacher, in colleges such as the Cork Municipal School of Music and the Leinster School of Music for the next twenty-five years. From 1924 onwards Annie was lecturer in

Irish music at University College Cork. She was also one of Dublin's outstanding church organists, conductor of the Dublin Choral Union, and composer and arranger of vocal, especially choral, and instrumental music. She wrote several books on music, including *The Story of Oratio, Schumann, Chats with Music Lovers, Native Music of Ireland* and *Six Original Gaelic Songs*. Her deep love of native Irish music (something rarely found at that time in musical circles in Dublin) found expression in her enthusiastic support of the Gaelic League. In 1894 she presented a proposal to that year-old organisation for 'the revival of the ancient Gaelic musical and literary festivals' and solicited support from various musical bodies in the capital. With the active participation of League members the first Feis Ceoil, a musical festival with competitions, was inaugurated in Dublin the same year. The wish expressed by the *Gaelic Journal*, 'to see justice done to our native language at the Feis,' was short-lived as non-League committee members were not enthusiastic. In response the League founded, in 1897, 'an Oireachtas or public assembly on behalf of the Irish language' to run in conjunction with the Feis. When the two committees separated completely Annie Patterson maintained her links with both. The Feis Ceoil in Dublin has remained, for more than one hundred years, as an important annual event in the Irish musical calendar; the Oireachtas has also continued annually to the present day as a major Irish-language festival and as the premier national competition for traditional music, song and dance.

PEARSE, MARGARET MARY (1878-1968), teacher, senator, sister of Patrick and Willie Pearse. Born August 4, 1878, in Dublin. The eldest of four children of James Pearse, an English monumental sculptor who lived and worked at Great Brunswick Street, Dublin,

where his business prospered. Her mother's family were Irish-speaking famine refugees from Co. Meath. Although her father wrote and published pamphlets at his own expense, one attacking a pro-Unionist pamphlet and the other attacking communism, it was her brother Patrick, future Commander-in-Chief of the Republican forces in 1916, who involved Margaret, her brother Willie, and their mother, in politics. Educated at the Holy Faith Convent, Glasnevin, Dublin, Margaret never entered paid employment although she may have had some training as a teacher. In 1904 she accompanied Patrick to Brussels where they examined education in a bilingual context. Her attempt to start an infants school failed but when Patrick founded the bilingual school, Scoil Éanna (St. Enda's), to advance his ideal of a free and Gaelic Ireland, she aided him and eventually became a full-time member of the school's staff along with her mother, brother Willie, and a female cousin. Despite the execution of her two brothers for their leading roles in the 1916 Rebellion, and in the face of debts and shortage of finance, Margaret and her mother kept the school going for a further two decades. She went on a lecture tour of the USA In 1926 to raise funds for the school. Margaret Pearse was elected TD for Co. Dublin, her deceased mother's seat, in 1933, having also taken her mother's place on the executive of Fianna Fáil. In spite of her efforts, her limited administrative and pedagogic abilities finally forced her to close St. Enda's in 1935. In 1938, she was elected to Seanad Éireann, remaining a member until her death in Dublin on November 7, 1968. Her career in politics resembled her mother's in that both women were little more than figure-heads for their political party. Both allowed themselves to be manipulated into playing more of a divisive part than a unifying one in Irish politics; they were also instrumental in the glorification of Patrick

Pearse at the expense of the other 1916 leaders. Always an uncritical follower of de Valera, Margaret, with two women deputies, supported his 1937 Constitution *in toto* although women's organisations throughout the country were unanimous in denouncing several articles in the proposal. Margaret Mary Pearse bequeathed St. Enda's, where she had lived virtually alone for many years, to the nation as a memorial to her brothers.

PIERCE, SOPHIE. See under HEATH, LADY MARY.

PLUNKETT, THE HONOURABLE KATHERINE (1820-1932), flower painter. Born at Kilsaran Rectory, Co. Louth, second daughter of the Bishop of Tuam, Kilalla and Achonry, and related on her mother's side to the Right Hon. John Foster, one of the founders of the Botanic Gardens in Dublin. She lived for most of her life at Ballymascanlon, outside Dundalk, Co. Louth, where, as was customary for a lady of her class, she maintained a large garden. Flower painting was also a fashionable pursuit but, from an early age, Katherine and her sister Frederica had the opportunity to extend the range and value of this recreation when travelling outside Ireland They visited the Black Forest in Germany, Zermatt and Murtan in Switzerland, San Remo in Italy and other parts of western Europe. A 'lady of leisure' all her life, Katherine had no need to paint professionally nor does she appear to have been motivated by scientific concerns as was her contemporary LYDIA SHACKLETON. In her eighties, following the death of her sister and collaborator, she presented a volume of twelve hundred different plants painted from nature to the National Museum of Ireland (then the Museum of Science and Art), being 'pleased to present them to a collection in my own country, rather than to any Botanical Society in England'.

59. 'Primula Marginata', *by the Hon.* **Katherine Plunkett.**

The volume is now preserved as an outstanding example of its kind in the Herbarium of the National Botanic Gardens, Glasnevin, Dublin. The Hon. Katherine Plunkett died at her home in Ballymascanlan at the extraordinary age of 112.

POPE, MARIA, née CAMPION (1775-1803), actress. Born Waterford city into a 'respectable merchant family'; her father died when she was still a child and Maria was reared by relatives away from her mother and sisters. She appears to have been given some education but was possibly something of an encumbrance on her adopters who encouraged her to approach a well-known theatre manager when, at sixteen, she became 'stage-struck' on her first visit to the Waterford Theatre. She was offered a trial on the Dublin stage and made her début as Monimia in the popular melodrama *The Orphan*. She greatly appealed to audiences and for several years appeared in different theatres in Dublin and also in York and Liverpool, in England, playing the Shakespearean tragic roles and those of the stock tragedies of the day. In 1797, Maria made her first London appearance at Covent Garden in the crowd-pulling role of Monimia and for the next half dozen years was the most popular tragedienne of her time. Respected for her propriety, she married a fellow-actor at twenty-two, and it is as Mrs. Pope she appears in theatrical histories. She died of a brain haemorrhage when she was twenty-eight having collapsed during a Covent Garden performance. She was buried in Westminster Abbey. A biographer noted that 'had Death spared her, there is every reason to believe that even to her great country-woman, Miss O'Neill, she would scarcely have stood second in the ranks as a tragic actress.' ELIZA O'NEILL, who had become the toast of the London stage within a decade of Maria Pope's death, was judged by her contemporaries to have been the greatest Irish-born tragedienne of all.

PRAEGER, (SOPHIA) ROSAMUND (1867-1954), sculptor and illustrator. Born Holywood, Co. Down. Her father was a linen merchant and her maternal grandfather, Robert Patterson, a noted naturalist who founded the Belfast Natural History Society in 1821; her brother Robert Lloyd Praeger was recognised as the foremost botanist in the Ireland of his day. She was educated locally before studying at the Belfast School of Art, the Slade School, London (where she won several prestigious awards), and in Paris. Returning to Ireland, in the late 1880s, Rosamund set up a

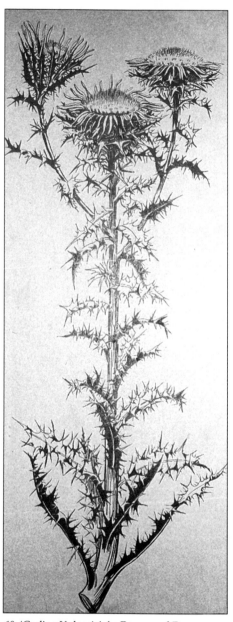

60. 'Carlina Vulgaris', *by **Rosamund Praeger**.

studio in Belfast and began to exhibit in 1891. From then on she proved herself to be an unusually versatile professional. She published, in 1896, the first of fifteen books of stories and rhymes for children that were illustrated and written, for the most part, by herself. About this time she also began to work on botanical line drawings, two hundred of which were used to illustrate at least two of her brother Robert's books; many of these drawings are now in the collection of the National Botanic Gardens, Dublin. Rosamund Praeger first established a reputation as a sculptor in 1913 with *The Philosopher*, a statue of a small boy which she exhibited at the Royal Academy in London. From this on she enjoyed continued success with a large output of sculptural works. She was much in demand for portraits but is perhaps best remembered for her numerous small scale pieces in plaster, many of them depicting children and whimsical subjects; several works such as *Fionnula, the Daughter of Lir*, were inspired by Irish mythology. She worked in various media, including marble and stone as well as bas-relief, terra cotta, and bronze, and carried out some large-scale monuments in stone, such as that commemorating the composer, Sir Hamilton Harty, in Hillsborough Church graveyard. Rosamund's work was exhibited widely, not only in Ireland, but also in England and France. She was elected an honorary member of the Royal Hibernian Academy in 1927 and later became president of the Royal Ulster Academy. Among other honours, Rosamund Praeger was awarded an MBE in 1939. At the age of eighty she produced, with illustrations, her last book *Oldfashioned Verses and Sketches*. Examples of her work are kept in the National Gallery of Ireland, the Ulster Museum, the Ulster Folk Museum and other public collections.

PRICE, DOCTOR DOROTHY, née STOPFORD (1890-1954), pioneer of BCG vaccination against tuberculosis in Ireland. Born Clonskeagh, Dublin. She studied medicine at Trinity College Dublin, and graduated in 1921. Professor William Boxwell, with whom she worked in the Meath Hospital, Dublin, encouraged Dorothy when she began to research the incidence of tuberculosis in children. She married in 1925 and began a private medical practice which brought her more into contact with the people of the city tenements where tuberculosis was rampant. This concern, coupled with her nationalist sympathies, allied her to Doctor KATHLEEN LYNN and Madeleine ffrench-Mullen who had founded St. Ultan's Infant Hospital in Charlemont Street, Dublin, in 1919. She was appointed to the Royal City of Dublin Hospital in 1932 and continued her research in regard to tuberculosis. Dorothy travelled to clinics in Germany, Sweden, Denmark and Switzerland to widen her knowledge of modern treatments as this area of medicine had been greatly neglected in Ireland. In agreement with Lynn and ffrench-Mullen she realised that while the disease was endemic in the slums of Dublin no political party was able or willing to take the necessary steps to improve the living conditions of the city's poor; therefore she concentrated her research work on vaccination. Although confronted with much hostility from her professional colleagues, Dorothy was the first doctor in Ireland to use the method of vaccination with an attenuated tubercle bacillus, now known as BCG. In 1938 she pioneered the method by injecting thirty-five children in St. Ultan's. The experiment proved to be remarkably successful and, after further demonstrations of the success of vaccination, led to Dublin Corporation setting up a major BCG system in 1938, the first of its kind in Ireland. For the rest of her life, Dr. Price worked to free Ireland from the scourge of tuberculosis, incurring opposition from the Roman Catholic hierarchy (which was to culminate in the 'Mother and Child' health scheme controversy of 1951) and being frustrated in her attempt to set up a nationwide Anti-Tuberculosis League. In 1942 she published *Tuberculosis in Childhood*, which gave significant impetus to the campaign against TB. Dr. Dorothy Price was made chairperson of the National BCG Committee in 1949. Ironically, she herself contracted tuberculosis in 1950 and was dead within four years, but had lived to see the killer disease being effectively tackled throughout the country, not least through the introduction of free BCG vaccination.

PURSER, SARAH (1848-1943), artist. Born March 22, 1848, in Kingstown (Dún Laoghaire), Co. Dublin, into a wealthy Anglo-Irish family. She was reared in Dungarvan, Co. Waterford, where her father had a flour milling business, and educated in Switzerland. Her father emigrated to America after his business failed and, at twenty-five, Sarah determined to make her living as a portrait painter. She studied at the College of Art, Dublin, and at the Académie Julian, Paris. She first exhibited at the Royal Hibernian Academy in 1880. Having painted CONSTANCE and EVA GORE-BOOTH that family found her the first of numerous commissions among the British aristocracy. Although not merely a portrait painter, as a handful of works in other genres prove, she continued her highly-paid portrait commissions for some twenty years and her artistic production, together with some shrewd investments, gained Sarah considerable wealth. Painting for Lane's proposed collection she contributed a great deal to the gallery of Irish national figures, including portraits of Edward Martyn, MAUD GONNE, and Douglas Hyde. An even more important stage of her career began in her early fifties and she was to remain a central figure in the Dublin art scene for the next four decades. Sarah was always generous to other artists and organised exhibitions for Jack Yeats and EVIE HONE; in 1903, with the guidance of Edward Martyn, she founded the famous co-operative glass and mosaic works An Túr Gloine (The Glass Tower) in Upper Pembroke Street, Dublin, which she ran until her death. With other distinguished artists, notably Evie Hone and Michael Healy, she took part in the decoration of Loughrea Cathedral. This, their first commission, was a milestone in Irish art history. Sarah's salon at Mespil House became a centre of artistic, literary, and intellectual life in Dublin. In 1924 she founded the Friends of the National Collections. Later, when the government vacated Charlemont House, she persuaded her friend W.T. Cosgrave, President of the Executive Council of the Irish Free State, to house the Municipal Gallery of Modern Art there. Sarah Purser was still painting in her eighties and took an active interest in An Túr Gloine until her death, at the age of ninety-five, on August 7, 1943, in Dublin.

QUINN, EDEL MARY (1907-1944), lay missionary. Born Kanturk, Co. Cork, September 14, 1907, of Galway-Clare extraction. Her father was a bank manager and the family transferred to several places in the south of Ireland. Educated in Clonmel and Enniscorthy Loreto schools, and later in an English Convent, Edel attended a commercial school in Dublin following family financial difficulties. Although intending to enter a contemplative order of nuns, she worked as a secretary in a tile factory to financially assist her family and joined the Legion of Mary. This recently-founded Roman Catholic lay organisation was devoted to apostolic and social work especially among the poor and underprivileged in Dublin's slums. Edel worked to help old people and prostitutes. The Legion's charismatic founder, Frank Duff, became her mentor. In 1932 she contracted tuberculosis and spent eighteen months in a sanatorium

61. A portrait of Kathleen Behan by **Sarah Purser.**

before returning to secretarial work and continuing with Legion activities. In view of her weakened state of health she finally abandoned her plan to enter a convent. The Legion had rapidly spread to Britain, the USA and India and now volunteers were required to set up branches in Africa. In 1936 Edel volunteered to become an envoy to Kenya and was accepted in spite of misgivings within the organisation on account of her ill health. The next seven years of her life were spent setting up Legion of Mary *praesidia* in Kenya, Uganda, Tanganyika, Nyasaland and Mauritius. Her apostolate brought her to cities, townships and villages, through jungles, swamps and leper colonies. In 1941, weakened by dysentery and pleurisy, she was admitted to a sanatorium in Johannesburg weighing only seventy-five pounds and suffering from advanced tuberculosis. After further hospitalisation, with the Dominican nuns in Cape Province, she resumed work in Nairobi in 1943 but, utterly burnt out, died the following year on May 12. Edel Quinn is buried beside another Irish Roman Catholic pioneer missionary, Bishop Shanahan, in the Missionaries Cemetery at Msongari, Nairobi.

REHAN, ADA (*c.* 1880-1916), actress. Born April 1860, Shannon Street, Limerick; real name Crehan. Her family emigrated to the USA when she was five years old and Ada followed her sisters onto the stage at thirteen. A printer's error led to her stage name. She quickly gained a reputation as a comedienne but also played serious roles and became the leading lady in Daly's Theatre, Broadway. She made her first appearance in London in 1884 and, three years later, took London audiences by storm as Katherina in Shakespeare's *Taming of the Shrew* and triumphed again in 1890 and 1895 in other Shakespearean productions. George Bernard Shaw considered her the only rival to Ellen Terry as a Shakespearean actress. Ada became a much-loved figure in New York and London and was asked to lay the foundation stone of Daly's new theatre at Leicester Square and to model for the Montana statue at the Chicago Exhibition which represented the ideal of loveliness. She never married and retired at the relatively young age of forty-five. Ada Rehan died in New York in 1916.

REID, NANO (1900-1981), painter. Born Drogheda, Co. Louth, where her family had a public house. Nano attended the local Dominican Convent before winning a scholarship to the Metropolitan School of Art in Dublin where she had Keating, Tuohy and Whelan among her tutors. However, she was most strongly influenced by Harry Clarke, that influence being most obvious in the early pictures she exhibited at the Royal Hibernian Academy exhibitions in the mid-twenties. Nano went to study in Paris in 1927 but, dissatisfied with her progress, moved on to the central School of Art in London where she was greatly encouraged by Bernard Meninsky. Her first one-woman show, in Dublin in 1934, was not a success. The second was a happier event and was even brought to her home town on the mayor's invitation. She exhibited mainly with the Royal Hibernian Academy at this period and, while her reputation as a mature painter grew, it was not until the mid 1940s that she began to develop into what many critics believe was 'one of the most significant Irish painters since Jack B. Yeats.' Basically a landscape painter, Nano's main subject matter was from the Boyne Valley of her home county and neighbouring Meath, Achill, Co. Mayo, and Donegal. Her early realism was said to have developed into an 'utterly Irish' form of abstract expressionism. She exhibited with the Irish Exhibition of Living Art and later with the Independent Artists. In 1950 she was chosen, with NORAH McGUINNESS, to represent Ireland at the Venice Biennale. Despite this, her reputation did not travel outside her own country and, although Nano received due critical recognition in Ireland, her work was not popular among the general public and sold poorly. Financial circumstances forced her to live with her sister in Drogheda. In 1972 she won the Douglas Hyde Gold Medal and the Arts Council Award at the Exhibition. Two years later there

*62. 'Cats in the kitchen', c.1953 by **Nano Reid**.*

were retrospective exhibitions of her work at the Dublin Municipal Gallery of Modern Art Museum. Up to her death, in a Drogheda Hospital on February 7, 1981, Nano Reid remained a private person and did not socialise outside a small bohemian coterie in Dublin. Critical acclaim, greater now than it was during her lifetime, has subsequently increased the value of her paintings. There are permanent exhibitions of her works in the Municipal Gallery of Modern Art, Dublin, in Santa Barbara Museum, California, and in the Irish Institute, New York.

RICHARDS, SHELAH (1903-1985), actress and producer. Born Dublin, May 1903, into a well-off family of Roman Catholic and protestant background. She was educated in Alexandra College, Dublin, and at a convent in Paris. While still in her teens, Shelah was introduced to acting by friends such as Lord and Lady Glenavy and became a member of the Dublin Drama League. She joined the Abbey Theatre in 1924 and soon attracted the attention of its co-director, W.B. Yeats, who insisted she take the lead in the revival of his *The Player Queen*. Later, at his request, she ran the Abbey School of Acting. Shelah played the role of Nora Clitheroe in the first production of Seán O'Casey's *The Plough and the Stars*, having already starred in his *Juno and the Paycock*. In 1938 she went to New York to play with Gladys Cooper and stayed in the US for almost two years. She formed her own company at the Olympia Theatre; among her more noted productions were those of Synge's *Playboy of the Western World* with SIOBHÁN McKENNA in the role of Pegeen Mike, and the world première of O'Casey's *Red*

Roses for Me. Having been a major figure in Irish Theatre for half a century, she became one of the first producers after RTÉ was set up in 1962 and worked mostly in this medium for two decades. She married playwright Denis Johnston and was the mother of novelist Jennifer Johnston. Shelah Richards died on January 19, 1985, at Ballybrack, Co. Dublin.

RIDGE, LOLA (ROSE EMILY) (1873-1941), poet and radical. Born December 12, 1873, in Dublin. Lola was taken by her mother to New Zealand in her mid teens. She studied art in Sydney, Australia, and in 1907, after her mother's death, moved to the USA. Settling in Greenwich Village, the bohemian quarter of New York, she supported herself, if poorly, as a copywriter and illustrator. From 1908 Lola published her poetry in various magazines, including the radical *Mother Earth*, but it was not until 1919, after her marriage, that she won acclaim with the publication of her first collection *The Ghetto and Other Poems*. By this time she was a supporter of radical, even anarchistic, causes and her imagist poetry reflected her compassion for the working class, the destitute, and her hostility to capitalism. *Sun-Up and Other Poems* appeared in 1920. Despite her radicalism she was awarded *Poetry Magazine's* Guarantor's Prize in 1923. Although suffering from ill health for most of her adult life Lola's energy was remarkable; she edited two small but important radical magazines, *Others* and *Broom*, while at the same time contributing a stream of poetry to both radical and non-political publications. In 1927 her third collection, *Red Flag and Other Poems*, celebrated many heroes of the struggle of the oppressed, ancient and modern, and was unashamedly communist in its sympathies. In the same year she took part in the unsuccessful campaign to prevent the execution of the Massachusetts anarchists Sacco and Vanzetti

and two years later *Firehead*, a collection based on the experience, voiced a protest not only against the executions but at injustices suffered by the American proletariat in general. She received several major literary awards, including a Guggenheim Fellowship in 1935, the year of the publication of her last collection *Dance of Fire*. Having been incapacitated by tuberculosis for the last decade of her life, Lola Ridge died on May 19, 1941, at her home in Brooklyn, New York. The high regard in which her poetry was held did not outlast the era of American radicalism that had helped to popularise it .

ROS, AMANDA McKITTRICK (1860-1939), novelist and poet, widely acclaimed as the world's worst writer. Born Drumaness, Co. Down. She trained in Dublin as a teacher and married the station master at Larne before the novels of Marie Corelli prompted her to write her own. Amanda's first offering, *Irene Iddesleigh*, was published in 1897 at her husband's expense as a wedding anniversary present. It was greeted with few sales and much amazement but, undaunted, she published two more in the same extravagantly florid style, *Delina Delaney* and *Donald Dudley*. These were so awful that a cult grew around them at Oxford and Amanda McKittrick Ros Clubs began to meet not only in London but, after Mark Twain had humorously reviewed her first work, all over the United States. Her novels were republished after Aldous Huxley had pronounced her 'an Elizabethan born out of her time'. It was also said of her that 'she had no standards, being below all possible standards'; some critics, believing her work to be impossibly bad, felt that they were deliberate satire, especially as the author harangued the 'sham and corruption of high society', lawyers and the clergy. *Punch Magazine* once devoted an entire issue to lampooning her work. Financial success served only to convince the author of her importance and she never seemed to become aware of the reason for the popularity of her books. In her writings she was an ardent imperialist and a Victorian prude, utterly devoid of humour. When not involved in writing or composing songs for broadsheets, she was engaged in numerous lawsuits and business quarrels. A woman of indomitable energy, she married again at sixty two to a well-to-do farmer and turned to publishing collections of verse, such as *Poems of Puncture* (1913) and *Poems of Fomentation* (1933) which were every bit as ridiculously high-flown as her prose but contained the same almost Rabelaisian vim. Her work has been reprinted from time to time and even a biography, *O Rare Amanda,* by Jack Loudan was published in 1954. Some of her couplets, such as the opening lines of her notorious 'Ode to Westminster Abbey', remain evergreen as literary curiosities:

Holy Moses! Take a look!
Brain and brawn in every nook!

ROSS, MARTIN, pen name of VIOLET FLORENCE MARTIN (1862-1915), novelist. Born June 11, 1862, at Ross House near Moycullen, Co. Galway, into a branch of the Martin family, one of the ancient 'tribes of Galway.' Violet was educated mostly at home by an aunt and a former hedge-school master and her youth was spent in the company of the children of estate workers and tenants. In 1886 she met her second cousin, EDITH SOMERVILLE (both were descended on their mother's side from Charles Kendal Bushe MP, orator and Lord Chief Justice of Ireland), and the women began a life-long friendship and literary partnership. From this time onwards

Violet lived, for the most part, with her cousin at Drishane House in Castletownshend, Co. Cork. Encouraged by her brother, a journalist and song writer, she and her cousin began to write amusing travel articles for *The Ladies Pictorial* about Ireland, Wales, the vineyards of the French Madoc and, later, Denmark where they were sent by the magazine. Some of these pieces appeared in book form in *The Vine Country* (1893). The women had earlier published a novel, *An Irish Cousin* (1889). A second novel followed before *The Real Charlotte* established their reputation in 1894; it is still acclaimed as a minor masterpiece. They had published several other travel books and another novel when, in 1898, a hunting accident left Violet a semi-invalid for the rest of her life. Nevertheless, the following year *Some Experiences of an Irish R.M.*, probably the authors' most popular novel, appeared. *Some Irish Yesterdays,* a book of memoirs, mostly Violet's, was published in 1908 and other novels followed, including *Further Experiences of an Irish R.M.* (1908), *Dan Russell the Fox* (1911), *In Mr. Knox's Country* (1915). These 'Anglo-Irish' novels pictured the last days of ascendancy Ireland in an ironic fashion, sometimes with cruel humour (which, it is generally agreed, was supplied mainly by Violet), and spared neither class nor person. The books were not only extremely popular in their day but have gained in stature in recent decades. Theirs was one of the most successful collaborations in the history of letters. Violet Ross died at Drishane on December 21, 1915. Further autobiographical essays, *Strayaways,* were published posthumously and she was honoured with an Hon. D. Litt. by Trinity College Dublin, in 1932. Edith Somerville continued to write under the name of Somerville and Ross, claiming that, even in death, her friend continued to work with her.

ROSS, MOTHER. See under CAVANAGH, KIT.

RUSSELL, MOTHER MARY BAPTIST (1829-1898), first Superior of the Sisters of Mercy in California, USA. Born April 18, 1829, at Killowen, near Newry, Co. Down. The Russells were a wealthy Roman Catholic family; her father an ex-sea captain turned brewer. She was an elder sister of the future Lord Russell of Killowen, the first Roman Catholic to be appointed Lord Chief Justice of England since the Reformation, and of Fr. Matthew Russell, SJ, founder of the influential Roman Catholic journal *Irish Monthly*. She was educated privately and, with a late vocation, entered the order of the Sisters of Mercy at Kinsale, Co. Cork, where she was professed in 1851. She worked among the poor, in an area devastated by the recent Great Famine and several cholera epidemics, before answering a call for volunteers from the Archbishop of San Francisco at the end of 1854. Appointed superior, she took a party of eight nuns and novices with the aim of caring for the sick, 'distressed young women', and 'instructing' the poor. San Francisco, in a state of disorder at this time, was overcrowded with an influx of emigrants many of which were destitute Irish. The following year cholera struck the city and, because of the nuns' experience in caring for fever victims in Ireland, they were given complete charge of the only hospital in the city, the County Hospital. Some years later difficulties with the civic authorities led Mother Russell to found, in 1860, St. Mary's Hospital, the first Roman Catholic hospital on the West Coast. From the beginning the order had attracted recruits and new foundations were set up in Sacramento as early as 1857 and in Grass Valley in 1863. During the forty-four years of Mother Russell's direction the Sisters of Mercy in San Francisco also set up refuges for unemployed women and unmarried mothers, an industrial school for young women, seven primary schools for boys and girls, and a home for the aged and infirm. The nuns were noted for feeding the poor during depressions and for visiting San Quentin State Prison, where they were especially welcome on death row. Mother Russell personally organised the fund-raising necessary to keep the order's institutions in existence. Financial support came from Roman Catholics and non-Catholics alike. The Californian State Legislature presented the order with five thousand dollars in gratitude for their work as volunteer nurses in the city fever hospital during the severe outbreak of smallpox in 1868. After she died, on August 6, 1898, the *San Francisco Bulletin* referred to Mother Russell as the 'best-known charitable worker on the Pacific Coast.'

SADLIER, MARY ANN, née MADDEN (1820-1913), novelist and business woman. Born December 31, 1820, in Cootehill, Co. Cavan. She emigrated to Montreal, Canada, in her twenties and soon after married Tipperary-born James Sadlier who, with his brother Denis, ran a publishing company that had its main branch in New York. Mary began to publish under the Sadlier imprint and her novels, some sixty in all and set for the most part in Irish historical backgrounds, were highly successful in their time. Many were published by Irish and British publishing houses. They include *The Red Hand of Ulster, The Hermit of the Rock of Cashel, The Confederate Chieftains* and *The Old House by the Boyne. The Blakes and Flanagans* (1896) was a novel illustrative of Irish life in the United States. In 1860, when the D. & J. Sadlier Company expanded to become one of the bigger Roman Catholic publishers in New York, she moved there with her husband and family. For two decades the New York *Tablet* carried many of her contributions. Even with her prolific literary output Mary became increasingly active in her husband's business. After his relatively early death, in 1869, she became more involved in the running of the company. Under her direction, the firm began a highly profitable line of Roman Catholic school textbooks. When her brother-in-law Denis died, in 1902, Mary Sadlier ran the company for another decade before selling it, at the age of ninety-three, to P.J. Kennedy & Sons.

ST. JOHN WHITTY, SOPHIA (1878-1924), co-op manager, wood carver, crafts teacher. Born in Dublin. Sophia studied wood carving at the South Kensington School of Art, London. She opened a studio in the centre of Dublin, with her sister, to give lessons in several crafts while attending the Dublin Metropolitan School of Art. She then studied wood carving in Belgium for a time. In 1902 Sophia was employed, as a teacher of woodwork, at Bray Technical School which was one of the first founded to address the lack of non-academic education. A woodwork class for Church of Ireland choirboys, which had been incorporated in the new Technical School, produced and sold so much work that a co-operative society, the Bray Art Furniture Industry, was formed and grant-aided by the Department of Agricultural and Technical Instruction. Sophia acted as manager, designer, and instructor in the enterprise, which specialised in cabinet making and carving. Employing about a dozen craftsmen full-time, and up to fifty on a part-time basis, the co-operative opened a shop in Bray's Main Street in 1907. Many of the more important commissions came from protestant churches while secular examples were exhibited by the Arts and Crafts Society of Ireland and Royal Dublin Society up to the outbreak of the First World War. The onset of the war brought about the closure of the business because of a sudden decline in orders. At this stage Sophia involved herself in working for the Society of United Irishwomen. This

*68. Prayer desk in Christ Church, Bray, Co. Wicklow, by **Sophia St. John Whitty** and Kathleen Scott.*

organisation, representing the women's counterpart of the contemporary co-operative movement in Ireland, addressed problems of education, domestic economy and public health. Sophia, attracted by the Society's aim to develop industries for women, remained with it during the difficult war years but resigned, as did many others, at the outbreak of the Civil War due to political tensions. Sophia St. John Whitty died three years later, hardly outliving the short by remarkable revival of wood carving coinciding with the general 'renaissance' of things Irish from the 1890s.

SAMTHANN (SAFANA), SAINT (died 739), virgin saint. Although the hagiography of this saint relates only that she led the simplest of lives and, unlike so many of her contemporary religious, was not given to travelling, she attained great stature after her death not only in the Irish Church but also in Salzburg, Austria.

Samthann was fostered by Críodán, king of Cairbre Gabhra in what is now Co. Meath, and is therefore assumed to have been of royal blood. Avoiding the marriage arranged for her, she went to Ernaide in Donegal where she took a woman anchorite, Cognat, as her spiritual mentor. Later, she set up her own foundation at Clonbroney, near Granard, Co. Longford, and remained abbess of this monastery until her death. Her simplicity of life provided an example to a church grown too worldly after ascetic beginnings. Samthann was renowned for her down-to-earth wisdom. When asked in what way prayer should be made, she replied that it ought to be made while standing, sitting, or lying. With regard to the Irish addiction to pilgrimage, especially to Rome, she remarked that heaven could be reached without crossing any sea. The scholar-scientist, Virgil, who came to Salzburg six years after Samthann's death and remained as abbot and bishop until 784, is presumed to have introduced her cult there. Her feast day is December 19.

SAYERS, PEIG (1873-1958), *seanchaí* or storyteller. Born Dún Chaoin, Co. Kerry, into a poverty-stricken family farming a smallholding on the seaboard. Her father, Tomás Mac an tSaoir (Sayers), and mother had moved there from Ventry, Co. Kerry, where nine of their family had died. Peig picked up her *seanchas* (folklore and traditional stories) from her father and from neighbours she visited as a child with an older brother. On leaving national school she worked as a serving girl in Dingle, Co. Kerry, for about six years before a match was made for her with a Blasket islander, Padraig Ó Guithín. She lived on the island for more than forty years. At first Peig's life, though difficult, was happy. Then four of her ten children died young, her husband lost his health, and her eldest son fell to his death from a cliff. When the fishing failed her surviving children emigrated and, after her husband's death, she lived with a blind brother-in-law in poor circumstances. Visiting scholars and students of the Irish language, many of them foreigners, were impressed by Peig's stories and folklore and her reputation as a *seanchaí* spread. Robin Flower, the English scholar and author, wrote that 'her words could be written down as they leave her lips and they would have the effect of literature.' In 1928, a neighbour. Tomás Ó Criomhthain, published his diary, *Allagar na hInise*, followed by his account of island life, *An tOileánach* (translated and published as *The Islandman* in 1934). Subsequently, Peig was encouraged by a Dublin teacher, Máire Ní Chinnéide, to relate her own life story, which was painstakingly written down by Peig's son, Micheál, who had returned from the USA. Under the title *Peig*, it was published in 1936; three years later a second volume of reminiscences, *Machnamh Seanmhná*, appeared. Both books were later translated into English. Further autobiography appeared posthumously in 1970, *Beatha Pheig Sayers*. Her greatest contribution may well be in the wealth of oral material, including some four hundred tales, recorded from her by the Irish Folklore Commission, especially by Seosamh Ó Dálaigh and Seán Ó Súilleabháin. By 1953, the viability of life on the island being in question, she and her son returned to Dún Chaoin with the remaining islanders under a government scheme. Peig Sayers spent the last years of her life in Dingle Hospital where she died at Christmas 1958.

SHACKLETON, LYDIA (1828-1914), botanic artist. Born into a large Quaker family that had come to Ireland more than a century previously; several Shackletons have been prominent in various areas of Irish life. Lydia went to the local Quaker school and stayed on for a time as a monitor or assistant teacher. In her early

*63. 'Helleborus Niger Macranthus', by **Lydia Shackleton**.*

twenties she studied at the Dublin School of Art before opening a small school for Quaker children in Lucan, a village in west Co. Dublin, where she taught for some twenty years. An amateur artist (painting being then a fashionable pursuit for 'genteel' ladies), she painted landscapes and pictures of wild flowers on two visits to North America which appear to have excited interest among a limited, if knowledgeable, circle. Frederick Moore, curator of the Dublin Royal Botanic Gardens in Glasnevin (now the National Botanic Gardens), commissioned Lydia to paint the Garden's pride when she was fifty: this was a collection of orchids which contained an enormous variety of species. She began work in September 1884 and did not retire until December 1907 when her eyesight failed. She executed, in watercolour, more than one thousand paintings of orchids and several hundred others of field plants found in the wild in Ireland. None of her work was published in Lydia's lifetime and it is thought she held only one exhibition, for the Limerick Field Club, when she was seventy-three. The work she did for the Botanic Gardens, unique in its own right, is still on display there; even if her free-flowing style was considered to be less suited to the depiction of smaller plants, Lydia Shackleton is widely considered to have been the greatest of all botanic artists born in Ireland.

SHEEHY SKEFFINGTON, HANNA, née SHEEHY (1877-1946), suffragist, socialist, republican, journalist. Born at 2, Belvedere Place, Dublin, into a family with prosperous farming and milling backgrounds in Limerick and Tipperary. Her father was an MP, a member of the IRB, and had been imprisoned for revolutionary activities; the Land League priest Fr. Eugene Sheehy was an uncle. Hanna attended the Dominican Convent in Eccles Street, Dublin, and was a brilliant student at the Royal University of Ireland, graduating in 1902 with a BA degree. She became a teacher in the Rathmines School of Commerce and, in 1903, married Francis Skeffington, a university registrar who was becoming prominent as a polemic journalist with socialist and pacifist sympathies. Five years later the pair, recognising the need for a separate Irish suffrage society founded, together with MARGARET COUSINS, the Irish Women's Franchise League (IWFL). Hanna contributed articles on education and feminist issues to the *Nation* and *Bean na hÉireann*, and, in 1912, she and her husband founded the influential paper *Irish Citizen*, aiming to promote the rights and responsibilities of citizenship for both sexes. Failing in their attempts to persuade Home Rule leaders to guarantee women's suffrage, Hanna led members of the IWFL into a militant protest which involved breaking windows in government buildings. She was arrested and, after making an opportune political speech in court, was sentenced to one month in Mountjoy Jail. Dismissed from her teaching post she devoted her time to the *Irish Citizen* and IWFL, and, increasingly, to the labour movement. She

64. Hanna Sheehy Skeffington.

and her husband became close associates of labour leader James Connolly and, during the protracted 1913 Lock Out, Hanna worked in the soup kitchen set up in Liberty Hall, the Dublin headquarters of the Irish Transport and General Workers Union, to support the locked-out union members. She was jailed again, this time for 'assaulting a policeman' (she was 5 feet 2 inches tall) while distributing suffragette pamphlets.

Hanna went on hunger strike and was released after five days. A pacifist like her husband, she supported him in the campaign against recruitment to the British armed forces at the onset of the First World War, for which activity he was imprisoned. During the 1916 Rising her husband was arrested and murdered at Portobello Barracks by British soldiers. Hanna immediately began to campaign for justice, forcing the Royal Commission to hold an inquiry, which led to the court martial of her husband's killer. By the end of the same year she toured the United States, to publicise the nationalist cause, and spoke at two hundred and fifty meetings; in January 1918, on behalf of Cumann na mBan, she personally presented Ireland's claim for self-determination to President Wilson. On her way home Hanna was again arrested, lodged in Holloway Jail with KATHLEEN CLARKE, COUNTESS MARKIEVICZ and MAUD GONNE, and again was released after hunger strike. In 1917 she was appointed to the executive of Sinn Féin and, during 1920, acted as judge in the Republican courts in South Dublin. She was also an executive member of the White Cross Fund set up to aid the needy families of Volunteers involved in the War of Independence. Along with many other republican suffragettes she rejected the Treaty but was involved in the joint attempt by women of both allegiances to bring a stop to the Civil War. She was appointed to the first executive of Fianna Fáil in 1926 but soon resigned when she realised there was no place for a committed feminist and radical in that party. In 1930 Hanna went on a six-week tour of Russia and following year took over as editor of the *Republican File*, a republican-socialist journal, after the jailing of its editor Frank Ryan; subsequently she became assistant editor of *An Phoblacht*, the organ of the Irish Republican Army (IRA). She was jailed, yet again, for a month for speaking at a public meeting in Newry, Co. Down, demanding release of republican prisoners and protesting against partition. In 1935, as a speaker for the Women's Graduates Association, she opposed the Conditions of Employment Bill which feminists considered a draconian measure against women workers. Hanna was a founder-member of the Women's Social and Progressive League, a party which came into being after a mass protest of women at the Mansion House, Dublin, following the passing of the bill; however, the party failed to win significant support despite initially campaigning strongly in the 1938 general elections. In 1943, at the age of sixty-six, Hanna stood as an independent candidate in the general elections, demanding equality for women, but none of the four feminist candidates received any support from the electorate. Hanna Sheehy Skeffington spent her life, until she died in 1948, fighting for equality of citizenship, for the rights of the individual, for workers and for a republic, and, most consistently, for the feminist cause.

SHERIDAN, FRANCES, née CHAMBERLAINE (1724-1766), novelist and dramatist. Born Dublin, the youngest child of a protestant clergyman. Her mother died at her birth and the father reared the family in a strict, puritan manner, even forbidding literacy for his daughters. An elder brother taught her in secret and at fifteen Frances wrote a romance that, in the circumstances, she could not publish. In 1745 Thomas Sheridan, a brilliant young actor already being compared to the great Garrick, acquitted himself well during a serious public riot in a Dublin theatre. When the story of his deportment reached Miss Chamberlaine she praised him in verse and pamphlet. The couple met and married two years later. The union appears to have been unusually happy despite the characteristic Sheridan improvidence. Thomas had

already written a life of his godfather, Dean Swift; later he published a number of works on education and elocution and gained a reputation as a lexicographer. The Sheridans moved to London in 1754. Here Thomas continued his successful career as actor-manager and he and Frances moved in the brilliant company of Dr. Samuel Johnson and other eminent men of the day in the Literary Club. Samuel Richardson, the great English novelist, then at the height of his career, recognised Frances' talents and encouraged her to write a novel. Her masterpiece, *Memoirs of Miss Sydney Biddulph* (1761) was warmly received and published in French and German versions. She wrote several lively comedies in the next few years, *The Discovery* (1783) being the most successful. The following year the couple emigrated to Blois in the Loire Valley, Brittany, to escape creditors. Frances Sheridan died here, aged forty-two, on September 26, 1766. The novel she wrote at fifteen, *Eugenia and Adelaide*, was published posthumously. Frances and Thomas Sheridan's second son was the dramatist Richard Brinsley Sheridan; their descendants have displayed remarkable literary talent over the several generations to the present time.

SHORTER, DORA SIGERSON (1866-1918), poet. Born in Dublin. Daughter of the physician, scientist, Gaelic scholar and man of letters, George Sigerson, a Roman Catholic from Co. Tyrone who practised in Dublin. Dora had no formal education but the family home in Clare Street, Dublin, was a noted gathering place for writers, artists and musicians. She was close friends with the writer and poet, KATHARINE TYNAN, and poet, Alice Furlong. Dora became an important member of the circle of writers and artists involved in the Literary Renaissance although she went to live in England from 1895 following her marriage to K.C. Shorter, English

*65. **Dora Sigerson Shorter** by Josephine Webb.*

critic and editor. From 1893 onwards she produced more than a dozen collections of poetry, four books of tales and sketches, and two novels, all very much in the nationalist spirit of the period. She was a skilled versifier and highly praised by the likes of Douglas Hyde and George Meredith for her ballad poetry. Her popularity is attested to by the fact that four volumes of her poetry were published posthumously, among them *Sad Years* (1918) and *The Tricolour* (1922). When Dora Shorter died, on January 6, 1918, her friend Katharine Tynan attributed her death to a broken heart caused by the failure of the 1916 Rising. Her work has dated and is now almost forgotten: however, 'Sixteen Dead Men', celebrating the executed 1916 leaders, remains an evergreen anthology piece:

Sixteen dead men! What on their sword?
'A nation's honour proved do they bear.'
What on their bent heads? God's holy word:
All of their nation's heart blended in prayer.'

SIGERSON, DORA. See under SHORTER, DORA.

SKINNIDER, MARGARET or **NÍ SCINNEADÓRA, MAIGHREAD** (1893-1971), revolutionary and president of the Irish National Teachers' Organisation. Born in Glasgow, Scotland, to which her parents had emigrated from Co. Monaghan. Margaret qualified as a teacher and joined the Glasgow branch of Cumann na mBan, the revolutionary Irishwomen's organisation. Like the Belfast branch, the Glasgow Cumann was greatly influenced by James Connolly, the republican socialist; his daughter, Nora Connolly O'Brien, became a life-long friend of Margaret's. She received some military training and appears to have been involved in raids for explosives. On her first visit to Ireland, at Christmas 1915, Margaret smuggled in detonators which she and COUNTESS MARKIEVICZ tested in the Dublin mountains. She became a trusted friend of the Countess and joined Connolly's Irish Citizen Army. With the Countess she served in the Citizen Army, under the command of Michael Mallin, in the fighting at St. Stephen's Green and the College of Surgeons during the 1916 Rebellion. Having acted both as sniper and scout, Margaret persuaded Mallin (arguing that, under the Constitution of the Irish Republic, women had "the same right to risk our lives as the men") to allow her lead a group to cut off the retreat of British snipers. She was wounded three times in the resulting action. Following the surrender, she was held in hospital custody, from which she eventually 'walked out.' Deceiving the British authorities with her Scots accent, Margaret obtained a special permit to return to Glasgow. As a member of a Cumann na mBan mission (which included Nora Connolly), she went to the USA in 1917 to publicise the situation in Ireland, and while there wrote a book, *Doing my Bit for Ireland*, to promote the republican cause. She was later involved in training members of the Volunteers in preparation for the War of Independence. During the Civil War (1922-1923), she was paymaster-general for the IRA until her arrest. Margaret was fortunate to obtain a teaching position following the formation of the Free State and, from this on until her retirement in 1961, she taught in a primary school run by the Irish Sisters of Charity at Kings Inns Street, Dublin. She was naturally drawn into the Irish National Teachers Organisation (INTO) and, as Máighréad Ní Scinneadóra, was a member of its central executive for many years. Ever since the Fianna Fáil Party had assumed power in 1932, the INTO was at odds with the government over pay, conditions, and compulsory teaching of the Irish language. During a protracted confrontation in 1946 she was a member of the strike working committee. Following the return to work, she was appointed to the salaries and arbitration committee which diffused much of the contention. Vice-president of the INTO in 1955, Máighréad Ní Scinneadóra was elected president the following year. During her presidency, she represented Ireland at the World Conference of the Organisation of the Teaching Profession in Manila, Philippines. Her union remembers her, in particular, for her fight for the rights of its women members which bore fruit in the introduction of common incremental salary scales for women and single men in 1949. Máighréad Ní Scinneadóra was buried in the Republican Plot, beside Countess Markievicz, in Glasnevin Cemetery, Dublin.

SMITHSON, ANNIE MP (1873-1948), novelist and nurse. Born September 26, 1873, at Sandymount, Dublin, into a protestant family with a grandfather who had been a revolutionary republican. Her father, a solicitor, died

when Annie was eight and, on her mother's remarriage, she went to live in England for some years before the family returned to Dublin. She trained as a nurse and midwife in London and Edinburgh and worked as a district nurse in several parts of Ireland and Glasgow. It was here, following an unhappy love affair, that Annie converted to Roman Catholicism. Back in Ireland, having become an ardent nationalist, she worked for Sinn Féin in the 1918 General Election and was active for Cumann na mBan nursing wounded Volunteers during the War of Independence. Annie was imprisoned but released after commencing a hunger strike. She began to write at a comparatively late age and her first novel, *Her Irish Heritage*, based on the experience of discovering her own 'Irishness', was published in 1917. It was sentimental and naïvely patriotic and, appealing to popular taste, became an immediate success. *By Strange Paths* followed in 1919, and *The Walk of a Queen*, in 1922. Taking the Republican side in the Civil War, she was present as a nurse in the siege of the Republican-held Moran's Hotel. Arrested and imprisoned, she was forced to resign from the Queen's Nurses Committee and turned to writing for her livelihood; the most popular romantic novelist of her time in Ireland, she published twenty more novels, all best-sellers, between 1925 and 1946. She assisted in the setting-up of the Irish Nurses' Union (later the Irish Nurses' Organisation) and worked as secretary and organiser of that union until 1942. Her autobiography, *Myself and Others*, was published in 1944. Annie Smithson died in Dublin on February 21, 1948.

SMITHSON, HENRIETTA (HARRIET) CONSTANCE or MADAME BERLIOZ (1800-1854), actress. Born Ennis, Co. Clare, on March 18, 1800, of English parents. Her father was an actor and theatre manager who worked mainly on the south eastern circuit with occasional visits to Ennis. Harriet spent her early childhood in the household of a protestant minister and later she went to boarding school in Waterford. Undoubtedly due to her father's influence, she made her first stage appearance in 1815 in Dublin's Crowe Street Theatre and, for the next nine years, played leading roles at theatres all over Ireland and Britain, including Drury Lane and the original Old Vic in London. In 1824 the young composer Hector Berlioz saw her during a performance in Paris and fell in love with her. 'No dramatic artist in France ever touched and excited the public as she did,' he wrote in his *Memoires*. Harriet remained in Paris where, for several years, her performances were acclaimed. Berlioz composed *Huit Scenes de Faust* (1829) expressly for her, followed by the autobiographical work *Symphonie Fantastique* which was an expression of his obsession with her. However, she never reciprocated his advances. By 1832 Harriet, who had never learned to speak French properly, found her career on the French stage in sudden decline and her finances in disarray. After Berlioz threatened suicide if she refused him the couple were married in 1833 much against the wishes of his family. The marriage was initially happy and a son was born the following year, but the strains caused by years of poverty, Harriet's frustration at the failure of her acting career and her subsequent heavy drinking led to the couple's separation in 1844. Madame Harriet Berlioz died on March 3, 1854, having been paralysed for the last four years of her life during which Berlioz contributed to her support.

SOMERVILLE, EDITH ANNA OENONE (1858-1949), novelist and artist. Born May 2 on the island of Corfu where her father, a lieutenant colonel in the British army, was stationed. From the age of one year she was raised on the family estates at Drishane, Castletownshend, near Skibbereen, Co. Cork. Educated privately and at Alexandra College, Dublin, Edith studied painting in Dusseldorf, London and Paris. Painting and illustrating, although soon overshadowed by her talent for writing, remained an abiding interest and she was still exhibiting at seventy-five. Another interest was horse-riding and hunting and, for some time, she was Master of the West Carbery Foxhounds. She already had some articles published, with her own illustrations, on student life in Paris before meeting her second cousin, VIOLET MARTIN, from Ross House, Co. Galway in 1886. A close friendship arose between the two and resulted in a most successful literary partnership. Encouraged by Violet's brother, a journalist and comic songwriter, Edith and Violet, published their first novel, *An Irish Cousin* in 1889 under the dual signature, 'Somerville and Ross'. When Violet died, twenty-six years later, they had produced more than a dozen titles, including novels, short story collections and travel books. In their fiction the women portray, to the point of caricature, the last days of the Anglo-Irish ascendancy in the late Victorian era. This world of decadent landlords and comic peasants, presented with an underlying ironic style, has been compared to that of Balzac. At the beginning the pair were mostly interested in travel writing, contributing essays to *The Ladies Pictorial* and publishing travel books such as *In the Vine Country* (1893). Their novel, *The Real Charlotte*, published in 1894, established the women in the forefront of Anglo-Irish fiction writers. Violet was seriously injured while hunting in 1898; permanently disabled, she was to spend most of her remaining years at Drishane. *Some Experiences of an Irish R.M.* was published the year after the accident and, along with two later collections of stories in the same vein, *Further Experiences of an Irish R.M* (1908) and

66. 'A trayful of burning sods of turf', *an illustration from* 'Further Experiences of an Irish R.M.', *by*
Edith E.O. Somerville.

In Mr. Knox's Country (1915), brought the authors lasting popularity. Other joint publications included *Some Irish Yesterdays* (1906), *Dan Russell the Fox* (1911), *The Discontented Little Elephant* (1912). When Violet Martin died, at the end of 1915, Edith wrote, 'my share of the world has gone with Martin and nothing can ever make that better.' Nevertheless, she continued to write

67. **The Hon. Mary Ellen Spring-Rice** (right) and Mary Childers on board the 'Asgard' near Howth, Co. Dublin, 1914.

and paint incessantly for the rest of her long life. During the 1920s she frequently exhibited oil paintings in London and New York. She insisted on publishing her books under the dual signature 'Somerville and Ross,' claiming that even death did not finish their collaboration. These later books included *Irish Memories* (1917), *Wheel Tracks* (1923), *Big House at Inver* (1925), *French Leave* (1928), *The Smile and the Tear* (1933), *The Sweet Cry of Hounds* (1936), *Sarah's Youth* (1938), and *Notions in Garrison* (1942). *An Incorruptible Irishman* (1932) was a biography of their great-grandfather, Charles Kendal Bushe, loyal member of the Irish Parliament and Lord Chief Justice of Ireland from 1822-1841. When Edith was in her seventies and short of money she accepted an invitation to go on a lecture tour of the USA which resulted in her last travel book, *The States through Irish Eyes* (1931). She was conferred with an honorary D. Litt. by Dublin University in 1922 and awarded the Gregory Gold Medal by the Irish Academy of Letters of which she had been a founder member in 1941. At eighty-five she took part in the Irish Exhibition of Living Art, Dublin. Her portrait of Violet Martin hangs in the National Portrait Gallery of London. Edith Somerville died on October 8, 1949, at Drishane and was buried with her cousin Violet in the churchyard of St. Barrahane, Castletownshend, Co. Cork.

SOSHIN. See under O'HALLORAN, MAURA.

SPERANZA OF THE NATION. See under WILDE, LADY JANE FRANCESCA.

SPRING RICE, THE HONOURABLE MARY ELLEN (1880-1924), nationalist and Gaelic Leaguer. Born October 14, 1880, into an old Jacobite family. Her father, the second Baron Monteagle, held estates in Co. Kerry and principally at Mount Trenchard, Foynes, Co. Limerick.

Her mother was a daughter of Dr. Butcher, Bishop of Meath. A cousin was British Ambassador to the USA. As a young girl Mary Ellen met Dr. Douglas Hyde, founder of the Gaelic League, while he was on a visit to her neighbour CHARLOTTE GRACE O'BRIEN. Hyde later recalled that Irish was then the common language in the Foynes area and that Mary Ellen was a fluent speaker. Influenced by the example of her first cousin, NELLIE O'BRIEN, who was an enthusiastic follower of Hyde, she joined the Gaelic League in Dublin and London, organised *scoraíochtaí* (festive assemblies) on the banks of the Shannon, and hired a native speaker from Kerry to teach classes in the local national school. Mary Ellen was an ardent supporter and member of the management board of Nellie's Coláiste Uí Chomhraí, an Irish-language summer college established in Carrigaholt, Co. Clare, in 1912, and many of the Spring Rices, including the British Ambassador, contributed to the founding of the college. Mary Ellen had by now become a committed nationalist. In 1914 she proposed the idea to Erskine Childers, the Irish-Englishman who espoused the cause of Irish Home Rule whom she met in London at a Gaelic League fair, that arms for the Irish Volunteers, then planning insurrection, could be run from Germany to Ireland using private yachts. After the Volunteer executive had agreed to the plan she was involved in setting up a committee (which included Roger Casement, ALICE STOPFORD GREEN and Mrs. Childers) in London to collect funds for the enterprise. Three yachts were involved, the *Asgard*, skippered by Childers, the *Kelpie* under her cousin Conor O'Brien and the *Chotah* under Sir Thomas Myles. Mary Ellen sailed on the *Asgard* which, on July 26, 1914, successfully carried one thousand five hundred rifles and seventy-four thousand rounds of ammunition from the Belgian Coast to Howth,

Dublin. During the War of Independence she nursed wounded Volunteers and set up first aid classes. Although in failing health, she remained active in the Society of the United Irishwomen, the women's agricultural organisation movement with which she had been associated from its inception in 1910. When Mary Ellen Spring Rice died, aged forty-four, her coffin carried by local republicans as a mark of their respect. She was buried at the family church, Loghill, near Foynes, Co. Limerick.

STARKIE, ENID MARY (1897-1970), scholar, biographer and critic. Born Killiney, Co. Dublin, into a family with a tradition of scholarship, her father, W.J.M. Starkie, was Resident Commissioner of National Education for Ireland and a distinguished classicist. Her brother Walter became an authority on the Romance languages and Gypsy culture. Enid was educated at Alexandra College, Dublin, and the Royal Irish Academy of Music, Dublin. She took a first-class degree in French at Oxford and, having gone to the Sorbonne as Gilchrist Student, gained a doctorate at the University of Paris and a prize from the French Academy in 1927 for a thesis on Émile Verhaeren, the Belgian poet and critic. She lectured at Exeter University before being appointed the first Sarah Smithson Lecturer in French literature at her old college, Somerville, Oxford and wrote biographies of Baudelaire (1933) and Rimbaud (1938) while pursuing her career at Somerville. Enid was elected Fellow and Tutor and awarded the first Doctorate of Letters conferred in her faculty (1939). In 1941 she wrote an autobiographical account of student life in Dublin and Oxford, *A Lady's Child*. In 1948 she was made a Chevalier of the French Légion d'Honneur, (an honour also awarded to her brother Walter). She published a book on the socially rebellious French author, Gide, in 1954, and produced two books on

Flaubert, *The Making of a Master* (1967) and *The Master* (1971). She was highly involved in university life and politics, lectured widely in the USA and was honoured with a CBE (1967). Enid Starkie died at Oxford in 1970.

STOKES, MARGARET MACNAIR (1832-1900), antiquarian, art historian, illustrator. Born York Street, Dublin, the eldest daughter of William Stokes, a noted Dublin physician who was president of the Royal College of Surgeons, a medical author, antiquarian and Young Ireland supporter. Her grandfather, Whitley Stokes, had been a United Irishman and Irish scholar. Her mother, Mary Black, was Scottish. Margaret was educated by governesses while her father nurtured her love of study. From childhood she was familiar with his close friends, especially the antiquarians George Petrie, the Earl of Dunraven and painter Frederick William Burton, who were her mentors in antiquarianism and art. She translated and edited her first volume of Didron's *Christian Iconography* while still in her teens. Margaret joined her father and his friends on an important field trip to the Aran Islands in 1857 where she studied the archaelogical remains with Petrie and painted with Burton. In 1861 she did the illustrations for Ferguson's *Cromlech of Howth*, a luxurious edition lavishly decorated in a Celtic style which greatly influenced the design and illustration of the later Celtic Revival. It is little known that she also influenced the neo-Hiberno/Romanesque style of architecture through her association with Franklin Fuller, official architect for the Church of Ireland and leading exponent of that style. She had brought out her second volume of Didron's work when Petrie died in 1866, and then undertook to finish the latter's incomplete research on inscriptions, a labour of a dozen years duration which culminated in her two-volume edition of *Christian Inscriptions of the Irish Language* (1872; 1879). In the

69. **Margaret Macnair Stokes** sketching the High Cross of Moone, Co. Kildare.

meantime Lord Dunraven died, having entrusted to Margaret the manuscript and other materials relating to his monumental work on Irish architecture, confident that 'he was placing them in hands thoroughly competent and most desirous to do justice to them.' The resulting two-volume Notes on Irish Architecture (1875; 1877) led to her being elected a member of the Royal Irish Academy, a rare occurrence for a woman in those days. In 1878 she published Early Christian Architecture in Ireland, a history of the era from stone forts to Romanesque architecture, illustrated by herself, Burton and others. She published numerous other articles and books including the significant Early Christian Art in Ireland and two illustrated travel books describing her pilgrimages made on the Continent 'in search of vestiges of the Irish saints', Six Months in the Appenines (1892) and

Three Months in the Forests of France (1895). The last ten years of Margaret Stoke's life were given in particular to the study of the high crosses. She wrote several ground-breaking essays on the subject but, before she could produce the monumental work to which she aspired, Margaret Stokes died on September 20, 1900.

SWANZY, MARY (1882-1978), painter. Born February 15, 1882, at Merrion Square, Dublin, where her father, Sir Henry Swanzy, was a distinguished ophthalmic surgeon. She was educated at Alexandra College, Dublin, and later in Versailles and Freiburg. She studied art at Miss Manning's School in Dublin with John Butler Yeats and the sculptor John Hughes among her tutors. Mary went to Paris in her early twenties and, while working in different studios, came

70. 'Honolulu Gardens', c.1924, by **Mary Swanzy**.

under a wide variety of influences while still thinking primarily of becoming a portrait painter. Soon after exhibiting a portrait at the Royal Hibernian Academy she was showing in Parisian group exhibitions with painters such as the young Picasso and Braque. In 1913 Mary held her first solo exhibitions in Dublin and in Paris at the Salon des Indépendants. Her work became noted for its variety of styles, themes, and subjects believed to be influenced by her extensive travels. After the death of her parents she spent a couple of years in St. Tropez, in the south of France, before going to live with her sister in eastern Europe where she painted continuously in Yugoslavia and Czechoslovakia. In 1924 she visited the west coast of America, then continued on to Honolulu and Samoa where her style now reflected these colourful tropical landscapes. She was back in the south of France in 1926 where an original 'lyrical' cubism became her characteristic. She continued to exhibit in Dublin and Paris. In the 1940s, confronted with the horrors of the Second World War, Mary's painting underwent another extraordinary change as and her expressionism mirrored that terrible period. She exhibited in London with Moore, Braque, Dufy, Chagall and Scott in 1946, and was elected to the Royal Hibernian Academy in 1949. In 1968, at the age of eighty-six, she held a retrospective at the Municipal Gallery, Dublin. Having continued to paint up to her final year, Mary Swanzy died in London on July 7, 1978, at the age of ninety-six.

TENNANT, MARGARET MARY EDITH (MAY), née ABRAHAM (1869-1946), pioneer promoter of workers rights and public health. Born April 5, 1869, Rathgar, Dublin, the daughter of a lawyer in the civil service. May received much of her education from her father. After his death she went to London, at the age of twenty-one, and became secretary to Lady Emily Dilke. Lady Dilke was a social reformer and advocate of trade unionism for women, especially in sweated and dangerous employment. This led to Margaret becoming treasurer of the Women's Trade Union League and, having played a prominent role in securing state inspection of laundries, becoming a member of the Royal Commission on Labour at the age of twenty-two. In 1893 the Commission appointed her as the first official woman factory inspector in Britain. Her reports on forced overtime, dangerous work practices and poor sanitation hastened the 1895 Factory and Workshop Act. In 1895 she was on a departmental committee monitoring dangerous trades. The following year May resigned her position and married the chairman, Harold John Tennant, a Liberal MP. Two years later she was appointed to the Chair of the Industrial Law Indemnity Fund which furnished compensation for victimised workers. In 1909 May served on the Royal Commission on Divorce and subsequently was instrumental in founding the Central Committee for Women's Employment, acting as its treasurer for twenty-five years. During the First World War she was chief adviser on women's welfare at the War Office and later became director of the Women's Section of the National Service Department for a time before serving in the Ministry of Munitions. The British Government awarded her the CH in recognition of her services. In 1917 her husband was appointed Secretary of State for Scotland. After the war she involved herself in public health matters, focusing on women's health issues, especially the lowering of maternal mortality and improving nursing care. During the Second World War, although her health was seriously impaired, she took an active part in the Royal Air Force Benevolent Fund. May Tennant died on July 11, 1946, at Cornhill, Rolvenden, Kent, England.

THOMPSON or THOMSON, ELIZABETH (mid-18th century), consort to Emperor Sidi Mohammed of Morocco and mother of Emperor Muli Ishmael. Born into a rich merchant family of British origin in Cork city. She wished to marry the son of Don Eugenio O'Shea, wine merchant and ship owner in Cadiz, and scion of an old Cork Gaelic family. Her parents, for political and religious reasons, refused her permission. With the Franciscans in Broad Lane, Cork, acting as go-betweens, Elizabeth's elopement to Spain was arranged and O'Shea sent a ship to Cork for the purpose. On the return journey the vessel was captured by a Moroccan corsair and Elizabeth and her man-servant were among the captives taken. Along with her servant she was sold in the slave market at the capital, Fez, and thus became part of the harem at the Imperial palace. In time, having converted to the Muslim religion, she became the favourite consort of Sultan Sidi Mohammed (styled 'Emperor' by Europeans) and mother of two of his sons. The assassination of the Emperor and the outbreak of civil war caused her to flee to Alicante on the Moorish east coast of Spain. When her eldest son, Moulay Yazid, was proclaimed Emperor she returned to the Imperial palace in Marrakech and remained there until her death.

THORNTON, BRIDGET, née LYONS (c. 1898-1987), republican, doctor, and first female commissioned officer in the Irish Army. She was born into a strongly republican family in

Longford of comfortable means. While still a medical student at University College Galway, together with two of her uncles (one of whom, Joe McGuinness, was later to win a landmark victory for Sinn Féin in the 1917 by-elections) she took part in the 1916 Rising, joining the rebels occupying the Four Courts building under Edward Daly's command. She was arrested and imprisoned in Kilmainham Jail, Dublin, but was given early release. During the War of Independence Bridget was attached to the Longford Brigade under General Seán MacEoin. Rising to the rank of Commandant, she was at times personally responsible to Michael Collins, Director of Organisation and Intelligence for the Volunteer military resistance to British rule. After she had qualified as a doctor in 1922, she accepted the invitation of Collins, now Commander-in-Chief of the Free State Government Forces, to join the Medical Service of the newly formed army. She was given the rank of First Lieutenant, thus becoming the first female commissioned officer in the Irish Army. (A half century would go by before another woman was commissioned). The Civil War had broken out and Bridget was given responsibility for the anti-Treaty prisoners in Kilmainham Jail, many of whom were her former comrades-in-arms. She married Captain Eddie Thornton in 1923 but they both contracted tuberculosis and he died within some months of the wedding. Having resigned her army commission, Bridget made her career in the public health sector, specialising in paediatrics and tuberculosis eradication. Following the lead of DOROTHY PRICE she played an important part, from the late 1930s, in pioneering the vaccination schemes using attenuated tubercle bacilli, now known as BCG, to combat the high incidence of tuberculosis in Ireland. The introduction of free BCG vaccination was a major factor in bringing the disease under control within twenty years.

TYNAN, KATHARINE (1861-1931), author, poet, journalist. Born January 21, 1861, at Clondalkin, Co. Dublin. Her father was a prosperous Roman Catholic gentleman farmer. Katharine's formal education, at the Dominican Convent, Drogheda, Co. Louth, was cut short by an eye condition which left her with a severe lifelong handicap. At twenty, she became a committee member (a self-confessed 'frivolous' one) of the Ladies Land League. At the same time she began to publish poems, particularily in the *Irish Monthly*. Her father paid twenty pounds to have her first poetry collection, *Louise de la Valliere* (1885), published. It was an immediate success and won her friends and a reputation among the leading figures of the Irish Literary Revival. For a time her escort to literary and political evenings was W.B. Yeats whom many of their associates felt she might surpass as a poet. Her *Ballads and Lyrics* (1891), a collection of nature poetry with a strong religious spirit, set the tone and standard of much of her verse which was prolific and popular but ultimately lightweight in comparison to the major poets of her time. In 1894 she married H. A. Hinkson, barrister and classic scholar. She lived in England for the next eighteen years, writing prolifically, while at the same time rearing three children and coping with an alcoholic husband. Daughter Pamela once claimed that her mother's works took up more space in the British Museum Library than those of any other writer. *Twenty Five Years* (1913), a five-volume autobiographical work, remains a valuable record of the personalities of her time. Her most famous poem, *Sheep and Lambs*, appeared in her collection, *Devotional Poetry* (1914). While writing for most of the influential journals and periodicals Katharine championed the rights of women and raised issues such as the working conditions of shop-girls and the plight of single mothers. Many of her novels are concerned with social and feminist issues. Before the start of the First World War she returned to Ireland, her husband having been appointed resident magistrate in Co. Mayo. She produced two volumes of patriotic war verse which attained widespread popularity in Britain. Her writings on Irish affairs evinced a thoroughly middle class, Roman Catholic rejection of republicanism. Left in somewhat impecunious circumstances after the death of her husband in 1918, Katharine travelled Europe on journalistic assignments with her teenage daughter, Pamela, who was to become, under her influence, an even more celebrated journalist and author. In a writing life of fifty-three years she produced more than one hundred novels, twelve short story collections, three plays, eighteen poetry collections, two poetry anthologies, seven books of devotional poems, twelve collections of memories, essays and criticisms, an autobiography in five volumes and numerous uncollected articles and stories. Katharine Tynan died after a brief illness in London on April 2, 1931.

TYRRELL, KATE (*c.* 1863-1921), ship's master and company director. Born at Arklow, Co. Wicklow, where her father had a small shipping firm (an unusual business at that time for a Roman Catholic), which did a coastal trade in the Irish Sea. Kate, one of four daughters, took an uncommon interest in the business and spent considerable time aboard ship from the age of fifteen. Especially after her mother's death, in 1882, she assisted in running the business on shore and at sea. In 1885, her father bought her a schooner, 'The Denbighshire Lass', only to find that the maritime authorities refused to allow the vessel to be registered in the name of a woman. She had to wait fourteen years before the laws were changed to enable her to do so. The 'Denbighshire Lass' was a sixty-two ton, two-masted vessel capable of carrying up to one hundred and twenty tons of cargo and could be sailed by a crew of four or five. After her father had a heart attack and died, when she was twenty-two, Kate took over the shipping firm and, with a family friend and old hand as nominal master, sailed the vessel, 'tramping' with cargo from port to port. Ten years later she married John Fitzpatrick who had joined her ship as a member of its crew and his name was registered as master for a time to appease the authorities. In 1899 she was able to register ownership under her own name. From this on, because of her young family and later ill health, Kate spent little time at sea. Nevertheless, she and her husband kept the business going in spite of intense competition from steamships. Kate Tyrrell died on October 4, 1921. The 'Denbighshire Lass,' with her husband as master and son as mate, continued working for only a further four years. However, on one of her last voyages, the 'Denbighshire Lass' had the distinction of being the first vessel to fly the Irish tricolour in a foreign port.

UÍ CHOISDEAILBH, EIBHLÍN BEAN or COSTELLO, EILEEN (ELLEN), née DRURY (1870-1962), folksong collector, Gaelic Leaguer and political activist. Born Edith Drury on June 27, 1870, most likely in the Strand Union Workhouse in St. Pancras, London. Her background remains obscure except for the fact that her father was a native of Co. Limerick and her mother was Welsh. Edith was educated, possibly through some protestant charitable society, and qualified as a teacher, later becoming principal of a Church of England school in London. She joined the Irish Literary Society, where she got to know the YEATS sisters, and was already collecting songs in Irish from emigrants before joining the London branch of the Gaelic League at its inaugural meeting in 1896. She played an active part in the

71. **Kate Tyrrell** *and her ship the* 'Denbyshire Lass'.

League for the next six years and in other related Irish-language organisations. In 1902 she was among the delegates sent to the League's Ard Fheis (national convention) in Dublin and stayed to assist in organising an *aeraíocht* or open-air festival on Inis Meáin, one of the Aran Islands, with ÚNA NÍ FHAIRCHEALLAIGH and Dr. Micheál Ó hIceadha. She was considered a prestigious enough personality to present the prizes at Tuam Feis, an important Gaelic League festival. About this time she had to resign from her post as school principal as she converted to Roman Catholicism. She returned to Ireland in 1903 to marry Dr. Tom Bodkin Costello. Having taken Eibhlín as her baptismal name, she became known as a folksong collector under the names of Eibhlín bean Uí Choisdeailbh and Mrs. Costello. Travelling in the Tuam area with her doctor husband, who was also an important antiquarian and Irish scholar, Eibhlín collected songs from Irish speakers and other people in Galway and Mayo who were interested in folksong and generously contributed to her collection. Eighty of these songs were chosen for the 1918 edition, Vol. XVI, of the *Irish Folksong Society Journal*. In 1923 her collection was published under the title of *Amhráin Mhuighe Seola*. She continued organising *feiseanna* and *aeraíochtaí* in Tuam and was involved in the Oireachtas na Gaeilge, the League's annual national festival. During the War of Independence Eibhlín stood for Sinn Féin and was elected as District Councillor for North Galway and as a Tuam Town Commissioner. She also acted as a judge in the Sinn Féin courts and because of frequently hiding Volunteers on the run, had her house raided by the Black and Tans, an infamous special force of British troops. Eibhlín supported the Treaty and joined with WYSE POWER, STOPFORD GREEN, GAVAN DUFFY and others in the new women's organisation, Cumann na Saoirse (League of Freedom), set up in March 1922 to support the establishment of the new Free State in opposition to the republican Cumann na mBan. She was elected to the first Free State Senate in the same year. With Jennie Wyse Power, she was instrumental in bringing about the Senate's rejection of the Civil Service Regulation Bill (1925) and in forcing the amendment of the Juries Bill (1927), on the grounds that both these bills discriminated against women. Eibhlín bean Uí Choisdealbh died on March 14, 1962.

UÍ DHIOSCA, ÚNA, née LEECH (1880-1958), Irish language revivalist and author. Born Elizabeth Rachael Leech in Danesfield House, Clontarf, Co. Dublin. Her father was a lawyer in the civil service. Elizabeth was sent to school in Switzerland and later to Alexandra College, Dublin. Living in the multilingual society of Switzerland had fuelled her desire to learn Irish and she persuaded the authorities in Alexander College to introduce Irish-language classes into the curriculum. She worked as a teacher for three

years in Canada before returning to Ireland and marrying Ernest McClintock Dix, a lawyer and bibliophile who was also an Irish language enthusiast. The couple lived in Rathfarnham, Dublin. From this time on she used the Gaelic form of her married name and converted from the Church of Ireland to Roman Catholicism in 1923. Úna was president of the Irish branch of War Resisters International and, in the early years of the Free State, founded and ran Na Cáirde Gael, an Irish language association which fostered interest in the United Nations and in foreign affairs. She began to write in her fifties and produced several novels and plays, including *Cailín na Gruaige Duinne* (1932) and *An Seod do-Fhágála* (1936). When her husband died in 1936, Úna moved with her family to Kildare and later to Wicklow, where she became absorbed with many aspects of rural community revival, especially in the Irish Countrywomen's Association and Muintir na Tíre. She died at her home in Co. Wicklow on November 2, 1958.

UÍ MHÁILLE, GRÁINNE (O'MALLEY, GRACE) (*c*. 1530-c. 1603), sea-queen. Born probably at Clare Island, Co. Mayo. Only daughter of the house of Ó Máille, hereditary chieftains of the maritime state of Umhall Uachtrach, (otherwise the Barony of Murrisk) on the Mayo coast, stretching from what is now Westport to Connemara, and including Clare Island. Her father was Dubhdara Ó Máille and her mother, Mairghréad, daughter of Conchobhar Óg Ó Máille, a kinsman. From an early age Gráinne's interest lay in the world of ships, trade and sea-power. At the age of sixteen she was married to Dónal a' Chogaidh Ó Flaitheartaigh (O'Flaherty), the warlike chief of Iar-Chonnacht and Connemara. They lived in Bunowen Castle, Co.Galway where Gráinne appears to have played an active part in the affairs of the estate. The couple had three children. There is evidence

72. **Gráinne Uí Mháille** *and Queen Elizabeth I, from an exhibition in the Louisburg Heritage Centre, Co. Mayo.*

that, after her husband was killed by the neighbouring Joyces, she captained O'Flaherty ships in attacks on British shipping and sailed on trading missions to Scotland and the Continent. She eventually returned to Umhall Uachtarach having failed to occupy her husband's influential place in O'Flaherty affairs. About 1566, a marriage was arranged between Gráinne and Risteard an Iarainn de Búrca, chief of the Burkes of Carra and Burrishoole, and tanist (successor in Brehon law) to the title of Mac William Íochtar as over-all lord of the Burkes of Mayo. Tradition holds that the marriage was only for 'one year certain' (an arrangement ratified by Brehon Law) and that, having installed herself at Carraig a' Chabhlaigh Castle near Newport on the north-east of Clew Bay and gaining

control of the surrounding territory for the O'Malleys, she terminated her marriage to Richard Burke. However, she and the Burkes remained allies all her life. In 1568 Gráinne and Risteard, with several other Connaught lords, submitted to Sydney, the invading Lord Deputy. Sydney recorded her offer of three galleys to aid him in both Ireland and Scotland and that 'she brought with her her husband, for she was, as well by sea as by land, more than Mrs. mate with him... This was a notorious woman in all the coasts of Ireland'. Encroachment by the English authorities forced the Burkes into rebellion and Gráinne was to support the latter over years of intermittent warfare. She was captured and imprisoned in Dublin Castle in 1577 and released the following year. In 1579 she defeated a goverment fleet and forced government troops to give up a siege at her castle, Carraig a' Chabhlaigh. Following the death of Risteard an Iarainn, in 1586, Gráinne was attacked and captured by the forces of Bingham, President of Connaught. She was brought to Dublin for hanging but her son-in-law Richard Burke, now at an uneasy peace with the government, demanded and obtained her release. Bingham's military excesses eventually brought Richard into open rebellion and during the war that followed (probably in 1592 when an English fleet penetrated Clew Bay and 'cleared' all of the O'Malley island-strongholds) Gráinne fled to Ulster, taking refuge with the Earl of Tyrone. In July 1593 she sailed to London to appeal to Queen Elizabeth I and, despite Bingham's evidence that she was a 'notorious traitoress and nurse to all the rebellions (in Connaught) for forty years,' Gráinne was granted restoration of one-third of her husband's estates. These estates were not restored to Gráinne personally but to her eldest son, Theobald (Tibbot-na-Long) Burke who was to become one of the main beneficiaries of the Composition of Connaught, the system by which lands were 'regranted' to chieftains surrendering to the Queen. Gráinne is said to have been reduced to great poverty but this is hardly credible given that her son regained a considerable amount of Burke possessions and was herself able to return to Clew Bay. At the age of seventy she captained a punitive expedition against the Donegal Mac Sweeneys whose fishing fleet were apparently poaching O'Malley waters. She beached her longship when chased by a British man-o'-war and, with her crew, reached safe refuge among the O'Donnells of Tyrconnell in Donegal. She returned to Clare Island, where she died some years later. In 1627 her son Theobald was created first Viscount of Mayo and the line

endures today in the Altamonts of Westport House. From the 17th to the 20th century the name 'Gráinne Uí Máille,' and its later anglicised form of 'Granuaile,' was used as an allegorical appellation for Ireland in the poems and songs of the *Aisling* genre.

ÚNA BHÁN. See under MacDERMOTT, ÚNA BHÁN.

WADDELL, HELEN (1889-1965), mediaeval scholar, poet and author. Born May 31, 1889, in Tokyo, Japan. After the death of her mother the two-year-old returned with her family to Banbridge, Co. Down. She was educated in Victoria College and Queens University, Belfast. Her brother Samuel was to become the well-known actor and playwright, Rutherford Mayne. Helen's expected academic career was delayed for eight years while she cared for her invalid stepmother. During this time she contributed reviews and articles on aspects of literature to reputable journals, published *Lyrics from the Chinese* (1915), and had her first play *The Spoilt Buddha* performed. In 1920 she registered at Somerville College, Oxford, for a research degree. Being awarded the Susette Taylor Travelling Fellowship enabled her to spend two years in Paris studying the *Carmina Burana* and other Low Latin Goliardic compositions by the *vagantes* or 'wandering scholars' of the Middle Ages. During this period Helen determined to spend her life in the study and dissemination of mediaeval Latin literature and humanism. Her first major book, *The Wandering Scholars* (1927), a study of the mediaeval Latin poets and scholars, took the academic and literary worlds by storm. She was awarded the A.C. Benson Silver Medal by the British Royal Society of Literature and was elected as that Society's first woman fellow. *Mediaeval Latin Lyrics* followed in 1929 and, in 1933, *Peter Abelard*, a historical novel remarkable for its insightful reconstruction of twelfth century France, went into the first of its thirty editions and nine subsequent translations. Helen also had written a play, *The Abbé Prévost*, and two further collections of Latin translations, *Beasts and Saints* and *The Desert Fathers*, before the outbreak of the Second World War. She had made her profound knowledge available to the public through teaching, lecturing, broadcasting and literary journalism; she also became assistant editor of the magazine *Nineteenth Century*. She began to suffer from a neurological disorder and, from 1950 on, this unusually great scholar became progressively oblivious of even her closest friends. Helen Waddell died in March 1965.

WALKER, MARY ELIZABETH (MOLLY). See under NIC SHIUBHLAIGH, MÁIRE.

WARD, MARY, née KING (1827-1889), naturalist, artist and astronomer. Born April 27, 1827, near Ferbane, Co. Offaly, the youngest child of a landed protestant minister; an aunt, Mary Lloyd, was married to the second Earl of Rosse. Mary King was educated at home by a governess and, as a frequent visitor to Birr Castle where her cousin William, the third Earl, was conducting astronomical experiments and building telescopes, was drawn into the world of science from her youth. Natural history was an early interest and her father obtained a Rosse microscope for her when she was eighteen, which led

73. *Mary Ward.*

to her making her own important scientific observations. Barred from university because of her sex Mary nevertheless became highly respected among contemporary scientists such as the mathematician, Sir William Rowan Hamilton, and Professor Richard Owen, founder of the British Museum (Natural History). She wrote several articles and books, the most popular of the latter being *The World of Wonders as Revealed by the Microscope*. Two of her books were displayed at the International Exhibition at London's Crystal Palace in 1862. Mary was a skilled artist who illustrated scientific books and articles, especially for Brewster, inventor of the kaleidoscope, and made many studies of fauna and insects. She married Henry William Crosby Ward of Castleward, Strangford, Co. Down, and had eight children, two of whom died in infancy. Mary met an untimely death on August 31, 1869, caused by falling off a steam-automobile driven by her husband in the grounds of Birr Castle. Until recently she was mainly remembered as the first victim of a motor accident on record rather than for her achievements. Mary Ward is buried in the Rosse family vault at Birr, Co. Offaly.

WHEELER, ANNA MASSEY, née DOYLE (1785-1848), radical social reformer and feminist. Born at Clonbeg in east Tipperary, where her father was a Church of Ireland dean. The Doyles were a military family which, during Anna's lifetime, gave six generals to the British army; her godfather was Henry Grattan, leader of the Patriot Party in the Irish Parliament. After the death of her father, Anna and her mother became part of her uncle's household, General Sir John Doyle. At fifteen she was married to the dissolute son of a Limerick landlord; after suffering abuse for twelve years she escaped, with her two children, to Guernsey in the English Channel where her uncle, Sir John, was Governor. She appears to have been financially

independent after his death. In 1818 she went to Caen, Normandy, and joined a group of social philosophers and reformers, followers of Saint-Simon, the founder of French socialism, 'to the support of whose doctrines she devoted both her purse and her pen.' After her husband's death in 1820 Anna returned to Ireland and made extended visits to London. There she met Robert Owen, the philanthropic manufacturer and leader of the co-operative movement, and Jeremy Bentham, leader of the philosophical radicals, and she mixed with Utilitarians and others who wished to reform society in the industrial era. Back in Paris in 1823, she presided over a notable salon frequented by the utopian socialist, François Fourier; Anna propagated his views widely through lectures and essays. She had previously begun a close friendship with William Thompson, a wealthy Cork landowner and leading economist in the Owenite movement. When the Utilitarian philosopher James Mill gave his opinion, in the treatise *On Government*, that since women's interests resembled children's in so much that they were those of their husband or father, there was no injustice in refusing them the vote and other rights. Anna and Thompson responded in 1825 with *An Appeal of One-Half of the Human Race, Women against the Pretensions of the Other Half, Men, to retain them in Political and thence in Civil Domestic Slavery*. This book contained the first explicit statement of the socialist case for equality of the sexes. Although the book appeared under Thompson's name he not only dedicated it to Anna, but also graciously acknowledged her input, describing himself merely as the 'scribe and interpreter' of her ideas. After her daughter died in Paris Anna moved to London suffering from a disabling 'nervous malady'. In 1833 her friend Thompson died. She overcame bouts of depression to lecture (often in dissenting chapels), write articles on women's rights for journals such as the *British Co-operator*, and engage in lengthy debates in their correspondence columns. In 1836 she had to endure the acrimonious public divorce of her surviving daughter, Rosina, and Bulmer Lytton, a notable literary figure. It is ironic that, in 1839, Anna Wheeler toured mental hospitals in England with Flora Triton, advocate of women's trade unions, in an attempt to expose conditions in these institutions, when Rosina was later to be kidnapped and incarcerated in one such place by her ex-husband to silence her attacks on him. Anna continued her contacts with the French socialists and lived to know of the 1848 socialist revolution in France. She is recognised as one of the more notable harbingers of the modern feminist movement. Her grandson, Edward Lytton, denigrated her views in his biography of his father, but Edward's daughter, Constance, was to become a prominent member of Emily Pankhurst's militant suffrage organisation.

WILDE, LADY JANE FRANCESCA, née ELGEE (*c.* 1821-1896), woman of letters, poet, 'Speranza of the Nation'. Born in Wexford into a protestant Unionist family of builders, clergymen and attorneys: spent her youth in Dublin. She was converted to the nationalism of Young Ireland through reading their publications and witnessing the emotional funeral of the patriot Thomas Davis, a fellow protestant. She began contributing verse and prose to the *Nation*, initially under a male pseudonym, then under the name Speranza. Her writings, both verse and essays, were not only vehemently nationalist and inflammatory but also sincerely concerned with the state of poverty in Ireland on the eve of the Great Famine. These rhetorical writings made a great impression on her contemporaries and at least one Young Irelander, Thomas Francis Meagher, quoted her in his speeches. In

1849 the editor of the *Nation*, Gavan Duffy, was prosecuted for seditious articles and accused especially of the authorship of 'Jacta Alea Est' because of which the paper had been suppressed. The young Jane Francesca Elgee stood up in court and admitted proudly to have been the author. The charges against Duffy were dismissed and the case dropped. In 1851 she married Dr. William Wilde, a distinguished eye and ear surgeon who was also a notable antiquarian and author. Their house in Merrion Square became a salon for those involved in the arts and sciences. They had three children, William, Oscar and a daughter who died young. Although her much older husband, who was to be knighted in 1804, was a notorious philanderer, Jane successfully held the marriage and family together. Sir William died in 1876 leaving the family in debt. His widow moved to London where her eldest son was a journalist. In her tiny Mayfair house she conducted one of the most brilliant salons of the time. Having published a volume of poems as Speranza a dozen years earlier, Lady Wilde now began writing under her own name on a wide diversity of subjects, in particular for the *Pall Mall Gazette*. In 1844 she published *Driftwood from Scandinavia*, a travel book based on her honeymoon tour some thirty years earlier. *Ancient Legends of Ireland,* an excellent and lasting work, appeared in 1887. *Ancient Cures* (1891), *Men, Women and Books* (1891) and *Social Studies* (1893) followed. In 1890 she was granted a badly-needed Civil List pension for, despite her publications and the extraordinary success of her son Oscar, she was gradually falling into poverty. Following the disgrace and imprisonment of Oscar, and the earlier estrangement with her alcoholic elder son, she became a recluse and died in poverty from bronchitis on February 3, 1896. She was buried in an unmarked grave in Kensal Green, London. Too often misrepresented as no more

74. *A portrait of* **Lady Jane Francesca Wilde** *by George Merosini.*

than a somewhat bizarre eccentric, Lady Jane Wilde's reputation has been deservedly restored in recent years.

WOFFINGTON, MARGARET (PEG) (*c.* 1715-1760), actress. Born Dublin, the daughter of a brick-layer and laundress, Peg is said to have been a watercress-seller before working in an amusement booth while still a child. At twelve, she played in Coffey's *The Beggar's Opera* at the Smock Alley Theatre, Dublin, and made an inauspicious appearance in London before becoming a major figure in the Dublin theatre world, particularly in the new Theatre Royal in Angier Street. Peg, a versatile and colourful actress, was especially successful in her 'breeches' part in Faraquhar's, *The Constant Couple.* She was taken to London, in 1740, by the impresario Rich, originator of pantomime and founder manager of Covent Garden Theatre, where she continued her success in Faraquhar's comedies. The following year she played Cordelia in Shakespeare's *King Lear* at Drury Lane with the renowned David Garrick as the King. The pair formed a successful professional partnership for some years, being lovers at the same time. On the break-up of their relationship Peg moved to Covent Garden; then, in 1751, she came to work at Dublin's Smock Alley, managed by Thomas Sheridan. She returned successfully to Covent Garden but her popularity was challenged by another Dublin-born actress, GEORGE ANNE BELLAMY, whom she stabbed in a fit of temper in 1756. Peg was apparently in ill health at the time and the following year she collapsed on stage while playing Rosamund in Shakespeare's *As You Like it.* It was to be her last appearance. From then until her death, in London on March 28, 1760, Peg Woffington spent much of her considerable wealth in charitable works such as endowing alms houses at Teddington, London.

*75. A portrait of **Margaret Woffington** painted 1753 by John Lewis.*

WYSE POWER JENNIE, née O'TOOLE (1858-1941), feminist, political activist and senator. Born May 1858, in Baltinglass, Co. Wicklow, where her father had a leather and provisions shop on the main street. When Jennie was two years old the business failed and her family moved to Dublin. The O'Tooles were strongly nationalist; an uncle had taken part in the Fenian Rising of 1867. Jennie joined the Ladies Land League in 1881, and became a member of the executive. She worked especially on the compilation of the so-called *Book of Kells* - eviction details used to great effect in co-ordinating the campaign on the ground. Jennie was also active as a League organiser in Carlow and Wicklow. In 1883 she married John Wyse Power, a journalist and member of the Irish Republican Brotherhood who joined the staff of the *Freeman's Journal* as political and leader writer. He was, later, one of the founders of the Gaelic Athletic Association. Jennie had four children in a decade but continued her political work, supporting Parnell in his declining period, and publishing a selection of his speeches, *Words of a Dead Chief* (1892). She was also involved with the Dublin Women's Suffrage Association and the Gaelic League. Jennie opened, in 1899, the Irish Farm and Produce Company - a shop and restaurant - at 21 Henry Street, Dublin which soon became a noted meeting place for Irish speakers and nationalists. The business prospered and she opened three other branches in the city. In 1900, at its inaugural meeting, Jennie was elected vice-president of the new separatist women's association, Inghinidhe na hÉireann. In 1903 she was elected to her first public office as Guardian in the Poor Law official relief system, a position she was to lose eight years later because vested interests opposed her attempts at reform. She was an executive member of Sinn Féin from its inception in 1906 and became joint treasurer in 1909 and a vice-president two years later with several other women including COUNTESS MARKIEVICZ. She helped organise the funeral of the Fenian, O'Donovan Rossa, the biggest nationalist demonstration of the time and was unanimously elected the first president of the radical militant women's organisation Cumann na mBan in 1914. Jennie's Henry Street restaurant was a meeting place of the revolutionaries planning the 1916 Rising and it was here that the Proclamation of the Republic was signed. During the Rising she supplied food to the insurgents until her premises were destroyed in the shelling. Following the surrender, with her daughter Nancy who had been active in preparations for the rebellion, she turned to organising relief for the prisoner's dependants. In 1918, as a member of the executive council of the re-constituted Sinn Féin, Jennie actively supported the successful election campaign of Countess Markievicz to the Westminster Parliament. During the War of Independence she was treasurer of Sinn Féin while her daughter Nancy worked for it in a secretarial capacity. In the 1920 municipal elections, Jennie was elected for the Inns Quay and Rotunda district, one of five women elected to Dublin Corporation. Despite much intimidation from the British armed forces she was particularly active in the areas of public health and technical education. While Cumann na mBan opposed the Treaty Jennie supported it and became an executive member of the new pro-Treaty women's organisation, Cumann na Saoirse. She also joined the pro-Treaty party, Cumann na nGael, of which she was a trustee. When appointed to the first Senate of the Free State, Jennie used her office to champion women's equality. In 1925 she withdrew her loyalty from the new government because she felt it had acquiesced in the continued partition of Ireland. She remained an independent senator until, impressed by Fianna Fáil's republicanism, she stood for that party in the Senate elections of 1934; however, she opposed their Conditions of Employment Bill the following year because it discriminated against women. In 1934, following the disbanding of the Senate, she retired after fifty-five years of active political life. Jennie Wyse Power died on January 5, 1941, in Dublin.

YEATS, ELIZABETH CORBET ('LOLLIE') (1868-1940), publisher, painter, and founder director of the Cuala Press. Born London into the talented family of John Butler Yeats the rector's son who had been called to the Bar but was then studying in London to become a painter. Her mother was Susan Pollexfen whose family were flour millers in Co. Sligo. Elizabeth's elder brother, William Butler Yeats, was to become the greatest Irish poet of his time, and the younger, Jack Butler Yeats, one of the greatest

THE NOBLE THREE
(To the air of 'The Black Horse')
One time when walking down a lane
As night was drawing nigh,
I met a colleen with three flowers
And she more young than I.
'Saint Patrick bless you, dear,' said I
'If you'll be quick and tell
The place where you did find those flowers
I seem to know so well.'

She took one flower and kissed it thrice
And softly said to me:
'This flower I found in Thomas Street,
In Dublin Fair,' said she;
'Its name is Robert Emmett
The youngest flower of all.
But I'll keep it fresh beside my breast
If all the world should fall.'

She took and kissed the next flower twice
And softly said to me,
'This flower I culled in Antrim's fields
Outside Belfast' said she;
'The name I call it is Wolfe Tone,
The bravest flower of all.
But I'll keep it fresh beside my breast
If all the world should fall.'

She took and kissed the next flower once
And softly said to me,
'This flower comes from the Wicklow hills,
Its name is Dwyer,' said she.
'But Emmett, Dwyer and Tone I'll keep
For I do love them all.
And I'll keep them fresh beside my breast
If all the world should fall.'

G. N. Reddin.

*76. A page from 'A Broadside' journal, Nov. 1914, published by **Elizabeth Corbet Yeats**, illustration by J.B. Yeats.*

painters. Between 1880 and 1887 the Yeats family lived in Dublin. On their return to London, she kept house in Bedford Park for her father, two brothers, Willie and Jack and older sister SUSAN MARY ('LILY') YEATS and an ailing mother. She trained as a teacher at the Bedford Park Kindergarten and taught art at Chiswick High School for five years after her mother's death and also lectured on painting and drawing at the London Froebel Institute. Besides being a talented painter in water colours Elizabeth also had acquired typesetting and printing skills while studying under the outstanding typographer, Emery Walker, and had done some work with the Women's Printing Society. She published two manuals, written and illustrated by herself, on the art of painting in water-colours, *Brushwork* (1896) and *Brushwork Studies of Flowers, Fruits and Animals* (1898). The Yeats sisters wished to return to Ireland but financial considerations prevented this until they met EVELYN GLEESON, a disciple of the craftsman and printer William Morris, at the Irish Literary Society in London. With the older Gleeson as head of the group the three women moved to Dublin determined to set up an arts and crafts guild. With borrowed money and grants they founded the Dun Emer Guild in Dundrum, then on the outskirts of Dublin. Having decided to focus on three main crafts, embroidery, printing, tapestry and rug making, they recruited local girls for training. The printing began early in 1903, under Elizabeth's direction, on a small second-hand hand-press and the first book from the Dun Emer Press, *In the Seven Woods* by W.B. Yeats, appeared in August 1903. Elizabeth's printing enterprise was the first to reach a notably high standard of design and printing in Ireland since the fine work produced in Dublin in the 18th century; later it became the Cuala Press and continued to set the standard consistently for thirty-seven years. Using only Irish materials and Irish female workers, it was the first private press to concentrate on publishing new work by living Irish writers and so had an incalculable impact on the Irish Literary Renaissance. In 1908 the sisters separated completely from Gleeson's Dun Emer Guild and set up Cuala Industries which incorporated the Cuala Press, at Rose Cottage, Churchtown, Co. Dublin. With W.B. Yeats as editor and Elizabeth responsible for design and production, the press concentrated on books with 'an intimate connection with the literary movement in contemporary Ireland', and also produced hand-coloured prints, cards, broadsides, embroidery design and even a Christmas stamp. Meanwhile, Elizabeth's sister Susan ('Lily') directed the embroidery and tapestry part of the Cuala Industries. The two women lived together for some forty years at their house, Gurteen Dhas, and much has been made of their incompatibility and highly strung temperaments since the time James Joyce caricatured them as 'the weird sisters.' However, although both possessed a strong personality, highly sensitive and individualistic, it must also be taken into account that they were perennially short of money and dogged by Susan's ill health. In the circumstances, the life-long achievement of the sisters must be considered all the more admirable. Elizabeth ('Lollie') died in 1940, survived by her chronically-ill sister.

YEATS, SUSAN MARY ('LILY') (1866-1949), craftswoman, designer, co-founder of the Cuala Press. Born Sandymount Avenue, Dublin, into the extraordinarily talented family of John Butler Yeats of Co. Down and Susan Pollexfen, a flour miller's daughter, from Co. Sligo. Her father was called to the Bar months after Susan's birth but moved to London the following year to become a painter. The family returned to Ireland in the early 1880s, but their father's inadequate income required they return to London in 1887. Here, the following year, Susan became an assistant embroiderer to May Morris in William Morris' famous design studio and before long was training assistants for the firm. In 1902 she returned to Dublin with her elder sister, ELIZABETH CORBET ('LOLLIE') YEATS, and their friend, EVELYN GLEESON, to set up an arts and crafts guild, initially financed by Gleeson and later by grants from the Department of Agriculture and Technical Instruction. The women set up the Dun Emer Guild in Dundrum on the outskirts of Dublin 'to find work for Irish hands in the making of beautiful things.' Local girls were recruited to train in printing, tapestry, rugmaking and embroidery, the latter section being under Susan's direction. One of her first large commissions was a set of twenty-four banners and vestments for Loughrea Cathedral, worked 'in the mediaeval style which was revived by William Morris.' After financial and other problems caused a split in the Guild, the Yeats sisters ran Dun Emer Industries until finally setting up the Cuala Industries at Rose Cottage, Churchtown, Co. Dublin. Here Susan abundantly designed and produced embroidery of a high calibre for liturgical and domestic. Though long overshadowed by her sister Elizabeth, it is Susan Yeats who is now credited by art and typographical historians as being principally responsible for setting-up Cuala Press and for creating the high standards of its publications which are still coveted by book collectors. It is possible Susan suffered more severely than other members of the Yeats family from the vein of neurosis which affected them. The sisters, dogged by emotional, financial and physical health problems, lived together at their house in Gurteen Dhas, for some forty years. Susan survived Elizabeth by nine years.

77. **Susan Mary Yeats** *(second from right) in the embroidery room of the Dun Emer Guild, c.1903.*

YOUNG, ROSE MABEL or NÍ ÓGÁIN, RÓIS (*c.* 1865-1947), Gaelic scholar. Born on October 30, 1865, at Castle Galgorm, Ahoghill, Co. Antrim, where her Scots forebears had been granted estates at the time of the Ulster Plantations (colonisation) in the early seventeenth century. Her father was High-Sheriff of the county and her siblings, several of whom became prominent in different fields, included Ella Young, a poet who not only collected much folklore in Ireland but also in Mexico and among native Americans. Having been educated by governesses Rose went to England to train as a teacher at Cambridge University. An interest in Irish history and language had previously been instilled in her by a family friend, Dr. William

Reeves, protestant Bishop of Down, Connor and Dromore, a noteworthy historian and translator. She joined the Gaelic League in London and studied Irish manuscripts in the Bodleian Library. When Rose returned to Ireland in the early 1900s she attended Irish-language classes in Belfast and, on extended visits to Dublin, associated with the leaders of the Gaelic League, with Dinneen the lexicographer, and Bergin, the Old Irish scholar. She became especially friendly with MARGARET DOBBS, who had come from the same landed protestant and Unionist background, and, through her, got involved in the Gaelic League in Antrim and in Feis na nGleann ('The Glens Festival', an annual Irish-language gathering). Rose never became converted to the nationalist movement to the same extent as her sister Ella, who actively supported Sinn Féin and the Irish Volunteers; however, she cultivated, as did her close friend Margaret Dobbs, a deep and public sense of 'Irishness' while remaining mildly Unionist in politics. She used a Gaelicised form of her name, Róis Ní Ógáin, in her writing and joined with ELLEN O'BRIEN in attempting to Gaelicise the Church of Ireland by infusing it with the spirituality of the Early Irish Church, to which end she contributed to O'Brien's *An tEaglaiseach Gaedhalach/The Gaelic Churchman*. Rose Young's distinction rests on her editing three remarkable volumes of Gaelic poetry and song, *Duanaire Gaedhilge*, (1901, 1924, 1930). These are collections of folksongs, of lyrics by poets between 1600 and 1800, and of Ossianic, religious, and mediaeval poetry, respectively. The material for the most part was gleaned from books published since the founding of the Gaelic League, in 1893 but, as a collection, with notes, vocabulary and translations, had a far-reaching effect. Not only was this particular body of songs and poems made more accessible to a wide readership but it also influenced Irish-language curricula and text-books in second-level schools for many decades. Rose Young spent the latter years of her life with Margaret Dobbs in Portnagolon, near Cushendun, Co. Antrim, where she died on May 28, 1947.

APPENDIX ONE

CLASSIFICATION according to occupations, pursuits, concerns, interests, etc.

PUBLIC AND PROFESSIONAL LIFE

PUBLIC LIFE AND POLITICS
Royalty and Aristocracy
Dervorgilla (wife of Ua Ruairc). Eirc (Queen). Fitzgerald, Bridget. Fitzgerald, Eleanor. Gormlaith (Queen, 10th century). Gormlaith (Queen, 11th century). Lynch, Eliza. McDonnell, Fionnghuala (Inghean Dubh). Medb, Queen. Ní Chearbhaill, Máigréd. Nic Shiubhlaigh, Máire. Ní Dhochartaigh, Róis. Ní Dhomhnaill, Nuala. O'Brien, Máire Rua. Thom(p)son, Elizabeth. Uí Mháille, Gráinne.

Public Figures and Politicians
Beere, Theckla. Clarke, Kathleen. Concannon, Helena. Green, Alice Stopford. Kearns, Linda. Lynn, Kathleen. MacSwiney, Mary. Markievicz, Countess. Pearse, Margaret Mary. Uí Choisdealbh, Eibhlín. Wyse Power, Jennie.

Revolutionaries, Patriots, Radicals
Bracken, Josephine. Broderick, Albinia. Carbery, Ethna. Carney, Winifred. Clarke, Kathleen. Comerford, Marie. Czira, Sydney. De Barra, Leslie. Despard, Charlotte. Devlin, Anne. Drumm, Máire. Gifford, Grace. Gonne, Maud. Gray, Betsy. Kearns, Linda. Lynch, Hanna. Lynn, Kathleen. Macardle, Dorothy. McCracken, Mary Ann. McSwiney, Mary. Markievicz, Countess. Milligan, Alice. Moloney, Helena. Nivedita, Bhagini. O'Leary, Ellen. Parnell, Anna. Parnell, Fanny. Ridge, Lola. Sheehy Skeffington, Hanna. Skinnider, Margaret. Spring Rice, Mary. Thornton, Bridget. Wyse Power, Jennie.

SOCIAL REFORM AND WELFARE
Education and Propagation of Ideas
Aylward, Margaret. Ball, Frances. Bryant, Sophie. Butler, Marie Joseph. Clarke, Mary Frances. Cousins, Margaret. Edgeworth, Maria. Herlihy, Nora. Jellicoe, Anne. McAuley, Catherine. Mulally, Teresa. Nagle, Nano. Skinnider, Margaret. Wheeler, Anna.

Charitable Relief, Social Welfare, Public Health
Aikenhead, Mary. Aylward, Margaret. Barry, Teresa. Bell, Laura. Bridgeman, Johanna. Cusack, Margaret. De Barra, Leslie. Fox, Evelyn. Hall, Anna Maria. Harrison, Sarah (Celia). Haughrey, Margaret (Gaffney). Herlihy, Nora. Kearney, Teresa (Mother Kevin). McCracken, Mary Ann. Martin, Mary. Meredith, Susanna. Morrogh-Bernard, Agnes. O'Brien, Charlotte. O'Connell, Mary (Anthony). Price, Dorothy Stopford. Russell, Mary Baptist. Tennant, Margaret. Thornton, Bridget.

Labour Organisation
Bennett, Louie. Blackburn, Helen. Carney, Winifred. Chenevix, Helen. Gore-Booth, Eva. Jones, Mary. Larkin, Delia. Moloney, Helena. Tennant, Margaret.

Rural Organisation
Gahan, Muriel. Lynch, Hanna. O'Leary, Ellen. Parnell, Anna. Parnell, Fanny. Tynan, Katharine. Wyse Power, Jennie.

Minority Rights and Issues
Bates, Daisy. Cusack, Margaret. Despard, Charlotte. Meredith, Susanna. O'Brien, Charlotte.

Feminism and Women's Rights
Beere, Theckla. Bennett, Louie. Blackburn, Helen. Chenevix, Helen. Cousins, Margaret. Despard, Charlotte. Gore-Booth, Eva. Haslam, Anna. Hayden, Mary. Jacob, Rosamund. Jameson, Anna. Sheehy Skeffington, Hanna. Wheeler, Anna.

RELIGION AND MORAL REFORM
Ascetics and Mystics
Attracta, St. Begha, St. Breage, St. Brigida, St. Brigid, St. Bruinseach, St. Caoilinn, St. De Burgo (Burke), Honoria. Dervilla, St. Ercnat, St. Fanchea, St. Gobnait, St. Íta, St. Kentigerna, St. Lelia, St. Maure and Brigida. Moninna, St. O'Halloran, Maura (Soshin). Osmanna, St. Samthann, St.

Evangelists and Missionaries
Begha, St. Breage, St. Bruinseach, St. Cosgrave, Mary Anne. Cousins, Margaret. Crida, St. Heck, Barbara. McLoughlin, Katherine. Modwena, St. Nivedita, Bhagini. Quinn, Edel.

Martyrs and Recusants
Ball, Margaret. Barnewell, Margery. De Burgo (Burke), Honoria. Dympna, St. Grimonia, St. Maure and Brigida. Nolan, Julian.

Founders and Administrators
Aikenhead, Mary. Attracta, St. Aylward, Margaret. Ball, Frances. Barry, (Mary) Gerald. Barry, Teresa. Breage, St. Brigid, St. Butler, Marie Joseph. Clarke, Mary Frances. Cosgrave, Mary Anne. Cusack, Margaret. Gobnait, St. Kearney, Teresa (Mother Kevin). Lelia, St. McAuley, Catherine. Martin, Mary. Modwena, St. Mulally, Teresa. Nagle, Nano. O'Connell, Mary (Anthony). Russell, Mary Baptist.

PROFESSIONS, OCCUPATIONS, PURSUITS
Teaching and Educational Administration
Aylward, Margaret. Ball, Frances. Barry, (Mary) Gerald. Butler, Marie Joseph. Clarke, Mary Frances. Duffy, Louise Gavan. Jellicoe, Anne. McAuley, Catherine. McGroarty, Julia. Maxwell, Constantia. Mulally, Teresa. Nagle, Nano. Pearse, Margaret Mary.

Medical Practice and Care
Bridgeman, Johanna. Barry, 'James' Miranda. Early, Biddy. Kearney, Teresa (Mother Kevin). Kearns, Linda. Lynn, Kathleen. Martin, Mary. O'Connell, Mary

(Anthony). Price, Dorothy Stopford. Russell, Mary Baptist. Smithson, Annie MP. Thornton, Bridget.

Business and Finance

Gleeson, Evelyn. Haughrey, Margaret (Gaffney). McCracken, Mary Ann. Morrogh-Bernard, Agnes. Sadlier, Mary Ann. Tyrell. Kate. Yeats, Susan (Lily). Yeats, Elizabeth (Lolly).

Law

Cousins, Margaret.

Communications and Media

Crawford, Emily. Czira, Sydney. Mitchell, Susan. Ridge, Lola. Tynan, Katharine.

Architecture

Gray, Eileen.

CULTURAL AND ACADEMIC LIFE

SCHOLARSHIP AND RESEARCH

Humanities, Arts, History

Bryant, Sophie. Concannon, Helena. Fox, Charlotte Milligan. Green, Alice Stopford. Grierson, Constantia. Hayden, Mary. Jameson, Anna. Kavanagh, Julia. Lawless, Emily. Macardle, Dorothy. Maxwell, Constantia. Starkie, Enid. Stokes, Margaret MacNair. Waddell, Helen.

Anthropology and Social Science

Bates, Daisy. Hall, Anna Maria.

Science and Chemistry

Ball, Mary. Blake, Edith. Clerke, Agnes. Hutchins, Ellen. Lonsdale, Kathleen. O'Brien, Charlotte. Ward, Mary.

Irish (Gaelic) revival and scholarship

Dobbs, Margaret. Duffy, Louise Gavan. Fox, Charlotte Milligan. Hull, Eleanor. Knott, Eleanor. Ní Fhaircheallaigh, Úna. Ní Raghallaigh, Maire. O'Brien, Ellen (Nellie). Patterson, Annie. Spring Rice, Mary. Uí Choisdealbh, Eibhlín. Uí Dhiosca, Young, Rose.

Folklore and Folk Song

Hull, Eleanor, MacNeill, Máire. Patterson, Annie. Uí Choisdealbh, Eibhlin. Fox, Charlotte Milligan.

ARTS AND ENTERTAINMENT

Literature

Barber, Mary. Barrington, Margaret. Blackburn, Helen. Blackburne, E. Owens. Blessington, Countess (Marguerite). Bowen, Elizabeth. Brayton, Teresa. Brooke, Charlotte. Browne, Frances. Bunbury, Selina. Carbery, Ethna. Centlivre, Susanna. Colum, Mary. Costello, Louisa. Cummins, Geraldine (G.D.). Davys, Mary. Deevy, Teresa. De Valera, Sinéad. Dillon, Eilís. Dufferin, Lady Helen. Edgeworth, Maria. Eva of 'The Nation.' Gore-Booth, Eva. Gormlaith (Queen, 10th century). Gregory, Lady. Grierson, Constantia. Grimshaw, E. Beatrice. Hall, Anna Maria. Jameson, Anna. Kavanagh, Julia. Laverty, Maura. Lavin, Mary. Lawless, Emily. Leadbetter, Mary. Líadain. Lindon,

Molly. Lynch, Hanna. Lynch, Patricia. Macardle, Dorothy. Martin, Mary Letitia. Maude, Caitlín. Milligan, Alice. Mitchell, Susan. Morgan, Sydney. Mulholland, Rosa. Ní Chonaill, Eibhlín Dubh. Ní Ghráda, Máiréad. Ní Laoghaire, Máire Bhuidhe. O'Brien, Kate. O'Neill, Mary. Parnell, Fanny. Ridge, Lola. Ros, Amanda McKittrick. Ross, Martin (Violet Martin). Sadlier, Mary Ann. Sheridan, Frances. Shorter, Dora Sigerson. Smithson, Annie MP. Somerville, Edith. Tynan, Katharine. Waddell, Helen. Wilde, Lady.

Visual Arts

Barton, Rose. Blake, Edith. Bowen, Gretta. Butler, Mildred. Bushe, Letitia. Costello, Louisa. Cranwell, Mia. Crilly, Margaret. Drury, Susanna. Geddes, Wilhelmina. Gifford, Grace. Gleeson, Evelyn. Gray, Eileen. Guinness, May. Hamilton, Letitia. Harrison, Sarah (Celia). Heron, Hilary. Hone, Evie. Houston, Mary. Hutchins, Ellen. Jellett, Mainie. Lynch, Concepta. McGuinness, Norah. O'Brien, Catherine (Kitty). Plunkett, Katherine. Praeger, Rosamund. Purser, Sarah. Reid, Nano. St. John Whitty, Sophia. Shackleton, Lydia. Somerville, Edith. Stokes, Margaret MacNair. Swanzy, Mary. Ward, Mary. Yeats, Susan (Lily). Yeats, Elizabeth (Lolly).

Performing Arts

Alexander, Cecil Frances. Allgood, Sara. Bellamy, George Anne. Burke Sheridan, Margaret. Centlivre, Susanna. Clive, Kitty. Craig, May. Crotty, Elizabeth. Farren, Elizabeth. Garson, Greer. Gregory, Lady. Hayes, Catherine. Linnane, Kitty. McKenna, Siobhán. Maude, Caitlín. Montez, Lola. Mooney, Ria. Mooney, Rose. Moriarity, Joan Denise. Murphy, Delia. Nic Shiubhlaigh, Máire. Ní Scolaí, Máire. O'Neill, Eliza. O'Neill, Máire. Patterson, Annie. Pope, Maria. Rehan, Ada. Richards, Shelah. Smithson, Henrietta (Harriet). Woffington, Margaret.

Folklore and Tradition

Sayers, Peig.

DOMESTIC ARTS

Fitzgibbon, Theodora. Laverty, Maura.

PHYSICAL FEATS AND UNDERTAKINGS

Exploration and Travel

Blessington, Countess (Marguerite). Bunbury, Selina. Cosgrave, Mary Anne. Costello, Louisa. Grimshaw, E. Beatrice. Jameson, Anna.

Sport and Pursuits

Bryant, Sophie. Grimshaw, E. Beatrice. Heath, Lady.

MISCELLANEOUS NOTABLES AND NOTORIETIES

Barnacle, Nora. Bates, Daisy. Behan, Kathleen. Bell, Laura. Betty, Lady. Bonny, Anne. Bourke, Honora. Bracken, Josephine. Barry, 'James' Miranda. Cavanagh, Kit (Mother Ross). Cleary, Bridget. Cummins, Geraldine (G.D.). Curran, Sarah. Dwyer, Mary. Early,

Biddy. Eva of 'The Nation.' Fitzgerald, Countess Katherine. Gray, Betsy. Hanley, Ellen. Heath, Lady. Kyteler, Alice. Leeson, Margaret. Lynch, Eliza. MacDermott, Úna Bhán. Misset, Madame. Montez, Lola. O'Brien, Máire Rua. Smithson, Henrietta (Harriet). Thom(p)son, Elizabeth. Tyrell, Kate. Uí Mháille, Gráinne (O'Malley, Grace). Ward, Mary.

APPENDIX TWO

GLOSSARY, NOTES AND ABBREVIATIONS

Abbey Theatre: Came into being in 1904 with W.B. Yeats, Lady Gregory and J.M. Synge as directors. Developed from the Irish Literary Theatre, an amateur group founded in 1899 by Yeats, Gregory, Edward Martin and George Russell (AE).

Aeraíocht: Open-air entertainment with music, song and dance; especially outings organised by the Gaelic League.

Aisling: A poetic form with roots in the pre-Christian period that reached its height in the eighteenth century. In this genre Ireland was symbolised as a woman, most often a beautiful queen, seeking her rightful mate, i.e., a Stuart prince. *Aisling* means 'a vision.'

American wake: Custom of holding a wake - as after a bereavement - with attendant lamentations and merry-making, the night before an emigrant left Ireland, as the chances of his or her return were minimal.

Anglo-Irish Literature: Irish literature written through the medium of the English language as distinct to that written in Irish Gaelic. Its great flowering as a recognised form came with the Irish Literary Revival (which see.)

Annals: Early Irish chroniclers or annalists were produced by monastic schools from as early as the sixth century when, as well as dating the various religious feasts, the monks jotted down secular events in the blank spaces. Probably the earliest extant compilation (based on several even earlier annals) was the *Ulster Chronicle* (mid-eight century). The best-known is the *Annals of the Four Masters*, compiled 1632-1636 from earlier sources.

Ascendancy: The small protestant landlord class. For the most part British colonists (the 'Anglo-Irish') who ruled Ireland and owned ninety percent of the arable land in the eighteenth and early nineteenth century.

BA: Bachelor of Arts degree.

BBC: British Broadcasting Corporation.

B.Comm: Bachelor of Commerce degree.

Bean na hÉireann: 'Women of Ireland.' Title of a nationalist-feminist journal launched in 1908. Official organ of Inghinidhe na hÉireann.

Black and Tans: Name given to a notorious British auxiliary force who wore a special uniform of these colours. Sent to Ireland in March 1920 to aid police and army against the IRA. The Black and Tans conducted a reign of terror throughout the country.

Boundary Commission (1925): The Government of Ireland Act of 1920, at the height of the War of Independence, provided for setting up two parliaments in Ireland. One for the six counties of Ulster (controlled by the Unionist Party) and the other for the remaining twenty-six counties, later to become the Irish Free State. The Anglo-Irish Treaty (1921) allowed for the Six County (Northern Ireland) Government to opt to remain outside the Free State and a Boundary Commission was set up to study the problem of partition. In December 1925 an agreement was signed between the governments of the Free State, Northern Ireland, and the United Kingdom that established, as a legal fact, the partition of Ireland into two states.

Breac-Ghaeltacht: *vide* Gaeltacht.

Brehon Laws: Indigenous laws of Ireland of pre-Christian origin. This ancient legal code, first recorded in writing by jurists in the sixth century, received its final and immutable form two centuries later; it was in use for almost a millennium.

Butlers of Ormond : One of the great Anglo-Norman families. Came to Ireland in the thirteenth century. Created Earls of Ormond in 1328. Ormond was an area which corresponded, approximately, to the present day counties of Kilkenny and Tipperary.

c.: circa.

Camogie (Camogaíocht): Women's equivalent of the ancient stick-game of hurling developed during the 'Irish Revival' period. The Camogie Association was formed under the auspices of the Gaelic Athletic Association (GAA) in 1904.

Catholic Emancipation: The Catholic Emancipation Act (1829) removed the majority of disabilities imposed on Roman Catholics following laws passed by the protestant Irish Parliament at the end of the seventeenth century. The Act was passed after a great constitutional movement led by Daniel O'Connell, the 'Liberator.'

CBE: Commander of the Order of the British Empire. Honour conferred by the British monarchy.

Celtic ('Art') Revival: A 'Celtic' revival in the visual arts as artists and craft workers explored their Irish identity and aspirations. Concurred with the Gaelic League revival of the Irish language and Irish Literary Revival at the turn of the twentieth century.

Cenél Cona(i)ll: Two sons of the high king, Niall of the Nine Hostages (d. 405), established the Kingdom of Ailleach in the north-west of Ulster. They decided to divide it between them and Conall, the younger brother, took the area known as Tír Conaill or Tyrconnell (Conall's Country). This roughly corresponds with contemporary Co. Donegal and gave the name Cinél Conall (Conall's Race) to his descendants. From the early thirteenth until the mid-seventeenth century the O'Donnells were the most powerful sept among the Cinél Conall.

CH: Companion of Honour. Honour conferred by the British monarchy.

Childers, Robert Erskine (1870-1922): Author, politician and republican. English-born. Had a distinguished career in the British army and navy and was awarded the Distinguished Service Cross. Converted to Irish nationalism, ran arms from Germany for the Irish Volunteers, elected to Dáil Éireann (1921). Joined the Republicans in the Civil War and was executed by the Free State in 1922.

Civil War, The (1922-1923): The Anglo-Irish Treaty, signed after the War of Independence (Anglo-Irish War) on December 6, 1921. It provided for the establishment of an Irish Free State as a Dominion of the British Commonwealth. It also allowed the parliament of the six north-eastern counties of 'Ulster' to opt to remain in the United Kingdom. The separatists split into those who were content, at least for the short term, with a large measure of Irish control over Irish affairs and those who sought a fully independent republic for the whole island of Ireland. Although the Treaty was approved by the Dáil, and British troops withdrew from Ireland, Civil War followed and ended with the defeat of the Republicans in May, 1922.

Collins, Michael (1890-1922): Revolutionary leader. Director of organisation and intelligence for the Irish Volunteers during the War of Independence. Member of the delegation which negotiated the Anglo-Irish Treaty, chairman of the Provisional Government, Commander-in-Chief of Free State Government forces during the Civil War: ambushed and shot during the War.

Conditions of Employment Bill (1935): Introduced by the Fianna Fáil Government to improve working conditions. Viewed by many as an attempt to remove women from the workplace and to give their jobs to men during the contemporary economic depression.

Congested District Board: Established in 1891 by the Chief Secretary for Ireland. Officially formed from concern for the problems of poverty and over-population in 'congested districts' mainly on the western seaboard. Its aim was to provide relief to the farming community by assisting the growth of home industries, to improve the standard of agricultural production, enlarge uneconomic holdings and assist emigration. It was also widely viewed as a British Government ploy to 'kill Home Rule by kindness.'

Connolly, James (1868-1916): Socialist and trade unionist. Organiser of the Irish Citizen Army and military commander of all Republican forces in Dublin during the 1916 Rebellion. One of the signatories of the Proclamation of the Irish Republic. Executed by firing squad in Kilmainham Jail, Dublin, May 12, 1916.

Constitution of Ireland (Bunreacht na hÉireann), 1937: The prime purpose of the 1937 Constitution, which superseded the 1922 'Treaty' Constitution, was to make the twenty-six counties of Ireland independent of British control; the Irish Free State became Éire, a republic in all but name. The 'new' Constitution has been perceived by many as less liberal and democratic, in particular with regard to the place given to the Roman Catholic Church, and to some articles that discriminated against women's rights and opportunities.

Cumann na mBan: Nationalist women's organisation. Formed to support the Irish Volunteers and to generally advance the cause of Irish independence.

Cumann na Saoirse: Women's organisation formed in 1922 to support the Treaty after Cumann na mBan rejected it.

Dáil (Éireann): First House of Irish parliament to which members, Teachtaí Dála (TDs), are elected.

Davitt, Michael (1846-1906): Organising secretary of the Irish Republican Brotherhood; founded the national Land League which led to the end of landlordism in Ireland.

DBE: Dame Commander of the Order of the British Empire. Honour conferred by the British monarchy.

de Valera, Éamon (1882-1975): Revolutionary, politician and President of Ireland. Joined the Irish Volunteers (1914), participated in the 1916 Rising, elected President of Sinn Féin (1917) and Príomh-Aire or President of the First Dáil (1919); did not accept the Treaty (1922), formed a new republican party, Fianna Fáil, in 1926 and took power in 1932. Elected President of Ireland in 1959 and retired from office in 1973.

DL: Deputy Lieutenant (of Ireland).

D. Lit: Doctor of Literature.

D. Litt: Doctor of Letters.

Emmet, Robert (1778-1803): United Irishman. Hanged in Dublin for leading the 1803 Rebellion.

Farquhar, George (1678-1707): Derry-born playwright. His plays were produced in London, particularly at the Drury Lane Theatre. One of the more important playwrights of his time in Britain.

Feis: Name given to an ancient Irish traditional gathering, to a parliament and its accompanying festivities in particular. Name for festivals or outings that include Irish language, music, cultural competitions or displays, especially as organised by the Gaelic League.

Feis Ceoil: A specific formal musical festival with competitions founded in 1894 by Annie Patterson and the Gaelic League, in Dublin, with the assistance of representatives of various music associations. Although its main aim of promoting indigenous music in an Irish-language context was soon overlooked, the Feis Ceoil has remained an important musical event for more than a century.

Fenians: An Irish republican organisation founded in America in 1858. The name was taken from that of a legendary Irish army, 'Na Fianna.' *vide* Irish Republican Brotherhood.

Fianna Fáil: A major political party in modern Ireland. Founded in 1926 by Éamon de Valera (which see).

File: A poet and/or scribe versed in native Irish learning. In early and mediaeval Ireland the *filí* were a powerful learned class and hereditary custodians of the national heritage of *seanchas* (lore, history, law, oral literature, etc.).

Fitzgerald, 'Silken' Thomas, tenth Earl of Kildare (1513-1537): Deputy-governor of Ireland but rebelled against the English government in 1535. Executed for this in the Tower of London.

Fleadh Ceoil: Festival of Irish traditional music and song with competitions.

Flower, Robin (1881-1946): English-born scholar. Educated in England. Studied the Irish language and made many translations of Irish poetry and studies of Irish life, literature and history. Popularised Irish-language literature.

Gaelic League (Connradh na Gaeilge): Organisation founded by Douglas Hyde and Eoin MacNeill, in 1893, to revive Irish Gaelic as the spoken language of the people. The League became a powerful cultural force and spearheaded the national revival. Despite Hyde's wish that it remain non-political, the Gaelic League led indirectly to the 1916 Rebellion by providing the most potent argument for the recognition of Ireland as a separate national identity.

Gaeltacht: Irish-speaking areas of Ireland. *Breac-Ghaeltacht* is the term used for districts containing pockets of Irish speakers.

Gallowglass: A corruption of the Gaelic term *gall-óglach* (foreign soldier). The gallowglasses, professional soldiers from the western isles of Scotland and from Antrim, were often hired by Irish lords and chieftains and sometimes formed part of a dowry for a Scottish or Scots-Irish noble lady. They were mentioned as early as 1258 and played an important role in events from the mid-fifteenth to early seventeenth century.

Garrick, David (1717-1779): Considered one of the greatest actors and theatrical personalities of the eighteenth century. Hired by Drury Lane Theatre in 1742, he became the manager in 1747.

German Plot (1918): The British Government alleged that Sinn Féin was in treasonable league with Germany during World War I and used this as a reason for mass arrest of Republicans. This was a fictitious plot conjured up as a reaction to Irish resistance to British conscription.

GPO: General Post Office (Dublin). Taken over by the Irish Volunteers as headquarters during the 1916 Rebellion.

Hon: Honourable. British courtesy title for MPs and children of nobility.

Hyde, Douglas (1860-1949): Pioneer of the Gaelic Revival. Co-founder and first President of the Gaelic League; unanimously selected by all political parties as the first President of Ireland (1937).

ICA: Irish Countrywomen's Association. Rural women's organisation that evolved in 1935 from the earlier Society of United Irishwomen.

Inghinidhe na hÉireann (Daughters of Ireland): Radical nationalist women's organisation founded in 1900 by Maud Gonne (MacBride) in opposition to a visit by the British monarch. It later evolved into Cumann na mBan.

IRA: Irish Republican Army. *vide* Irish Volunteers.

Irish Citizen: Organ of the militant Irish Women's Franchise League. Founded by Francis Sheehy Skeffington and James Cousins, in 1912, 'to win for men and women equally the rights of citizenship and to claim for men and women equally the duties of citizenship.'

Irish Citizen Army: Founded by James Connolly following the 1913 'Lock Out' of workers by their employers in Dublin. Connolly, hoping to establish a socialist republic, took part in the preparations for the 1916 Rebellion in which the Citizen Army played a significant role.

Irish Literary Revival: Name given to a non-political cultural movement that originated at the end of the nineteenth century. When translations of early Irish legends, poetry and folklore became available in English at this time many writers, led by W.B. Yeats, drew inspiration from this material and a rediscovery of Ireland's culture pervaded most aspects of Irish life, cultural and political.

Irish Literary Society (of London): Founded by W.B. Yeats in 1891. Among its aims was to publicise the literature and legends of Ireland. It provided an impetus to the Irish Revival movement.

Irish Republican Army: *vide* Irish Volunteers.

Irish Republican Brotherhood (Fenian movement): Secret military organisation. Founded in New York in 1856, and in Dublin two years later, with the aim of establishing an Irish Republic by physical force. Although an attempted invasion of Canada and the 1867 Rebellion in Ireland failed, it influenced the movement to end landlordism. Many leaders of the 1916 Rebellion and of the Irish Volunteers in the War of Independence (1919-1921) were members of the Brotherhood.

Irish Volunteers: Founded by Eoin MacNeill in October 1913 and backed by the Irish Republican Brotherhood (IRB). Intended to ensure that the British Government kept its promise to grant Home Rule. Large numbers of Volunteers followed the Home Rule Party's call to join the British Army following the outbreak of World War I. The IRB-controlled remnant took part in the 1916 Rebellion and, in 1919, the reorganised force, now called the Irish Republican Army (IRA), began the War of

Independence. Civil War (1922) split the IRA. The defeated anti-Treaty force retained the name IRA and went underground and the Free State Government eventually took special powers to suppress it. This policy was continued in the 1930s by the Fianna Fáil Government. The IRA conducted a bombing campaign in Britain in 1939 and a military offensive on Northern Ireland, between 1956 and 1962, in an attempt to force an end to partition. Following the suppression of the Civil Rights Movement in Northern Ireland (*c.* 1970), the IRA began another military campaign against Britain.

Irish Women's Franchise League: Militant suffrage organisation founded in 1908 by Hanna Sheehy Skeffington and Margaret Cousins.

Irish Worker: Radical anti-capitalist weekly newspaper founded by labour leader, James Larkin, in 1911. It sold 20,000 copies weekly and exerted immense influence on the growing trade union movement. It was suppressed by the British authorities in 1914. Larkin revived it in 1930.

KBE: Knight of the British Empire. Honour conferred by the British monarchy.

Ladies Land League: Auxiliary body of the Land League. Founded in 1881 by the Parnell sisters, Anna and Fanny, when the Land League was suppressed and its leaders imprisoned.

Land League: Organisation campaigning for land reform. Founded by Michael Davitt in 1879 when crop failure and falling prices threatened disaster for tenant farmers. The League developed into a mass movement and, with the support of the Irish Party in the British Parliament, resulted in the Land Acts that, after 1903, transferred ownership of the land from the landlords to the farmers who worked it.

Lane Collection: *vide* Sir Hugh Lane.

Lane, Sir Hugh (1875-1915): Art dealer and collector. Through the influence of his aunt, Lady Gregory, and that of W.B. Yeats he became interested in the Irish Renaissance. He offered his valuable art collection, mostly comprising French impressionists, to the Dublin Municipal Gallery on the condition a permanent gallery be built to house it. When Dublin City Council refused he bequeathed the paintings to the English National Gallery, in 1913. But, in 1915 he added an unwitnessed codicil to his will restoring the collection to Dublin. Following his death in 1915 a lengthy dispute arose between the Irish Government and London's National Gallery over ownership of the Lane Collection. It was agreed, in 1959, that the paintings be divided into two collections and each exhibited alternatively, over five-year periods, in the National Gallery of Ireland, Dublin.

LL.D: Doctor of Laws.

Lord Deputy: Title usually given to the principal representative of the British monarchy in Ireland from the twelfth to the mid-seventeenth century.

Lord Lieutenant: Title given to the principal representative of the British monarchy in Ireland from the mid-seventeenth century until 1922. Also called *Viceroy*.

MA: Master of Arts degree.

Mathew, Father Theobald (1790-1856): Apostle of temperance. Began a total abstinence crusade, especially among the poor, in 1838. The Crusade had extraordinary success in Ireland and areas of Irish immigration in Britain.

McCormack, John (1884-1945): Operatic and concert singer. Born Athlone, Co. Westmeath. His career began with winning a gold medal at the 1902 Feis Ceoil in Dublin. Internationally recognised as one of the greatest tenors of his day.

Martyn, Edward (1859-1924): Playwright. An important figure in the Irish Literary revival. He was associated with W.B Yates and Lady Gregory in founding the Irish Literary Theatre (1899) later to become the Abbey Theatre Company. He wrote several successful plays for these companies and set up the short-lived Irish Theatre in 1914.

MBE: Member of the Order of the British Empire. Honour conferred by the British monarchy.

Meredith, George (1828-1909): British novelist and poet. Much acclaimed writer in his time.

Meyer, Kuno (1858-1919): Celtic scholar and translator. Born in Hamburg, Germany and educated at Edinburgh and Leipzig Universities. Devoted his life to the study of vernacular literature of ancient Ireland; founded the School of Irish Learning in Dublin (1903). He established several Celtic journals and published five books of translations from Early Irish.

MP: Member of Parliament. Elected member of the British House of Commons.

Muintir na Tíre: Rural community organisation. Founded by Canon John Hayes in 1931 to improve the quality of life in rural communities through a spirit of co-operation and social principles as expressed in Papal Encyclicals.

Nation, The: Official weekly organ of the Young Ireland Movement. Founded in 1842 by Thomas Davis, Gavan Duffy and J.B. Dillon.

National League: Inaugurated in 1882 by Charles Stewart Parnell. It succeeded the Land League when the agrarian crisis had receded. Less radical than the Land League, and dominated by the Irish Party, it had a broader programme.

OBE: Order of the British Empire. Honour conferred by the British monarchy.

O'Casey, Seán (1880-1964): Playwright. Dublin-born, working class, self-educated. Established his reputation with *Shadow of a Gunman* (1923), *Juno and the Paycock* (1924), and *Plough and the Stars* (1926). All three plays were first produced in the Abbey Theatre.

O'Connell, Daniel (1775-1847): The 'Liberator.' Lawyer who founded the Catholic Association (1823) with the object of gaining Catholic emancipation (from Penal laws, which see) through constitutional means. The British Government conceded when confronted with one of the greatest mass crusades in the history of democracy (1829). O'Connell attempted to repeal the Act of Union, as an MP, and set up a parliament in Dublin through a similar mass crusade. The government eventually confronted the movement head-on and O'Connell was jailed for conspiracy in 1843.

O'Connor, Frank (1903-1966): Cork-born author and translator. His first book of short stories, *Guests of the Nation,* was published in 1939. Internationally recognised as a master of the short story. Novelist, playwright, biographer, Irish-language scholar and translator of Irish poetry.

O'Donovan Rossa, Jeremiah (1831-1915): Fenian organiser and author. Cruelly treated in penal servitude (1865-1871). Became a symbol of indomitable rebellion.

O'Faoláin, Seán (1900-1991): Limerick-born author and man of letters. His first collection of short stories, *Midsummer Night Madness* (1932), established his international reputation. Recognised as one of the greatest of all Irish short story writers. Also published novels, biographies, books of travel, criticism, etc.

O'Flaherty, Liam (1897-1984): Author. Born to an Irish-speaking family on the Aran Islands. Published many novels and collections of short stories, from 1923, to international acclaim.

Oireachtas: (1) Annual festival of Gaelic culture, particularly that held by the Gaelic League; (2) ancient assembly or convocation; (3) Irish national parliament, i.e. combined legislatures of the Dáil and Seanad (Senate).

Pale, The: In an attempt to rationalise English control in Ireland an 'English Land' was planned at the end of the fourteenth century. This area in eastern Ireland comprised counties Louth, Meath, Kildare, Dublin, Wicklow, Wexford, Carlow and Waterford. A new colony was to be planted from Britain in this 'Pale.' The aspiration was not fulfilled although the Pale became a foothold and bridgehead for the English. In the sixteenth century, prior to the Tudor conquest of Ireland, the Pale had been reduced to Dublin, Louth and east Meath. Origin of term, 'beyond the Pale.'

Parnell, Charles Stewart (1846-1891): Political leader, 'Uncrowned King of Ireland.' Leader of the Irish Party in the British House of Commons. Became President of the National Land League. Won a balance-of-power advantage in the British Parliament and worked to promote land reform and Home Rule for Ireland.

Pearse, Patrick or Mac Piarais, Pádraig (1879-1916): Poet, educator, writer, revolutionary. Significant member of the Gaelic League. Founded Scoil Éanna (St. Enda's) the influential bilingual school. Member of the Supreme Council of the Irish Republican Brotherhood and on the Provisional Committee of the Irish Volunteers (1915). Commander-in-Chief of the Republicans in the 1916 Rebellion, and President of Provisional Government. He was executed in Kilmainham Jail, Dublin, May 3, 1916.

Penal laws: Penal laws against Roman Catholics existed for most of the period between the Act of Supremacy (1560) and Catholic Emancipation (1829). The term refers in particular to those laws enacted following the defeat of the Jacobites in 1691 which barred the practice of the Roman Catholic religion and deprived Catholics of their civil rights. The bulk of the population suffered from such poverty as to culminate in the Great Famine of the 1840s. This poverty is largely attributed to the general enforcement of Penal laws in areas of land ownership and livelihood.

Poor Law: Official relief agency to combat poverty. Extended to Ireland by the British Government in 1836. The country was divided into Poor Law Districts or Unions. A workhouse, administered by a Board of Guardians, was built for each. The Poor Law Government Act (1896) allowed women to elect and become Poor Law Guardians.

RDS: Royal Dublin Society (which see).

Royal Dublin Society: Originally 'The Dublin Society.' Founded in 1731 for 'the improvement of husbandry, the manufactures and other useful arts.' It encouraged a wide variety of arts, crafts and other skills by grants and instruction. Its role in training artists and architects is almost forgotten today. Became the Royal Dublin Society in 1820 under the patronage of King George IV.

Royal Institute: British organisation founded in London (1799) for 'the promotion, diffusion, and extension of science and useful knowledge.'

RHA: Royal Hibernian Academy (which see).

Royal Hibernian Academy: Founded in 1823. First exhibition (open to artists, sculptors and architects) held in 1826. Once contained an art school. Its annual exhibition remains one of the most prestigious in Ireland.

Royal University of Ireland: Established in Dublin, in 1880, by the British Conservative Government as a compromise between Roman Catholic demands for higher education and government education policy for Ireland. In 1908 it made way for the National University of Ireland.

RTE: Radio Telefís Éireann. The national radio and television broadcasting service.

Russell, George (AE) (1867-1935): Poet, painter, apostle of the co-operative movement. Editor of the *Irish Homestead* and *Irish Statesman.*

Senate (Seanad Éireann): Second House of Irish parliament.

School of Irish Learning: Founded in Dublin by the renowned German Celtic scholar, Kuno Meyer, in 1903.

Scoil Éanna (St. Enda's School): Founded at Cullenswood House, Ranelagh, Dublin, in 1908 by Patrick Pearse. Intended to promote his ideal of a Gaelic and free Ireland. The school moved to 'The Hermitage,' Rathfarnham, Dublin, in 1910.

Sinn Féin: Political movement founded by Arthur Griffith in 1904. Called for passive rejection of British rule and of political and economic self-reliance. Following the failure of the Home Rule movement, and increased anti-British feeling after the 1916 Rebellion, a new Sinn Féin party emerged in 1917 committed to work for an Irish Republic.

Synge, John Millington (1871-1909): Playwright. One of the foremost writers of the Irish Literary Revival. His genius lay in bringing rural life and speech effectively to the stage. He was literary advisor and, later, co-director of the Abbey Theatre.

Taoiseach: Prime Minister of the government of the Republic of Ireland.

TD: Teachta Dála (which see).

Teachta Dála: Member of the Dáil or First House of Irish parliament.

Treaty, The: Following a truce in the War of Independence (Anglo-Irish War), and peace negotiations between Irish and British Governments, a Treaty was signed on December 6, 1921. It provided for the establishment of an Irish Free State as a Dominion of the British Commonwealth, but allowed for the Stormont Parliament in Belfast (which governed six northeastern counties) the choice of remaining within the United Kingdom. The Treaty resulted in Civil War between those who accepted Free State status and those who wished to establish a republic.

UCC: University College Cork.

UCD: University College Dublin.

UCG: University College Galway.

United Arts Club (Dublin): Founded in 1905 by Ellen Duncan and Countess Markevicz to bring together people who were interested in the arts and to 'crystallise the renaissance movement' happening in Dublin at that time.

United Irishmen: Political society founded in 1791 by Wolfe Tone and others to demand reform of the Irish parliament and equality for all Irishmen of all religious persuasions. When it was suppressed by the government, in 1793, the society went underground and plotted revolution with French help. In 1798 it was forced into open rebellion and crushed with extreme cruelty. The United Irishmen attempted another unsuccessful insurrection, in 1803, under the leadership of Robert Emmet.

United Irishwomen: Rural organisation formed in 1910, by Anita Lett and others, to improve the life of women in rural Ireland and to complement the work of the Irish Agricultural Organisation Society. Following the tensions of the Civil War it was replaced by the Irish Countrywomen's Association.

War of Independence (Anglo-Irish War): A continuation of the 1916 rebellion attempting to establish an Irish Republic with country-wide organisation. This war against British occupation of Ireland began in January 1919 and ended, with the Truce and ceasefire, in July 1921.

Whiteboys: A widespread agrarian movement against the evils of the colonial landlord system took root in Ireland, particularly in Munster, following the ending of Jacobite hopes in the mid-eighteenth century. Those anonymously involved in attacks on livestock, property, and persons, were known by many names but initially and especially by that of *Buachaillí Bána* or Whiteboys. Sporadic and desperate outbreaks of 'Whiteboyism,' in various forms, continued throughout the country for a further one hundred and fifty years.

White Cross: Following an American Commission investigation into the state of Ireland's civilian population, an American Committee for Relief in Ireland was established, in December 1920. Irish-Americans organised a huge fund-raising operation. The White Cross Fund was the Irish response, distributing food and funds to approximately one hundred thousand people.

Womens Prisoners Defence League: Protest group organised by Maud Gonne (secretary) and Charlotte Despard (president). Formed to help Republican prisoners and their families during the Civil War and to protest against the appalling conditions and executions of Republican prisoners.

Yeats, William Butler (1865-1939): Poet and dramatist. Main leader of the Irish Literary Revival. Founded the Irish Literary Society (1891), the National Literary Society (1892) and was co-founder of the Abbey Theatre (1904). Appointed to the Senate of the newly-established Irish Free State (1922). Awarded the Nobel Prize for Literature in 1923.

Yeats, Jack Butler (1871-1952): Painter and illustrator. Member of the distinguished Yates family and acclaimed as one of Ireland's greatest artists. The 1916 Rebellion and the struggle for independence inspired some of his best-known works.

SELECT BIBLIOGRAPHY

HISTORIES, REFERENCE AND GENERAL WORKS

Annals of the Kingdom of Ireland by the Four Masters, (John O'Donovan, trans.), Dublin 1858, Dublin 1990.

Arnold, Bruce, *A Concise History of Irish Art,* London 1969.

Blackburne, E. Owens, *Illustrious Irish Women,* London 1877.

Boylan, Henry, *A Dictionary of Irish Biography,* Dublin 1988.

Brady, Anne M. and Cleeve, Brian, *A Biographical Dictionary of Irish Writers,* Mullingar 1985.

Breathnach. D. and Ní Mhurchú, Máire, *Beathaisnéis a hAon,* Dublin 1986.

Breathnach. D. and Ní Mhurchú, Máire, *Beathaisnéis a Do,* Dublin 1990.

Burke's Irish family Records, London 1976.

Butler, Patricia, *300 Years of Irish Watercolours and Drawings,* London 1990.

Byrne, Art and McMahon, Sean, *Lives of 113 Great Irishwomen and Irishmen,* Dublin 1990.

Byrne, Francis John, *Irish Kings and High Kings,* London 1973.

Clear, Caitriona, *Nuns in Nineteenth Century Ireland,* Dublin 1987.

Collins, Tim, *Some Irish Women Scientists,* pp 39-53, UCG Women's Studies Centre Review, Vol 1, Galway 1992.

Concannon, Helena, *Daughters of Banba,* Dublin 1930.

Concannon, Mrs. Thomas, *Defenders of the Ford,* Dublin 1925.

Concannon, Mrs. Thomas, *The Poor Clares in Ireland (1629-1929),* Dublin 1929.

Concannon, Mrs. Thomas, *Irish Nuns in Penal Days,* Dublin 1931.

Corish, Patrick J., *The Irish Martyrs,* Dublin 1989.

Coxhead, Elizabeth, *Daughters of Erin,* London 1965.

Crookshank and the Knight of Glin, *The Painters of Ireland c. 1660-1920,* London 1978.

Cullen, Mary and Luddy Maria (eds.), *Women, Power and Consciousness in 19th Century Ireland,* Dublin 1995.

Cullen Owens, Rosemary, *Smashing Times. A History of the Irish Women's Suffrage Movement 1889-1922,* Dublin 1984.

Curtis, Edmund, *A History of Ireland,* London 1936.

Curtis, P.J., *Notes from the Heart. A Celebration of Irish Traditional Music,* Dublin 1994.

Daches, David, *The Penguin Companion of Literature,* London 1971.

D'Alton, Rev. E.A., *History of Ireland, From the Earliest Times to the Present Day,* London n.d.

Davitt, Michael, *The Fall of Feudalism in Ireland, or The Story of the Land League Revolution,* London and New York 1904.

Deane, Ciaran, *Guinness Book of Irish Facts and Feats,* Dublin 1994.

de Breffny, Brian, *The Irish World. The History and Cultural Achievements of the Irish People,* London 1977.

de hÍde, Dubhglas, *Abhráin Ghrádha Chúige Chonnacht,* Dublin 1931, 1950.

Dictionary of American Biography, Oxford 1936.

Dictionary of National Biography, London 1890, 1960.

Dolan, Rev. James, *Women Saints of the Gael. Miniature Lives of Irish Female Saints,* Dublin 1923.

Drabble, Margaret and Stringer, Jenny, *The Concise Oxford Companion to English Literature,* Oxford 1987

Duncan, Alastair, *Art Deco Furniture,* London 1984.

Ellis, Beresford, *Celtic Women,* London 1995.

Encyclopaedia Americana, New York 1977.

Europa Biographical Dictionary, British Women, London 1983.

Farmer, David Hugh, *Oxford Dictionary of Saints,* Oxford 1978.

Fox, R.M., *Rebel Irishwomen,* Dublin 1935 (1967).

Gallagher, John, *Courageous Irishwomen,* Mayo 1995.

Green, Alice Stopford, *The Making of Ireland and its Undoing 1200-1600,* London 1908.

Hennessy, Maurice, *The Wild Geese. The Irish Soldier in Exile,* London 1973.

Henry, Noel, *From Sophie to Sonia, 75 Years of Irishwomen's Athletics,* Dublin 1996.

Hickey, D.J. and Doherty, J.E., *A Dictionary of Irish History since 1800,* Dublin 1988.

Hill, Myrtle and Pollack, Vivienne, *Image and Experience. Photographs of Irish Women c. 1880-1920,* Belfast 1993.

Hogan, Robert (ed.), *The Macmillan Dictionary of Irish Literature,* Conn. 1979, London 1980.

Hunt, Hugh, *The Abbey: Ireland's National Theatre. 1904-1979,* Dublin 1979.

Jones, Mary, *These Obstreperous Lassies. A History of the Irish Women Workers' Union,* Dublin 1988.

Kelly, A.A. (ed.), *Pillars of the House,* Dublin 1988.

Kelly, A.A., *Wandering Women. Two Centuries of Travel Outside Ireland,* Dublin 1995.

Kennelly, Brendan (ed.), *The Penguin Book of Irish Verse,* London 1970.

Kunitz, Stanley and Haycroft, Howard (eds.), *British Authors Before 1800, A Biographical Dictionary,* New York 1952.

Larmour, Paul, *The Arts and Crafts Movement in Ireland,* Belfast 1992.

Lucy, Sean, *Love Poems of the Irish,* Cork 1967.

Lyons, F.S.L., *Ireland Since the Famine,* London 1971.

Macardle, Dorothy, *The Irish Republic,* London 1937.

McConkey, Kenneth, *Irish Art - A Free Spirit (1860-1960),* London 1990.

McCormack, Eugene, *The INTO And the 1946 Teachers' Strike,* Dublin 1996

MacCurtain, Margaret and O'Dowd, Mary (eds.), *Women in Early Modern Ireland,* Dublin 1991.

MacCurtain, Margaret and Tierney, Mark, *The Birth of Modern Ireland,* Dublin 1969.

MacE. A.A., *Calendar of Irish Saints*, Dublin 1931.

Mac Lochlainn, Alfred and Sheehy Skeffington, Andrée, *Writers, Raconteurs and Notable Feminists*, Dublin n.d.

Mollan, Charles; Davis, William and Finucane, Brendan (eds.), *Some People and Places in Irish Science and Technology*, Dublin 1985.

Moody, T.W. and Martin, F.X., *The Course of Irish History*, Cork 1967.

Moran, Rev. P.F., *Persecutions of Irish Catholics (Under the Cromwellians and the Puritans)*, Dublin 1884.

New Catholic Encyclopaedia, Washington 1967, New York 1967.

New Encyclopaedia Britannica, Chicago 1994.

Newman, P.R., *Companion to Irish History 1603-1921*, Oxford and New York, 1991.

Newmann, Kate, *Dictionary of Ulster Biography*, Belfast 1993.

Nicholls, Kenneth, *Gaelic and Gaelicised Ireland*, Dublin 1977.

Ó Corráin, Donnchadh and Maguire, Fidelma, *Gaelic Personal Names*, Dublin 1981.

O'Hanlon, Rev. John, *Lives of the Irish Saints* (10 vols.), London 1875.

O'Neill, Capt. Francis, *Irish Minstrels and Musicians*, Chicago 1913, Wakefield, 1973.

O'Neill, Sr. Rose, O.P., *A Rich Inheritance. Galway Dominican Nuns 1644-1944*, Galway 1994.

Owens Weeks, Ann, *Unveiling Treasures*, Dublin 1993.

Ryan-Smolin, Wanda; Mayes, Elizabeth and Rogers, Jenni (eds.), *Irish Women Artists. From the Eighteenth Century to the Present Day*, Dublin 1987.

Sheehy, Jeanne, *The Rediscovery of Ireland's Past: the Celtic Revival 1830-1930*, London 1980.

Uglow, Jennifer, *The Macmillan Dictionary of Women's Biography (2nd Ed.)*, London 1989.

Wallace, Martin, *Famous Irish Lives*, Belfast 1991.

Ward, Margaret, *Unmanageable Revolutionaries. Women and Irish Nationalism*, Dingle and London 1983.

Ward, Margaret, *In Their Own Voice. Women and Irish Nationalism*, Dublin 1995.

Women's Community Press and Irish Feminist Information Publications, *Missing Pieces*, Dublin 1983.

SELECT BIOGRAPHIES AND AUTOBIOGRAPHIES

Barry, Michael, *Great Aviation Stories, Vol. 1*, Cork 1993.

Blackburn, Julia, *Daisy Bates in the Desert*, London 1994.

Coogan, Tim Pat, *De Valera. Long Fellow, Long Shadow*, London 1993.

Chambers, Anne, *Granuaile: The Life and Times of Grace O'Malley c. 1530-1603*, Dublin 1983.

Chambers, Anne, *Eleanor, Countess of Desmond c. 1545-1638*, Dublin 1986.

Chambers, Anne, *La Sheridan, Adorable Diva*, Dublin 1989.

Culloty, A.T., *Nora Herlihy, Irish Credit Union Pioneer*, Dublin 1990.

Donoghue, Denis, (ed.), *W.B. Yeats: Memoirs*, London 1972.

Dudley Edwards, Ruth, *Patrick Pearse. The Triumph of Failure*, London 1977.

Elliot, Marianne, *Wolfe Tone, Prophet of Irish Independence*, New Haven and London 1989.

Fallon, Charlotte H., *Soul of Fire, A Biography of Mary MacSwiney*, Cork 1986.

ffrench Eager, Irene, *Margaret Anna Cusack, A Biography*, Dublin 1970, 1979.

Field Parton, Mary (ed.), *The Autobiography of Mother Jones*, Chicago 1990.

Fitzgibbon, Theodora, *With Love*, London 1982, 1983.

Foster, R.F., *Charles Stewart Parnell, The Man and His Family*, Sussex 1976.

Fox, R.M., *Louie Bennett: Her Life and Times*, Dublin 1957.

Gaddis Rose, Marilyn, *Katharine Tynan*, New Jersey 1974.

Geel, *Psychiatric Family Care*, Geel n.d.

Hardwick, Joan, *The Yeats Sisters: A Biography of Susan and Elizabeth Yeats*, London 1996.

Kohfeldt, Mary Lou, *Lady Gregory - The Woman Behind the Irish Renaissance*, London 1984.

Larkin, Babe, *In the Footsteps of Big Jim*, Dublin 1995.

Larkin, Emmet, *James Larkin, Irish Labour Leader 1876-1947*, Dublin 1961.

Leahy, J.K., *The Spiritual Writings of Mother Butler*, New York 1954.

Lenihan, Edmund, *In Search of Biddy Early*, Cork 1987.

Levinson, Leah, *With Wooden Sword*, Boston and Dublin 1983.

Litton, Helen (ed.), *Revolutionary Woman, Kathleen Clarke, An Autobiography*, Dublin 1991.

Louis, Sr. M. OSF, *Love is the Answer*, Dublin n.d.

Lyons, F.S.L., *Charles Stewart Parnell*, London 1977.

Lyons, Mary (ed.), *The Memoirs of Mrs. Leeson, Madam*, Mullingar 1995.

Mahon, John, *Kate Tyrrell, Lady Mariner*, Dublin 1995.

Medical Missionaries of Mary, *The Seed of an Idea*, Dublin 1984.

Mulvihill, Margaret, *Charlotte Despard, A Biography*, London 1989.

Mac Liammoir, Sandra, *The Secret Life of Joan Denise Moriarty*, Dublin 1995.

Mac Neill, M., *Maire Rua, Lady of Leamaneh*, Ballinakella 1990.

McNeill, Mary, *The Life and Times of Mary Ann McCracken, 1770-1866*, Belfast 1960.

Ní Chearbhaill, Máire, Margaret Aylward, *Foundress of the Sisters of the Holy Faith*, Dublin 1989.

Ní Ghráda, Máiréad, *An Triail/Breithiúnas (Introduction by Éamon Ó Cíosáin)*, Dublin 1978.

Ó Coigligh, Ciarán (ed.), *Caitlín Maude, Dánta*, Dublin 1984.

Ó Donnchú, An tAth. Donncha, *Filíocht Mháire Bhuidhe Ní Laoghaire*, Dublin 1931.

O'Halloran, Maura 'Soshin', *Pure Heart, Enlightened Mind*, 1995.

Ó hAodha, Micheál, *Siobhan - A Memoir of an Actress*, Dingle 1984.

O'Hara, Sr. S. OSF., *Dare to Live. A Portrait of Mother Kevin*, Dublin 1979.

O'Neill, Marie, *From Parnell to de Valera; A Biography of Jennie Wyse Power 1858-1941*, Dublin 1991.

Ormsby, Frank (ed.), *Amanda McKittrick Ros Reader, Thine in Storm and Calm*, Belfast 1988.

Ó Tuama, Seán, *Caoineadh Airt Uí Laoghaire*, Dublin 1961.

Robinson, Hilary, *Somerville and Ross*, Dublin 1980.

Robinson, Lennox, *Palette and Plough, A Pen-and-Ink Drawing of Dermot O Brien*, Dublin 1948.

Roper, Esther, *Poems of Eva Gore-Booth, with Biographical Introduction*, London 1929.

Rynne, Catherine, *Mother Mary Aikenhead, 1787-1885*, Dublin 1980.

Rynne, Etienne (ed.), *A Shrine of Celtic Art. The Art of Sr. Concepta Lynch O.P.*, Dublin n.d.

Sayers, Peig, *Peig*, Dublin 1936.

Suenens, Cardinal Leon Joseph, *Edel Quinn*, Dublin 1952.

Turner Johnston, Sheila, *Alice. A Life of Alice Milligan*, Omagh 1994.

Van Voris, Jacqueline, *Constance Markievicz. In the Cause of Ireland*, Massachusetts 1967.

Walsh, T.J., *Nano Nagle and the Presentation Sisters*, Kildare 1959 .

NEWSPAPERS, PERIODICALS, REVIEWS

Béaloideas (Dublin).
Capuchin Annual (Dublin).
Cork Examiner (Cork).
Dal gCais (Clare).
Irish Art Review (Dublin).
Ireland's Eye (Westmeath).
Irish Historical Studies (Dublin).
Irish Independent (Dublin).
Ireland of the Welcomes (Dublin).
Ireland's Own (Wexford).
Irish Press (Dublin).
Irish Times (Dublin).
Journal of Irish Archaeology (Dublin).
North Munster Antiquarian Journal (Limerick).
Old Limerick Journal (Limerick).
Sunday Independent (Dublin).
Sunday Tribune (Dublin).
The Word (Roscommon).
This Other Clare (Clare).
UCG Women's Studies Centre Review (Galway).

The authors believe they have taken every reasonable precaution to avoid infringement of copyright; if any involuntary infringement of copyright or inadvertant ommission of acknowledgement has occurred, the authors offer sincere apologies and will be pleased to receive any information which would enable matters to be rectified in a future edition.

INDEX

ABOUT THE AUTHORS
of

Women of Ireland
A Biographic Dictionary

Kit Ó Céirín SRN. SCM.
Born Co. Westmeath, Ireland; trained as a nurse, worked in health care and social services; part-time journalist; co-author (with husband Cyril Ó Céirín) of two books.

Cyril Ó Céirín B.A. H.Dip.Ed.
Born Dublin, Ireland; trained as secondary school teacher (Hist., Irish, English), worked as teacher, lecturer, freelance journalist; painter, poet, author, translator, editor.

Published works:

Poetry: *Le hAer's le Fuacht* (1986)
Breith (1974), ed. and contributor
Saltair Muire (1988), ed.

Poetry published in 'Poetry Ireland', 'Innti', 'New Irish Writing' et al.

Awards: Oireachtas (three times)
Listowel Writers Week

Others: *My Story*, by Peter O'Leary (1970 /87), transl.
An tOilithreach Gaelach (1973)
Séadna (1989), transl. and ed. (with Kit Ó C.)
Wild and Free (1978), (with Kit Ó C.)

Tír Eolas is a publishing firm based in Kinvara, Co. Galway.

Since it was established in 1985, **Tír Eolas** has published six Guides and Maps, covering the Burren, South Galway, Kinvara and Medieval Galway.

Tír Eolas Books

The Book of the Burren, edited by Jeff O'Connell and Anne Korff, 1991.
ISBN 1-873821-00-X PB
1-873821-05-0 HB

The Shannon Floodlands, by Stephen Heery, 1993. A Natural History of the Shannon Callows.
ISBN 1-873821-02-6 PB

Not a Word of a Lie, by Bridie Quinn-Conroy, 1993. A portrait of 'growing up' in the West of Ireland.
ISBN 1-873821-01-8 PB

The Book of Aran, edited by John Waddell, J.W. O'Connell and Anne Korff, 1994.
ISBN 1-873821-03-4 PB
1-873821-04-2 HB